Lecture Notes in Artificial Intelligence 3366

Edited by J. G. Carbonell and J. Siekmann

Subseries of Lecture Notes in Computer Science

———

Iyad Rahwan   Pavlos Moraitis
Chris Reed (Eds.)

Argumentation in Multi-Agent Systems

First International Workshop, ArgMAS 2004
New York, NY, USA, July 19, 2004
Revised Selected and Invited Papers

 Springer

Series Editors

Jaime G. Carbonell, Carnegie Mellon University, Pittsburgh, PA, USA
Jörg Siekmann, University of Saarland, Saarbrücken, Germany

Volume Editors

Iyad Rahwan
The British University in Dubai, Institute of Informatics
P.O. Box 502216, Dubai, United Arab Emirates
E-mail: irahwan@acm.org
University of Melbourne, Dept. of Information Systems
E-mail: i.rahwan@pgrad.unimelb.edu.au

Pavlos Moraitis
University of Cyprus, Dept. of Computer Science
75 Kallipoleos Str., 1678 Nicosia, Cyprus
E-mail: moraitis@cs.ucy.ac.cy

Chris Reed
University of Dundee, Division of Applied Computing
Dundee DD1 4HN, Scotland, UK
E-mail: chris@computing.dundee.ac.uk

Library of Congress Control Number: 2004118426

CR Subject Classification (1998): I.2.11, I.2, C.2.4, H.5.2-3

ISSN 0302-9743
ISBN 3-540-24526-X Springer Berlin Heidelberg New York

Springer is a part of Springer Science+Business Media

springeronline.com

© Springer-Verlag Berlin Heidelberg 2005
Printed in Germany

Typesetting: Camera-ready by author, data conversion by Scientific Publishing Services, Chennai, India
Printed on acid-free paper   SPIN: 11384885   06/3142   5 4 3 2 1 0

Preface

The theory of argumentation is a rich, interdisciplinary area of research lying across philosophy, communication studies, linguistics, and psychology (at least). Its techniques and results have found a wide range of applications in both theoretical and practical branches of artificial intelligence and computer science. Several theories of argumentation with various semantics have been proposed in the literature. Multi-agent systems theory has picked up argument-inspired approaches and specifically argumentation-theoretic results from many different areas.

The community of researchers in argumentation and multi-agent systems is currently presented with a unique opportunity to integrate the various understandings of argument into a coherent and core part of the functioning of autonomous computational systems. The benefits range from extended semantics of arguments construed as relationships between epistemic atoms, through conversation protocols for argumentation with serendipitous information exchange, to models of dialectical practical reasoning, both intra- and inter-agent (and a mixture of the two). In all these cases argumentation is used to structure knowledge representation, reasoning and agent interaction, and offers a potential means of better integrating these disparate problems.

In recognition of this increasing interest, the 1st International Workshop on Argumentation in Multi-agent Systems (ArgMAS) was conceived. The workshop was the first forum that brought together researchers interested in applying argumentation to problems faced by the Autonomous Agents and Multi-agent Systems (AAMAS) community. Hence, the workshop was held in conjunction with the 3rd International AAMAS Conference, in July 2004 at Columbia University, New York. The workshop received 20 full-paper submissions and 2 position statements, which was a very encouraging sign for a new workshop. After a thorough reviewing process by at least 2 anonymous referees per paper, 13 full papers were selected for presentation at the workshop. The workshop also included an invited talk by Prof. Jonathan Adler from the Faculty of Philosophy, City University of New York. In this volume, we included revised and expanded versions of the 13 workshop papers. In addition, we included 4 invited contributions, which range from relevant papers that appeared at the main AAMAS conference to contributions from prominent researchers in the field who did not make it to the workshop. Invited contributions were also fully refereed, either by the AAMAS or ArgMAS reviewers. As a result, the book provides a strong representation of the state of the art in the emerging field. Papers range from specific technical contributions to discussions of overarching issues in the area.

The papers were roughly divided into the following main themes:

- Foundations of dialogues
- Belief revision
- Persuasion and deliberation

– Negotiation
– Strategic issues

Although these topics are not completely distinct, they indicate some main directions of research. We have therefore arranged the papers in the book according to these themes.

The first five papers (Part I) address foundational issues in argumentation-based multi-agent dialogues. The first paper (by *Simon Parsons, Peter McBurney* and *Michael Wooldridge*) sets down some preliminary but important steps towards a meta-theory of inter-agent dialogues by examining different classes of protocols and how they may lead to different interaction outcomes. The next paper (by *Chris Reed* and *Doug Walton*) looks at formalizing and implementing argumentation schemes, a form of non-deductive reasoning. This is followed by another paper (by *Simon Wells* and *Chris Reed*) which explores the specification of formal dialectic Hamblin-type systems, and presents an implemented system that makes use of the formal framework. The fourth paper (by *Jamal Bentahar, Bernard Moulin, John-Jules Ch. Meyer* and *Brahim Chaib-draa*) provides an approach based on modal logic for providing semantics for commitments during argumentation dialogues. This paper was invited after being accepted for presentation at the main conference. The last paper in Part I (by *Antonis Kakas, Nicolas Maudet* and *Pavlos Moraitis*) explores the interplay between dialogue protocols and agent internal strategies, and analyzes these within a single theoretical framework.

Part II focuses on the use of argumentation as a reasoning mechanism for revising beliefs in the context of a changing environment. The first paper in this section (by *Fabio Paglieri* and *Cristiano Castelfranchi*) provides the reader with a good scoping of the research field of the workshop. In particular, it argues that belief revision and argumentation are complementary components of belief change in multi-agent systems. Next, a specific model for argumentation-based belief revision is presented in a separate paper by *Marcela Capobianco, Carlos I. Chesñevar* and *Guillermo R. Simari*. The final paper in this section is an invited contribution (by *Gerard Vreeswijk*) on the relationship between argumentation-based reasoning and Bayesian probabilistic inference. This contribution promises to open up new avenues of research to bridge the gap between the symbolic and probabilistic views of communication.

Part III of this volume presents three contributions to multi-agent persuasion and deliberation dialogues. The first paper (by *Jamal Bentahar, Bernard Moulin* and *Brahim Chaib-draa*) presents a persuasion dialogue game protocol and studies the dynamics of the commitments of agents using the protocol. The following two papers contribute to deliberation dialogues, interactions where participants jointly decide on a course of action. The first of those (by *Katie Atkinson, Trevor Bench-Capon* and *Peter McBurney*) presents a dialogue game protocol for deliberation dialogues. This is followed by another paper (by *Peter McBurney* and *Simon Parsons*) which proposes a denotational semantics for deliberation dialogues, based on mathematical category theory.

Part IV concentrates on argumentation-based negotiation dialogues, an area receiving increasing interest in the multi-agent systems community. The first paper (by *Iyad Rahwan*, *Liz Sonenberg* and *Peter McBurney*) discusses the difference between argumentation-based negotiation and traditional bargaining, in which agents simply exchange offers. This is followed by a paper by *Leila Amgoud* and *Souhila Kaci*, who present an argumentation-based approach to generate desires and goals. This approach has potential benefit for negotiation dialogues as it provides a means for allowing agents to influence each others' preferences during negotiation. The third paper in this part (by *Sabyasachi Saha* and *Sandip Sen*) presents an approach for argumentation-based negotiation based on Bayesian networks. This is a slightly different treatment from that presented in the paper by *Gerard Vreeswijk* in Part II, since it uses Bayesian networks in order to model the negotiation opponent's behavior. The last paper, by *Fernando A. Tohmé* and *Guillermo R. Simari*, presents a framework for negotiation based on defeasible logic programming (DeLP) augmented with utility functions.

Finally, Part V contains papers that explore various issues related to agent decision-making in dialogues, i.e., their strategies. The first paper (by *Nishan C. Karunatillake* and *Nicholas R. Jennings*) uses empirical simulation to investigate whether and when argumentation improves negotiation. They demonstrate that argumentation is useful when resources are relatively scarce, but provide marginal benefit when resources are abundant. The second paper (by *Elizabeth Sklar*, *Simon Parsons* and *Mathew Davies*) explores the issue of lying in multi-agent dialogues and shows that lying can be useful, and even acceptable, in certain circumstances.

Together the papers in the five parts capture the current landscape of uses of argumentation in multi-agent systems. As a young and dynamic field of research, fresh with vitality, advances are being made extremely rapidly, but nevertheless there are some few trends that are worth identifying in trying to understand where the research is heading. Perhaps the first and most striking is that there is an increasing appeal from more informal areas of argumentation theory. Thus rhetoric, with its focus on audiences, values and context-dependence, is becoming more visible as agents become more sophisticated in their communication structures and reasoning capabilities. The more complex such capabilities become, the more susceptible those systems become to rhetorical techniques. Similarly, argumentation schemes, which encompass a wide range of humanistic reasoning techniques, are being harnessed for internal agent reasoning and inter-agent communication. As the structure of agent knowledge bases becomes more refined, the reasoning techniques that can be leveraged become more detailed and more specific.

Another clear trend is the emergence of the need for objective comparisons between systems. In some cases, such evaluation can be carried out using tools from earlier multi-agent systems research or distributed computing. Yet, much more commonly, the tools for evaluation simply do not exist and need building from scratch. As the range of argumentation-based techniques for reasoning and communicating expands, benchmarking and evaluation will become an increasingly important requirement in comparing and assessing those techniques.

A very important research trend, which we are only beginning to see glimpses of, is the integration of argumentation-theoretic and economic-theoretic conceptions of rationality. Attempts to integrate notions of economic preference (e.g., via the notion of *utility*) into argumentation systems is an important step towards integration.

Finally, and looking to the longer term, we foresee the emergence of richer argumentation models such as those that move away from the so-called "standard treatment" (such as formalizations of Toulmin's model). These will be driven by the limitations of expressivity identified in dialectical models (e.g., refutations versus negations; distinctions between undercutting and rebutting; and distinctions between warrants and implications). As agent reasoning becomes more sophisticated, the limits of the propositional model come ever more to the fore. Perhaps it is the ArgMAS community that will be at the vanguard of engineering solutions that tackle induction, categorical syllogism, the interrogative and imperative, and a whole host of Aristotelian basic concepts that might yield concrete computational gains in implemented agent systems.

We conclude this preface by extending our gratitude to the members of the steering committee, members of the program committee, and the auxiliary reviewers, who together helped make the ArgMAS workshop a success. We also thank the authors for their enthusiasm in submitting papers to the workshop, and for revising their papers on time for inclusion in this book.

October 2004   Iyad Rahwan, Pavlos Moraitis, and Chris Reed
                                                            Program Chairs
                                                               ArgMAS 2004

Organization

Program Chairs

Iyad Rahwan   University of Melbourne, Australia
The British University in Dubai, UAE
Pavlos Moraitis   University of Cyprus, Cyprus
Chris Reed   University of Dundee, UK

ArgMAS Steering Committee

Antonis Kakas   University of Cyprus, Cyprus
Nicolas Maudet   Université Paris Dauphine, France
Peter McBurney   University of Liverpool, UK
Pavlos Moraitis   University of Cyprus, Cyprus
Simon Parsons   City University of New York, USA
Iyad Rahwan   University of Melbourne, Australia
Chris Reed   University of Dundee, UK

Program Committee

Leila Amgoud   IRIT, France
Frank Dignum   Utrecht University, Netherlands
Rogier van Eijk   Utrecht University, Netherlands
Antonis Kakas   University of Cyprus, Cyprus
Nicolas Maudet   Université Paris Dauphine, France
Peter McBurney   University of Liverpool, UK
Pavlos Moraitis   University of Cyprus, Cyprus
Xavier Parent   King's College, London, UK
Simon Parsons   City University of New York, USA
Henry Prakken   Utrecht University, Netherlands
Iyad Rahwan   University of Melbourne, Australia
Chris Reed   University of Dundee, UK
Carles Sierra   IIIA, Spain
Paolo Torroni   Università di Bologna, Italy
Bart Verheij   Maastricht University, Netherlands
Gerard Vreeswijk   Utrecht University, Netherlands
Mike Wooldridge   University of Liverpool, UK

Auxiliary Referees

Evelina Lamma
Paola Mello

Table of Contents

Part IV: Negotiation

Part V: Strategic Issues

Some Preliminary Steps Towards a Meta-theory for Formal Inter-agent Dialogues

Simon Parsons[1], Peter McBurney[2], and Michael Wooldridge[2]

[1] Department of Computer and Information Science, Brooklyn College,
City University of New York, 2900 Bedford Avenue, Brooklyn,
New York, NY 11210, USA
`parsons@sci.brooklyn.cuny.edu`
[2] Department of Computer Science, University of Liverpool,
Chadwick Building, Liverpool L69 7ZF, UK
`{p.j.mcburney, m.j.wooldridge}@csc.liv.ac.uk`

Abstract. This paper investigates the properties of argumentation-based dialogues between agents. It takes a previously defined system by which agents can trade arguments, and examines how different classes of protocols for this kind of interaction can have profoundly different outcomes. Studying such classes of protocol, rather than individual protocols as has been done previously, allows us to start to develop a *meta-theory* of this class of interactions.

1 Introduction

Research into the theoretical properties of protocols for multi-agent interaction can be crudely divided into two camps. The first camp is broadly characterised by the application of game and economic theory to understanding the properties of multi-agent protocols; this camp includes, for example, research on auction protocols and algorithmic mechanism design [12]. The second camp may be broadly characterised by an understanding of agents as practical reasoning systems, which interact in order to to resolve differences of opinion and conflicts of interest; to work together to resolve dilemmas or find proofs; or simply to inform each other of pertinent facts. As work in the former camp has been informed by game and economic theory, so work in this latter camp has been informed in particular by research in the area of *argumentation* and *dialogue games*. Examples of argumentation-based approaches to multi-agent dialogues include the work of Dignum *et al.* [4], Kraus [13], Reed [20], Schroeder *et al.* [21] and Sycara [22].

The work of Walton and Krabbe has been particularly influential in argumentation-based dialogue research [23]. They developed a typology for inter-personal dialogue which identifies six primary types of dialogues and three mixed types. The categorization is based upon: what information the participants each have at the commencement of the dialogue (with regard to the topic of discussion); what goals the individual participants have; and what goals are shared by the participants, goals we may view as those of the dialogue itself. This *dialogue game* view of dialogues overlaps with work on conversation policies (see, for example, [3, 6]), but differs in considering the entire dialogue rather than dialogue segments. As defined by Walton and Krabbe, the three types of dialogue

I. Rahwan et al. (Eds.): ArgMAS 2004, LNAI 3366, pp. 1–18, 2005.

we have considered in our previous work are: *Information-Seeking Dialogues* (where one participant seeks the answer to some question(s) from another participant, who is believed by the first to know the answer(s)); *Inquiry Dialogues* (where the participants collaborate to answer some question or questions whose answers are not known to any one participant); and *Persuasion Dialogues* (where one party seeks to persuade another party to adopt a belief or point-of-view he or she does not currently hold). Persuasion dialogues begin with one party supporting a particular statement which the other party to the dialogue does not, and the first seeks to convince the second to adopt the proposition. The second party may not share this objective.

Our previous work investigated capturing these types of dialogue using a formal model of argumentation [2], and the basic properties and complexity of such dialogues [16]. Most recently, we have looked at how the outcomes of these dialogues can depend upon the order in which agents make utterances [17]. Here we extend this investigation, by moving from the study of particular protocols to the study of *classes of protocols*, and the properties of those classes. These results, then, are (very preliminary) results about the *meta-theory* of argumentation-based dialogues. The advantage of this change in perspective is that our results are robust—they hold for a wider range of possible dialogues—and more wide-reaching that we have been able to obtain hitherto, permitting a more complete analysis of argumentation-based dialogues. Note that, despite the fact that the types of dialogue we are considering are drawn from the analysis of human dialogues, we are only concerned here with dialogues between *artificial* agents. Unlike Grosz and Sidner [10] for example, we choose to focus in this way in order to simplify our task—dealing with artificial languages avoids much of the complexity of natural language dialogues.

2   Background

In this section, we briefly introduce the formal system of argumentation that underpins our approach [1], a system that extends Dung's [5] with preferences. We start with a (possibly inconsistent) knowledge base Σ with no deductive closure. We assume Σ contains formulas of a propositional language $\mathcal{L}$, that $\vdash$ stands is the classical inference relation, and $\equiv$ stands for logical equivalence. An argument is a proposition and the set of formulae from which it can be inferred:

Definition 1. *An* argument *is a pair $A = (H, h)$ where h is a formula of $\mathcal{L}$ and H a subset of Σ such that:*

1. *H is consistent;*
2. *$H \vdash h$; and*
3. *H is minimal, so no proper subset of H satisfying both (1) and (2) exists.*

H is called the support *of A, written $H = Support(A)$ and h is the* conclusion *of A, written $h = Conclusion(A)$.*

We thus talk of h being *supported* by the argument (H, h)

In general, since Σ is inconsistent, arguments in $\mathcal{A}(\Sigma)$, the set of all arguments which can be made from Σ, will conflict, and we make this idea precise with the notion of *undercutting*:

Definition 2. *Let A_1 and A_2 be two arguments of $\mathcal{A}(\Sigma)$. A_1 undercuts A_2 iff $\exists h \in Support(A_2)$ such that $h \equiv \neg Conclusion(A_1)$.*

In other words, an argument is undercut iff there is another argument which has as its conclusion the negation of an element of the support for the first argument.

To capture the fact that some facts are more strongly believed than others, we assume that any set of facts has a preference order over it. We suppose that this ordering derives from the fact that the knowledge base Σ is stratified into non-overlapping sets $\Sigma_1, \ldots, \Sigma_n$ such that facts in Σ_i are all equally preferred, and are more preferred than those in Σ_j where $j > i$. The preference level of a nonempty subset H of Σ, $level(H)$, is the number of the highest numbered layer which has a member in H.

Definition 3. *Let A_1 and A_2 be two arguments in $\mathcal{A}(\Sigma)$. A_1 is* preferred *to A_2 according to* Pref, $Pref(A_1, A_2)$, *iff $level(Support(A_1)) \leq level(Support(A_2))$.*

By $\gg^{Pref}$, we denote the strict pre-order associated with $Pref$. If A_1 is preferred to A_2, we say that A_1 is *stronger* than A_2[1]. We can now define the argumentation system we will use:

Definition 4. *An argumentation system (AS) is a triple $\langle \mathcal{A}(\Sigma), Undercut, Pref \rangle$ such that:*

- *$\mathcal{A}(\Sigma)$ is a set of the arguments built from Σ,*
- *Undercut is a binary relation representing the defeat relationship between arguments, $Undercut \subseteq \mathcal{A}(\Sigma) \times \mathcal{A}(\Sigma)$, and*
- *Pref is a (partial or complete) preordering on $\mathcal{A}(\Sigma) \times \mathcal{A}(\Sigma)$.*

The preference order makes it possible to distinguish different types of relation between arguments:

Definition 5. *Let A_1, A_2 be two arguments of $\mathcal{A}(\Sigma)$.*

- *If A_2 undercuts A_1 then A_1 defends itself against A_2 iff $A_1 \gg^{Pref} A_2$. Otherwise, A_1 does not defend itself.*
- *A set of arguments S defends A iff: $\forall$ B undercuts A and A does not defend itself against B then $\exists$ $C \in S$ such that C undercuts B and B does not defend itself against C.*

We write $C_{Undercut, Pref}$ to denote the set of all non-undercut arguments and arguments defending themselves against all their undercutting arguments. The set $\underline{S}$ of acceptable arguments of the argumentation system $\langle \mathcal{A}(\Sigma), Undercut, Pref \rangle$ is the least fixpoint of a function $\mathcal{F}$ [1]:

$$S \subseteq \mathcal{A}(\Sigma)$$
$$\mathcal{F}(S) = \{(H, h) \in \mathcal{A}(\Sigma) \mid (H, h) \text{ is defended by } S\}$$

---

[1] We acknowledge that this model of preferences is rather restrictive and in the future intend to work to relax it.

Definition 6. *The set of* acceptable *arguments for an argumentation system* $\langle \mathcal{A}(\Sigma),$
Undercut, Pref $\rangle$ *is:*

$$\underline{\mathcal{S}} = \bigcup \mathcal{F}_{i \geq 0}(\emptyset)$$
$$= C_{Undercut, Pref} \cup \left[\bigcup \mathcal{F}_{i \geq 1}(C_{Undercut, Pref}) \right]$$

An argument is acceptable *if it is a member of the acceptable set, and a proposition is* acceptable *if it is the conclusion of an acceptable argument.*

Definition 7. *If an agent A has an acceptable argument for a proposition p, then the* status *of p for that agent is* accepted, *while if the agent does not have an acceptable argument for p, the status of p for that agent is* not accepted.

An acceptable argument is one which is, in some sense, proven since all the arguments which might undermine it are themselves undermined.

3   Locutions and Attitudes

As in our previous work, agents put forward propositions and accept propositions put forward by other agents based on their acceptability. The exact locutions and the way that these locutions are exchanged define a formal *dialogue game* which agents engage in.

Dialogues are assumed to take place between two agents, for example called P (for "pro") and C ("con"). Each agent $i \in \{P, C\}$ has a knowledge base, Σ_i, containing its beliefs. In addition, each agent i has a further knowledge base $CS(i)$, visible to both agents, containing *commitments* made in the dialogue. We assume an agent's *commitment store* is a subset of its knowledge base. Note that the union of the commitment stores can be viewed as the state of the dialogue at a given time. Since each agent has access to their private knowledge base and both commitment stores, agent i can make use of $\langle \mathcal{A}(\Sigma_i \cup CS(j)), Undercut, Pref \rangle$ where $i, j \in \{P, C\}$ and $i \neq j$.

All the knowledge bases contain propositional formulas and are not (necessarily) closed under deduction, and moreover all are stratified by degree of belief as discussed above. Here we assume that these degrees of belief are static and that both the players agree on them (acknowledging that this is a limitation of this approach).

With this background, we can present a set of dialogue moves, based on those first introduced in [16], and then modified in [15]. Each locution has a rule describing how to update commitment stores after the move, and groups of moves have conditions under which the move can be made—these are given in terms of the agents' assertion and acceptance attitudes (defined below). For all moves, player P addresses the ith move of the dialogue to player C.

$assert(p)$ where p is a propositional formula.

$$CS_i(P) = CS_{i-1}(P) \cup \{p\} \text{ and } CS_i(C) = CS_{i-1}(C)$$

Here p can be any propositional formula, as well as the special character $\mathcal{U}$, discussed below. This makes a statement that the agent is prepared to back up with argument.

$assert(S)$ where S is a set of formulas representing the support of an argument.

$$CS_i(P) = CS(P)_{i-1} \cup S \text{ and } CS_i(C) = CS_{i-1}(C)$$

$accept(p)$ p is a propositional formula.

$$CS_i(P) = CS_{i-1}(P) \cup \{p\} \text{ and } CS_i(C) = CS_{i-1}(C)$$

This explicitly notes that P agrees with something previously stated by C.

$reject(p)$ p is a propositional formula.

$$CS_i(P) = CS_{i-1}(P) \text{ and } CS_i(C) = CS_{i-1}(C)$$

This explicitly notes that P disagrees with something previously stated by C.

$challenge(p)$ where p is a propositional formula.

$$CS_i(P) = CS_{i-1}(P) \text{ and } CS_i(C) = CS_{i-1}(C)$$

A challenge is a means of making the other player explicitly state the argument supporting a proposition that they have previously asserted[2]. In contrast, a question can be used to query the other player about any proposition.

$question(p)$ where p is a propositional formula.

$$CS_i(P) = CS_{i-1}(P) \text{ and } CS_i(C) = CS_{i-1}(C)$$

$question$ is used to start an information-seeking dialogue. The last two locutions are used to start particular types of dialogue [15]:

$know(p)$ where p is a propositional formula.

$$CS_i(P) = CS_{i-1}(P) \text{ and } CS_i(C) = CS_{i-1}(C)$$

$know(p)$ is a statement akin to "do you know that p is true", which kicks off a persuasion dialogue.

$prove(p)$ where p is a propositional formula.

$$CS_i(P) = CS_{i-1}(P) \text{ and } CS_i(C) = CS_{i-1}(C)$$

$prove(p)$ is an invitation to start an inquiry dialogue to prove whether p is true or not. This is the set of moves, $\mathcal{M}_{DC}^{PK}$ from [15], an expansion of those in [16] that allows for more elegant dialogues[3].

---

[2] In this system it is only possible to issue a challenge for a proposition p following an $assert(p)$ by the other agent.

[3] The locutions in $\mathcal{M}_{DC}^{PK}$ are similar to those discussed elsewhere, for example [7, 19], though there is no $retract$ locution.

The way in which these locutions are used will be determined by the protocol used (examples of which are given below) and the *attitudes* that control the assertion and acceptance of propositions. Following our previous investigation [16, 17], we deal with "thoughtful/skeptical" agents that can assert any proposition p for which they can construct an acceptable argument, and will accept any proposition p for which they can construct an acceptable argument. Whatever the protocol, no agent is allowed to repeat exactly the same locution (down to the proposition or propositions that instantiate it) without immediately terminating the dialogue.

We refer to the system described here as $\mathcal{DG}$, irrespective of the protocol that controls the exchange of locutions.

4   Types of Dialogue

Previously [16], we defined three basic protocols for information seeking, inquiry and persuasion dialogues. These were subsequently updated in [15], and despite their apparent simplicity, have proved to be theoretically very rich.

4.1   Information-Seeking

The following protocol, denoted $\mathcal{IS}$, is unchanged from [16] and captures basic information seeking:

1. A asks $question(p)$.
2. Depending upon the contents of its knowledge-base and its assertion attitude, B replies with either $assert(p)$, $assert(\neg p)$, or $assert(\mathcal{U})$, where $\mathcal{U}$ indicates that, for whatever reason, B cannot give an answer.
3. A either *accepts* B's response, if its acceptance attitude allows, or *challenges*. $\mathcal{U}$ cannot be *challenge*d, and as soon as it is asserted, the dialogue terminates without the question being resolved.
4. B replies to a *challenge* with an $assert(S)$, where S is the support of an argument for the last proposition challenged by A.
5. Go to (3) for each proposition in S in turn.

When the dialogue terminates with A *accept*ing the subject of the dialogue, the dialogue is said to be *successful*.

Note that A *accepts* whenever possible, only being able to *challenge* when unable to *accept*.

4.2   Inquiry

The inquiry protocol $\mathcal{I}''$ from [15] is:

1. B proffers $prove(p)$, inviting A to join it in the search for a proof of p.
2. A asserts $q \rightarrow p$ for some q or $\mathcal{U}$.
3. B accepts $q \rightarrow p$ if its acceptance attitude allows, or *challenges* it.
4. A replies to a *challenge* with an $assert(S)$, where S is the support of an argument for the last proposition challenged by B.

5. Go to (2) for each proposition $s \in S$ in turn, replacing $q \to p$ by s.
6. B *asserts* q, or $r \to q$ for some r, or $\mathcal{U}$.
7. If $\mathcal{A}(CS(A) \cup CS(B))$ includes an argument for p that is acceptable to both agents, then first A and then B *accept* it and the dialogue terminates successfully.
8. If at any point one of the propositions is not acceptable to an agent, it issues a *reject*, and the dialogue ends unsuccessfully.
9. Go to 6, reversing the roles of A and B and substituting r for q and some t for r.

This protocol has some core steps in common with $\mathcal{IS}$ dialogues, and we discuss these below.

4.3 Persuasion

The persuasion protocol $\mathcal{P}'$ from [15] is:

1. A issues a $know(p)$, indicating it believes that p is the case.
2. A *asserts* p.
3. B *accepts* p if its acceptance attitude allows, else B either *asserts* $\neg p$ if it is allowed to, or else *challenges* p.
4. If B asserts $\neg p$, then go to (2) with the roles of the agents reversed and $\neg p$ in place of p.
5. If B has *challenged*, then:
   (a) A asserts S, the support for p;
   (b) Go to (2) for each $s \in S$ in turn.
6. If B does not *challenge*, then it issues either $accept(p)$ or $reject(p)$, depending upon the status of p for it.

Note that this kind of persuasion dialogue does not assume that agents necessarily start from opposite positions, one believing p and one believing $\neg p$. Instead one agent believes p and the other may believe $\neg p$, but also may believe neither p nor $\neg p$. This is perfectly consistent with the notion of persuasion suggested by Walton and Krabbe [23].

   Protocols $\mathcal{IS}$, $\mathcal{I}''$, and $\mathcal{P}'$ define a range of possible sequences of locutions, and we call these sequences *dialogues* (the relationship between the two is explored more in [15]). Here a protocol is a blueprint for many different dialogues, depending on the beliefs of the agents who use the protocol. We will refer to any dialogue under the X protocol as an "X dialogue".

5   Classes of Protocol

We have previously [16, 17] studied the properties of these three individual protocols. Here we extend this work, investigating whether there are properties, especially properties related to the outomes of dialogues under these protocols, that are determined by the structure of the dialogues.

A: $question(p)$
B: $assert(p)$
    A: $challenge(p)$
    B: $assert\left(\bigcup_i \{s_i\}_{i=1...n}\right)$
        A: $challenge(s_1)$
        B: $assert(\{s_1\})$
        A: $accept(s_1)$
        A: $challenge(s_2)$
        B: $assert(\{s_2\})$
        A: $accept(s_2)$
        $\vdots$
        A: $challenge(s_n)$
        B: $assert(\{s_n\})$
        A: $accept(s_n)$
    A: $accept\left(\bigcup_i \{s_i\}_{i=1...n}\right)$
A: $accept(p)$

Fig. 1. An example information-seeking dialogue

5.1   The General Shape of Dialogues

We start by considering the structure of an $\mathcal{IS}$ dialogue, the general form of which will be as in Fig. 1. The dialogue is written to emphasize that one way to think of it is as a set of sub-dialogues. There is an outer dialogue of three locutions, inside that there is another 3 locution dialogue, which in turn has a sequence of three-locution dialogues inside it. Looking at the other kinds of dialogue defined above reveals that they not only do they have a similar structure [15], but that the sub-dialogues they contain have the same structure. We can exploit this structure to obtain general results about dialogues constructed in this way.

We can consider the repeated sub-dialogue in Fig. 1 to be an *atomic protocol*[4], which, along with some additional ones identified in [15] (along with a set of rules for combining them) are sufficient to construct the protocols given above. These are similar in concept to conversation policies [8], being fragments from which a dialogue can be created. The atomic protocol distilled from the repeated sub-dialogue in Fig. 1 we call **A**. This starts following an $assert(X)$ and runs:

A: $challenge(X)$
B: $assert(Y)$
A: $accept(X)$ or $reject(X)$

where X and Y are variables, and Y is the support for whatever proposition instantiates X. By analogy with the $\mathcal{IS}$ dialogue, we say that an **A** dialogue is *successful* if it concludes with an $accept$.

Additional **A** dialogues may be nested inside the dialogue generated by this protocol, and typically we will have a series of such dialogues after the $assert$ (just as in Fig. 1).

---

[4] In the sense that it cannot be broken down further and yield a recognisable protocol.

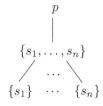

Fig. 2. An A dialogue

This corresponds to the construction of a *proof tree* for X. Thus if the X is instantiated with p and Y with $S = \{s_1, \ldots s_n\}$, then the proof tree unfolded by the instance of A above, and subsequent A dialogues about each s_i will build the proof tree in Fig. 2. This figure denotes that the set $\{s_1, \ldots, s_n\}$ is the set of grounds for p, and that each s_i has a set of grounds $\{s_i\}$.

Definition 8. *The subject of a dialogue is p iff the first locution in the dialogue concerns p.*

Definition 9. *Consider two dialogues D and E. D is said to be* embedded *in E if the sequence of locutions that make up D is a subsequence of those that make up E.*

Definition 10. *Consider two dialogues D and E. D is said to be* directly embedded *in E if D is embedded in E and there is no dialogue F such that D is embedded in F and F is embedded in D.*

If D is embedded in E but is not directly embedded in E, then there are one or more *intermediate* dialogues F, such that D is embedded in F and F is embedded in E. In such a case every F is said to be *between* D and E. In Fig. 1, the dialogue:

A: $challenge(s_1)$
B: $assert(\{s_1\})$
A: $accept(s_1)$

is embedded in the dialogue:

A: $question(p)$
B: $assert(p)$
   $\vdots$
A: $accept(p)$

and directly embedded in the A dialogue:

A: $challenge(p)$
B: $assert\left(\bigcup_i \{s_i\}_{i=1\ldots n}\right)$
   $\vdots$
A: $accept\left(\bigcup_i \{s_i\}_{i=1\ldots n}\right)$

If both D and E are carried out under **A** then the only reasonable ways to embed D in E is to have D follow the *assert* in E, or to follow another dialogue F that is already embedded in E.

Definition 11. *Consider two dialogues D and E, where D is directly embedded in E. If E has a level of embedding of n, then D has a level of embedding of $n + 1$. A dialogue that is not embedded in another has a level of embedding of 0.*

We can then show:

Proposition 1. *If E is an **A** dialogue with subject p and a level of embedding n, and D is an **A** dialogue embedded in E such that all intermediate dialogues between D and E are **A** dialogues, then the maximum level of embedding of D is $n + 1$.*

*Proof. The maximum level of embedding will occur when dialogues are nested as deeply within one another as possible, so we proceed by constructing the deepest possible nesting. If E has subject p, then the second locution of E will be the assertion of the grounds for p. This will be some set of propositions S which are a subset of the knowledge base of the agent replying to the assertion (by definition). Each member of this set can then be challenged by a new dialogue D_i with subject $s_i \in S$. The only possible response to such a challenge is to assert $\{s_i\}$ (the agent that asserts this has nothing else to back s_i with), and either D_i will end without another **A** dialogue being embedded in it, or E will terminate because of repetition. Either way there will be no **A** dialogues embedded in D_i.* $\qquad\qquad\Box$

In other words we can only have two levels of direct embedding of **A** dialogues. With this result, we are ready to start analysing combinations of atomic protocols.

5.2   Simple Dialogues

We will start by just considering combinations of **A** dialogues. Since we can only have two levels of direct embedding of **A** dialogue, a dialogue under $\mathcal{IS}$ will never end up building a proof tree deeper that in Fig. 2. This is the reason we can obtain termination results like those in [18]—the dialogue must terminate once the elements of the tree have been enumerated.

What do the proof trees look like for other kinds of dialogue? Well, dialogues conducted under $\mathcal{I}''$ will consist of a sequence of $\mathcal{IS}$ dialogues linked by their subject. If the subject of the nth dialogue is $r \rightarrow q$, then the subject of the $n + 1$th is r or $s \rightarrow r$. The subject of the first dialogue is $q \rightarrow p$, for some q, where p is the subject of the $\mathcal{I}''$ dialogue. This creates a structure like that in Fig. 3. In an $\mathcal{IS}$ dialogue, the key thing is the acceptance, or otherwise, of the subject of the dialogue and hence the subject of the top-level **A** dialogue. In an $\mathcal{I}''$ dialogue, the focus is much more on whether it is possible to prove something about the subject of the dialogue. In other words, for a dialogue with subject p, we are interested in whether $\cup_i \{a_i\} \vdash p$ where a_i is the subject of the ith top-level **A** dialogue. We refer to all logically distinct and non-tautological propositions like p that can be inferred from things that have been the subject of a successful **A** dialogue as being *agreed conclusions* of the dialogue. Obviously the subjects of all successful **A** dialogues are themselves agreed conclusions. The following result justifies the name:

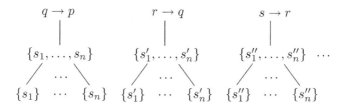

Fig. 3. An $\mathcal{I}''$ dialogue

Proposition 2. *Given a dialogue D between agents F and G, where D consists of one or more **A** dialogues, and where p is an agreed conclusion of D, then both agents have an acceptable argument for p.*

*Proof. The subject of each **A** dialogue that has the status of agreed conclusion is acceptable to both agents by definition—any proposition that is not acceptable will have been* rejected. *Any agreed conclusion p is a logical consequence of these subjects a_i, and therefore an agent can build an argument $(\cup_i \{a_i\}, p)$. Because the a_i are acceptable, there are no acceptable undercutting arguments for the a_i, and hence none for $(\cup_i \{a_i\}, p)$. So both agents have an acceptable argument for p.* □

The idea of agreed conclusions allows us to talk about outcomes other than those considered in [17]. There, we focused on *acceptance outcomes*—those propositions which one agent *assert*ed and the other later *accept*ed. Such acceptance outcomes include all the propositions in Fig. 2 and 3.

The relationship between acceptance outcomes and agreed conclusions is captured by the following results.

Proposition 3. *For any dialogue under a protocol which permits only one **A** dialogue, the set of agreed conclusions is exactly the set of acceptance outcomes.*

*Proof. The subject p of the **A** dialogue can be an acceptance outcomes, and if so the only acceptance outcome—since the grounds for p that are asserted are not accepted if there is only one **A** dialogue they can't be accepted. If is an acceptance outcomes, then p is also an agreed conclusion, and if p is not an acceptance outcome, there are no agreed conclusions, so the result holds.* □

Proposition 4. *Given any dialogue between agents F and G that has two **A** dialogues D and E embedded in it, such that D is directly embedded in E, or so that D and E are in sequence, then the set of acceptance outcomes is a subset of the agreed conclusions of the dialogue.*

Proof. Consider D and E in sequence and imagine both are successful. For both dialogues, Proposition 3 tells us that the acceptance outcomes are exactly the set of agreed conclusions. Let's call these acceptance outcomes p and q. Then $p \wedge q$, which need not be an acceptance outcome, is an agreed conclusion and the result holds for D and E in *sequence. Exactly the same argument holds if one of D and E is embedded in the other. If either, or both, of D and E are not successful, then the the set of agreed conclusions is exactly the set of acceptance outcomes for this dialogue, ∅, and the result holds.* □

So, if there is only one A, then acceptance outcomes and agreed conclusions coincide; but if a second A is included in the dialogue, then the set of agreed conclusions expands beyond the acceptance outcomes.

The reason that agreed conclusions and the A protocol are important ideas is that they give us a route to producing meta-theoretic results about the kinds of dialogue system we have been studying in [16, 17] that relate to dialogue structure. The above results are results about general classes of protocol—those that do and do not allow multiple A dialogues—rather than results about particular protocols. These are the kind of first, tentative, steps towards a meta-theory that we make in this paper.

The previous results suggest that it makes sense to classify protocols by the number of A dialogues that they permit. Since protocols that permit at most one A dialogue are not very interesting, we won't consider these to be a separate class. Instead we will classify protocols into those that do and do not permit sequences of A at the lowest level of embedding of such dialogues. (This is the only level at which it makes sense to discuss protocols which do not allow sequences—as soon as a set of grounds are asserted, as they must be in a A protocol, it does not make sense to prevent an embedded sequence of As testing the validity of the propositions in the grounds—so there is no point in considering restrictions on A dialogues at higher levels of embedding.)

Protocols like $\mathcal{I}''$ that allow sequences of A dialogues at the top level we will call *A-sequence* protocols and those like $\mathcal{IS}$ that do not allow such sequences of A dialogues we will call *A-singleton* protocols. Note that classifying a dialogue as A-singleton says nothing about whether it has embedded A dialogues. An A-sequence dialogue will in general generate more agreed conclusions than an A-singleton dialogue.

5.3   More Complex Dialogues

We are now ready to consider combinations of A with other atomic protocols, and will start by looking at the $\mathcal{P}'$ dialogue (since this neatly introduces another atomic protocol). There are two ways that a $\mathcal{P}'$ dialogue with subject p can unfold. In one, which in [15] we called *persuasion*$_1$, the initial combination of $know, assert$ is followed by a single A dialogue (which, of course, may have other A dialogues embedded in it). In the other, which in [15] we called *persuasion*$_2$, $know(p)$, $assert(p)$ is followed by $know(\neg p)$, the assertion of $\neg p$ and then by a A dialogue with subject $\neg p$. Clearly, then $\mathcal{P}'$ is an A-singleton protocol (though it can still have a set of agreed conclusions which is a superset of its set of acceptance outcomes). Since the atomic protocol:

A: $know(x)$
A: $assert(x)$
B: $reject(x)$ or $accept(x)$

was called K in [15], we will classify protocols like $\mathcal{P}'$ which have K and A protocols embedded in K-protocols (but no K protocols embedded in the As, and no sequences

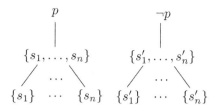

Fig. 4. An extended $\mathcal{P}$ dialogue

of Ks) as K-embedded protocols. Such protocols are rather limited. If the sequence of embedded K protocols concern the same proposition p, and so start with $know(p)$ then $know(\neg p)$, and so on we will call this a $K(p)$-embedded dialogue. Clearly the rule about repetition in $\mathcal{DG}$ implies that in practice there is no "and so on":

Proposition 5. *In $\mathcal{DG}$, $K(p)$-embedded dialogues can be composed of at most two K dialogues.*

Although this limiting result—which restricts $K(p)$-embedded dialogues to basically be identical to $\mathcal{P}'$—doesn't hold for other kinds of K-embedded dialogue, it isn't clear that such dialogues makes sense—they would involve a $know/assert$ pair about two unconnected propositions (they might, however, be a basis for eristic dialogues—quarrels).

Since $\mathcal{P}'$ summarises all the possibilities for $K(p)$-embedded dialogues, we have:

Proposition 6. *A $K(p)$-embedded dialogue where the lowest level of embedding of K is n has the same set of agreed outcomes as an A-singleton dialogue with a level of embedding of $n + 1$ and a subject of p, or an A-singleton dialogue with a level of embedding of $n + 2$ and a subject of $\neg p$.*

Proof. Follows immediately from the unfolding of a dialogue under $\mathcal{P}'$.   □

Thus $\mathcal{P}'$ and the whole class of $K(p)$-embedded dialogues capture a much narrower range of interactions than A-sequence dialogues.

It is possible to extend $\mathcal{P}'$ to obtain a similar kind of dialogue that is in the A-sequence class, but only in a limited way. Consider a dialogue that is a hybrid of $persuasion_1$ and $persuasion_2$ (which isn't possible under $\mathcal{P}'$, but would be under a close relative of it) with subject p in which the assertion of p is followed by the same A dialogue as in $persuasion_1$, but which doesn't stop[5] once the grounds for p have been found acceptable by both agents. Instead, the agent to which the initial $assert(p)$ was addressed is now allowed to $assert \neg p$, and there is another A dialogue about the grounds for $\neg p$. The result is the construction of the proof tree in Fig. 4. At this point, both agents judge the overall acceptability of p and $\neg p$ (which will depend in the limit on the strengths with which propositions are believed) and one will $accept(p)$ or the other will $accept(\neg p)$. This new persuasion dialogue will be called e$\mathcal{P}$.

---

[5] What we are describing here is the fullest extent of a dialogue under such a protocol—what [15] calls the *extensive form*. Clearly, a dialogue under this protocol might stop at this point.

We will classify protocols like $e\mathcal{P}$—protocols in which there are successive K dialogues at a level of embedding of 1—we will relax this restriction later—as K-sequence protocols. Such protocols are allowed to have A protocols embedded in the K protocols, just as in $\mathcal{P}$, and maybe other protocols around the K-protocols.

It turns out that it is useful to distinguish K-sequence protocols in which successive K dialogues start with $know(p)$ then $know(\neg p)$, and so on. We call such dialogues K(p)-sequence dialogues. Clearly the limitation on repetition in $\mathcal{DG}$ again means that:

Proposition 7. *In $\mathcal{DG}$, K(p)-sequence dialogues can have at most two K dialogues at a level of embedding of 1.*

We this notation, we can study the outcomes of dialogues like $e\mathcal{P}$. K(p)-sequence dialogues are rather different to $\mathcal{P}'$ dialogues. A $persuasion_1$ dialogue between F and G in which F utters the first locution will result in G either accepting or not accepting p, but there will be no change in F's beliefs about p. Similarly, a $persuasion_2$ dialogue will either result in F accepting $\neg p$ or not accepting $\neg p$, but there will be no change in G's beliefs about $\neg p$. In an $e\mathcal{P}$ dialogue, either of the agents may change the status of p, but we can't tell which from the form of the dialogue. Indeed we won't be able to say anything about the outcome of the dialogue until the end. However, we do know that both agents cannot change their minds in this way:

Proposition 8. *In $\mathcal{DG}$, an K(p)-sequence dialogue between agents F and G under a protocol in which the only dialogues at a level of embedding of 1 are K dialogues cannot result in one agent changing the status of p and the other changing the status of $\neg p$.*

Proof. For both agents to persuade the other to change the status of p we need the following scenario, or some symmetric variant, to take place. Before the dialogue, p is acceptable to F and $\neg p$ is acceptable to G. F starts a K dialogue with subject p and has p as an acceptance result. G has then changed status. G now has to get F to change the status of p. Consider the course of the dialogue unfolding in the best way to allow both agents to change the status of p. F asserts p, and may need to support this, and G accepts. The only remaining sub-dialogue requires that G assert $\neg p$ at this point, which it cannot do thanks to F's argument. The only time G can succeed in its persuasion is when F fails to make G change the status of p. $\quad\square$

This result hinges on the fact that both K dialogues are about the same proposition, and a G that has been persuaded that p is the case cannot then turn around and persuade F that $\neg p$ is the case. More general K-sequence dialogues, in which sucessive persuasions are about different propositions, can result in both agents changing the status of the subjects of successive sub-dialogues.

We can extend the kinds of dialogue we can assemble with the K dialogue, by allowing K dialogues to be embedded in A dialogues. Denoting protocols that allow K dialogues within A dialogues as well as A dialogues within K dialogue as *AK-embedded* protocols, it is no surprise to find that:

Proposition 9. *Every K-sequence protocol is an AK-embedded protocol. Some AK-embedded protocols are not K-sequence protocols.*

Proof. Immediate from the definition of K-sequence and AK-embedded protocols. $\quad\square$

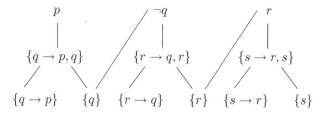

Fig. 5. An **AK**-embedded dialogue

However, the range of additional dialogues that are enabled by this extra embedding is maybe startling:

Proposition 10. *The class of **AK**-embedded protocols can generate dialogues which include embedded dialogues at arbitrarily large levels of embedding.*

Proof. *Since **K** dialogues are allowed to be embedded in **A** dialogues, we can keep deepening the proof tree (if the knowledge bases of the agents suffice) by answering every $assert(p)$ in a **K** dialogue with an **A** dialogue with subject p, and then meeting the assertion of one of the grounds s of the argument for p with an **K** dialogue that begins $know(\neg s)$.* □

In other words, the argument can now continue as long as the participants have something new to say.

Such dialogues now make a new kind of persuasion possible—A can propose p, B can come up with an undercutter (attacking the grounds of p), but this can then be over-ruled by another argument from A which is undefeated and undercuts the undercutter. The proof tree for such a dialogue is given in Fig. 5. However, despite the fact that they support this new kind of persuasion, **AK**-embedded protocols still have significant commonality with **K**-sequence dialogues:

Proposition 11. *Consider two agents F and G, with databases Σ_F and Σ_G. If F and G engage in a **K**-sequence dialogue, their agreed conclusions will be a subset of their agreed conclusions under a **AK**-embedded dialogue.*

Proof. *The result holds because **K**-sequence and **AK**-embedded dialogues start out in the same way—they only differ in terms of assertions (which are the locutions that give rise to agreed conclusions) once the dialogue gets to the first embedded **K**-dialogue. So while **AK**-embedded dialogues may have agreed conclusions that aren't achieved by **K**-sequence dialogues, they will have all the agreed conclusions (which may be the empty set of agreed conclusions) of the **K**-sequence dialogue up to that first embedded **K**-dialogue.* □

At this point it makes sense to ask whether we have a kind of monotonicity result for **AK**-embedded dialogues that says, just as Proposition 8 does for $\mathbf{K}(p)$-sequence dialogues, that once both agents agree on a proposition, it remains agreed throughout the dialogue. In fact, we can show the opposite of Proposition 8 for **AK**-embedded dialogues:

Proposition 12. *A dialogue between agents F and G under an **AK**-embedded protocol can result in one agent changing the status of p and the other changing the status of $\neg p$.*

Proof. For this result we only need an existence proof. An instance occurs in following scenario, or some symmetric variant. Before the dialogue, p is acceptable to F and ¬p is acceptable to G. F starts a K dialogue with subject p and has p as an acceptance result. G has then changed status. G now has to get F to change the status of p. It can't do this by asserting ¬p, since it no longer has an acceptable argument for ¬p, but it can now assert some q (if there is such a proposition) that allows F to create an acceptable argument for ¬p. If this q does not, so far as G knows, bear upon p or ¬p, then G remains convinced of the acceptability of p and both agents have changed status as required by the result.   □

This is a critical point, and it is worth considering it in more detail. As an example of how we can have the kind of situation in the proof of Proposition 12, consider the dialogue outlined in Fig. 5. Consider further that F starts the dialogue by stating p, G challenges, F replies with $\{q \rightarrow p, q\}$ and so on. By the time that the dialogue finishes with the statement of $\{s\}$, G has an acceptable argument for p and so changes status. However, a later assertion by G (and such an assertion is not ruled out in an AK-embedded dialogue), t, which is unrelated to the proof tree in Fig. 5 provides the final piece of a convincing argument from Σ_F (and thus invisible to G) against p. Then F will change the status of p.

Note that t cannot be part of the chain of argument about p. If it were, if t was part of the grounds for $\neg q$, say, and also a crucial part of some argument against p the rest of which was only known to F, then this argument would also be an argument against t and so be objected to by F. If it were able to cause F to find p not acceptable, then it would also prevent G changing the status of $\neg p$.

The important thing that is happening here is that, unlike what happens in the simple dialogues we have been studying up until now, both agents are making assertions and then further assertions in their defence, and later assertions need not be directly related—that is related in a way that is visible to both agents—to earlier ones. As the commitment stores grow, the set of new arguments that both agents can make as a result of the dialogue is growing, and, in particular, the non-overlapping part of this is growing. As this happens, the non-monotonicity of the notion of acceptability is coming to the fore. An obvious question then is, doesn't Proposition 8 contradict Proposition 12? Doesn't the non-monotonicity of the agreed conclusions (they are non-monotonic because they are determined by acceptability) mean that two agents can have an K-sequence dialogue about p and obtain agreed outcomes that are not agreed outcomes of an AK-embedded dialogue about p between the same two agents?

The answer is that the result of Proposition 8 holds *across the course of the dialogue* rather than *at the end of the dialogue*. In other words, it is possible for those agents to have an AK-embedded dialogue about p that ends up with a set of agreed outcomes that do not include the agreed outcomes of a K-sequence dialogue about p, but along the way they will have agreed on exactly the same outcomes, only to later reject them when they considered additional information.

The notion that we have to consider results across the course of the dialogue, and so take the non-monotonicity of the agreed outcomes properly into account, will be the focus of our future work.

6   Conclusions

This paper has extended the analysis of formal inter-agent dialogues in [15, 16, 17]. The main contribution of this extension has been to begin to provide a meta-theory for such dialogues based on structural classification, making it possible to establish results for whole classes of dialogue protocol. This, in turn, allows us to classify the whole space of possible protocols, establishing relations between them, and giving us ways of identifying good and bad classes. An early attempt in this direction was a second major contribution of this paper—giving a more extensive analysis of the relation between types of protocol and the outcome of dialogues under different protocols than has previously been possible [17].

In this paper we have only scratched the surface of the work that needs to be done in this area. There are a number of future directions that we are taking. First, we are deepening the analysis in this paper, extending the work to handle the notion of "across the course of the dialogue", and investigating other kinds of dialogue, such as the deliberation (in the terminology of [23]) dialogues [9]. Second, we are looking to strengthen our meta-theory using techniques from dynamic logic [11], to come up with tools that allow us to analyse dialogues in a way analogous to that in which dynamic logic is currently used to analyse program correctness. From this perspective we can think of each locution as a "program" in the usual program correctness sense, and then identify the effect of combinations of these. Finally, we are developing a denotational semantics for our dialogues using category theory [14]. This allows us to talk about properties of dialogues at a very abstract level.

Acknowledgments. This work was partially supported by NSF #REC-02-19347, NSF #IIS-0329037 and IST STREP-002307. Thanks are due to Frank Dignum for suggesting we look at proof trees.

References

[1] L. Amgoud and C. Cayrol. On the acceptability of arguments in preference-based argumentation framework. In *Proceedings of the 14th Conference on Uncertainty in Artificial Intelligence*, pages 1–7, 1998.

[2] L. Amgoud, N. Maudet, and S. Parsons. Modelling dialogues using argumentation. In E. Durfee, editor, *Proceedings of the Fourth International Conference on Multi-Agent Systems*, pages 31–38, Boston, MA, USA, 2000. IEEE Press.

[3] B. Chaib-Draa and F. Dignum. Trends in agent communication language. *Computational Intelligence*, 18(2):89–101, 2002.

[4] F. Dignum, B. Dunin-Kȩplicz, and R. Verbrugge. Agent theory for team formation by dialogue. In C. Castelfranchi and Y. Lespérance, editors, *Seventh Workshop on Agent Theories, Architectures, and Languages*, pages 141–156, Boston, USA, 2000.

[5] P. M. Dung. On the acceptability of arguments and its fundamental role in nonmonotonic reasoning, logic programming and n-person games. *Artificial Intelligence*, 77:321–357, 1995.

[6] R. A. Flores and R. C. Kremer. To commit or not to commit. *Computational Intelligence*, 18(2):120–173, 2002.

[7] T. F. Gordon. The pleadings game. *Artificial Intelligence and Law*, 2:239–292, 1993.

[8] M. Greaves, H. Holmback, and J. Bradshaw. What is a conversation policy? In F. Dignum and M. Greaves, editors, *Issues in Agent Communication*, Lecture Notes in Artificial Intelligence 1916, pages 118–131. Springer, Berlin, Germany, 2000.

[9] B. J. Grosz and S. Kraus. The evolution of sharedplans. In M. J. Wooldridge and A. Rao, editors, *Foundations of Rational Agency*, volume 14 of *Applied Logic*. Kluwer, The Netherlands, 1999.

[10] B. J. Grosz and C. L. Sidner. Attention, intentions, and the structure of discourse. *Computational Linguistics*, 12(3):175–204, 1986.

[11] D. Harel, D. Kozen, and J. Tiuryn. *Dynamic Logic*. MIT Press, 2000.

[12] M. O. Jackson. Mechanism theory. In U. Devigs, editor, *Optimization and Operations Research*, The Encyclopedia of Life Support Science. EOLSS Publishers, Oxford, UK, 2003. The working paper version of this article includes a more comprehensive bibliography and some bibliographic notes.

[13] S. Kraus, K. Sycara, and A. Evenchik. Reaching agreements through argumentation: a logical model and implementation. *Artificial Intelligence*, 104(1–2):1–69, 1998.

[14] P. McBurney and S. Parsons. A denotational semantics for deliberation dialogues. In *3rd International Conference on Autonomous Agents and Multi-Agent Systems*. IEEE Press, 2004.

[15] S. Parsons, P. McBurney, and M. Wooldridge. The mechanics of some formal inter-agent dialogue. In F. Dignum, editor, *Advances in Agent Communication*. Springer-Verlag, Berlin, Germany, 2003.

[16] S. Parsons, M. Wooldridge, and L. Amgoud. An analysis of formal inter-agent dialogues. In *1st International Conference on Autonomous Agents and Multi-Agent Systems*. ACM Press, 2002.

[17] S. Parsons, M. Wooldridge, and L. Amgoud. On the outcomes of formal inter-agent dialogues. In *2nd International Conference on Autonomous Agents and Multi-Agent Systems*. ACM Press, 2003.

[18] S. Parsons, M. Wooldridge, and L. Amgoud. Properties and complexity of formal inter-agent dialogues. *Journal of Logic and Computation*, 13(3):347–376, 2003.

[19] H. Prakken. Relating protocols for dynamic dispute with logics for defeasible argumentation. *Synthese*, 127:187–219, 2001.

[20] C. Reed. Dialogue frames in agent communications. In Y. Demazeau, editor, *Proceedings of the Third International Conference on Multi-Agent Systems*, pages 246–253. IEEE Press, 1998.

[21] M. Schroeder, D. A. Plewe, and A. Raab. Ultima ratio: should Hamlet kill Claudius. In *Proceedings of the 2nd International Conference on Autonomous Agents*, pages 467–468, 1998.

[22] K. Sycara. Argumentation: Planning other agents' plans. In *Proceedings of the Eleventh Joint Conference on Artificial Intelligence*, pages 517–523, 1989.

[23] D. N. Walton and E. C. W. Krabbe. *Commitment in Dialogue: Basic Concepts of Interpersonal Reasoning*. State University of New York Press, Albany, NY, 1995.

Towards a Formal and Implemented Model of Argumentation Schemes in Agent Communication

Chris Reed[1] and Doug Walton[2]

[1] Division of Applied Computing, University of Dundee,
Dundee DD1 4HN Scotland, UK
chris@computing.dundee.ac.uk
http://www.computing.dundee.ac.uk/staff/creed
[2] Department of Philosophy, University of Winnipeg,
Winnipeg R3B 2E9 Manitoba, Canada
d.walton@uwinnipeg.ca
http://www.uwinnipeg.ca/~walton

Abstract. Argumentation schemes are patterns of non-deductive reasoning that have long been studied in argumentation theory, and have more recently been identified in computational domains including multi-agent systems as holding the potential for significant improvements in reasoning and communication abilities. By focusing on models of natural language argumentation schemes, and then building formal systems from them, direct implementation becomes possible that not only has advantages in flexibility and scope, but also computational efficiency.

1 Introduction

Argumentation schemes capture stereotypical patterns of reasoning. Their study constitutes an ancient part of argumentation theory that has recently been attracting increasing attention (Walton, 1996), *inter alia*. Very early expositions laid out schemes as types of proofs -- a handy guide to the ways and means of persuading an audience (see, e.g. (Quintilian, 1920)). In this context, they are treated as a form of rhetoric. Later, they were adopted as a means of identifying bad argument -- this is very much the Aristotelian approach, in which schemes form a foundation stone for fallacy theory. Both of these traditions, the fallacy-theoretic and rhetorical, have had much more recent exponents, such as Grennan (1997) and Perelman and Olbrechts-Tyteca (1967). But a new approach has also emerged from informal logic, whereby a more analytical, more objective approach has been taken to the characterisation of these reasoning patterns. Good examples include Kienpointner (1986) and Walton (1996) who both attempt to sketch means for the classification of schemes.

Schemes have also been attracting the attentions of those who are interested in exploiting the rich interdisciplinary area between argumentation and AI (Reed & Norman, 2003; Verheij, 2003). Of course, AI has long been interested in non-deductive forms of reasoning (for a good review of a large proportion of the area, see (Prakken & Vreeswijk, 2002)). But schemes, as construed by argumentation theory, seem to provide a somewhat more fine-grained analysis that is typical within AI. One example

I. Rahwan et al. (Eds.): ArgMAS 2004 LNAI 3366, pp. 19–30, 2005.

lies in the granularity of classification of types: Kienpointner introduces over a dozen, Walton, almost thirty, Grennan, over fifty, Katzav and Reed (2004), over one hundred -- and none claim exhaustivity. By comparison, AI systems are more typically built with a small handful (Pollock's (1995) OSCAR, for example identifies less than ten -- with an uneven amount of work spread between them). This profligacy in philosophical classification might be argued to be as much a problem as an advantage - this is explored further below - but it serves to demonstrate that more detail is in some way being adduced. In particular, the propositional logic upon which a great deal of multi-agent argumentation is based is being further analysed to yield more refined structures of reasoning. It is the contention of this paper that those refined structures of reasoning yield well to a computational interpretation, and can be implemented to useful effect.

The aim of this paper is to employ conventional techniques (demonstrated in (Dung, 1995; McBurney and Parsons, 2002; Amgoud and Cayrol, 2002; *inter alia*) to handle the structure of argumentation schemes in such a way that (a) individual agents can reason about and develop arguments that employ schemes, and (b) that communication structures can be built up around those schemes. A formal account is an important objective servicing this aim, but equally important is a concrete implementation that demonstrates that both (a) and (b) can be achieved in practice. Although the implementation necessarily makes specific choices with regard to development, the formal component guarantees the broader applicability of the approach.

This paper represents a work in progress and sketches the framework, both theoretical and applied, around which development continues.

2   Argumentation Schemes in Natural Discourse

Argumentation schemes are forms of argument (structures of inference) representing common types of argumentation. They represent structures of arguments used in everyday discourse, as well as in special contexts like legal argumentation or scientific argumentation. They represent the deductive and inductive forms of argument that we are so highly familiar with in logic. But they can also represent forms of argument that are neither deductive nor inductive, but that fall into a third category, sometimes called abductive or presumptive. This third type of argument is defeasible, and carries weight on a balance of considerations in a dialogue. Perelman and Olbrechts-Tyteca, in *The New Rhetoric* (1969) identified many of these defeasible types of arguments used to carry evidential weight in a dialogue. Arthur Hastings' Ph.D. thesis (1963) carried out a systematic analysis of many of the most common of these presumptive schemes. The scheme itself specified the form of premises and conclusion of the argument. Hastings expressed one special premise in each scheme as a Toulmin warrant linking the other premises to the conclusion. Such a warrant is typically a defeasible generalization. Along with each scheme, he attached a corresponding set of critical questions. These features set the basic pattern for argumentation schemes in the literature that followed.

Many of these argumentation schemes were described and analyzed by van Eemeren and Grootendorst (1992). Kienpointner (1992) developed a comprehensive listing of argumentation schemes that includes deductive and inductive forms in addition to presumptive ones. In (Walton, 1996), twenty-five argumentation schemes for common types of presumptive reasoning were identified. Following Hastings' format, a set of critical questions is attached to each scheme. If an argument put forward by a proponent meets the requirements of a scheme, and the premises are acceptable to the respondent, then the respondent is obliged to accept the conclusion. But this acceptance, or commitment as it is often called, is provisional in the dialogue. If the respondent asks one of the critical questions matching the scheme, the argument defaults and the burden shifts back to the proponent. The weight of the argument is only restored when the proponent gives a successful answer to the question.

An argumentation scheme that can be used as an example is that for argument from sign. An example would be a case in which Helen and Bob are hiking along a trail in Banff, and Bob points out some tracks along the path, saying, "These look like bear tracks, so a bear must have passed along this trail." In the argumentation scheme below, one premise is seen to function as a Toulmin warrant.

Argument from Sign (Walton, 1996, p. 49).

Minor Premise: Given data represented as statement A is true in this situation.

Major (Toulmin Warrant) Premise: Statement B is generally indicated as true when its sign, A, is true, in this kind of situation.

Conclusion: Therefore, B is true in this situation.

The major premise is a presumptive conditional stating that if A is true, then generally, but subject to exceptions, B is also true. In the case cited, the tracks could have been "planted" on the trail by tricksters. But in the absence of evidence of such trickery, it is reasonable to provisionally draw the conclusion that a bear passed along the trail. Argument from sign is closely related to abductive inference, or inference to the best explanation. The best explanation of the existence of the observed tracks is the hypothesis that a bear walked along the trail producing the tracks. Of course, there could be other explanations. But in the absence of additional evidence, the bear hypothesis could be plausible as a basis for proceeding carefully.

3   A Theory of Argumentation Schemes

Unfortunately, though the argumentation literature includes a wide variety of approaches to definition, classification, collection, analysis and specification of schemes, there is none that represents either a definitive or a consensual view. Any current computational work on schemes must therefore position itself somewhere in the space of theoretical work.

If argumentation schemes capture types of argument, perhaps the first theoretical issue is to resolve the scope of our study by answering the question, 'What is argument?' The question is interesting, and has direct impact on models in multi-agent systems. Does, for example, the bid-counter-bid protocol of many auctions count as argument? For most MAS people, this is too trivial to count, though for some argumentation theorists who take an inclusive view (such as Walton) it certainly could. Alternatively, would the exchange of sets of acceptable theorems (in the sense of Dung (1995)) count as argument? For most MAS people using argumentation, the answer is that it is, self-evidently, argument. Yet argumentation theorists of a communication theoretic or pragma-dialectic stripe would beg to differ. If we want a theory of argumentation in multi-agent systems, we need to delimit what that theory should account for.

There are, as might be expected, almost as many definitions of argument as there are argumentation theorists. At one end, the all encompassing taxonomy of Gilbert (1997) covers a panoply of situated action that can count as argument, from artistic creation, through non-linguistic communication, to physical activity. At the other end, van Eemeren and Grootendorst's (1992) pragma-dialectics associates argument with the notion of critical discussion, a closely bounded, tightly specified linguistic activity whose definition rests upon speech act theory.

In multi-agent systems, the majority of recent work exploring notions of argumentation has a propositional foundation. Thus one of the foremost examples, (McBurney and Parsons, 2002), offers brief description of the "topic layer": "Topics are matters under discussion by the participating agents, and we assume that they can be represented in a suitable logic L. Topics are denoted by the lower case Roman letters p, q, r, etc. ... Topics may refer to either real-world objects or to states of affairs". They go on to explain that L may also include modalities, but even though the concept of "real-world objects" is a little ambiguous, it is clear that the intention here is to use something rather close to a (possibly modal) propositional logic as the language for expressing the content of locutions. There is little more said in (McBurney and Parsons, 2002) – or in work that takes a very similar approach (of which a good example is (Amgoud & Cayrol, 2002)) – on the topic layer.

If there is a need to stay close to natural language use (in order, for example, to exploit theories of communication that have been developed for natural languages), then such a propositional basis starts to falter – or at least, starts to be inadequate on its own.

The aims of a formalisation should therefore be (a) to remain sufficiently close to linguistic practice that the richness and flexibility of natural argumentation can be exploited, whilst aiming (b) to render a model that is straightforwardly implementable, both in generation and understanding. The focus here is upon the definition, representation and manipulation of scheme-based structures. There are many and rich interplays between argumentation schemes and the progress and conduct of dialogue. Some of these are explored in (Prakken et al., 2003).

With these aims, and this focus in mind, and building on the multi-agent systems tradition of the propositional underpinning, the theoretical basis here borrows heavily from (Katzav and Reed, 2004). Arguments themselves are construed as (non-atomic) propositions[1]. These propositions refer to facts that "wholly convey" other facts through a variety of relations of conveyance. That is, the communicative structures refer to relationships that exist in the world between fully specified states. Examples of these relationships include causal relations, class-membership relations, constitutive relations and others (and these relation types can form the basis of a system of classification).

---

[1] This apparently simple starting point has various ramifications, some of which are convenient (such as the fact that it any argument R can be referred to with an appropriate 'that' clause – the argument that R: this is a property of propositions) and some of which are less so (such as the requirement to exclude interrogatives and imperatives from the concept of argument for now). Further discussions can be found in (Katzav and Reed, 2004).

An example will serve to clarify. The following extract, Ex1, is taken from the *The United Kingdom Commons Hansard Debate Text* for 21 October 2002: Vol. No. 391, Part No. 192, Column 2:

> (Ex1) *Confidence in personal and occupational schemes will have been severely damaged this week by news that the Government are abolishing higher-rate tax relief on pension contributions.*

The analysis in Figure 1 is taken from the AraucariaDB online corpus[2]:

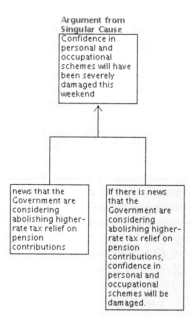

Fig. 1. An *Araucaria* analysis of the structure of the *Pensions* argument. Vertical arrows indicate support; joined arrows indicate linked support (Freeman, 1991); shaded areas around diagram components show schemes, named at their conclusions; and shaded boxes show enthymemes

This is one of the simpler examples in the corpus. Figure 1 shows an instantiation of a scheme in the Katzav-Reed taxonomy called *Argument from Singular Cause*. The implicit conditional is presumed in this analysis to express a causal relationship between premise as cause and conclusion as effect. Thus the fact that there is news from the Government (...) conveys via a causal relation of conveyance the fact that confidence (...) will have been damaged. This ('compound') fact is the one identified by the proposition that is the argument in Ex1 and Figure 1.

---

[2] Available at http://www.computing.dundee.ac.uk/staff/creed/araucaria

The final component is to notice that there is a relationship between the type of argumentation scheme and the type of atomic propositions that instantiate it. Thus, in the example above, of the three atomic components, one expresses a causal relation (the major premise), and the other two express the sort of facts that can stand as cause and effect, respectively. (Note that the task here is not to develop an all encompassing ontology. Nor is it to claim that some propositions can be uniquely labelled as 'causes' or 'effects' – such a position would be absurd. But nevertheless, it is self evident that some types of propositions can stand in such places, and that others cannot, and it is merely this distinction that is being drawn here). Individual propositions may have numerous attributes that characterise their type.

In this way, a conventional propositional database of intentional attitudes such as beliefs, is stratified by typing the propositions that it contains. This typing then supports autonomous reasoning mechanisms by which agents can identify and communicate arguments constructed from schemes instantiated by propositions of the appropriate type.

This approach to the theoretical basis has the benefit of not only providing a means for exploiting theories of argumentation from empirical sources, but also makes possible reuse of analysed data within implemented multi-agent communities.

4   Elements of a Formalisation of Argumentation Schemes

The starting point is propositional logic, *PL*, from which we take our propositions (*Props*) and propositional variables, and all the usual operators. Next, we define a set of attributes, *T*. This set contains any number of arbitrary tokens. Attributes are associated with propositions by the typing relation, τ, thus: $\tau: Props \rightarrow P(T)$. That is, the typing relation associates with every proposition a set of attributes, or "type".

The next step is to define scheme structures formally. The approach presented here is based on the implementation of the Argument Markup Language DTD (Reed and Rowe, 2001), and is designed to facilitate practical and reusable implementation.

The set, Ξ, of schemes in a particular system is comprised of a set of tuples of the following form: *<SName, SConclusion, SPremises>*, where *SName* is some arbitrary token, *SConclusion* $\in P(T)$, and *SPremises* $\subset P(T)^3$. If $\exists \xi \in \Xi$ such that $\xi = <\sigma_0, \sigma_1, \sigma_2>$ then $\neg\exists\xi' \in \Xi / \{\xi\}$ such that $\xi' = <\sigma_0, \sigma_3, \sigma_4>$ or $\xi' = <\sigma_5, \sigma_1, \sigma_2>$, for any $\sigma_3, \sigma_4, \sigma_5$. In this way, a scheme is uniquely named and is associated with a conclusion type, and a set of premise types.

---

[3] In fact, the picture for *SPremises* is rather more complicated. Clearly, an argument scheme can include more than one premise of the same type. Thus *SPremises* can have multiple identical elements. Hence *SPremises* is not a set, but a bag. In order to keep the presentation simple, and to focus on the broad structural aspect of the formalism, it is here simplified and restricted such that there can only be one premise of each type. In detail, extra machinery can be added quite simply such that each element of *SPremises* is a tuple in which the first element is a unique natural number, and the second element the set of attributes that constitute a premise type. In this way, *SPremises* remains a set and yet multiple instances of a given premise type are permitted

Finally, an instantiation is an argument based upon one of the schemes. An instantiation is thus a tuple, *<Name, Conclusion, Premises>* such that for some *<SName, t, SPremises>* $\in \Xi$, where *SName = Name*,

$$Conclusion \in Props \qquad \wedge \quad \tau(Conclusion) = t, \qquad\qquad and$$
$$\forall p \in Premises, \; p \in Props \wedge \quad \text{the set } \{\pi \mid \pi = \tau(p)\} = SPremises^4$$

In this way, an instantiation of a scheme named *SName* must have a conclusion of the right type, and all the premises, each of which is also of the right type. (Note that this latter requirement is actually a little too strong for most natural models of scheme usage, as schemes often involve some premises being left implicit, to form enthymematic arguments. The simplification is useful at this stage of development, and does not preclude more sophisticated handling later).

This model supports a straightforward mechanism for representation of schemes. It does not, as it stands, give an agent a mechanism for reasoning with schemes and for building (that is to say, chaining) arguments using schemes. Through structures such as critical questions (Walton, 1996), argumentation schemes offer the potential for a sophisticated model of dialectical argument-based nonmonotonic reasoning. Such a model is currently under development (see (Prakken *et al.*, 2003) for some preliminary steps in this direction). In the meantime, a simple solution suffices to support development of both theory and implementation.

To sketch how this works, we define a new operator, $\Rrightarrow$, that corresponds to implication extended to schemes. That is, in this system, if $\alpha \supset \beta$, then $\alpha \Rrightarrow \beta$, but also, if there exists an instantiation of an argument scheme *<N, C, P>* in which $\beta = C$ and $\alpha \in P$, then $\alpha \Rrightarrow \beta$. Dung-style definitions of acceptability, admissibility are then formed using deductive closure on $\Rrightarrow$ rather than $\supset$, and everything else remains as before. Thus, the representation of argumentation schemes is brought in to standard models of defeasible argumentation of Dung, Prakken, Vreeswijk, Verheij, etc.

5   Towards Implementation

There are two distinct facets to implementation that can handle schemes. The first is the ability to represent and manipulate scheme based structures in the one-agent setting in a flexible and scalable way. The second is to utilise that representation in the multi-agent case, and exploit representational structure in communication design.

5.1   Representation

Following work examining the diagramming of natural argument – an important topic from the practical, pedagogic point of view (van Gelder & Rizzo, 2001), but also a driver of theoretical development in informal logic (Walton & Reed, 2004) – Reed and Rowe (2001) developed *Araucaria*, a system for aiding human analysts and students in marking up argument. Araucaria adopts the 'standard treatment' (Freeman, 1991) for argument analysis, based on identification of propositions (as vertices in a diagram) and the relationships of support and attack holding between them (edges in a

---

[4] Set equivalence here is taken to mean identical membership.

diagram). It is thus similar to a range of argument visualisation tools (see (Kirschner *et al.*, 2003) for an overview), and familiar from AI techniques such as Pollock's (1995) inference graphs. As well as having a number of features that make it particularly well suited to teaching and research in argumentation, it is also unique in having explicit support for argumentation schemes.

Araucaria's underlying representation language is an XML language, the Argument Markup Language. AML is defined using a DTD, a simple and straightforward language-design mechanism. One of the basic components of arguments from Araucaria's point of view is a proposition or PROP - loosely, a text-box in Figure 1, above. The definition for this component is as follows:

```
<!ELEMENT PROP (PROPTEXT, OWNER*, INSCHEME*)>
```

The PROPTEXT component details the text or, roughly, the propositional content of a given PROP. The OWNERs of a PROP allow analysts to distinguish between viewpoints in an argument (and lay a foundation for marking up argumentative dialogue, which is currently work in progress). Finally, the INSCHEME component allows the analyst to indicate that a PROP belongs to a given scheme. Notice that the Kleene star in the definition allows multiple INSCHEME tags for a given PROP - that is, a given proposition can be in more than one argumentation scheme.

The definition of the (empty) INSCHEME tag, below, includes two references, one to a unique scheme name, the *scheme* attribute, and one to a unique identifier, *schid*. It is important to include both so that any given PROP can be marked as belonging not only to a scheme of a particular type, but also a particular instance of that scheme within the current text (so that multiple instances of a given scheme can be identified uniquely).

```
<!ATTLIST INSCHEME scheme   CDATA #REQUIRED
                   schid    CDATA #REQUIRED>
```

Finally, the *scheme* attribute in the definition above corresponds (in processing, not in AML definition) to an element in the SCHEMESET tag of the AML file. For ease of exchange and independence, each AML analysis includes the complete set of scheme definitions that are used in the analysed text. The SCHEMESET (which can also be saved separately, and thereby adopted in different analyses) is composed of a series of SCHEME elements.

```
<!ELEMENT SCHEME (NAME, FORM, CQ*)>
```

Thus each scheme has a unique name (e.g., 'Argument from Expert Opinion' in the schemeset corresponding to (Walton, 1996)). The CQ elements allow specification of critical questions, and the FORM element supports specification of the formal structure of a scheme thus:

```
<!ELEMENT FORM (PREMISE*, CONCLUSION)>
```

where both PREMISEs and CONCLUSIONs are ultimately just propositions expressed in text.

In this way, AML supports the specification of argumentation schemes in a machine readable format. It is flexible enough to capture various types of argumentation schemes, including examples from (Kienpointner, 1986), (Walton, 1996), (Grennan,

1997) and (Katzav and Reed, 2004). Similarly, it is flexible enough to handle and match other types of argumentation analysis in diverse domains including Wigmore charts in reasoning about legal evidence (Prakken *et al.*, 2003), and representing Pollock-style inference graphs (Pollock, 1995). At the same time, the language is simple enough to support manipulation by a number of systems, tools and utilities, including, of course, Araucaria. But AML is also used by several other utilities, and its schemes are being employed in the construction of a large online corpus[5] of natural argumentation, available online at http://www.computing.dundee.ac.uk/staff/creed/araucaria.

5.2   Agent Communication

Implementing scheme-based communication situated in a multi-agent system is currently a work in progress. We have adopted a flexible, lightweight and easily deployed agent platform called Jackdaw[6], primarily because it offers great flexibility in the design and implementation of both mentalistic structures and communication languages and protocols.

The belief database is populated at start up. Beliefs are stored as directed by the model of section 4, with a propositional component and a type component, the latter comprised of a number of attributes. The "invention" of the argument is beyond the scope of the current work – in implementation, the agent simply has the user select a proposition to argue for. The agent then selects a supporting argument at random. That is, by chaining through the belief database, it identifies instantiations of schemes, replete with appropriately typed propositions, and selects one of them. The argument is then rendered as a fragment of AML, and communicated to an opponent.

Following in the spirit of Parsons and Jennings' (1996) style interaction, agents determine responses on the basis of acceptability classes. Specifically, if the hearer has an argument (that is, an instantiation of a scheme) that attacks a component of the speaker's argument, they can return such an argument as a counter[7]. If the hearer has no such argument, it simply updates it belief database with both premises and conclusions of the speakers argument. Such a dialogic protocol is extremely simple: the focus here is not upon how argumentation schemes interact with protocols (which is being pursued in companion work), nor on how argumentation-based dialogue games can structure inter-agent communication (which is the topic of much current research) – but rather, on the contents of the moves as schemes.

6   The Role of Schemes in Agent Communication

There are several key advantages that are delivered by using argumentation schemes in inter-agent argument. The first is that the belief database is stratified. As agents become larger, and have larger belief databases, and as agent systems are deployed in more real world situations, deduction and search through that database – even by the

---

[5] Clearly the use of a markup language and the presentation here is suggestive of other work in corpus linguistics. There is not space here to explore the relationships between AML and corpus research; the interested reader is directed to the website for further details.

[6] See http://www.calicojack.co.uk/

[7] We abstract here from the distinction between undercutting and rebutting arguments.

very fastest theorem provers – becomes extremely computationally expensive. Tackling this problem is going to require a battery of techniques. One of those techniques could be to partition or stratify the database to guide the search process. That particular schemes (i.e. particular ways of reaching conclusions) can only take certain types of proposition cuts the processing required to generate arguments by substantially reducing the branching factor. A second, analogous advantage reduces load for the hearer – processing an incoming argument to assess its acceptability (or some other standard for validity, reasonableness, or sufficiency) is similarly computationally intensive. It too is simplified by reducing search through scheme-based stratification. A third advantage also becomes manifest at this step in the process of inter-agent argumentation. For not only is the computational load of judging incoming arguments reduced, but further, the mechanisms by which that judging can be carried out and much broader. Individual argument schemes might have their own standards of validity by which they might be judged (in a similar way to the distinction between deductive validity and inductive strength). The way in which particular schemes are judged is then a feature of the community or society in which that agent resides (demonstrating a close analogy to human communities).

There are also broader, practical advantages of equipping agents, both autonomous and those working directly on behalf of users, with the ability to formulate and handle argumentation schemes as fragments of AML. The first is that it offers the opportunity to re-use increasingly rich resources of existing argumentation, such as AraucariaDB, that could provide a way of overcoming some of the limitations of the "knowledge bottleneck", that limits many real world deployments of interesting AI and MAS models. The second advantage is that with wide heterogeneity in the types of arguments used in domains such as law, pedagogy and e-government, it is important to have communication and reasoning models that are as theory-neutral as possible.

Finally, it becomes possible to envisage heterogeneous environments in which completely autonomous agents can interact with humans, or agents representing humans, through the medium of natural language restricted through structural constraints and ontological limits – but not requiring natural language understanding and generation. Though an ambitious aim, such systems are being hinted at by increasingly sophisticated models of CSCW and CSCA in particular (Kirschner *et al.*, 2003), and scheme-based communication represents a further step in that direction.

7   Concluding Remarks

There are several tasks that require immediate attention in implementation. Empirical evaluation is then planned for the implementation to show the advantages discussed in section 6 in situ, and to provide quantitative justification for the currently qualitative, theoretical claims.

In conjunction with parallel work, an important next step is to tie the internal representation and thence communication structures with larger scale characterisations of dialogue and the dynamics of dialogue. So, for example, critical questions have a key role to play in capturing the shifting burden of proof and dialectical obligations in discourse. Investigation of these topics will be aided by having a simple, sound foundation for representation and exchange of the schemes and their instantiations.

One further exciting opportunity is to have agents configure their reasoning capabilities on the basis of schemeset definitions. There are many alternative ways of defining schemes (Walton, 1996), (Kienpointner, 1986) and (Katzav and Reed, 2004) represent three divergent theoretical views, and (Norman et al., 2003) indicate that it is likely that more will be developed in the computational domain. It was for these reasons that Araucaria was designed to support the definition, manipulation and exploitation of "schemesets" that use the same AML language to characterise different sets of schemes. These schemesets essentially represent a more or less complete way of performing reasoning, and so could be used to reconfigure agent reasoning capabilities on the fly.

But despite the work that remains to be done, it is already clear that there is a need for a model of scheme-based communication that builds on the successes of (McBurney and Parsons (2003), Amgoud and Cayrol (2002), et al., but integrates work on argumentation schemes, both the more mature research in argumentation theory, and the nascent results with a more computational bent (Norman et al., 2003; Verheij, 2002). This paper has aimed to lay out some groundwork for such an integration at a conceptual level, arguing for the importance of including naturalistic models; at the formal level, sketching the formal framework; and at the implementation level, showing how implemented components are being slotted together to provide testable systems. In this way, our objective is to develop models and systems of inter-agent behaviour for a wide class of agents and a wide class of reasoning structures.

Acknowledgements

The authors would like to acknowledge grant support from the Leverhulme Trust in the UK, and SSHRC in Canada, for supporting their collaborative work in the area. They would also like to thank Henry Prakken for stimulating discussions on closely related issues. Finally, grateful acknowledgement is made to the anonymous reviewers who through their comments have aided significant improvements to this presentation.

References

1. Amgoud, L. & Cayrol, C. (2002) "A model of reasoning based on the production of acceptable arguments." *Annals of Mathematics and Artificial Intelligence* **34**, pp. 197-216.
2. Dung, P.M. (1995) "On the acceptability of arguments and its fundamental role in non-monotonic reasoning, logic programming and n-person games", *Artificial Intelligence* **77** pp 205-219.
3. Eemeren, F.H. Van & Grootendorst, R. (1992) *Argumentation, Communication and Fallacies*, LEA.
4. Freeman, J.B. (1991) *Dialectics and the Macrostructure of Argument*, FORIS.
5. Gilbert, M.A. (1997) *Coalescent Argumentation*, LEA.
6. Grennan, W. (1997) *Informal Logic*, McGill-Queens University Press.
7. Hastings, A.C. (1963) *A Reformulation of the Modes of Reasoning in Argumentation*, Evanston, Illinois, Ph.D. Dissertation.
8. Katzav, J. and Reed, C.A. (2004) "On Argumentation Schemes and the Natural Classification of Argument", *Argumentation* to appear.

9.   Kienpointner, M. (1986) "Towards a Typology of Argument Schemes" in *Proceedings of ISSA 1986*, Amsterdam University Press.

10. 10. Kienpointner, M. (1992) *Alltagslogik: Struktur und Funktion von Argumentationsmustern*, Stuttgart, Fromman-Holzboog.

11. Kirschner, P.A., Buckingham Shum, S.J., Carr, C.S. (2003) *Visualizing Argument*, Springer

12. McBurney, P. and Parsons, S. (2002) "Games that Agents Play", *Journal of Logic, Language and Information* **11** (**3**) pp315-334.

13. Norman, T.J., Carbogim, D.V., Krabbe, E.C. & Walton, D. (2003) "Argument and Multi-Agent Systems" in (Reed and Norman, 2003)

14. Pollock, J.L. (1995) *Cognitive Carpentry: A Blueprint for How to Build a Person*, MIT Press.

15. Prakken, H., Reed, C.A. and Walton, D. (2003) "Argumentation Schemes and Generalisations in Reasoning about Evidence" in *Proceedings of the 9th International Conference on AI & Law*, ACM Press.

16. Prakken, H. and Vreeswijk, G. (2002) "Logics for defeasible argumentation", in Gabbay, D. and Guenther, F. (eds) *Handbook of Philosophical Logic*, Vol. 4, Kluwer, pp218-319.

17. Quintilian (1920) *Institutio Oratoria*, Harvard University Press, Translated H.E. Butler.

18. Parsons, S. & Jennings, N. R. (1996) "Negotiation through argumentation: A Preliminary Report", in *Proceedings ICMAS'96*.

19. Perelman, C. & Ohlbrechts-Tyteca, L. (1969) *The New Rhetoric: A Treatise on Argumentation,* University of Notre Dame Press.

20. Reed, C.A. & Norman, T.J. (2003) *Argumentation Machines*, Kluwer.

21. Reed, C.A. & Rowe, G.W.A. (2001) "Araucaria: Software for Puzzles in Argument Diagramming and XML", *Department of Applied Computing, University of Dundee Technical Report* available at http://www.computing.dundee.ac.uk/staff/creed/

22. Verheij, B. (2003) Dialectical argumentation with argumentation schemes: towards a methodology for the investigation of argumentation schemes. *Proceedings of the Fifth Conference of the International Society for the Study of Argumentation (ISSA 2002)* (eds. F.H. van Eemeren, J.A. Blair, C.A. Willard & F. Snoeck Henkemans), pp. 1033-1037. Sic Sat, Amsterdam.

23. van Gelder, T. & Rizzo, A. (2001) "Reason!Able across the curriculum", in *Is IT an Odyssey in Learning? Proceedings of the 2001 Conference of the Computing in Education Group of Victoria*

24. Walton, D. (1996) *Argumentation Schemes for Presumptive Reasoning*, LEA.

25. Walton, D. and Reed, C.A. (2004) "Argumentation Schemes and Enthymemes", *Synthese* to appear.

Formal Dialectic Specification

Simon Wells and Chris Reed

Division of Applied Computing, University of Dundee, Dundee, UK, DD1 4HN
{swells, chris}@computing.dundee.ac.uk

Abstract. Formal dialectic systems have been suggested as a means to model inter-agent communication in multi-agent systems. The formal dialectic systems of Hamblin are practical models for the computational implementation of such a system of argumentative dialogue.

This paper introduces a formal framework for the specification of Hamblin-type systems that has a range of benefits for theoretical work in the area including: yielding concise sets of clearly defined moves; allowing the moves of both existing and new games to be specified in a consistent manner; facilitating the use of dialectical shifts and dialogue embeddings independent of ruleset; facilitating the investigation of the coupling between sets of moves and dialogue situations; defining the attributes possessed by the general Hamblin-style formal dialectical system and thereby enabling the systematic exploration of the types of moves that these systems might encompass; and facilitating the rapid development of software applications that use formal dialectic to regulate communications.

1 Introduction

The formal dialectic systems after [1] have been proposed as a practical means to model the interactions between the participants in a dialogue. In computational environments, such dialectical systems have found application in various domains including the design, specification and implementation of conversation protocols in multi-agent systems. The dialogue in a formal dialectic system is conceived as a turn-taking game between two players whose utterances are constructed in terms of the types of moves allowed in the game. Games are traditionally specified in terms of sets of locutional rules, structural rules, commitment rules and, occasionally, completion rules. The locutional rules specify the possible moves that a player might make, the structural rules regulate which moves are allowed at a given point in the dialogue and the commitment rules govern how dialectical commitment is incurred or retracted as a result of the players moves.

The original Hamblin-style formal dialectic system, H in [1], was suggested primarily but not solely as a means to investigate some of the logical fallacies. As a practical investigational tool H was seen as an antidote to what Hamblin called the 'Standard treatment of fallacies' in which, he claimed, the common fallacies were listed without any deep examination of their underlying causes and the conditions from which they arose.

I. Rahwan et al. (Eds.): ArgMAS 2004, LNAI 3366, pp. 31–43, 2005.

This dialectical approach to fallacy research was very productive yielding several families of games including those of Woods and Walton [2], Mackenzie [3] and Walton [4]. From fallacies the focus of dialectical systems research moved towards general theories of dialogical argumentation utilising commitment in the work of [5], commitment as a means to model belief in artificial intelligence in [6] and joint activities in [7].

Contemporary work with formal dialectical systems has concentrated on applying the theory to various aspects of computational systems. Mackenzie's game DC was used in [8] and [9] to research computer based learning systems. The application of formal dialectical systems to multi-agent systems is investigated in [10]. A theoretical basis for dialectical shifts within dialogues, the means to move from one dialogue type, as typified in [5], to another during a single dialogue is introduced in [11]. Some of the most recent work on argumentation in AI is presented in [12], which lays out new collaborative ventures not only in multi-agent systems, but also decision support, natural language, law, and knowledge representation.

2   Motivation

Formal-dialectic systems exhibit certain useful properties. These include explaining sequences of human utterances, a means to make decisions that can be less computationally intensive than game-theoretic based decision making [11] and allowing reasoning to occur in domains where knowledge is uncertain or limited.

Making use of a formal-dialectic game in a multi-agent system requires that a set of rules be devised and implemented as conversation protocols in agents. There are many games in the argumentation and multi-agent systems literature including [1], [3], [4], [5], [7], [6], [13], [14], [15], [16], [17], [18], that might make good candidates for protocols to regulate argumentative inter-agent communication. Unfortunately many of these have been suggested as means to tackle particular problems within argumentation, such as fallacious reasoning, rather than as general models of argumentative dialogue. Even where games have been formulated primarily as models of argumentative dialogue. it is difficult to efficiently compare the performance of the many different systems. Therefore it is not readily identifiable which games are better than others and under which circumstances and conditions this is so.

One way to determine which system of rules is most suitable is to compare them under a variety of conditions to determine particular properties that each set of rules might possess. Testing through implementation as suggested in [19] compliments our original intent of producing a computational implementation of a formal-dialectic system for inter-agent communication.

The problem with this though is that the games are specified in different ways, usually in natural language. This is sufficient to expose details of argumentative discourse for a theoretical audience but inadequate when the systems are implemented in software where ambiguity in the original specification can alter the overall behavior of the implemented system. A second problem is that the different specifications mean that multiple implementations are required, one for each formal-dialectic system which is both time and effort intensive. Each implementation would be limited to a single set of rules. This assumes that the set of rules selected are those most appropriate to governing inter-agent communication. A deeper concern with this approach is the lack of an examination of the underlying principles of a formal-dialectic system and the space of possible behaviors that such a system might exhibit.

A more efficient approach would be to draw out the common elements of the existing formal-dialectic systems and codify them in terms of a specification format that would enable a single computational implementation to afford the behaviour of any existing Hamblin-type formal-dialectic system. Some steps have been made towards a general framework for dialogue games, notably in [20] which suggests a theoretical framework but lacks the implementational detail and in [21] which looks at dialectical systems more generally and does not examine the entire family of games due to Hamblin. The aim of the current work is to develop not only a broad theoretical framework, but also an implementation that can act as a rapid application development tool for dialectical agents.

An initial approach would be to define the characteristics of the general formal-dialectic system and through examination of existing sets of rules determine the requirements for a framework and specification format in which the legal moves of any existing formal dialectic system can be specified. The formal dialectic systems, both those embodied in existing sets of rules and those suggested through examination of the properties of formal-dialectic systems in general, could then be compared and contrasted using a single framework which would eliminate behaviors introduced by differing implementations of the various systems. Ultimately this would allow an examination of the space of the possible sets of rules that might be embodied in a formal-dialectic system.

In order to allow the flexible definition, implementation, assessment of fit-for-purpose, and evaluation of dialogue systems, and classes of dialogue systems, what is required is a single, simple framework that can not only handle the full richness, diversity and expressive power of games described in the argumentation literature, but that can also form a direct bridge to rapid design and development of systems that implement those games in AI systems.

3   Towards a Framework for Game Specification

3.1   Hamblin's Formal-Dialectic and Successors

Hamblin conceived of the formal-dialectic as a means to investigate phenomena that occur in natural dialogue. This was achieved through the design of simple systems of precise rules which could be used to plot the properties of dialogue played out according to the rules. The formal dialectic can be generally defined thus;

> A regulated dialogue involving a number of participants who speak in turn in accordance with a set of rules that specify the form of what is said relative to the context and previous utterances in the dialogue.

On the surface this does not set the formal-dialectic of Hamblin much apart from the dialectic of [22] or the obligation game of medieval philosophy (see [1] chapter 8) but Hamblin further specifies some elements of the possible systems. The number of participants is set at two, the dialogue context refers to the specification of an interaction between the players and the previous occurences refer either to previous locutional acts within the dialogue or to the contents of the players commitment stores.

Practically this requires that the rules of a formal-dialectic system specify contexts of interaction, for example, that move X_1 must follow move X_0. Further a rule may prescribe that a players commitment store maintain a particular commitment for that interaction to be legal, or that a specific move has been made at an earlier point in the dialogue. A system of formal-dialectic therefore has three core characteristics which must be reflected in a formalisation of that system:

1. Interaction contexts
2. Commitment store contents
3. Dialogue history

Hamblin's game, H, specifies a set of moves that embody these characteristics. The rules of H are presented in two categories, those that describe the syntactical structure of the dialogue, and those that operate on a players commitment stores. Successive games in [4], [5], [3] and in [7], reutilse the format of H with additional categories of rules such as the locutional rules that specify what can be said, the structural rules which are the syntactical rules renamed, and the closure rules, a seldom used group of rules that suggest a means to determine when a dialogue is at an end.

3.2   Specifying Sets of Moves

Common to the formal dialectic systems of [1], [3], [4], [5] and [7] is the notion of the legal move. The only way to alter the state of the dialogue is to make a legal move specified in terms of a locution and usually some propositional content. Usually the order in which moves can be made depends heavily upon which move was made in the previous players turn. This is the primary mechanism that allows the dialectical systems to regulate the flow of conversation and thereby allow the conversants to engage in realistic dialogues by restricting which moves are valid at any given point. In practice, only a subset of the possible moves is available for the current players to use depending upon earlier moves.

Hamblin introduces the notion of commitment as a means to maintain consistency in a player's utterances. Through making a move in a formal-dialectic system a player can incur some form of propositional commitment. The commitments incurred are added to a public record of all commitments incurred in the dialogue by each player, this record is called the commitment store. Hamblin suggested that it be required of each new commitment that it can be added without inconsistency to the incurring player's store. The notion of commitment and stores of incurred commitments has been applied to multi-agent systems research in [23], [24] [25] and [26]. [27] presents the DIAGAL agent communication language and a series of games that use player incurred commitment to regulate flexible conversation policies.

Each player maintains a set of commitment stores. There are two basic types of commitment store, the static commitment store and the dynamic commitment store. The static commitment store, also called the veiled [4] or dark-side [5] commitment-store is not altered by moves in the dialogue and it's contents are fixed before the dialogue commences. The dynamic commitment store [1] is a set of propsitional commitments that alter depending upon the moves the players make in the dialogue. The dynamic commitment stores are indexed by turn so that each player's set of commitments at each turn in the dialogue can be examined.

An examination of the existing rules yields a set of parameters that govern whether a particular move is admissible, and a set of effects that take place as a result of the move being made. If the specification of individual moves is made in terms of their legality requirements and effects, then the separate specification of commitment, structural and locutional rules is not required. The legality requirements and effects can be structured in terms of the pre-conditions and post-conditions required by the move. The pre-conditions state the conditions that must hold for the move to be legally made, for example, the contents of the players commitment stores and the previous moves made in the dialogue. The post-conditions specify the alterations that should be made to the players commitment stores as a result of the move and the set of moves that is allowed in response to the current move. This specification is therefore reminiscent of a planning style approach to dialogue, such as was developed in early work by [28].

Specifying Individual Moves. An individual move can be modelled thus;

Move *Name of move*
Pre-Conditions *Conditions that must hold for the move to be legally made*
Post-Conditions *Conditions that must hold for the move to be satisfactorily completed*

In order to specify the pre-conditions and post-conditions that an individual move may possess, some game variables must be defined;

A game comprises a set of players, $\Pi=\{P,O\}$ for the proponent and opponent, a set of propositions Λ (of arbitrary atomic tokens), a set of locutions Φ. A given dialogue is a sequence of turns, that can be constructed as a relation R mapping $\mathbb{N} \rightarrow T$, where T are possible turns, i.e. T: Φ x Λ x Π . For syntactic convenience T_n refers to the triple $\langle \Phi, \Lambda, \Pi \rangle$ identified by R(n).

The player's commitments are recorded in commitment stores designated $C\pi_n$ where $\pi \in \Pi$ identified here for an arbitrary agent S, and form a sequence of sets of commitments. The player's may maintain any number of individually labelled commitment stores as set out in the rules for the game being played.

There are several general classes and subclasses of both pre- and post-conditions. These are outlined below with an explanation of each.

Pre-Conditions

1. Commitment Store Contents
   (a) $C \in CS_n$
      Commitment C is currently in commitment store CS
   (b) $C \notin CS_n$
      Commitment C is not currently in commitment store CS
   (c) $\exists m, m \in \mathbb{N}.C \in CS_{n-m}$
      Commitment store CS has previously contained commitment C
   (d) $\exists m, m \in \mathbb{N}.C \notin CS_{tn-m}$
      Commitment store CS has not previously contained commitment C
2. Previous Moves
   (a) $T_{n-1} = \langle \Phi, \Lambda, \Pi \rangle$
      The immediate previous turn comprised locution Φ made with content Λ by player Π
   (b) $T_{n-1} \neq \langle \Phi, \Lambda, \Pi \rangle$
      The immediate previous turn did not comprise locution Φ made with content Λ by player Π
   (c) $\exists m, m \in \mathbb{N}, m < n.T_{n-m} = \langle \Phi, \Lambda, \Pi \rangle$
      A previous turn comprised locution Φ made with content Λ by player Π
   (d) $\forall m, m \in \mathbb{N}, m < n.T_{n-m} \neq \langle \Phi, \Lambda, \Pi \rangle$
      A previous turn did not comprise locution Φ made with content Λ by player Π

Post-Conditions

1. Alterations to Commitment Stores
   (a) $CS_{n+1} = CS_n \cup \{C\}$
      Commitment C is added to commitment store CS
   (b) $CS_{n+1} = CS_n \setminus \{C\}$
      Commitment C is removed from commitment store CS
2. Legal Responsive Moves
   (a) $T_{n+1} = \langle \Phi, \Lambda, \Pi \rangle$
      The next turn must comprise locution Φ made with content Λ by player Π
   (b) $T_{n+1} \neq \langle \Phi, \Lambda, \Pi \rangle$
      The next turn must not comprise locution Φ made with content Λ by player Π
   (c) $\exists m, m \in \mathbb{N}.T_{n+m} = \langle \Phi, \Lambda, \Pi \rangle$
      A future turn must comprise locution Φ made with content Λ by player Π

(d) $\forall m, m \in \mathbb{N}.T_{n+m} \neq \langle \Phi, \Lambda, \Pi \rangle$

   A future turn must not comprise locution Φ made with content Λ by player Π

Due to the manner in which each turn is constructed, any combination of move, propositional content and player can be specified as a past or future condition of a move. This is because a fully formed legal move is made by a player and comprises a locution and some propositional content. This means that the space of possible moves in a Hamblin-style formal dialectical system can be delineated through application of the dialogue variables.

By utilising this format, the number of rules required to specify a set of moves for a dialectical system is reduced merely to the number of legal moves in the system. For example, the legal moves of DC can be specified as follows: N.B. The proponent is denoted P and the opponent O. The proponent's commitment store is denoted CP and the opponent's commitment store, CO.

1. **Move** Statement(S_x)
   Pre $\varnothing$
   Post $CP_{n+1} = CP_n \cup \{S_x\}$
       $\wedge\ CO_{n+1} = CO_n \cup \{S_x\}$
2. **Move** Denial(S_x)
   Pre $\varnothing$
   Post $CP_{n+1} = CP_n \cup \{\neg S_x\}$
       $\wedge\ CO_{n+1} = CO_n \cup \{\neg S_x\}$
3. **Move** Defense(S_y)
   Pre $\varnothing$
   Post $CP_{n+1} = CP_n \cup \{S_y\}$
       $\wedge\ CP_{n+1} = CP_n \cup \{S_y {\rightarrow} S_x\}$
       $\wedge\ CO_{n+1} = CO_n \cup \{S_y\}$
       $\wedge\ CO_{n+1} = CO_n \cup \{S_y {\rightarrow} S_x\}$
4. **Move** Withdrawal(S_x)
   Pre $\varnothing$
   Post $CP_{n+1} = CP_n \setminus \{S_x\}$
5. **Move** Challenge(S_x)
   Pre $\varnothing$
   Post $CP_{n+1} = CP_n \setminus \{S_x\}$
       $\wedge\ CP_{n+1} = CP_n \cup \{WhyS_x?\}$
       $\wedge\ CO_{n+1} = CO_n \cup \{S_x\}$
       $\wedge\ (\ T_{n+1} = \langle \text{Defense}, S_x, O \rangle$
       $\vee\ T_{n+1} = \langle \text{Resolve}, S_x, O \rangle$
       $\vee\ T_{n+1} = \langle \text{Withdrawal}, S_x, O \rangle\ )$
6. **Move** Question(S)
   Pre $\varnothing$
   Post $T_{n+1} = \langle \text{Denial}, S_x, O \rangle$
       $\vee\ T_{n+1} = \langle \text{Statement}, S_x, O \rangle$
       $\vee\ T_{n+1} = \langle \text{Withdrawal}, S_x, O \rangle$

7. **Move** Resolve(S)
   Pre Ø
   Post $T_{n+1} = \langle \text{Statement, } S_x, O \rangle$
   $\qquad \vee \; T_{n+1} = \langle \text{Withdrawal, } S_x, O \rangle$

Through using this framework the game DC can be modified easily to yield the variant game DD [3] by replacing the post-conditions of the Statement(S_x) move with the following:

Post $CS_{n+1} = CP_n \cup \{S_x\}$
$\qquad \wedge \; CS_{n+1} = CP_n \setminus \{\text{WhyS}_x?\}$
$\qquad \wedge \; CH_{n+1} = CO_n \cup \{S_x\}$

3.3 Specifying Dialogue Stages

The use of dialogue stages allows the practical implementation of dialectical shifts, the movement from one type of dialogue to another [5], and dialogue embeddings [11], the functional encapsulation of an entire child dialogue within a parent dialogue. [29] identifies four stages that dialogue might proceed through including the confrontation stage, opening stage, argumentation stage and the concluding stage.

A practical example of the use of stages can be seen in the specification of the game PPD$_0$ in [5]. In PPD$_0$ the moves allowed in the opening stage of a dialogue are restricted and this situation continues until the contents of the players commitment stores match a particular set of conditions. This is an example of a dialogue shift because the dialogue moves from an expository situation in which the conversants are laying out their initial commitments to a more structured dialogue in which the conversants may explore each others arguments. This is not exactly the same as a dialogue shift though, the dialogue type according to the Walton and Krabbe typology [5] remains the same, persuasion dialogue, but the persuasion dialogue may move through several stages before completion.

A practical means to implement this type of shift is to bind each set of moves into a stage which specifies a set of entry and exit conditions. In single stage games such as H, DC et al where the set of rules is fixed throughout the entire dialogue, the entry-conditions set out the point of issue between the conversants and the exit-conditions can be used to specify when the dialogue is complete, this allows games to make use of win-loss completion conditions that were not specified in the original rules. In PPD$_0$ this is sufficient to allow an opening stage in which the players commitment stores are set up and the legal moves are restricted. When the exit-conditions of the opening stage of PPD$_0$ are met the entry-conditions for the next stage, the persuasive dialogue stage, are examined and if met the dialogue proper begins. The exit conditions of the persuasive dialogue stage set out the win/loss conditions of the dialogue as a whole. This mechanism allows the dialogue to proceed in a series of discrete stages with a complete set of rules defined and tailored to suit the requirements of each stage.

A stage therefore consists of a set of permissible moves and a set of conditions under which the stage can be opened and closed. An effect of this formulation is that a dialogue-stage can be set up to embed entirely within another dialogue-stage through a careful formulation of the rules governing the entry and exit to the embedded sub-stage. As a result the stages that a dialogue might move through need not be linear. Dependent upon earlier occurrences in the dialogue and the formulation of entry- and exit-conditions, differing paths through the graph of stages might arise.

3.4   Implementation

The current implementation of the framework can be seen in figures 1 and 2. It is written in Java and makes use of XML to specify the sets of legal moves that constitute a formal-dialectic system. The use of XML allows sets of rules to be swapped between conversants and means that some degree of run-time code generation can occur. This means that the dialectic system governing a dialogue is not hard-coded but flexible, allowing sets of rules to be tailored towards specific dialogue contexts, whether the dialogue types in [5] or those pertaining to social or cultural situations. This avoids the situation found in [8] and [9] in which a lot of work is expended on implementing and refining a single formal-dialectic system.

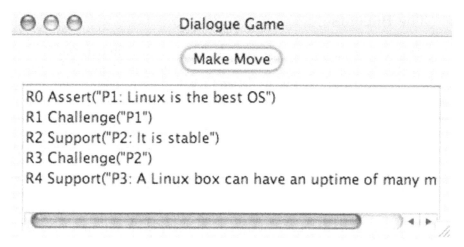

Fig. 1. The main dialogue window showing a dialogue in progress

Development is now under way to refine the implementation in the form of a module for the JackDaw agent framework [30] a lightweight, flexible, industrial-strength agent platform. JackDaw agents make use of software modules to provide added functionality to the core agent capabilities. This development work will set the formal-dialectic framework firmly within the scope of multi-agent systems allowing agents that embody the resulting module to engage argumentative dialogue governed by formal-dialectic.

By utilising a specification framework the rapid development, implementation and evaluation of Hamblin-type formal-dialectic systems is possible without the need to develop an individual implementation for each game.

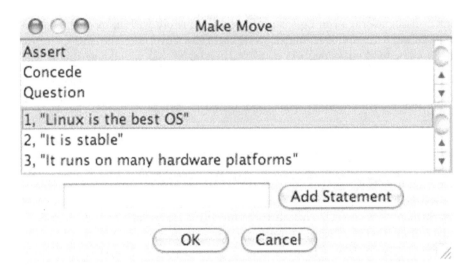

Fig. 2. The make move dialogue

4   The Benefits

The immediate benefits of this are that a single implementation can be constructed that uses concisely written, exactly specified and consistent rulesets that may be altered as required at design-time or run-time to suit the current context of dialogue. The implementation of dialogue shifts and embeddings is catered for through the use of dialogue stages which can be applied to any ruleset regardless of whether the original formulation of rules supported them.

The computational implementation of dialectical systems, especially if they are to communicate with other systems utilising the same set of rules, require that the results of each individual move be explicitly specified. Otherwise each implementation is subject to the system designer's interpretation of the rules which can lead to differences between the way systems would react given identical circumstances. Use of the suggested framework for the specification of formal-dialectic systems means that all existing systems can be written using a single nomenclature that exactly specifies what the effect of each variable should be. Any existing game can be specified merely by selecting the correct set of moves and specifying the appropriate pre-conditions and post-conditions for those moves. Related games can then be created simply by changing an individual rule or a component of that rule.

From here the space of possible rulesets for Hamblin-style formal dialectic systems may be examined. If a particular dialogue type is embodied in a particular set of rules governing how the dialogue should proceed then dialectical shifts and embeddings can be implemented as a means to shift between those types merely by altering the rules to that required by the particular dialogue type during runtime and by agreement between the conversants. The generic framework allows varying sets of rules to be compared and evaluated as to their applicability to particular dialectical situations. This continues the work outlined in [5] which suggests that new rules for PPD_0 type dialogues be formulated as required. It also extends earlier work by allowing, for example, games such as DC to make use of win/loss conditions to determine the result of a dialogue. A survey of dialogue situations and the rules applicable therein leads to a tighter coupling of rules to situation and facilitates improvements in the expressive capabilities of implemented systems.

A partial typology of dialogue types is established in [5]. Dialogue types are characterised by their initial situation, overall goal and individual participants aims. Sets of rules should be tailored to particular instances of a dialogue type. Further distinctions might be drawn between rulesets applicable in differing social situations. For example, in a legal setting the rules by which a dialogue might proceed are very different from those that obtain at a hotel bar.

One set of rules will not suffice to govern all of the types of possible dialogues. When an agent uses a single agent-communication language (ACL) to govern all of its communicative interactions, the primitives of the ACL will necessarily be of the lowest common denominator. They will be applicable to as many situations as possible but not well suited to providing the best set of primitives for every dialogue context [31]. Analogously, were one set of rules proposed to govern all types of dialogue it could only service the common elements of each dialogue and would not necessarily embody the best set of rules for that situation. As the dialogue changes so the rules should change to suit. This is dealt with implicitly in the game PPD_0, where the opening stage shifts to the persuasive stage in response to the changing factors of the dialogue, with a resulting change in the set of legal moves. This concept could be extended to meet the needs of a diverse set of dialogue situations where the set of legal moves would be kept fluid depending upon the character of the dialogue currently underway. As the dialectical situation alters with the flow of dialogue, so the rulesets pertaining to the current dialectical situation should also change. A framework for formal dialectical systems that allows rulesets to be loaded at runtime gives formal-dialectic increased flexibility to handle a wide range of communicative situations, broadening the scope of computational implementations and their ability competency during differing dialogues as the goals and situations of the participants change.

5   Conclusions

The framework outlined herein sets out a means to utilise both existing formal dialectic systems after [1] and new formulations of rules within a single computational implementation. Where formal dialectic systems have been used as conversation protocols to govern the interactions between systems, there is now a common format within which sets of rules can formulated and exchanged. This allows researchers to easily explore new sets of rules within the context of a Hamblin-type formal dialectic system and it allows systems to swap sets of rules at runtime so that the conversation protocol governing the systems interactions can be tailored to the situation, dialogical or social, that it is engaged in.

Provision is made for existing games to take advantage of newer developments in argumentation research such as the dialogue stages of [5] and the dialogue embeddings of [11]. This not only extends the scope of many of the existing systems, including H, DC and CB, but also any Hamblin-type formal-dialectic system to make use of many sets of rules, each tightly coupled to a particular dialogue situation or context, and to move between those rulesets as needed.

The framework and associated implementation provide a means for multi-agent systems to make practical use of the rich, diverse and expressive systems presented in the argumentation literature. A single, simple, consistent approach is provided toward the specification, implementation and evaluation of dialogue systems that can meet the growing demands of sophisticated agents in complex domains.

Acknowledgements

This research is funded by EPSRC under the Information Exchange project (GR/S03706/01). Gratitude is expressed to Calico Jack Ltd. for their JackDaw agent framework and JUDE development environment.

References

1. Hamblin, C.L.: Fallacies. Methuen and Co. Ltd. (1970)
2. Woods, J., Walton, D.N.: Arresting circles in formal dialogues. Journal Of Philosophical Logic **7** (1978) 73–90
3. Mackenzie, J.D.: Question begging in non-cumulative systems. Journal Of Philosophical Logic **8** (1979) 117–133
4. Walton, D.N.: Logical Dialogue-Games And Fallacies. University Press Of America (1984)
5. Walton, D.N., Krabbe, E.C.W.: Commitment in Dialogue. SUNY series in Logic and Language. State University of New York Press (1995)
6. Girle, R.A.: Knowledge organized and disorganized. Proceedings of the 7th Florida Artificial Interlligence Research Symposium by the Florida AI Research Society (1994)
7. Girle, R.A.: Commands in dialogue logic. Practical Reasoning: International Conference on Formal and Applied Practical Reasoning, Springer Lecture Notes in AI (1996)
8. Moore, D., Hobbes, D.: Computational uses of philosophical dialogue theories. Informal Logic **18** (1996) 131–163
9. Yuan, T., Moore, D., Grierson, A.: A conversational agent system as a test-bed to study the philosophical model dc. In: 3rd Workshop on Computational Models of Natural Argument (CMNA'03). (2003)
10. McBurney, P., Parsons, S.: Agent ludens: Games for agent dialogues. In: Game-Theoretic and Decision-Theoretic Agents (GTDT 2001): Proceedings of the 2001 AAAI Spring Symposium. (2001)
11. Reed, C.: Dialogue frames in agent communication. In: Proceedings of the 3rd International Conference on Multi Agent Systems, IEEE Press (1998)

12. Reed, C., Norman, T.: Argumentation Machines. Kluwer Academic Publishers (2003)
13. Amgoud, L., Parsons, S.: Agent dialogues with conflicting preferences. Pre-Proceedings of the Eighth International Workshop on Agent Theories (2001)
14. Amgoud, L., Parsons, S., Maudet, N.: Arguments, dialogue, and negotiation. Proceedings of the Fourteenth European Conference on Artificial Intelligence (2000)
15. Dignum, F., Dunin-Keplicz, B., Verbrugge, R.: Agent theory for team formation by dialogue. Intelligent Agents VII: Proceedings of the Seventh International Workshop on Agent Theories, Architectures and Languages (ATAL 2000) (2000)
16. Dignum, F., Dunin-Keplicz, B., Verbrugge, R.: Creating collective intention through dialogue. Logic Journal of the IGPL (2001)
17. Hitchcock, D., McBurney, P., Parsons, S.: A framework for deliberation dialogues. Proceedings of the Fourth Biennial Conference of the Ontario Society for the Study of Argumentation (2001)
18. McBurney, P., van Eijk, R.M., Parsons, S., Amgoud, L.: A dialogue-game protocol for agent purchase negotiations. Journal of Autonomous Agents and Multi-Agent Systems 7 (2001) 235–273
19. Maudet, N., Moore, D.: Dialogue games as dialogue models for interacting with, and via, computers. Informal Logic 3 (2001)
20. Maudet, N., Evrard, F.: A generic framework for dialogue game implementation. In: roceedings of the Second Workshop on Formal Semantics and Pragmatics of Dialog. (1998)
21. Bench-Capon, T.J.M., Geldard, T., Leng, P.H.: A method for the computational modelling of dialectical argument with dialogue games. Artificial Intelligence and Law 8 (2000) 233–354
22. Rescher, N.: Dialectics, "A Controversy-Oriented Approach to the Theory of Knowledge. State University of New York Press, Albany. (1977)
23. Singh, M.P.: Multi-agent systems as spheres of commitment. International Conference on Multi-Agent Systems (ICMAS) (1996)
24. Singh, M.P.: Commitments among autonomous agents in information-rich environments. 8th European Workshop on Modelling Autonomous Agents in a Multi-Agent World (MAAMAW) (1997)
25. Singh, M.P.: An ontology for commitments in multi-agent systems. Artificial Intelligence and Law (1998)
26. McBurney, P., Parsons, S.: The posit spaces protocol for multi-agent negotiation. Advances in Agent Communication (2004)
27. Maudet, N., Chaib-draa, B., Labrie, M.A.: Request for action reconsidered as dialogue game based on commitments. Workshop on Agent Communication Language (AAMAS'02) (2002)
28. Cohen, P.R., Perrault, R.: Elements of a plan-based theory of speech acts. Cognitive Science 3 (1979) 177–212
29. van Eemeren, F.H., Grootendorst, R.: Argumentation, Communication, and Fallacies. A Pragma Dialectical Perspective. Lawrence Erlbaum Associates (1992)
30. http://www.calicojack.co.uk: Calico jack website (2004)
31. Reed, C., Norman, T., Jennings, N.: Negotiating the semantics of agent communication languages. Computational Intelligence (2002)

A Modal Semantics for an Argumentation-Based Pragmatics for Agent Communication

Jamal Bentahar[1], Bernard Moulin[1], John-Jules Ch. Meyer[2],
and Brahim Chaib-draa[1]

[1] Laval University, Department of Computer Science and Software Engineering,
Ste Foy, QC, G1K 7P4, Canada
jamal.bentahar.1@ulaval.ca
{bernard.moulin, brahim.chaib-draa}@ift.ulaval.ca
[2] University Utrecht, Department of Computer Science,
PO Box 80.089 3508TB, Utrecht, The Netherlands
jj@cs.uu.nl

Abstract. In this paper we present a modal semantics for our approach based on social commitments and arguments for conversational agents. Our formal framework based on this approach uses three basic elements: social commitments, actions that agents apply to these social commitments and arguments that agents use to support their actions. This framework, called Commitment and Argument Network (CAN), formalizes the agents' interactions as a network in which agents manipulate commitments and arguments. More precisely, we propose a logical model (called DCTL*$_{CAN}$) based on CTL* and on dynamic logic for this framework. The advantage of this logical model is to bring together social commitments, actions, argumentation relations, and the relations existing between these three elements within the same framework. Our semantics makes it possible to represent the dynamics of agent communication. It also allows us to establish the important link between social commitments as a deontic concept and arguments. The final objective of this paper is to propose a unified framework for pragmatics and semantics of agent communication by defining logic-based protocols.

1 Introduction

In the domain of agent communication, semantics is one of the most important aspects, particularly in the current context of open and interoperable multi-agent systems (MAS) [7]. Although a certain number of significant research works were done in this field [13, 22, 24, 25], the definition of a clear and global semantics is an objective yet to be reached. Agent communication pragmatics is another important aspect to be addressed. While semantics is interested in the meaning of communication acts, pragmatics deals with the way of using these acts. Pragmatics is related to the dynamics of agent interactions and to the way of relating the isolated acts to build conversations. Pragmatics was also addressed by several researchers [9, 18, 20, 21]. However, only few attempts have been made to address these two facets of agent communication in the same framework.

I. Rahwan et al. (Eds.): ArgMAS 2004, LNAI 3366, pp. 44–63, 2005.

The objective of this paper is to propose a general framework to capture pragmatic and semantic issues of an approach based on social commitments and arguments for agent communication. Indeed, this work is a continuation of our previous research in which we addressed in detail the pragmatic aspects [2, 3]. Thus, the paper highlights the semantic issues of our approach and the link with pragmatic ones. The semantics that we define here deals with all the aspects used in our approach.

In addition to proposing a unified framework for pragmatic and semantic issues, this work presents two results: 1) it semantically establishes the link between social commitments and arguments; 2) it uses both a temporal logic (CTL* with some additions) and a dynamic logic to define a complete and unambiguous semantics.

Paper overview. In Section 2 we address the pragmatic aspects by introducing the main ideas of our approach. In Section 3 we present the syntax and the semantics of the main elements of our logical model. Other details will be described in an extended version of the paper. In Section 4 we define protocols using our logical model. In Sections 5 and 6 we compare our approach to related work and conclude the paper.

2   Social Commitments and Argument-Based Approach

2.1   Social Commitments

A social commitment SC is a commitment made by an agent (called the *debtor*), that some fact is true [5]. This commitment is directed to a set of agents (called *creditors*). The social commitment content is characterized by time t_φ, which is generally different from the utterance time denoted t_u and from the time associated with the social commitment denoted t_{sc}. t_φ is the time described by the utterance, and thus by the content φ. Time t_{sc} refers to the time during which the social commitment holds. When it is an interval, this time is denoted $[t_{sc}^{\inf}, t_{sc}^{\sup}]$. If the social commitment is satisfied or violated we have $t_{sc}=[t_u, t_\varphi]$. However, if the social commitment is withdrawn, we have: $t_{sc}=[t_u, t_w]$, with t_w the withdrawal time. Time t_{sc} indicates the time during which the social commitment holds, i.e. the time during which the social commitment is *active* (we will return to this notion later). Time t_φ indicates the moment at which the social commitment must be satisfied.

In order to model the dynamics of conversations, we interpret a speech act SA as an action performed on a social commitment or on the content of a social commitment. A SA is an abstract act that an agent, the speaker, performs when producing an utterance U and addressing it to another agent, the addressee. The actions that an agent can perform on a social commitment are: Act ∈ {Create, Withdraw, Reactivate, Violate, Satisfy}. The actions performed on the content of a social commitment are Act-content ∈ {Accept-content, Refuse-content, Challenge-content, Change-content}. Thus, a SA leads either to an action on a social commitment when the speaker is the debtor, or to an action on a social commitment content when the speaker is the debtor or the creditor. Formally, in our framework a SA can be defined in BNF form as follows:

Definition 1. $SA(i_k, Ag_1, Ag_2, t_u, U) =_{def}$
  $Act(Ag_1, t_u, SC(id_n, Ag_1, Ag_2, t_{sc}, \varphi, t_\varphi))$
  $\mid Act\text{-}content(Ag_k, t_u, SC(id_n, Ag_i, Ag_j, t_{sc}, \varphi, t_\varphi))$

where $i, j \in \{1, 2\}$ and $(k = i \text{ or } k = j)$, $=_{def}$ means "is interpreted by definition as", i_k is the identifier of the SA. The definiendum $SA(i_k, Ag_1, Ag_2, t_u, U)$ is defined by the definiens $Act(Ag_1, t_u, SC(id_n, Ag_1, Ag_2, t_{sc}, \varphi, t_\varphi))$ as an action performed by the debtor Ag_1 on its social commitment. The definiendum is defined by the definiens $Act\text{-}content(Ag_k, t_u, SC(id_n, Ag_i, Ag_j, t_{sc}, \varphi, t_\varphi))$ as an action performed by an agent Ag_k (the debtor or the creditor) on the social commitment content.

2.2 Taxonomy

In this section, we explain the various types of social commitments we use in the logical model:

A. Absolute Commitments (ABCs): They are social commitments whose fulfillment does not depend on any particular condition. Two types can be distinguished:

A1. Propositional Commitments (PCs): They are related to the state of the world and expressed by assertives.

A2. Action Commitments (ACs): They are always directed towards the future and are related to actions that the debtor is committed to carrying out. This type of social commitments is typically conveyed by promises.

B. Conditional Commitments (CCs): In several cases, agents need to make social commitments not in absolute terms but under given conditions. CCs allow us to express that if a condition β is true, then the creditor will be committed towards the debtor to making γ or that γ is true.

C. Commitment Attempts (CTs): The social commitments described so far directly concern the debtor who commits either that a certain fact is true or that a certain action will be carried out. These social commitments do not allow us to explain the fact that an agent asks another one to be committed to carrying out an action. To solve this problem, we propose the concept of CT. We consider a CT as a request made by a debtor to push a creditor to be committed.

  We notice that there is no explicit relation between PCs and ACs. When the current state of the world does not satisfy a PC we speak about a violation of this social commitment. There is no rule indicating that the agent develops an AC to make the content of a PC true when this PC becomes violated.

2.3 Argumentation and Social Commitments

In the domain of agent communication, several argumentation-based approaches have been put forward, for example [1, 15]. An argumentation system essentially includes a logical language L, a definition of the argument concept, a definition of the attack relation between arguments and finally a definition of acceptability [1]. In our model, we adopt the following definition from [10]. Here Γ indicates a possibly inconsistent knowledge base with no deductive closure. ⊢ Stands for classical inference and ≡ for logical equivalence.

Definition 2. *An argument is a pair (H, h) where h is a formula of L and H a sub-set of Γ such that : i) H is consistent, ii) H $\vdash h$ and iii) H is minimal, so that no subset of H satisfying both i and ii exists. H is called the support of the argument and h its conclusion.*

The link between social commitments and arguments enables us to capture both the public and reasoning aspects of agent communication. This link is explained as follows. Before committing to some fact h being true (i.e. before creating a social commitment whose content is h), the speaker agent must use its argumentation system to build an argument (H, h). On the other side, the addressee agent must use its own argumentation system to select the answer it will give. For example, an agent Ag_1 accepts the social commitment content h proposed by another agent Ag_2 if it is able to build an argument which supports this content from its knowledge base. If Ag_1 has an argument neither for h, nor for $\neg h$, then it must ask for an explanation.

The argumentation relations that we use in our model are thought of as actions applied to social commitment contents. The set of these relations is: {*Justify, Defend, Attack, Contradict*}.

We used this approach in [2] to propose a formal framework called Commitment and Argument Network (CAN). The idea is to reflect the dynamics of agent communication by a network in which agents manipulate social commitments and arguments. In the following section we propose a formal semantics of this formalism in the form of a logical model.

3   The Logical Model

3.1   Syntax

In this section we specify the syntax of the main elements we use in our framework. The details of the other elements are described in an extended version of the paper. Our formal language $\mathcal{L}$ is based on an extended version of CTL* [11] and on dynamic logic [14]. We use a branching time for the future and we suppose that the past is linear. We also suppose that time is discrete. Let Φp be the set of atomic propositions and Φa the set of action symbols. The set of the agents is denoted A and the set of time units is denoted TU. The various types of social commitments, the actions of the agents on social commitments and on their contents and the argumentation relations are introduced as modal operators. We denote $\mathcal{L}sc$ a sub-language of $\mathcal{L}$ for social commitments. To simplify the notation, a social commitment, independently of its type, is denoted: $SC(Id_0, Ag_1, Ag_2, \varphi)$. $Id_0 \in N$ is the social commitment identifier, Ag_1 and Ag_2 are two agents and φ the social commitment content. The language $\mathcal{L}$ can be defined by the following syntactic rules.

3.1.1   Propositional Elements
R1. $\forall \phi \in \Phi p$, $\phi \in \mathcal{L}$: *Atomic formula*
R2. $p, q \in \mathcal{L} \Rightarrow p \wedge q \in \mathcal{L}$: *Conjunction*

R3. $p \in £ \Rightarrow \neg p \in £$: *Negation*
R4. $p, q \in £ \Rightarrow p \therefore q \in £$: *Argumentation*

This means that p is an argument for q. We can read this formula: p, *so* q. At this level, our definition of the argument does not take into account the defeasible aspect. This aspect will be introduced into our model by the argumentation relations (Section 3.1.6).

R5. $p \in £ \Rightarrow ?p \in £$: *Is p true?*
R6. $p \in £ \Rightarrow Ap \in £$: *Universal path-quantifier*
R7. $p \in £ \Rightarrow Ep \in £$: *Existential path-quantifier*
R8. $p, q \in £ \Rightarrow p\ U^+ q \in £$: *Until (in the future)*

Informally, $p\ U^+ q$ (*p until q*) means that on a given path from the given moment, there is some future moment in which q will eventually hold and p holds at all moments until that future moment.

R9. $p \in £ \Rightarrow X^+p \in £$: *Next moment (in the future)*
X^+p holds at the current moment, if p holds at the next moment.
R10. $p, q \in £ \Rightarrow p\ U^- q \in £$: *Since (in the past)*

The intuitive interpretation of $p\ U^- q$ (*p since q*) is that on a given path from the given moment, there is some past moment in which q eventually held and p holds at all moments since that past moment.

R11. $p \in £ \Rightarrow X^-p \in £$: *Previous moment (in the past)*
X^-p holds at the current moment, if p held at the previous moment.

3.1.2 Actions
R12. $p \in £/£sc,\ \alpha \in \Phi a \Rightarrow Perform(\alpha)p \in £$: *Action performance (about propositions)*

Perform(α)p is an operator from dynamic logic. It indicates that the achievement of action α makes the proposition p true.

R13. $SC(Id_0, Ag_1, Ag_2, \varphi) \in £sc, \alpha \in \Phi a \Rightarrow$

$Perform(\alpha)SC(Id_0,\ Ag_1,\ Ag_2,\ \varphi) \in £$: *Action performance (about social commitments)*

This indicates that the achievement of action α makes the social commitment $SC(Id_0, Ag_1, Ag_2, \varphi)$ true in our model.

3.1.3 Social Commitments
R14. $p \in £/£sc \wedge Id_0 \in N \wedge \{Ag_1, Ag_2\} \subseteq A \Rightarrow$
$PC(Id_0, Ag_1, Ag_2, p) \in £sc$: *Propositional commitment*
R15. $\alpha \in \Phi a \wedge p \in £/£sc \wedge Id_0 \in N \wedge \{Ag_1, Ag_2\} \subseteq A \Rightarrow$
$AC(Id_0, Ag_1, Ag_2, \alpha)p \in £sc$: *Action commitment*

R16. $\beta \in £/£sc \wedge \gamma \in £/£sc \cup \Phi a \wedge Id_0 \in N \wedge \{Ag_1, Ag_2\} \subseteq A \Rightarrow CC(Id_0, Ag_1, Ag_2, \beta \Rightarrow \gamma) \in £sc$: *Conditional commitment*

In order to formally introduce the notion of CT we need some definitions from first order logic.

Definitions.

TerC: a set of constant terms. A constant term can be a number, a name, etc.

Var: a set of variables.

Val: $Var \mapsto TerC$: a valuation function associating a variable to a constant term.

Let Ξ_{Val} be a substitution that makes it possible to substitute each free variable x that appears in a formula φ by a constant term, i.e. by $Val(x)$. We denote a formula φ in which appears a sequence of free variables X by $?X\varphi$. The expression $?X\varphi \bullet \Xi_{Val}$ indicates the formula φ in which each variable x of the sequence of free variables X is substituted by a corresponding value (i.e. by $Val(x)$). Thus, we can define the syntax of a CT as follows:

R17. $?X\varphi \in £/£sc \wedge Id_0 \in N \wedge \{Ag_1, Ag_2\} \subseteq A \Rightarrow CT(Id_0, Ag_1, Ag_2, ?X\varphi) \in £sc$: *Commitment attempt*

3.1.4 Actions Applied to Commitments

R18. $SC(Id_0, Ag_1, Ag_2, \varphi) \in £sc \Rightarrow$
$Create(Ag_1, SC(Id_0, Ag_1, Ag_2, \varphi)) \in £sc$: *Creation of a social commitment*

R19. $SC(Id_0, Ag_1, Ag_2, \varphi) \in £sc \Rightarrow$
$Withdraw(Ag_1, SC(Id_0, Ag_1, Ag_2, \varphi)) \in £sc$: *Withdrawal of a social commitment*

R20. $SC(Id_0, Ag_1, Ag_2, \varphi) \in £sc \Rightarrow$
$Satisfy(Ag_1, SC(Id_0, Ag_1, Ag_2, \varphi)) \in £sc$: *Satisfaction of a social commitment*

R21. $SC(Id_0, Ag_1, Ag_2, \varphi) \in £sc \Rightarrow$
$Violate(Ag_1, SC(Id_0, Ag_1, Ag_2, \varphi)) \in £sc$: *Violation of a social commitment*

R22. $SC(Id_0, Ag_1, Ag_2, \varphi) \in £sc \Rightarrow Active(SC(Id_0, Ag_1, Ag_2, \varphi)) \in £sc$: *An active social commitment*

3.1.5 Actions Applied to Commitment Contents

R23. $SC(Id_0, Ag_1, Ag_2, \varphi) \in £sc \Rightarrow$
$Accept\text{-}content(Ag_2, SC(Id_0, Ag_1, Ag_2, \varphi)) \in £sc$:   *Acceptance of a social commitment content*

R24. $SC(Id_0, Ag_1, Ag_2, \varphi) \in £sc \Rightarrow$
$Challenge\text{-}content(Ag_2, SC(Id_0, Ag_1, Ag_2, \varphi)) \in £sc$:   *Challenge of a social commitment content*

3.1.6 Argumentation Relations

R25. $SC(Id_0, Ag_1, Ag_2, \varphi) \in £sc \wedge \varphi' \in £/£sc \Rightarrow$
$Justify\text{-}content(Ag_2, SC(Id_0, Ag_1, Ag_2, \varphi), \varphi') \in £sc$: *Justification*

R26. $SC(Id_0, Ag_1, Ag_2, \varphi) \in £sc \Rightarrow$
$Contradict\text{-}content(Ag_1, SC(Id_0, Ag_1, Ag_2, \varphi)) \in £sc$: *Contradiction.* This relation means that an agent contradicts the content of its social commitment.

R27. SC(Id$_0$, Ag$_1$, Ag$_2$, φ) ∈ £sc ∧ φ' ∈ £/£sc ⇒
Attack-content(Ag$_2$, SC(Id$_0$, Ag$_1$, Ag$_2$, φ), φ') ∈ £sc: *Attack of a social commitment content*

R28. SC(Id$_0$, Ag$_1$, Ag$_2$, φ) ∈ £sc ∧ φ' ∈ £/£sc ⇒
Defend-content(Ag$_2$, SC(Id$_0$, Ag$_1$, Ag$_2$, φ), φ') ∈ £sc: *Defense of a social commitment content against an attacker*

Abbreviations: We use in our model the following abbreviations:

A1. p ∨ q (disjunction) is the abbreviation of ¬(¬p ∧ ¬q)
A2. p ⇒ q (implication) is the abbreviation of ¬p ∨ q
A3. F$^+$p (sometimes in the future) is the abbreviation of true U$^+$ p
A4. G$^+$p (globally in the future) is the abbreviation of ¬F$^+$¬p
A5. F$^-$p (sometimes in the past) is the abbreviation of true U$^-$ p
A6. G$^-$p (globally in the past) is the abbreviation of ¬F$^-$¬p

3.2 Semantics

In this section, we define the formal model in which we evaluate the well-formed formulas of our framework. Thereafter, we give the semantics of the different elements that we specified syntactically in the previous section.

3.2.1 The Formal Model

Let S be a set of states. A path *Pa* is an infinite sequence of states <s_0, s_1,...> where $T(s_0) < T(s_1) <$.... The function T gives us for each state s_i the corresponding moment t (this function will be specified later). Generally, for all i and j of N, if $i < j$ and s_i and s_j belong to the same path *Pa*, then $T(s_i) < T(s_j)$. We denote the set of all paths by σ. The set of all paths starting from the state s_i are denoted: σ^{si}. In our vision of branching future, we can have several states at the same moment. Only along a given path (for example the real path) there is one and only one state at one moment. Indeed, in our framework, s_i does not indicate (necessarily) the state at moment i. Therefore, it is necessary to specify the state s and the moment t i.e. a couple $(s, t) \in S \times TU$. According to this formalization, we can use the notation: M, s_i, $T(s_i)$ ⊢ ψ to indicate that ψ is satisfied in the Kripke model M at the state s_i at the moment $T(s_i)$. To simplify this notation, we will use in the rest of the paper the following notation: M, s_i ⊢ ψ. In this notation: M, s_i ⊢ ψ there is a "hidden" time.

Following this simplification we can write:
M, s_i, $T(s_i)$ ⊢ ψ *iff* M, s_i ⊢ ψ.
The formal model for £ is defined as follows:
$M(S, A, Np, Np?, Fap, Rpc, Rac, T)$ where
S : a nonempty set of states.
A : a nonempty set of agents.
$Np : S \mapsto 2^{\Phi ap}$: function relating each state $s \in S$ to the set of the atomic propositions that are true in this state.

$Np? : S \mapsto 2^{\Phi ap}$: function relating each state $s \in S$ to the set of the atomic propositions that are neither true nor false in this state (i.e. we do not know if they are true or false).

$Fap : S \times \Phi a \mapsto 2^S$: function that gives us the state transitions caused by the achievement of an action.

$Rpc : A \times A \times S \mapsto 2^S$: function producing the accessibility modal relations for PCs.

$Rac : A \times A \times S \mapsto 2^S$: function producing the accessibility modal relations for AC.

$T : S \mapsto TU$: function associating to any state s_i the corresponding time.

The functions Rpc and Rac give us the states that correspond to the time t_φ, i.e. the states in which the social commitment created by an agent Ag_1 towards another agent Ag_2 must be satisfied. These functions allow us to define a deadline for determining whether a violation or a satisfaction occurs. They give us all the states corresponding to the time t_φ on all paths starting from the state at moment t_u. The fact that these two functions give us a set of states means that the social commitment must be satisfied whatever the future. Since there is only one real path, the social commitment is satisfied or is violated only in one state of the set given by Rpc and Rac. Indeed, the outputs of the functions Rpc and Rac are known only after the creation of the social commitment. Thus, this depends on the state in which the social commitment is created. For example, if we have: $s_j \in Rpc(Ag_1, Ag_2, s_i)$, then this means that at moment $T(s_i)$ agent Ag_1 is committed towards agent Ag_2 to satisfy a certain social commitment at moment $T(s_j)$. We can see that Rpc depends on the current moment $T(s_i)$.

The algebraic properties of these two relations are as follows:

1- *Rac is not reflexive*, i.e.:

$$\forall Ag_1, Ag_2 \in A, \forall s_i \in S, s_i \notin Rac(Ag_1, Ag_2, s_i)$$

The reason is that this accessibility relation defines a deadline and that action commitments are always directed towards the future. For the same reason, we have: Rpc^f is not *reflexive* and Rpc^p is *reflexive*, where: Rpc^f is the restriction of Rpc to the propositional commitments directed to the future, and Rpc^p is the restriction of Rpc to the propositional commitments directed towards the past and the present.

2- *Rpc and Rac are serial*, i.e.:

$$\forall Ag_1, Ag_2 \in A, \forall s_i \in S : \exists s_j \in R(Ag_1, Ag_2, s_i)$$

where R = Rpc or R = Rac

This property fits with the notion of infinite path in CTL*.

3- *Rpc and Rac are transitive*, i.e.:

$$\forall Ag_1, Ag_2 \in A, \forall s_i, s_j, s_k \in S : s_j \in R(Ag_1, Ag_2, s_i) \wedge s_k \in Rac(Ag_1, Ag_2, s_j)$$
$$\Rightarrow s_k \in R(Ag_1, Ag_2, s_i)$$

where R = Rpc or R = Rac.

Consequently, social commitments in our model are *S4* modal logic operators. The interpretation of this property is as follows: if an agent commits that a proposition is true, or so that an action will be performed, this implies that the agent commits so that it commits that the proposition is true or so that the action will be performed.

4- Because *Rpc* and *Rac* allow us to define a deadline, these relations are *not symmetric*, i.e.:$\forall Ag_1, Ag_2 \in A, \exists s_i, s_j \in S : s_j \in R(Ag_1, Ag_2, s_i) \wedge s_i \notin R(Ag_1, Ag_2, s_j)$ *where R = Rpc or R = Rac.*

5- *Rpc* and *Rac* are not *euclidean*, i.e.:

$$\forall Ag_1, Ag_2 \in A, \exists s_i, s_j, s_k \in S : s_j \in R(Ag_1, Ag_2, s_i) \wedge s_k \in R(Ag_1, Ag_2, s_i)$$
$$\wedge s_k \notin R(Ag_1, Ag_2, s_j) \wedge s_j \notin R(Ag_1, Ag_2, s_k)$$

where R = Rpc or R = Rac.

Therefore, the *negative introspection* schema *S5* is not verifiable in our model.

We notice here that we do not impose a model to be *asymmetric*, but we only emphasize the fact that *Rpc* and *Rac* are *not symmetric*. For this reason we use the existential quantifier in 4.

As in CTL*, we have in our model path formulas and state formulas. We propose to evaluate the static formulas (the different types of social commitments) as state formulas. These formulas can also be interpreted on paths in which case one considers satisfaction in the first state of a path. On the other hand, we propose to evaluate dynamic formulas (the actions on social commitments) on paths. These path formulas can become state formulas if they are true on all the paths starting from a given state. $M, s_i \vdash \psi$ indicates that the formula ψ is evaluated in the state s_i of the model *M*. *M, Pa, $s_i \vdash \psi$* indicates that the formula ψ is evaluated on the path *Pa* starting from the state s_i of the model *M*. We can now define the semantics of the elements of £.

3.2.2 Propositional Elements

S1. M, $s_i \vdash \psi$ iff $\psi \in Np(s_i)$ with $\psi \in \Phi p$

S2. M, $s_i \vdash p \wedge q$ iff M, $s_i \vdash p$ & M, $s_i \vdash q$

S3. M, $s_i \vdash \neg p$ iff $\neg($ M, $s_i \vdash p)$

S4. M, $s_i \vdash p \therefore q$ iff M, $s_i \vdash p$ & $(\forall j : M, s_j \vdash p$ $\Rightarrow M, s_j \vdash q)$

In S4 we add the first clause (M, $s_i \vdash p$) to capture the following aspect: when an agent presents an argument p for q (i.e. p$\therefore$ q) for this agent p is true and if p is true then q is true. Indeed, p so q is stronger than just stating that both p and q are true. The implication is much stronger since it holds in all the states of the model M. The idea is to express that p is the support of the conclusion q.

S5. M, $s_i \vdash ?p$ iff $p \in Np?(s_i)$.

S6. M, $s_i \vdash Ap$ iff $(\forall Pa : Pa \in \sigma^{si} \Rightarrow M, Pa, s_i \vdash p)$

S7. M, $s_i \vdash Ep$ iff $(\exists Pa \in \sigma^{si}$ & M, Pa, $s_i \vdash p)$

S8. M, Pa, $s_i \vdash p$ iff M, $s_i \vdash p$: *Propositional path formulas*

S9. M, Pa, $s_i \vdash p \wedge q$ iff M, Pa, $s_i \vdash p$ & M, Pa, $s_i \vdash q$

S10. M, Pa, $s_i \models \neg p$ iff $\neg($ M, Pa, $s_i \models p)$

S11. M, Pa, $s_i \models p \, U^+ q$ iff $(\exists j : i \leq j \, \& \, M, Pa, s_j \models q$
$\& \, (\forall k : i \leq k < j \Rightarrow M, Pa, s_k \models p))$

S12. M, Pa, $s_i \models X^+ p$ iff M, Pa, $s_{i+1} \models p))$

S13. M, Pa, $s_i \models p \, U^- q$ iff $(\exists j : j \leq i \, \& \, M, Pa, s_j \models q$
$\& \, (\forall k : j < k \leq i \Rightarrow M, Pa, s_k \models p))$

S14. M, Pa, $s_i \models X^- p$ iff M, Pa, $s_{i-1} \models p))$

3.2.3 Actions

S15. M, Pa, $s_i \models \text{Perform}(\alpha)p$ iff $\forall s_j : s_j \in \text{Fap}(s_i, \alpha) \wedge s_j \subset Pa \Rightarrow M, Pa, s_j \models p$.

where $s_j \subset Pa$ indicates that Pa, s_j is a *suffix* of Pa, s_i.

S16. M, $s_i \models \text{Perform}(\alpha)p$ iff $\forall Pa : Pa \in \sigma^{si} \Rightarrow M, Pa, s_i \models \text{Perform}(\alpha)p$.

Action performance (related to social commitments)

S17. M, Pa, $s_i \models \text{Perform}(\alpha)SC(Id_0, Ag_1, Ag_2, \varphi)$ iff

$\forall s_j : s_j \in \text{Fap}(s_i, \alpha) \wedge s_j \subset Pa \Rightarrow M, Pa, s_j \models SC(Id_0, Ag_1, Ag_2, \varphi)$.

This formula indicates that the achievement of action α makes the social commitment true in all the accessible states from the state s_i. As for S15, the accessible states are defined by the function *Fap*. The evaluation of this operator in a state is given by the following formula:

S18. M, $s_i \models \text{Perform}(\alpha)SC(Id_0, Ag_1, Ag_2, \varphi)$ iff

$\forall Pa: Pa \in \sigma^{si} \Rightarrow M, Pa, s_i \models \text{Perform}(\alpha)SC(Id_0, Ag_1, Ag_2, \varphi)$.

3.2.4 Social Commitments

Social commitment as a path formula

S19. M, Pa, $s_i \models SC(Id_0, Ag_1, Ag_2, \varphi)$ iff M, $s_i \models SC(Id_0, Ag_1, Ag_2, \varphi)$

S20. M, $s_i \models PC(Id_0, Ag_1, Ag_2, p)$ iff $(\forall s_j : s_j \in \text{Rpc}(Ag_1, Ag_2, s_i) \Rightarrow M, s_j \models p)$

S21. M, $s_i \models AC(Id_0, Ag_1, Ag_2, \alpha)p$ iff

$\forall s_j : s_j \in \text{Rac}(Ag_1, Ag_2, s_i) \Rightarrow M, s_j \models \text{Perform}(\alpha)p))$.

The formula S21 indicates that agent Ag_1 is committed towards agent Ag_2 to do α and that in all accessible states s_j performing α makes p true. According to formulas S20 and S21, the semantics we give to the social commitments requires their fulfillment. Thus, if it is created, a social commitment must be held. However, it is always possible to violate or withdraw such a social commitment. For this reason, these two operations (violation and withdrawal) are explicitly included in our framework. Thus, it is possible to have wrong social commitments in the model. The reason is that *Rpc* and *Rac* give us the states that correspond to the states in which the social commitment *must* be satisfied. These states are not conceived as merely "possible", but as states when the content of a social commitment *must* be true.

We notice that although *Rpc* and *Rac* are dynamic functions, we do not need to change the Kripke model M to capture this dynamics. This way of modeling is different from that used for example in KARO framework [19]. In our model which fits in naturally with CTL* the whole dynamics is represented in one unique model.

S22. $M, s_i \vdash CC(Id_0, Ag_1, Ag_2, \beta \Rightarrow \gamma)$
iff $(M, s_i \vdash EF^+\beta \Rightarrow M, s_i \vdash ABC(Id_0, Ag_1, Ag_2, \gamma))$

This formula indicates that agent Ag_1 commits to perform γ (or that γ is true) only if the condition β is true (or is satisfied).

In order to define the semantics of CTs, we define the binary relation $\vdash^{\Xi Val}$ between a pair (M, s_i) and a formula $CT(Id_0, Ag_1, Ag_2, ?X\varphi)$ as follows:

S23. $M, s_i \vdash^{\Xi Val} CT(Id_0, Ag_1, Ag_2, ?X\varphi)$ iff
$(M, s_i \vdash EX^+F^+ABC(Id_0, Ag_2, Ag_1, ?X\varphi\bullet\Xi_{Val})$
$\vee (\exists\beta \in £/£sc : M, s_i \vdash EX^+F^+CC(Id_0, Ag_2, Ag_1, \beta \Rightarrow ?X\varphi\bullet\Xi_{Val}))$

This formula indicates that a CT whose content is $?X\varphi$ is satisfied in the model M according to a substitution Ξ_{Val} iff the creditor (i.e. Ag_2) will commit that a content $?X\varphi\bullet\Xi_{Val}$ is true. In other words, the CT is satisfied iff the interlocutor will commit that the substitution Ξ_{Val} for the sequence X of free variables appearing in the formulae φ is true. The social commitment of the interlocutor can be absolute (ABC) or conditional (CC). We suppose here that agents are "dialogically" co-operative in so far as an agent accepts to offer a substitution Ξ_{Val} for the sequence X.

3.2.5 Actions Applied to Commitments

S24. $M, Pa, s_i \vdash Create(Ag_1, SC(Id_0, Ag_1, Ag_2, \varphi))$ iff
$\exists\alpha \in \Phi a \ \& \ M, Pa, s_i \vdash Perform(\alpha)SC(Id_0, Ag_1, Ag_2, \varphi) \wedge G^-\neg SC(Id_0, Ag_1, Ag_2, \varphi)$

This formula indicates that the creation of a social commitment is satisfied in the model M along a path Pa iff there is an action α whose performance makes true the social commitment (i.e. the social commitment holds after the performance of the action α) and if in the past (before the creation moment of the social commitment), the social commitment was never satisfied in this model. This formula highlights the fact that the creation of a social commitment is an action in itself. Indeed, the action α corresponds to the agent's utterance which creates the social commitment.

S25. $M, Pa, s_i \vdash Withdraw(Ag_1, SC(Id_0, Ag_1, Ag_2, \varphi))$ iff
$\exists\alpha \in \Phi a, M, Pa, s_i \vdash X^-F^-Create (Ag_1, SC(Id_0, Ag_1, Ag_2, \varphi))$
$\wedge Perform(\alpha)\neg SC(Id_0, Ag_1, Ag_2, \varphi).$

This formula indicates that an agent withdraws its social commitment for φ iff: (1) The agent has already created this social commitment. (2) The agent performs an action α so that this social commitment does not hold at the current moment.
The semantics of the satisfaction operation depends on the type of the social commitment. In this paper we give only the semantics of the satisfaction of a PC as follows:

S26. $M, Pa, s_i \vdash Satisfy(Ag_1, PC(Id_0, Ag_1, Ag_2, p))$ iff
$\exists j : j \leq i \ \& \ M, Pa, s_j \vdash Create(Ag_1, PC(Id_0, Ag_1, Ag_2, p))$
$\wedge M, Pa, s_i \vdash p \wedge s_i \in Rpc(Ag_1, Ag_2, s_j).$

A PC is satisfied iff it was already created and the propositional content is true in the moment that corresponds to the moment where the social commitment must be satisfied. This moment is denoted by s_i that defines the deadline. For example, if an agent commits at 14PM that it will rain at 16PM, we say that the social commitment is satisfied if it really rains at 16PM, if not, the social commitment is violated.

We can think of satisfaction and violation as two dual relations. Hence, we can express the relation between satisfaction and violation for any social commitment type. For example, for a PC this relation is specified by the formula:

S27. $M, Pa, s_i \vdash \text{Violate}(Ag_1, PC(Id_0, Ag_1, Ag_2, \varphi))$ iff

$\exists j : j \leq i$ & $M, Pa, s_j \vdash \text{Create}(Ag_1, PC(Id_0, Ag_1, Ag_2, \varphi)) \wedge s_i \in \text{Rpc}(Ag_1, Ag_2, s_j)$

$\wedge M, Pa, s_i \vdash \neg\text{Satisfy}(Ag_1, PC(Id_0, Ag_1, Ag_2, \varphi))$.

This formula expresses the following property: If an agent violates its social commitment in the state s_i (which represents the deadline) along the path Pa, then this agent does not satisfy this social commitment in this state along this path and vice versa.

After introducing the different actions that the debtor can apply to its social commitments, we can define the semantics of an active social commitment as follows:

S28. $M, Pa, s_i \vdash \text{Active}(SC(Id_0, Ag_1, Ag_2, \varphi))$ iff

$M, Pa, s_i \vdash ((\neg\text{Violate}(Ag_1, SC(Id_0, Ag_1, Ag_2, \varphi))$

$\wedge \neg\text{Satisfy}(Ag_1, SC(Id_0, Ag_1, Ag_2, \varphi)) \wedge \neg\text{Withdraw}(Ag_1, SC(Id_0, Ag_1, Ag_2, \varphi)))$

$U^- \text{Create}(Ag_1, SC(Id_0, Ag_1, Ag_2, \varphi)))$

This property indicates that a social commitment is active iff: (1) This social commitment was already created. (2) Until the current moment, the social commitment was neither violated, withdrawn nor satisfied. Therefore, once the social commitment is satisfied, violated or withdrawn, it becomes inactive.

3.2.6 Actions Applied to Commitment Contents

S29. $M, Pa, s_i \vdash \text{Accept-content}(Ag_2, SC(Id_0, Ag_1, Ag_2, \varphi))$ iff

$M, Pa, s_i \vdash \text{Active}(SC(Id_0, Ag_1, Ag_2, \varphi)) \wedge \text{Create}(Ag_2, SC(Id_1, Ag_2, Ag_1, \varphi))$

This formula indicates that the acceptance of the social commitment content φ by agent Ag_2 is satisfied in the model M along a path Pa iff: (1) The social commitment is active on this path because we cannot act on a social commitment content if the social commitment is not active. (2) Agent Ag_2 creates a social commitment whose content is φ. Therefore, Ag_2 becomes committed towards the content φ.

S30. $M, Pa, s_i \vdash \text{Challenge-content}(Ag_2, SC(Id_0, Ag_1, Ag_2, \varphi))$ iff

$\exists \alpha \in \Phi a, \exists \varphi' \in £/£sc$ & $M, Pa, s_i \vdash \text{Perform}(\alpha)PC(Id_1, Ag_2, Ag_1, ?\varphi)$

$\wedge \text{Active}(SC(Id_0, Ag_1, Ag_2, \varphi)) \wedge EX^+F^+\text{Justify-content}(Ag_1, SC(Id_0, Ag_1, Ag_2, \varphi), \varphi')$

This formula indicates that the challenge of the social commitment content φ by an agent Ag_2 is satisfied in the model M along a path Pa iff: (1) Agent Ag_2 commits that $?\varphi$. Indeed, $PC(Id_1, Ag_2, Ag_1, ?\varphi)$ states that "Ag_2 does not know φ but it would like to know it". (2) The challenged commitment is active on this path. (3) Agent Ag_1

justifies in the future its social commitment for φ. Indeed, when we challenge a statement, we expect an answer from the speaker. Thus, in our semantics the fact that there is a possibility of having an answer is included in the meaning of the challenge. The operator E in $(EX^+F^+Justify\text{-}content(Ag_1, SC(Id_0, Ag_1, Ag_2, \varphi), \varphi'))$ allows us to capture the concept of possibility i.e. that there is a path along which Ag_1 will justify its social commitment. This formula highlights the fact that the challenge of a social commitment content is an action in itself. As for the creation operation, the action α corresponds to the production of the utterance that challenges the social commitment content.

3.2.7 Argumentation Relations

S31. M, Pa, $s_i \models$ Justify-content(Ag_1, $SC(Id_0, Ag_1, Ag_2, \varphi)$, φ') iff

M, Pa, $s_i \models$ Active($SC(Id_0, Ag_1, Ag_2, \varphi)$) $\wedge$ Create(Ag_1, $SC(Id_1, Ag_1, Ag_2, \varphi' \therefore \varphi)$).

This formula indicates that the justification of the social commitment content φ by an agent Ag_1 is satisfied in the model M on a path Pa iff: (1) This social commitment is active on this path. (2) This agent creates on this path a social commitment whose content is φ' that supports the conclusion φ. In other words, an agent's social commitment towards another agent to make a content φ true is justified (by means of φ') iff the social commitment exists (has been created) and moreover a social commitment is created to establish an argument (φ', φ), where φ' is committed to be true because according to the definition of the connector $(\therefore)$, φ' is true for Ag_1. The fact that this operator is included in the social commitment indicates that the agent is committed that φ' is true and then φ is true, i.e. φ is true because φ' is true. Indeed, agents have knowledge bases and the propositions that are not challenged can be used for justification (i.e. as supports of arguments). Hence, to end the chain of argumentation, agents use PCs that are not challenged any further. The justification operation is the basis of other argumentation operations. As shown by the following properties (S33 and S34), this is due to the fact that all the other operations are defined using this operation.

S32. M, Pa, $s_i \models$ Contradict-content(Ag_1, $SC(Id_0, Ag_1, Ag_2, \varphi)$) iff

$(\exists \varphi' \in$ £/£sc: (M, Pa, $s_i \models$ Active($SC(Id_0, Ag_2, Ag_1, \varphi)$)

$\wedge$ Create(Ag_1, $SC(Id_1, Ag_1, Ag_2, \varphi')$))) $\wedge (\varphi' \therefore \neg\varphi))$

This formula indicates that an agent contradicts its previous social commitment whose content is φ if it creates another social commitment whose content is a logical conclusion of $\neg\varphi$, whereas its social commitment for φ is still active.

Properties:

S33. M, Pa, $s_i \models$ Attack-content(Ag_2, $SC(Id_0, Ag_1, Ag_2, \varphi)$, φ') iff

M, Pa, $s_i \models$ Active($SC(Id_0, Ag_1, Ag_2, \varphi)$)

$\wedge$ Justify-content(Ag_2, $SC(Id_1, Ag_2, Ag_1, \neg\varphi)$, φ')

This formula indicates that the attack of the social commitment content φ by an agent Ag_2 is satisfied in the model M along a path Pa iff: (1) This social commitment is active on this path. (2) This agent justifies along this path its social commitment whose content is $\neg\varphi$.

S34. M, Pa, $s_i \models$ Defend-content(Ag_1, SC(Id_0, Ag_1, Ag_2, φ), φ') iff
$\exists\varphi'' \in £/£sc$ & M, Pa, $s_i \models$ Active(SC(Id_0, Ag_1, Ag_2, φ))
$\wedge$ X¯F¯Attack-content(Ag_2, SC(Id_0, Ag_1, Ag_2, φ), φ''))
$\wedge$ Attack-content(Ag_1, SC(Id_1, Ag_2, Ag_1, φ''), φ'))

This formula indicates that the defense of the social commitment content φ by an agent Ag_1 is satisfied in the model M along a path Pa iff: (1) This social commitment is active on this path. (2) This agent attacks the attacker of the content of its social commitment.

3.2.8   Link Between Commitments and Arguments
Until now we gave the seman- tics of the main elements of our formalism. We can now formally establish the link between social commitments and arguments. This link is shown by the two following formulas:

S35. A(Create(Ag_1, SC(Id_0, Ag_1, Ag_2, φ))$\Rightarrow$
(($\neg$(F$^+$Contradict-content(Ag_1, SC(Id_0, Ag_1, Ag_2, φ)))))
$\wedge$(F$^+$(Challenge-content(Ag_2, SC(Id_0, Ag_1, Ag_2, φ))$\Rightarrow$$\exists\varphi'$:
AX$^+$F$^+$Justify-content(Ag_1, SC(Id_0, Ag_1, Ag_2, φ), φ')))
$\wedge$(F$^+$Attack-content(Ag_2, SC(Id_0, Ag_1, Ag_2, φ), φ')$\Rightarrow$$\exists\varphi''$:
AX$^+$F$^+$Defend-content(Ag_1, SC(Id_0, Ag_1, Ag_2, φ), φ''))))

This formula provides the conditions generated by the creation of a social commitment on all paths. The agent must be in a position to check these conditions before creating a social commitment. Indeed, if an agent creates a social commitment, then it should not contradict itself during the conversation. It must also be able to justify its social commitment if it is challenged and to defend it if it is attacked. By establishing the link between social commitments and arguments, this formula reflects the deontic aspect of social commitments. These conditions are also valid for withdrawal, acceptance and refusal because their semantics is expressed in terms of the creation operation. On the other hand, an agent challenges a social commitment content if it has no argument for or against this content. Therefore, An agent challenges a social commitment content if it cannot accept or refuse it. Formally:

S36. A((Active(SC(Id_0, Ag_1, Ag_2, φ)) $\wedge$ $\neg$Accept-content(Ag_2, SC(Id_0, Ag_1, Ag_2, φ))
$\wedge$ $\neg$Refuse-content(Ag_2, SC(Id_0, Ag_1, Ag_2, φ)))
$\Rightarrow$ Challenge-content(Ag_2, SC(Id_0, Ag_1, Ag_2, φ)))

4   Logic-Based Protocols

Until now we defined a modal semantics for our approach in order to give a meaning to the different communicating actions. The purpose behind the definition of this semantics using temporal and dynamic logic is to be able to verify the correctness of the agent communication protocols. A protocol is correct iff it satisfies given properties specified using our logic. Thus, the correctness problem is a model-checking one. In this section, we show how we can define these protocols on the basis of our approach. This definition enables us to establish the link between the semantics and the pragmatics.

$$R1 \ \wedge: \frac{\psi_1 \wedge \psi_2}{\psi_1 \ \psi_2} \quad R2 \ \vee: \frac{\psi_1 \vee \psi_2}{\psi_1 \ \psi_2} \quad R3 \ \vee: \frac{E(\psi)}{\psi} \quad R4 \ \neg: \frac{\neg \psi}{\psi} \quad R5 \ ?: \frac{?\psi}{\psi}$$

$$R6 \ \neg: \frac{A(\Phi)}{E(\neg\Phi)} \quad R7 <\alpha_p>: \frac{E(\Phi, Perform(\alpha)\varphi)}{E(\Phi, \varphi)}$$

$$R8 <C>: \frac{E(\Phi, Create(Ag_1, SC(Id_0, Ag_1, Ag_2, \varphi))}{E(\Phi, SC(Id_0, Ag_1, Ag_2, \varphi))}$$

$$R9 <S_{PC}>: \frac{E(\Phi, Satisfy(Ag_1, PC(Id_0, Ag_1, Ag_2, \varphi))}{E(\Phi, \varphi)}$$

$$R10 \ <V_{PC}>: \frac{E(\Phi, Violate(Ag_1, PC(Id_0, Ag_1, Ag_2, \varphi))}{E(\Phi, \neg\varphi)}$$

$$R11 <Ch>: \frac{E(\Phi, Challenge-content(Ag_2, PC(Id_0, Ag_1, Ag_2, \varphi))}{E(\Phi, PC(Id_1, Ag_2, Ag_1, ?\varphi))}$$

$$R12 <Acc>: \frac{E(\Phi, Accept-content(Ag_2, SC(Id_0, Ag_1, Ag_2, \varphi))}{E(\Phi, SC(Id_1, Ag_2, Ag_1, \varphi))}$$

$$R13 <Att>: \frac{E(\Phi, Attack-content(Ag_2, PC(Id_0, Ag_1, Ag_2, \varphi), \varphi')}{E(\Phi, PC(Id_1, Ag_2, Ag_1, \varphi' \therefore \neg\varphi))}$$

$$R14 <Def>: \frac{E(\Phi, Defend-content(Ag_1, PC(Id_0, Ag_1, Ag_2, \varphi), \varphi')}{E(\Phi, PC(Id_1, Ag_1, Ag_2, \varphi' \therefore \varphi))}$$

$$R15 \ [PC_{Ag1}]: \frac{E(\Phi, PC(Id_0, Ag_1, Ag_2, \varphi))}{E(\Phi, \varphi)} \quad R16 <>: \frac{E(\Phi, l)}{l, \ E(\Phi)}$$

$$R17 \ \wedge: \frac{E(\Phi, \varphi_1 \wedge \varphi_2)}{E(\Phi, \varphi_1, \varphi_2)} \quad R18 \ \vee: \frac{E(\Phi, \varphi_1 \vee \varphi_2)}{E(\Phi, \varphi_1) \ E(\Phi, \varphi_2)} \quad R19 \ ?: \frac{E(\Phi, ?\varphi)}{E(\Phi, \varphi)}$$

$$R20 \ X^+: \frac{E(\Phi, X^+\varphi_1, ..., X^+\varphi_n)}{E(\Phi, \varphi_1, ..., \varphi_n)} \quad R21 \ \wedge: \frac{E(\Phi, \varphi_1 \therefore \varphi_2)}{E(\Phi, \varphi_1, X^+(\neg\varphi_1 \vee \varphi_2))}$$

$$R22 \ \vee: \frac{E(\Phi, \varphi_1 U^+ \varphi_2)}{E(\Phi, \varphi_2) \ E(\Phi, \varphi_1, X^+(\varphi_1 U^+ \varphi_2))}$$

Fig. 1. Some tableau rules for DCTL*$_{CAN}$ logic

Agent communication protocols are specified as a set of rules describing the entry condition, the dynamics and the exit condition of these protocols[4]. Using our logic, these rules can be specified as action formulas: actions on social commitments, actions on social commitment contents and argumentation relations. These protocols can be specified using transition systems. The purpose of these transition systems is to describe not only the sequence of the allowed actions (like classical transition systems), but also the semantics of these actions. The semantics we use here is a tableau semantics [6] that we can consider as a simplification of the semantics defined in Section 3.2. This semantics is specified in terms of the decomposition of action formulas to sub-formulas using a set of inference or *proof rules* called *tableau rules*. The tableau rules are designed so that the formula is true if all the sub-formulas are true. The tableau semantics enables us to define *top-down proof systems*. The idea is: given a formula, we apply a proof rule and determine the sub-formulas to be proven. Fig. 1 shows some examples of tableau rules of our DCTL*$_{CAN}$ logic. Φ is a set of path formulas φ_i and ψ is a state formula. The definition of the tableau rules is based on the semantics defined in Section 3.2.

The states of the transition systems are sub-transition systems that we call *semantic transition systems*. These automata describe the semantics of the actions labeling the entry transitions. Defining protocols using transition systems in such a way allows us to verify:

1- The correctness of the protocol (if the model of the protocol satisfies the properties that the protocol should specify).
2- The compliance to the semantics (if the specification of the protocol respects the semantics).

The definition of the transition systems of agent communication protocols is given by the following definitions:

Definition 3. *A semantic transition system T' describing the semantics of an action formula is a 6-uple* $<S', F, L', R, \rightarrow^R, s'_0>$ *where:S' is a set of states, F is a sub-set of the set of formulas from DCTL*$_{CAN}$ (F does not include the action formulas), L' : S'* $\mapsto$ F *is the labeling state function,* $R \in \{\wedge, \vee, \neg, ?, <>, X^+, X^-, PC_{Ag}, AC_{Ag}\}$ *is the set of rule labels,* $\rightarrow^R \subseteq S' \times R \times S'$ *is the transition relation, s'$_0$ is the start state.*

Intuitively, states s' contain the sub-formulas of the action formulas, and the transitions are labeled with operators associated with the formula of the source state. Semantic transition systems enable us to describe the semantics of formulas using sub-formulas connected by logical operators. Thus, there is a transition between states s'_i and s'_j iff $L'(s'_j)$ is a sub-formula or a semantically equivalent formula of $L'(s'_i)$.

Definition 4. *A transition system T for an agent communication protocol is a 6-uple* $<S, \wp, L, Act, \rightarrow^{Act}, s_0>$ *where: S is a set of states,* $\wp$ *is a set of semantic transition systems, L : S* $\rightarrow$ *T' is the function associating a state s* $\in$ *S to a semantic transition system T'* $\in$ $\wp$ *describing the semantics of the action labeling the entry transition, Act* $\in$ *{ Create, Withdraw, Satisfy, Accept-content, Refuse-content, Challenge-content, Justify-content, Defend-content, Attack-content} is the set of actions,* $\rightarrow^{Act} \subseteq S \times Act \times S$ *is the transition relation, s$_0$ is the start state.*

The transitions are labeled with the actions applied to social commitments and to social commitment contents and the argumentation actions. We write $s \rightarrow^* s'$ in lieu of $<s,*, s'> \in \rightarrow$ where $* \in Act$.

4.1 Logical Properties to be Verified

The properties to be verified in the protocols specified by DCTL$^*_{CAN}$ are action and temporal properties. For example we can verify if a model of an agent communication protocol satisfies the following property:

$AG^+(Challenge\text{-}content(Ag_2, PC(Id_0, Ag_1, Ag_2, \varphi)) \Rightarrow$
$\exists \varphi': F^+Justify\text{-}content(Ag_1, PC(Id_0, Ag_1, Ag_2, \varphi), \varphi'))$

This property indicates that if an agent Ag_2 challenges the content of an Ag_1's propositional commitment (PC), then Ag_1 will justify this content. Another property capturing the deontic notion of social commitments is given by the following formula:

$AG^+(Attack\text{-}content(Ag_2, PC(Id_0, Ag_1, Ag_2, \varphi), \varphi')) \Rightarrow \exists \varphi'':$
$(F^+Defend\text{-}content(Ag_1, PC(Id_0, Ag_1, Ag_2, \varphi), \varphi'')$
$\vee F^+Attack\text{-}content(Ag_1, PC(Id_1, Ag_2, Ag_1, \varphi'), \varphi''))$
$\vee F^+Accept\text{-}contentt(Ag_1, PC(Id_1, Ag_2, Ag_1, \varphi')))$

Thus we can verify if a protocol satisfies the fact that if an agent Ag_2 attacks the content of an Ag_1's propositional commitment, then Ag_1 will defend its commitment content, attack the Ag_2's argument or accept it.

We are currently developing a model checking technique to verify these properties and the underlying semantics using a combination of tableau-based and automata-based model checking technique. This technique enables us to verify temporal and action properties by exploring the product graph of a labeled tableau automata representing the logical property and the transition system describing the protocol. The advantage of this technique is that the state space is explored in a need-driven fashion. The algorithm searches only the part of the state space that needs to be explored to prove or disprove a certain formula.

5 Related Work

Semantical considerations for agent communication have recently begun to find a significant audience in the MAS community. We can distinguish three kinds of semantics:

1- Mentalistic semantics: This subjective semantics is based on so-called agent's mental states. The best-known formalisms describing it are [8, 16, 19, 22]. KQML [12] and FIPA-ACL use this semantics to define a pre/post conditions semantic of communication acts. The advantage of this semantics is its compatibility with the formalisms used for reasoning about rational agents. However, the verification of such a semantics is not possible if we cannot have access to the agents' programs. In addition, this pre/post condition semantics offers no dynamic or operational description of agent communication. Because our approach is based on public and argumentative concepts, the compliance verification can be made without having access to the agents' programs. The satisfaction and the violation of agents' social

commitments make it possible to determine if the agent respects our semantics. In addition, the agents' ability to justify their social commitments facilitates this verification. In addition, our semantics treats more explicitly the dynamic aspect of agent communication using the agents' actions on social commitments and on their contents.

2- Social semantics: This objective semantics was proposed by Singh [23, 24] as an alternative to the mentalistic one. Singh used CTL to propose a formal language and a model in which the notion of social commitment is described. Verdicchio and Colombetti [25] proposed an interesting logical model of social commitments by extending CTL*. This model is based on the fact that agent communication should be analyzed in terms of communicative acts. Mallya et al. [17] used the temporal commitment structure specified by [13] to define some constraints in order to capture some operations on social commitments. Our logical model uses some ideas of [25] and it belongs to this kind of semantics, but it differs from these propositions in the following respects: 1) In our approach the social commitment semantics is not defined as an abstract accessibility relation, but as an accessibility relation that takes into account the satisfaction of the social commitment. The semantics is defined in terms of the deadline at which the social commitment must be satisfied. This way is more intuitive than the semantics defined by Singh. 2) We differentiate social commitments as static structures evaluated in states from the operations applied to social commitments as dynamic structures evaluated on paths. This enables us to describe more naturally the evolution of the agent communication as a system of states / transitions which reflects the interaction dynamics. 3) In our model, the strength of social commitments as a basic principle of agent communication does not result only from the fact that they are observable, but also from the fact that they are supported by arguments. The social commitment notion we formalize is not only a public notion but also a deontic one. The deontic aspect is captured by the fact that social commitments are considered as obligations. The agent is obliged to satisfy its social commitments, to behave in accordance with these social commitments and to justify them. It is also obliged not to contradict its social commitment contents during the conversation. 4) We capture in our semantics not only PCs, but the various types of social commitments. This enables us to have a greater expressivity and to capture the different types of SAs.

3- Argumentation-based semantics: This semantics is defined in [1] to capture the meaning of certain communication acts. It is based upon an argumentation system and on the formal dialectics. This semantics has the advantages of being simple and of taking into account the argumentation aspect of agent communication. In addition to the fact that this semantics does not take into account temporal and dynamic aspects in its formalization, it is different from our approach on several points: 1) It is based on an informal logic. 2) It is described in terms of pre/post conditions and it does not offer the meaning of the different communication acts. 3) The commitment notion used in this semantics captures only the propositions stated by the agents. 4) Contrary to our approach, the satisfaction, violation, cancellation, attack and defense notions do not appear.

6 Conclusion and Future Work

In this paper we developed a formal semantics for our approach based on social commitments and arguments to model agents' interactions. We proposed a logical model (DCTL*$_{CAN}$) based on a combination of CTL* and dynamic logic. The model captures different social commitment types, different actions applied to these social commitments and various argumentation relations. We showed how we can define protocols using DCTL*$_{CAN}$ logic in order to be able to check the correctness and the semantic compliance using a model-checking algorithm. We used the tableau semantics as a simplified semantics for the compliance verification. The tableau rules based on this semantics are needed for the translation of the logical properties to be verified to a tableau automata. Thus, our CAN formalism includes both pragmatic and semantic issues of agent communication.

We plan as future work to develop efficient model-checking algorithm for logic-based protocols. The idea we are investigting is to use an automata theoretic model-checking based on the empiteness problem of graphs. We intend to implement this algorithm using the CWB-NC verification tool.

Acknowledgments. We would like to thank Josée Desharnais from Laval University for her valuable comments about the logical model. We would also like to thank the three anonymous referees of AAMAS'04 for their detailed and very interesting comments that allowed us to improve the quality of this paper.

References

1. Amgoud, L., Maudet, N., and Parsons, N. An argumentation-based semantics for agent communication languages. 15th Euro. Conf. on AI (2002) 38-42.
2. Bentahar, J., Moulin, B., and Chaib-draa, B. Commitment and Argument Network: a formal framework for representing conversation dynamics Logic and Dialogue. Kluwer (2004) (to appear).
3. Bentahar, J., Moulin, B., and Chaib-draa, B. Commitment and argument network: a new formalism for agent communication. Dignum, F. (ed.). Advances in Agent Communication. Lecture Notes in Artificial Intelligence, Vol. 2922. Springer-Verlag (2003) 146-165.
4. Bentahar, J., Moulin, B., and Chaib-draa, B. Specifying and Implementing a Persuasion Dialogue Game using Commitments and Arguments. Rahwan, I., Moraitis, P., and Reed, C. (eds.). Argumentation in Multi-Agent Systems. Springer Verlag (2004), in this volume.
5. Castelfranchi, C. Commitments: from individual intentions to groups and organizations. The Int. Conf. ICMAS. (1995) 41-48.
6. Cleaveland, R. Tableau-based model checking in the propositional mu-calculus. In Acta Informatica, Vol. 27(8). (1990) 725-747.

7. Chaib-draa, B., and Dignum, F. Trends in agent communication language. Computational Intelligence, Vol. 18(2). Oxford (2002) 89-101.

8. Cohen, P.R., and Levesque, H.J. Persistence, intentions and commitment. Cohen, P.R., Morgan. J., and Pollack, M.E. (eds.). Intentions in Communication. Cambridge (1990) 33-70.

9. Dastani, M., Hulstijn, J., and der Torre, L.V. Negotiation protocols and dialogue games. The Belgium/Dutch AI Conf. Kaatsheuvel (2000) 13-20.

10. Elvang-Goransson, M., Fox, J., and Krause, P. Dialectic reasoning with inconsistent information. The 9th Conf. on Uncertainty in AI (1993) 114-121.

11. Emerson, E.A. Temporal and Modal logic. Handbook of Theoretical Computer Science. van Leeuwen, J. (eds). Elsevier Science Publishers (1990) 995-1072.

12. Finin, T., Labrou, Y., and Mayfield, J. KQML as an agent communication language. Bradshaw, J.M. (ed.). Software Agent. MIT Press (1997) 291-316.

13. Fornara, N., and Colombetti, M. Operational specification of a commitment-based agent communication language. The First Int. Conf. on AAMAS (2002) 536- 542.

14. Harel, D. Dynamic logic. Handbook of Philosophical Logic. Gabbay, D.M., and Guenther, F. (eds), Vol. 2 (1984) 497-604.

15. Rahwan, I., Ramchurn, S.D., Jennings, N.R., McBurney, P., Parsons, S., and Sonenberg, L. Argumentation-based negotiation. Knowledge Engineering Review (2004) (to appear).

16. Van der Hoek, W., and Wooldridge, M. Towards a logic of rational agency. Logic Journal of the IGPL, Vol. 11(2) (2003) 133-157.

17. Mallya, A.U., Yolum, P., and Singh, M. Resolving Commitments Among Autonomous Agents. Dignum, F. (ed.). Advances in Agent Communication. Lecture Notes in Artificial Intelligence, Vol. 2922. Springer Verlag (2003) 166-182.

18. McBurney, P., Parsons, S., and Wooldridge, M. Desiderata for agent argumentation protocols. The First Int. Conf. on AAMAS (2002) 402-409.

19. Meyer, J.-J. Ch., van der Hoek, W., and van Linder, B. A logical Approach to the dynamics of commitments. AI Journal, Vol. 113 (1-2) (1999) 1-40.

20. Parsons, S., Sierra, C., and Jennings, N. Agents that reason and negotiate by arguing. Journal of Logic and Computation, Vol. 8(3) (1998) 261-292.

21. Pitt, J., and Mamdani, A. Communication protocols in multi-agent systems: a development method and reference architecture. Dignum, F., and Greaves, M. (eds.). Issues in Agent Communication. Lecture Notes in Artificial Intelligence, Vol. 1916. Springer Verlag (2000) 160-177.

22. Rao, A.S., and Georgeff, M.P. BDI agents: from theory to practice. The Int. Conf. ICMAS (1995) 312-319.

23. Singh, M.P. Agent communication languages: rethinking the principles. IEEE Computer, Vol. 31(12) (1998) 40-47.

24. Singh, M.P., A social semantics for agent communication language. Dignum, F., and Greaves. M. (eds.). Issues in Agent Communication. Lecture Notes in Artificial Intelligence, Vol. 1916. Springer Verlag (2000) 31-45.

25. Verdicchio, M., and Colombetti, M. A logical model of social commitment for agent communication. The Second Int. Conf. on AAMAS (2003) 528-535.

Layered Strategies and Protocols for Argumentation-Based Agent Interaction

Antonis Kakas[1], Nicolas Maudet[2], and Pavlos Moraitis[1]

[1] Department of Computer Science,
University of Cyprus,
CY-1678 Nicosia, Cyprus
{antonis, moraitis}@cs.ucy.ac.cy
[2] LAMSADE
Univ. ParisIX-Dauphine,
75775 Paris Cedex 16, France
maudet@lamsade.dauphine.fr

Abstract. Communication between agents needs to be flexible enough to encompass together a variety of different aspects such as, conformance to society protocols, private tactics of the individual agents, strategies that reflect different classes of agent types (or personal attitudes) and adaptability to the particular external circumstances at the time when the communication takes place. In this paper we propose an argument-based framework for representing communication theories of agents that can take into account in a uniform way these different aspects. We show how this approach can be used to realize existing types of dialogue strategies and society protocols in a way that facilitates their modular development and extension to make them more flexible in handling different or special circumstances.

1   Introduction

Communication is one of the main features of multiagent systems. Society *protocols* regulate the communicative behaviour agents should conform to by defining what dialogue moves are legal in any given situation. Private *strategies*, as adopted by an individual agent, specify the dialogue move(s) the agent is willing to utter, according to its own objectives and other personal characteristics. Ideally, dialogue moves selected by the agent's strategy will fall within the legal moves defined by the protocol.

In this paper, we investigate how to represent communication patterns using an argumentation-based framework with dynamic preferences. The behaviour of an agent participating in a dialogue is conditioned on two theories in this framework each one of which is expressed as a preference policy on the dialogue moves.

The first theory captures the society protocol describing the legal moves at two levels, normal (or default) and exceptional, as the preferred moves given a current set of circumstances within the society the agent belongs to. The context-dependent protocols, afforded by our representation framework, will give a high degree of flexibility to encompass together in one uniform theory, the different aspects of the protocol under different

I. Rahwan et al. (Eds.): ArgMAS 2004, LNAI 3366, pp. 64–77, 2005.

circumstances as perceived by the different agents in the society that share this commnon protocol. The second theory describes, again as a preference policy, the personal strategy of the agent. This can be influenced by application domain tactics but also by the agent's personal *profile or attitude* characteristics. As with the society protocols, this theory is context-dependent in order to take into account the variety of situations under which a dialogue can take place (e.g. the different *roles* of the interlocutors and the *context* of the dialogue) as well as the dynamically changing circumstances of the dialogue. The overall decision of which move to utter next is based on the integration of these theories by suitably exploiting the sceptical and credulous forms of argumentation-based reasoning. Our approach therefore allows the modulal separation of concerns: professional tactics of dialogue strategy, personal attitudes influencing the strategy and legality of strategy decisions required by societal protocols.

Several works have studied the problem of dialogue strategies in interactions governed by social protocols, many of which [1, 2], use like we do, argumentation as their basis. Our work can be viewed as providing an approach where these notions can be modularly realized and in cases extended to allow a wider class of problems to be addressed. This stems from the fact of greater flexibility and expressivity provided to define private strategies and public protocols uniformly within the same highly expressive representation framework which in addition possesses a viable computational model. Communication theories can be easily implemented directly from their declarative specification in the Gorgias system [3] for this framework.

Paper Overview. Section 2 gives the background framework on agent argumentative reasoning used in this paper. Section 3 studies the representation of agent private strategies while section 4 explores in turn the representation of social protocols in the same framework. Section 5 studies in some detail the connection to existing approaches.

2   The Agent Reasoning Framework

This section gives the basic concepts of the underlying argumentation framework in which an agent represents and reasons with its communication theory. This framework was proposed in [4] and developed further in [5], in order to accommodate a dynamic notion of priority over the rules (and hence the arguments) of a given theory [6, 7].

As proposed in [8] we can distinguish three languages in the representation of an agent's communication theory. A language, $\mathcal{L}$, to describe the background information that the agent has about its world at any moment and the basic rules for deciding its communication moves; a language, $\mathcal{ML}$, for expressing preference policies pertaining to its decision of these moves; and a language, $\mathcal{CL}$, which is a common communication language for all agents.

Furthermore, we will see that (components of) an agent's theory will be layered in three levels. *Object-level decision rules*, in the language $\mathcal{L}$, are defined at the first level. The next two levels, represented in the language $\mathcal{ML}$, describe priority rules on the decision rules of the first level and on themselves thus expressing a preference policy for the overall decision making of the agent. This policy is separated into two levels: level two to capture the *default* preference policy under normal circumstances while level three is concerned with the *exceptional* part of the policy that applies under specific contexts. Hence we will assume that agents are always associated with a (social) environment of interaction in which they can distinguish normal (or default) contexts from specific (or exceptional) contexts. Their argumentation-based decision making will then be sensitive to context changes.

In general, an argumentation theory is defined as follows.

Definition 1. *A theory is a pair* $(\mathcal{T}, \mathcal{P})$. *The sentences in* $\mathcal{T}$ *are propositional formulae, in the background monotonic logic* $(\mathcal{L}, \vdash)$ *of the framework, defined as* $L \leftarrow L_1, \ldots, L_n$, *where* $L, L_1, \ldots, L_n$ *are positive or explicit negative ground literals. Rules in* $\mathcal{P}$ *are defined in the language* $\mathcal{ML}$ *which is the same as* $\mathcal{L}$ *apart from the fact that the head* L *of the rules has the general form* $L = h\_p(rule1, rule2)$ *where* $rule1$ *and* $rule2$ *are ground functional terms that name any two rules in the theory. This higher-priority relation given by* h_p *is required to be irreflexive. The derivability relation,* $\vdash$, *of the background logic for* $\mathcal{L}$ *and* $\mathcal{ML}$ *is given by the single inference rule of modus ponens.*

For simplicity, it is assumed that the conditions of any rule in the theory do not refer to the predicate h_p thus avoiding self-reference problems. For any ground atom $h\_p(rule1, rule2)$ its negation is denoted by $h\_p(rule2, rule1)$ and vice-versa.

An *argument* for a literal L in a theory $(\mathcal{T}, \mathcal{P})$ is any subset, T, of this theory that derives L, i.e. $T \vdash L$ under the background logic. The subset of rules in the argument T that belong to $\mathcal{T}$ is called the *object-level* argument. Note that in general, we can separate out a part of the theory $\mathcal{T}_0 \subset \mathcal{T}$ and consider this as a non-defeasible part from which any argument rule can draw information that it might need. We call $\mathcal{T}_0$ the background knowledge base.

The notion of attack between arguments in a theory is based on the possible conflicts between a literal L and its negation and on the priority relation of h_p in the theory.

Definition 2. *Let* $(\mathcal{T}, \mathcal{P})$ *be a theory,* $T, T' \subseteq \mathcal{T}$ *and* $P, P' \subseteq \mathcal{P}$. *Then* (T', P') *attacks* (T, P) *iff there exists a literal* L, $T_1 \subseteq T'$, $T_2 \subseteq T$, $P_1 \subseteq P'$ *and* $P_2 \subseteq P$ *s.t.:*

(i) $T_1 \cup P_1 \vdash_{min} L$ *and* $T_2 \cup P_2 \vdash_{min} \neg L$
(ii) $(\exists r' \in T_1 \cup P_1, r \in T_2 \cup P_2 \text{ s.t. } T \cup P \vdash h\_p(r, r')) \Rightarrow (\exists r' \in T_1 \cup P_1, r \in T_2 \cup P_2$
$\text{s.t. } T' \cup P' \vdash h\_p(r', r)).$

Here $S \vdash_{min} L$ means that $S \vdash L$ and that no proper subset of S implies L. When L does not refer to h_p, $T \cup P \vdash_{min} L$ means that $T \vdash_{min} L$. This definition states that a "composite" argument (T', P') is a counter-argument to another such argument when it derives a contrary conclusion, L, and $(T' \cup P')$ makes the rules of its counter proof at least "as strong" as the rules for the proof by the argument that is under attack. Note that the attack can occur on a contrary conclusion $L = h\_p(r, r')$ that refers to the priority between rules.

Definition 3. *Let* $(\mathcal{T}, \mathcal{P})$ *be a theory,* $T \subseteq \mathcal{T}$ *and* $P \subseteq \mathcal{P}$. *Then* (T, P) *is admissible iff* $(T \cup P)$ *is consistent and for any* (T', P') *if* (T', P') *attacks* (T, P) *then* (T, P) *attacks* (T', P'). *Given a ground literal* L *then* L *is a credulous (respectively skeptical) consequence of the theory iff* L *holds in a (respectively every) maximal (wrt set inclusion) admissible subset of* $\mathcal{T}$.

Hence when we have dynamic priorities, for an object-level argument (from $\mathcal{T}$) to be admissible it needs to take along with it priority arguments (from $\mathcal{P}$) to make itself at least "as strong" as the opposing counter-arguments. This need for priority rules can repeat itself when the initially chosen ones can themselves be attacked by opposing priority rules and again we would need to make now the priority rules themselves at least as strong as their opposing ones.

An agent's argumentation theory will be defined as a theory $(\mathcal{T}, \mathcal{P})$ which is further layered in separating $\mathcal{P}$ into two parts as follows.

Definition 4. *An agent's* argumentative policy theory, T, *is a theory* $T = (\mathcal{T}, (\mathcal{P}_R, \mathcal{P}_C))$ *where the rules in* $\mathcal{T}$ *do not refer to h_p, all the rules in* $\mathcal{P}_R$ *are priority rules with head* $h\_p(r_1, r_2)$ *s.t.* $r_1, r_2 \in \mathcal{T}$ *and all rules in* $\mathcal{P}_C$ *are priority rules with head* $h\_p(R_1, R_2)$ *s.t.* $R_1, R_2 \in \mathcal{P}_R \cup \mathcal{P}_C$.

We therefore have three levels in an agent's theory. In the first level we have the rules $\mathcal{T}$ that refer directly to the subject domain of the theory at hand. We call these the *Object-level Decision Rules* of the agent. In the other two levels we have rules that relate to the policy, under which the agent uses its object-level decision rules, associated to normal situations (related to a default context) and specific situations (related to specific or exceptional contexts). We call the rules in $\mathcal{P}_R$ and $\mathcal{P}_C$, *Default* or *Normal Context Priorities* and *Specific Context Priorities* respectively.

2.1   The Communication Framework

We assume that agents interact using *dialogue moves or performatives*. Once performed, these dialogue moves are added directly (or via commitment stores) to the agent background knowledge, $\mathcal{T}_0$, that is, we assume that all these moves are perfectly perceived by the agents of the society. The shared communication language, $\mathcal{CL}$, of the agents contains a set of communication performatives (see e.g. [9]) of the form $P(X, Y, S)$ where:

- P is a performative type belonging to the set $\mathcal{P}$;
- X and Y are the sender and the receiver of the performative, respectively;
- S is the subject (i.e., body) of the performative;

The subject S can contain elements (facts, rules, etc.) expressing arguments supporting the message. The details of this are not important for this paper as here we will be primarily concerned with how we express the argumentation policies of how an agent decides to move next based on these policies. What is important is to have all the different parameters, P, X, Y and S, that can influence the definition of these policies. For simplicity of presentation, we have omitted the utterance time parameter.

In particular, the set of *performative types* ($\mathcal{P}$) of the communication language adopted will play a significant role in this. We may take this to be one of the current standards , e.g. proposed by the FIPA consortium [10]. However, as these standards do not include moves devoted to argumentation (see [11] for a discussion), we shall use instead a set suited to our purpose that is in the lines of those used in [2, 12], e.g. $\mathcal{P} = \{request, propose, accept, refuse, challenge\}$. In what follows, this set will also be used as a *label set*. As mentioned above we will assume that both the society and the agents interacting in the society share the same set of performative types $\mathcal{P}$.

3   Flexible Agent Strategies

Based on the argumentation framework described in the previous section we can compose a *private or personal strategy* theory of an agent in three parts which modularly capture different concerns of the problem. These parts are:

- the *basic component*, T_{basic}, that defines the private *dialogue steps* of the dialogue
- the *tactical component*, $T_{tactical}$, that defines a private preference policy of (professional) tactics
- the *attitude component*, $T_{attitude}$, that captures general (application independent) characteristics of personal strategy of the agent type

We call $T_{basic} \cup T_{tactical}$ the *tactical theory* and $T_{basic} \cup T_{attitude}$ the *attitude theory*. Let us examine in turn these different components.

The Basic Component (T_{basic}). This component contains object-level rules in the language $\mathcal{L}$, defining the private *dialogue steps*, and are (for an agent X) of the form:

$$r_{j,i}(Y, S', S) : p_j(X, Y, S') \leftarrow p_i(Y, X, S), c_{ij}$$

where i, j belong to the label set $\mathcal{P}$ and c_{ij} (which can be empty) are called the *enabling conditions* of the dialogue step from the performative p_i to p_j. In other words, these are the conditions under which the agent X (whose theory this is) *may* utter p_j upon receiving p_i from agent Y. These conditions thus correspond to the rationality rules of [2] or the conditions of the dialogue constraints of [12]. These rules and their names, $r_{j,i}(Y, S', S)$, are written in Logic Programming style representing compactly all the propositional rules obtained by ground these over the Herbrand universe of the theory.

For simplicity, we will assume that the enabling conditions are evaluated in the non-defeasible part, T_0, of the theory containing the background knowledge that the agent X has about the world and the dialogue so far. This essentially simplifies the attacking relation of the argumentation but this is not a significant simplification for the purposes of the work of this paper. The background knowledge base T_0 also contains the rules:

$$\neg p_j(X, Y, S) \leftarrow p_i(X, Y, S), i \neq j$$
$$\neg p_i(X, Y, S') \leftarrow p_i(X, Y, S), S' \neq S$$

for every i and j in $\mathcal{P}$ and every subject S', S to express the general requirement that two different utterances are incompatible with each other.

This means that any argument for one specific utterance is potentially (depending on the priority rules in the other parts of the theory) an attack for any other different one. Hence any admissible set of arguments cannot contain rules that derive more than one utterance. In fact, with the basic component alone the theory can (easily) have several credulous conclusions for which could be the next utterance as the following example illustrates.

Example 1. Let us consider an agent Bob equipped with a basic component containing the following simplified rules.

$$
\begin{aligned}
r_{acc,req}(Y,P) \quad &: accept(X,Y,P) \quad \leftarrow request(Y,X,P), \\
&\qquad\qquad\qquad\qquad\quad have(X,P) \\
r_{ref,req}(Y,P) \quad &: refuse(X,Y,P) \quad \leftarrow request(Y,X,P) \\
r_{chall,req}(Y,P) \quad &: challenge(X,Y,P) \leftarrow request(Y,X,P) \\
r_{prop,req}(Y,P,Q) &: propose(X,Y,Q) \quad \leftarrow request(Y,X,P), \\
&\qquad\qquad\qquad\qquad\quad altern(P,Q)
\end{aligned}
$$

Now assume that Bob has just received the dialogue move $request(Al,Bob,nail)$ and that Bob currently has a nail, ie $T_0 = \{request(Al,Bob,nail), have(Bob,nail)\}$. Then $accept(Bob,Al,nail), refuse(Bob,Al,nail)$ and $challenge(Bob,Al,nail)$ are the different credulous consequences of the theory, and hence these are all possible reply moves, with no further information to discriminate them. Note that if T_0 contained also $alternative(Bob,nail,hook)$, then we would also have the credulous conclusion $propose(Bob,Al,hook)$.

The extra information needed to discriminate between these equally possible moves will typically come from the preference policies described in the other two components (tactical and attitude) of the private strategy theory.

The Tactical Component ($T_{tactical}$). This component defines a private preference policy that captures the professional tactics of the agent for how to decide amongst the alternatives enabled by the basic part of the theory. It consists of two sets $\mathcal{P}_R, \mathcal{P}_C$ of priority rules, written in the language $\mathcal{ML}$, at the two higher levels as defined in section 2.

The rules in $\mathcal{P}_R$ express priorities over the dialogue step rules in the basic part. A simple pattern that one can follow in writting these rules is to consider the dialogues steps that refer to the same incoming move $p_i(Y,X,S)$ and then have rules of the following form.

$$
\begin{aligned}
R^i_{k|j} &: h\_p(r_{k,i}, r_{j,i}) \leftarrow true \\
R^i_{j|k} &: h\_p(r_{j,i}, r_{k,i}) \leftarrow SC_{jk}
\end{aligned}
$$

where SC_{jk} are specific conditions that are evaluated in the background knowledge base of the agent and could depend on the agent Y, the subject of the incoming move and indeed the types j and k of these alternative moves. Note that these R rules can have additional superscripts in their names if there is a need to distinguih them further.

The first rule expresses the default preference of responding with p_k over responding with p_j while the second rule states that under some specific conditions the preference is the other way round. More generally, we could have conditions NC_{kj} in the first rule that specify when the normal conditions under which the default preference applies.

Using this level, it is then possible to discriminate between the dialogue moves by simply specifying that the agent will usually prefer his default behaviour, unless some special conditions are satisfied. Typically, the later situation can capture the fact the strategy should vary when exceptional conditions hold (for example when the others agents have specific roles). More generally this would cover any tactics pertaining to the roles of the agents Y, the subject, S, and other relevant factors of the current situation.

Example 2. Consider the following rules defining the tactic component of the agent *Bob*.

$$R^{requ}_{acc|chall}(Y,S) : h\_p(r_{acc,requ}(Y,S), r_{chall,requ}(Y,S))$$
$$\leftarrow true$$
$$R^{requ}_{chall|acc}(Y,S) : h\_p(r_{chall,requ}(Y,S), r_{acc,requ}(Y,S))$$
$$\leftarrow unknown(Y,X)$$
$$R^{requ}_{acc|ref}(Y,S) : h\_p(r_{acc,requ}(Y,S), r_{ref,requ}(Y,S))$$
$$\leftarrow manager(Y,X)$$
$$R^{requ}_{chall|ref}(Y,S) : h\_p(r_{chall,requ}(Y,S), r_{ref,requ}(Y,S))$$
$$\leftarrow true$$

Now assuming in the background knowledge, T_0, of *Bob* that *Al* is known to be a manager of *Bob*, then this tactical theory together with the basic component introduced in the previous example would give $accept(Bob, Al, nail)$ as the only credulous and indeed skeptical consequence of the theory for the next reply move of *Bob*. The normal default preferences apply. If though T_0 of *Bob* contained $unknown(Al, Bob)$ (and so *Al* was not a manager of *Bob*) then clearly both $accept(Bob, Al, nail)$ and $challenge(Bob, Al, nail)$ would be credulously admissible and hence possible reply moves.

In order to overturn the default of accepting over challenging, in this specific context of unknown requesters, a rule at the third specific context level of the tactical theory would be needed. We would have the set in $\mathcal{P}_C$ of the tactical component the higher-level priority rule:

$$C^{tactical}_{chall|acc} : h\_p(R^{requ}_{chall|acc}, R^{requ}_{acc|chall}) \leftarrow true$$

Then the only possible move for *Bob* would be to challenge.

Note that the $T_{tactical}$ component of the personal strategy theory could change from application to application as the tactic that an agent may want to apply could be different. A designer may hold different tactic components and equip its agent with the relevant one, depending on the application. Alternatively, this flexibility could be captured in one theory $T_{tactical}$ by introducing suitable *tactical conditions* in these priority rules to separate the cases of different applications. For instance, in one application the role of manager could be important but in another it is not. In this case the priority rule will be written as:

$$R^{requ}_{acc|ref} : h\_p(r_{acc,requ}(Y,S), r_{ref,requ}(Y,S))$$
$$\leftarrow manager(Y,X), context(S)$$

where the $context(S)$ is the tactical condition that defines in T_0 the situations (applications) where the management relation is significant.

The Attitude Component $T_{attitude}$. This third component of the private strategy theory of an agent captures general, typically application independent, charateristics of personal strategy that the agent applies. This consists of priority rules R and C (like the $T_{tactical}$ component) on the rules of the first component T_{basic}. They are again of the form:

$$R^{name}_{j|k} : h\_p(r_{j,i}, r_{k,i}) \leftarrow b_{jk}$$

where i, j, k belong to the performative types label set, $\mathcal{P}$. Here $name$ is an identifier name for this personal strategy and b_{jk} are called *behaviour* conditions under which a particular personal strategy is defined. Higher-level C rules can be included on these R rules as above to allow the flexibility to deviate from a normal personal stradegy under special circumstances.

Example 3. Let us now consider the following attitute theory, we call $T_{altruistic}$, whereby agent Bob prefers to accept a request when it does not need the resource. This theory has the priority rule:

$$R_{acc|chall}^{altruistic} : h\_p(r_{acc,requ}, r_{chall,requ}) \leftarrow \neg need(P, X)$$

Hence if the background theory is now extended to $T_0 = T_0 \cup \{\neg need(nail, Bob)\}$, then Bob will give preference to the rule $r_{acc,requ}$, and $accept(Bob, Al, nail)$ will be the skeptical conclusion.

Conflicts Between Components. It is now important to note that the latter two components may have different priorities, that is the tactical component may give priority to a rule while the attitude component does the reverse. Consider for example an attitude theory, called $T_{argumentative}$, specifying the personal attitude that Bob prefers to challenge whenever possible as specified by [2]. We will examine later on in more details the link between our attitude components and the agent type strategies proposed in [2].

Example 4. $T_{argumentative}$ would contain rules of the form:

$$R_{chall|acc}^{argumentative} : h\_p(r_{chall,requ}, r_{acc,requ}) \leftarrow true$$

Then Bob under its personal attitude theory will always give preference to challenge. Hence both $accept(Bob, Al, nail)$ and $challenge(Bob, Al, nail)$ are credulous consequences of the overall strategy theory containing the tactic and attitude components.

Therefore dilemmas (non-determinism) in the overall decision of our theory can exist. We can then use higher-level priority rules in the attitude component to resolve conflicts either way, in favour of *attitude dominance* or of *tactic dominance*. These special higher-order rules would then refer to R-rules in any of the components, i.e. also in $T_{tactical}$. In the case of our example, if we wanted to impose the attitude strategy we would then have a higher-order rule:

$$C^{argumentative} : h\_p(R^{argumentative}, R^K)$$
$$\leftarrow K \neq argumentative$$

Such a rule gives flatly priority of the attitute preference rules over those of the tactical component. This can be make more specific to apply only on some subset of rules. e.g. that refer to only some performatives. Also we again have the flexibility to make this dominance conditional on specific conditions pertaining to the current knowledge of the agent about its world, e.g. that the dominance of the argumentative attitude in our example is only when there is a danger involved in the request.

3.1   Properties of Private Strategies

An agent upon receipt of a performative from a fellow agent will typically dispose of several options in order to reply. These options are obtained by computing (credulous or skeptical) conclusions of its strategy theory.

Often a desirable theoretical property of the strategy theory is that this is *non-concurrent*, namely that at most one dialogue move is generated at any time. In our framework, this is guaranteed by construction because every strategy includes rules making concurrent moves conflicting with each others. In others words, there is no admissible argument that would support two different moves. Observe that this property is often called *determinism* in similar frameworks [12], because the semantics used does not allow concurrent sets of admissible arguments. In our case, non-concurrency does not guarantee determinism in the usual sense. For instance, a *credulous* would typically pick up an admissible argument at random when facing different alternatives (and may then respond differently to the same performative).

To guarantee that at least one such admissible argument exists, we need to inspect the conditions that appear at the first level of the strategy. In other words, we need to check that the strategy is *exhaustive* in the sense that the conditions of at least one of its rules at level 1 are always satisfied. Again, this does not coincide exactly with the *existence* of a reply move [12]. For instance, a *skeptical* agent would not choose between different candidate moves (admissible arguments), and remain silent (if there are no moves generated then we can have a special utterance $\mathcal{U}$ (see [8]) indicating that this is the case and either the dialogue would terminate or suspend until more information is acquired by the agent).

One way to ensure that all these notions actually coincide is to require that the complete strategy theory, comprising of all its three components together, has a *hierarchical* form defined as follows.

Definition 5 (Hierarchical Policy). *An agent's argumentative policy theory, S, is hierarchical iff for every pair of rules s_i, s_j in S whose conclusions are incompatible, there exists a priority rule, p_i^j in S, that assigns higher priority to one of these two rules, such that, whenever both the conditions of s_i, s_j are satisfiable (in the background theory of S) so is the condition of p_i^j.*

Note that in this definition the rules s_i, s_j could be themselves priority rules in which case the rule p_i^j is a priority rule at a higher level. Basically, the hierarchical structure prevents the existence of concurrent sets of admissible arguments. In this case, of course, the (unique) credulous conclusion and the skeptical conclusion would coincide. As a consequence, non-concurrency implies determinism, and exhaustivness implies existence. This leads to the following result:

Theorem 1 (Uniqueness). *If the strategy theory is exhaustive, hierarchical and its priority relation does not contain any cycles of length > 2, then the agent will always have exactly one move to utter in its reply.*

4   Flexible Society Protocols

We now turn to the representation of society protocols. Protocols specify what is deemed legal for a given interaction, that is which dialogue moves can follow up after a (sequence of) dialogue move(s). We shall see how protocols can be specified using the same logical framework as for the private strategies in an analogous way, as argumentation theories divided in three parts. Note that there is no issue of determinism here. A protocol will typically allow an arbitrary number of legal continuations: any credulous consequence of the society protocol theory would be a legal move. However, exploiting the flexibility of our framework to take into account exceptional situations that may arise in interactions, we shall introduce different notions of legality.

In the first part (P_0), we specify all the dialogue moves that may be legal in some circumstances, namely the possible legal follow-ups after a dialogue move $p_i(Y, X, S)$. By defining one such a rule

$$r_{j,i}(Y, S) : p_j(X, Y, S') \leftarrow p_i(Y, X, S), S_{ij}$$

for each possible legal continuation under the conditions S_{ij} which in the simplest case can be taken to be empty. Note that this lower-level part of the protocol is completely analogous to the basic component of the private strategy theory of an agent and in some cases it can be replaced by it. At this level then we have several single moves as credulous conclusions and hence legal moves. We will refer to this set as the set of *potentially legal* moves.

Example 5. Consider for instance the following protocol which regulates requesting interactions (observe that this protocol does not cater for counter-proposals).

$$\begin{aligned}
r_{acc,req} &: \ accept(X, Y, P) &&\leftarrow request(Y, X, P) \\
r_{ref,req} &: \ refuse(X, Y, P) &&\leftarrow request(Y, X, P) \\
r_{chal,req} &: challenge(X, Y, P) &&\leftarrow request(Y, X, P)
\end{aligned}$$

The set of potentially legal moves clearly contains accept, refuse and challenge.

The main task of the protocol is then to specify which of the potentially legal moves are in fact legal under normal circumstances. This is done by representing a preference policy at the next part (P_1) of the society protocol theory. whose rules have the form

$$R^l_{j|k} : h\_p(r_{ji}, r_{ki}) \leftarrow N_{jk}, \mathrm{l}= 1, 2...$$

where N_{jk} are conditions that hold in a normal situation. Such a rule gives priority of the move p_j over p_k under the conditions N_{jk} and hence in the absence of any other rule it will renders p_k illegal, as this is not a credulous conclusion of the full $(P_0 \cup P_1)$ protocol theory now. Note that unlike conditions appearing in the agents' strategies, these protocol conditions are assumed to be objective and verifiable. We will assume that these conditions should hold in the (shared) commitment store (CS) of the agents involved in the interaction.

We can then define the set of *normal (or default) legal* moves as those moves that are credulous consequences of the theory $CS \cup P_0 \cup P_1$.

Example 6. The (normal) preference policy rules regulating the delivering of drug are the following: (i) if the prescription is shown then you can accept to give the drug, (ii) if the request is from a child then refuse to provide the drug, and (iii) in any case you are allowed to challenge the request. This protocol can be captured by the rules ($k \in \mathcal{P}$):

$$R^1_{accept|k} : \quad h\_p(r_{accept,request}(Y,P), r_{k,request}(Y,P))$$
$$\leftarrow prescription(Y,P), k \neq accept$$
$$R^2_{refuse|k} : \quad h\_p(r_{refuse,request}(Y,P), r_{k,request}(Y,P))$$
$$\leftarrow child(Y), k \neq refuse$$
$$R^3_{challenge|k} : h\_p(r_{challenge,request}(Y,P), r_{k,request}(Y,P))$$
$$\leftarrow k \neq challenge$$

Let us now consider different cases: if $prescription(Al, drug)$ holds in CS, then $accept(Bob, Al, drug)$ and $challenge(Bob, Al, drug)$ are credulous conclusions. If $child(Al)$ holds in CS then both $refuse(Bob, Al, drug)$ and $challenge(Bob, Al, drug)$ are credulous conclusions. If both $prescription(Al, drug)$ and $child(Al)$ holds in CS then all the potentially legal moves are again credulous conclusions. Hence under these respective normal circumstances these are the normal or default legal moves.

In some particular situations we may want the protocol to impose a special requirement that could render some normal legal moves illegal, or even some illegal moves legal. To have this added flexibility we can complete our protocol theory with a third part (P_3) that contains priority rules that apply under special situations. Some of these are higher-order priority rules on the other priority rules. The rules of P_3 will have the form:

$$C_{k|j} : h\_p(R^m_{k|j}, R^n_{j|k}) \leftarrow E^C_{kj}, \text{m,n}= 1,2...$$
$$R_{k|j} : h\_p(r_{ki}, r_{ji}) \leftarrow E^R_{kj}$$

where E^R_{kj} are conditions describing *special conditions* and similarly E^C_{kj} are *special situations* that give priority of $R^m_{k|j}$ over $R^n_{j|k}$.

We are now in position to define the set of *exceptional legal* moves as those moves that are credulous consequences of the theory obtained by conjoining CS together with the overall society component ($P_0 \cup P_1 \cup P_2$).

Example 7. The protocol is now refined by requiring that if the drug is toxic then a child should be refused. This is captured by:

$$C^{toxic}_{ref|chall} : h\_p(R^2_{ref|chall}(Y,P), R^3_{chall|ref}(Y,P))$$
$$\leftarrow toxic(P)$$

Then in full protocol theory the move $challenge(Bob, Al, drug)$ when Al is a child is not a credulous consequence any more and the only exceptional legal move is then $refuse(Bob, Al, drug)$.

Observe that it is possible that moves normally illegal become exceptionally legal, as illustrated by the following example.

Example 8. The protocol is now refined by specifying that (i) if the request is urgent then it should be allowed to accept it, and (ii) if it is also critical then the seller must accept the request.

$$R^{urgent}_{acc|k} : h\_p(r_{acc,requ}(Y,P), r_{k,requ}(Y,P))$$
$$\leftarrow urgent(P), k \neq accept$$
$$C^{critical}_{acc|j} : h\_p(R^{urgent}_{acc|j}(Y,P), R^{m}_{j|acc}(Y,P))$$
$$\leftarrow critical(P)$$

With this added to the protocol theory, the move $accept(Bob, Al, drug)$ when Al is a child becomes a credulous consequence if $urgent(P)$ holds in CS. If $critical(P)$ also holds, then it is even a skeptical conclusion.

In our framework, the reference to conditions allows us to define the circumstances under which the potentially legal moves are normally or exceptionnaly legal. Interestingly, the status of legality is non monotonic under new information on these conditions. As this information kept in the commitment stores will evolve during the dialogue, it can even become a matter of discussion for the agents.

5   Related Work and Conclusions

There is an increasing lot of work on argument-based interaction, mainly focused on negotiation —see [13] for a survey. More generally, according to [8], apart from its naturalness, an argumentation-based approach has two major advantages: rationality of the agents, and a social semantics in the sense of [14]. Our argumentation-based approach inherits these advantages in adressesing both the private aspects of agents' strategies, along with the social aspects of interaction protocol and providing added flexibility. Agent strategies give adaptable behaviour according to the context of the dialogue and the particular roles of the participating interlocutors. At the social level, flexible protocols can be defined that can cater for a wide variety of interactions, including specific circumstances that may come up as the dialogue evolves.

Agents' Profiles. Different notions of agent profiles have been proposed in the literature. Amgoud *et. al.* [2], for instance, have proposed five profiles of dialogues to discriminate between different classes of agent types with varying degree of "willingness to cooperate" in the personal attitude of an agent. The enhanced flexibility of our approach allows us to capture these profiles as special cases.

Theorem 2. *The agent type strategies (agreeable, disagreeable, argumentative, open-minded, elephant child) defined in [2] can be captured as private agent strategies.*

To see this consider for example the first one of these where agreeable is given by [2] as *accept whenever possible.* We can capture this as folllows: whenever the (or a) dialogue step leading to accept is enabled (so its rationality conditions are satisfied) then this would have higher priority than other dialogue steps. This is easily expressed by the following rules in the second level of the attitude component of a strategy:

$$R^{agreeable}_{accept|k} : h\_p(r_{i,accept}, r_{i,k}) \leftarrow k \neq accept$$

for every $i, k \in \mathcal{P}$. This then gives the agreeable strategy in the cases when the second component, $T_{tactical}$, of the private strategy theory is empty. Otherwise, we could have rules, $R^{tactical}_{k|accept}$, in this that could make the move also possible. To impose the agreable strategy we include in the attitude component the higher-order rule

$$C^{agreeable} : h\_p(R^{agreeable}_{accept|k}, R^{tactical}_{k|accept}) \leftarrow k \neq accept$$

for every rule $R^{tactical}_{k|accept}$ of the tactical component. Similarly, we can capture the other agent type strategies.

We also conjecture that it would be possible to formalize the different "assertion and "acceptance" attitudes and consequently the different agent profiles (i.e. confident, careful thoughtful and credulous, cautious, skeptical, respectively) proposed in the recent collected work of [8].

Cognitive agent architectures. Another related work is that of the *BOID architecture* [15]. This defines several agents types (e.g. realistic, selfish, social, etc) depending on the priority the agent gives to these different *mental attitudes* (Beliefs, Obligations, Intentions, Desires). This is related to our approach whereby the agent can solve conflicts between components of its theory. The society protocols can be considered as the normative aspect of the system, whereas the tactical component is more related to intentions and desires. Different meta-level preferences of these components would give agents of different types. Note that our framework allows for argumentation to be carried out also on the conditions in agents' strategies. These can then be considered as part of the agent's beliefs and hence our agents are *realistic* in the sense of [15].

Logic-based protocols. In [16], protocols are translated into integrity constraint rules, in Abductive Logic Programming (ALP), of the form $p_i \Rightarrow \vee p_j$. These can easily be translated into rules at the first level of our protocols. It is instructive though to ask the reverse question of how would this ALP-based approach capture our seemingly more expressive theories. The two approaches use different logical notions for the semantics of the protocol: logical consistency for the ALP-based and (non-deterministic) admissibility for our argumentation-based approach. The non-locality of the consistency requirement (any one conflict in the integrity constraints would render the whole protocol theory protocol inconsistent and all moves illegal) suggests that in order to tranlate our theories into ICs of ALP an exponential growth of the theory would be required resulting in a highly non-modular representation of the protocol.

Commitment machines. In [17], *social commiments* are used as a way to specify protocols by refering to the content of the actions. By allowing reference to the content of the moves (and other relevant information in the commitment store), we cater for the kind of flexibility discussed in [17]. However, our approach is closer to in spirit to *dialogue games* approaches where dialogue rules and conditions on the commitment stores are used in combination to define the notion of legality. Further work is needed to evaluate how our approach compares to these hardcore commitment-based approaches.

In conclusion, our approach provides a way of realizing together several notions of argumentation-based communication that combines the merits of (a) modular separation of concerns, (b) added expressivity of the theories and (c) feasible implementation directly from their declarative specification. Further work is needed to develop a more systematic methodology for building these theories, for instance the design issue of how criteria should be distributed amongst the three components of the framework. Preliminary rules of thumb can be given, (e.g. the attitude component relates to the domain independent personality of the agent that captures generic strategies of decision, like selfish), but a more comprehensive account needs to be worked out.

Acknowledgments. We would like to thank Ulle Endriss and the anonymous referees of this paper for their comments. This work was supported by the European Commission FET Global Computing Initiative, within the SOCS project (IST-2001-32530).

References

1. Parsons, S., Sierra, C., Jennings, N.R.: Agents that reason and negotiate by arguing. Journal of Logic and Computation **8** (1998)
2. Amgoud, L., Parsons, S.: Agent dialogue with conflicting preferences. In: Proceedings of ATAL01. (2001)
3. GORGIAS: A system for argumentation and abduction. http://www.cs.ucy.ac.cy/ nkd/gorgias (2002)
4. Kakas, A., Mancarella, P., Dung, P.M.: The acceptability semantics for logic programs. In: Proceedings of the International Conference on Logic Programming. (1994)
5. Kakas, A., Moraitis, P.: Argumentation based decision making for autonomous agents. In: Proceedings of AAMAS03. (2003)
6. Brewka, G.: Dynamic argument systems: a formal model of argumentation based on situation calculus. Journal of logic and computation **11** (2001)
7. Prakken, H., Sartor, G.: A dialectical model of assessing conflicting arguments in legal reasoning. Artificial Intelligence and Law **4** (1996) 331–368
8. McBurney, P., Parsons, S.: Argumentation-based communication between agents. In: Communication in Multiagent Systems. Volume 2650 of LNAI., Springer-Verlag (2004)
9. Karacapilidis, N., Moraitis, P.: Engineering issues in interagent dialogues. In: Proceedings of ECAI02. (2002)
10. FIPA: Foundation for intelligent physical agents. Communicative act library specification (xc00037h). http://www.fipa.org/spec (2001)
11. McBurney, P., Parsons, S., Wooldridge, M.: Desiderata for agent argumentation protocols. In: Proceedings of AAMAS02. (2002)
12. Sadri, F., Toni, F., Torroni, P.: Dialogues for negotiation: agent varieties and dialogue sequences. In: Intelligent Agent series VIII. Volume 2333 of LNAI., Springer-Verlag (2001)
13. Rahwan, I., Ramchurn, S.D., Jennings, N.R., McBurney, P., Parsons, S., Sonenberg, L.: Argument-based negotiation. Knowledge Engineering Review (2004) To appear.
14. Singh, M.P.: A social semantics for agent communication language. In: Issues in Agent Communication. Number 1916 in LNCS. Springer-Verlag (2000)
15. Broersen, J., Dastani, M., Hulstijn, J., Huang, Z., van der Torre, L.: The BOID architecture: conflicts between beliefs, obligations, intentions and desires. In: Proceedings of AGENTS01. (2001)
16. Endriss, U., Maudet, N., Sadri, F., Toni, F.: Protocol conformance for logic-based agents. In: Proceedings of IJCAI03. (2003)
17. Yolum, P., Singh, M.P.: Flexible protocol specification and execution: applying event calculus planning using commitments. In: Proceedings of AAMAS02. (2002)

Revising Beliefs Through Arguments: Bridging the Gap Between Argumentation and Belief Revision in MAS

Fabio Paglieri[1] and Cristiano Castelfranchi[2]

[1] University of Siena, Piazza S. Francesco 8, 53100 Siena, Italy
paglieri@media.unisi.it
[2] Institute of Cognitive Sciences and Technologies, National Research Council
(ISTC-CNR), Viale Marx 15, 00137 Roma, Italy
c.castelfranchi@istc.cnr.it

Abstract. This paper compares within the MAS framework two separate threads in the formal study of epistemic change: belief revision and argumentation theories. Belief revision describes how an agent is supposed *to change his own mind*, while argumentation deals with persuasive strategies employed *to change the mind of other agents*. These are two sides (cognitive and social) of the same epistemic coin: argumentation theories are incomplete, if they cannot be grounded in belief revision models – and vice versa. Nonetheless, so far the formal treatment of belief revision mostly neglected any systematic comparison with argumentation theories. In MAS such problem becomes evident and inescapable: belief change is usually triggered by communication and persuasion from other agents, involving deception, trust, reputation, negotiation, conflict resolution (all typical issues faced by argumentation-based models). Therefore, a closer comparison between belief revision and argumentation is a necessary preliminary step towards an integrated model of epistemic change in MAS.

1 Belief Revision Without Argumentation

Following the seminal work in [14], belief revision has recently become an extremely active area of research at the confluence between AI, logic, cognitive science, and philosophy. Notwithstanding the impressive amount and quality of studies devoted to this topic (including many researches in the MAS community, e.g. [1, 9, 12, 13, 31]), belief revision has been mainly addressed in a rather single-minded fashion, isolating the issue of belief change from other related features of cognitive processing. As remarked in [26], current theories of belief revision have been put forward and discussed in a sort of epistemological vacuum, without providing a more comprehensive account of epistemic states and dynamics. Moreover, the process of belief change has been usually conceived as an isolated activity, neglecting even the most obvious connections with other cognitive tasks: e.g. inferential reasoning, communication, argumentation (significant exceptions to this trend are in [10, 13]). On the contrary, we claim that belief revision should be investigated as a specific function (albeit a crucial one) in the cognitive processing of epistemic states, integrating formal models of belief change in a more comprehensive epistemological theory, and providing systematic connections with related cognitive tasks.

I. Rahwan et al. (Eds.): ArgMAS 2004, LNAI 3366, pp. 78–94, 2005.
© Springer-Verlag Berlin Heidelberg 2005

1.1 Limitations of Current Theories

The AGM paradigm [14] has been the most influential model of belief revision so far, serving as a frame of reference for both refinements and criticisms of the original proposal. Roughly summarizing (see [21] for further discussion), this model was first conceived as an idealistic theory of rational belief change: belief states were characterized as sets of propositions (infinite and deductively closed), three basic types of change were described (expansion, contraction, revision), and rationality was expressed by a set of postulates binding these operators. To decide between different outcomes of the revision process (i.e. different sets of propositions consistent with the rationality postulates), an ordering criterion was introduced in the original belief state, ranking propositions for their importance (epistemic entrenchment).

This approach to belief revision fails to integrate with argumentation theories for two reasons: (1) it does not make any predictions or assumptions about how and why some propositions come to be believed, rather than others; (2) there is a deliberate lack of structural properties in the characterization of epistemic states. Argumentation theories capture how a desired change in the audience's beliefs is brought about by the arguer: therefore, without an explicit theory of *the reasons to believe something*, the whole point of argumentation is lost. AGM-style approaches to belief revision simply lack the necessary internal structure to describe argumentative strategies (for a philosophically oriented discussion of justification in belief revision, see [15]).

In this respect, the so called *foundation theories* of belief revision fare better than AGM, since they provide a precise account of the reasons supporting a given belief, e.g. using Truth Maintenance Systems [8]. Similar proposals have also been advanced in the field of multi-agent systems [9, 12, 13, 18], and there are several analogies between the criticisms to the AGM approach discussed in this paper and objections raised within the TMS community (e.g. the need for detailed analysis of the reasons that support and determine the agent's beliefs), although our approach is more cognitive-oriented, while TMS put greater emphasis on computational issues.

Since a detailed comparison between our approach and TMS is beyond the aim of this work (cf. 4 on future developments in the direction), here we will provide only a short comment on belief change and argumentation in TMS. In spite of the richer framework outlined by TMS for belief revision in MAS, only few of these theories explicitly address argumentation and/or communication (e.g. [18]), and the structural properties of epistemic states are restricted to factual supports for the agent's beliefs, to ensure an accurate weighting of unreliable and/or contrasting sources of information. Although such structures are essential to integrate belief revision and argumentation, they are not enough: a fairly rich picture of argumentative strategies must include motivational and emotional features [7, 11, 16, 17], not only factual credibility. Since also belief revision is affected by similar considerations, a more comprehensive cognitive model of epistemic change must be devised (cf. 2.1-2.4).

2 A Cognitive Model of Data-Oriented Belief Revision (DBR)

The following sections provide a short outline of an alternative model of belief revision, i.e. Data-oriented Belief Revision (DBR): for further details, see [6, 21]. Although this model is still mainly theoretical and far from implementation in MAS, it is conceived as a realistic cognitive framework for understanding belief revision in agent-based social simulation[1]. Special emphasis is given to the representation of *individual variation in belief revision* (cf. 2.2, 2.4): it is extremely important, for the sake of cognitive plausibility and social simulation, to be able to model different strategies of epistemic change for different agents, and to represent all of them within the same conceptual framework. This has a significant impact on argumentation as well, since it allows to model different argumentation strategies and to distinguish between local and global arguments (cf. 3.5).

2.1   Data and Beliefs: Properties and Interactions

Two basic epistemic categories, *data* and *beliefs*, are put forward in this model, to account for the distinction between pieces of information that are simply *gathered and stored* by the agent (data), and pieces of information that the agent considers *reliable bases for action, decision, and specific reasoning tasks*, e.g. prediction and explanation (beliefs). Clearly, the latter are a subset of the former: the agent might well be aware of a datum that he does not believe (i.e. he does not consider reliable enough); on the other hand, the agent should not be forced to forget (i.e. to lose as a datum) a piece of information which he temporarily rejects as a belief [6]. Moreover, a rejected piece of information retains significant epistemic properties (e.g. its own unreliability, and the reasons for it) that will often be crucial in future revisions and should be preserved by a formal model of belief change [9, 26].

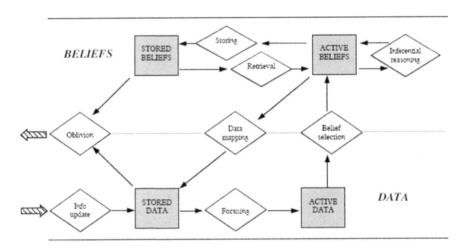

Fig. 1. Epistemic processing in Data-oriented Belief Revision

The distinction between data and beliefs yields a number of consequences for the formal study of epistemic dynamics: to start with, it leads to conceive *belief change as a two-step process*. Let us consider external belief change (cf. 2.3): whenever a new piece of evidence is acquired through perception or communication, it affects *directly*

---

[1] Broader accounts of belief revision have been advocated also for epistemic change in communication [13] and in defeasible reasoning [10, 26].

the agent's data structure, and only *indirectly* his belief set. In other words, the effects (if any) of the new datum on the agent's beliefs depend (1) on its effects on the other data, and (2) on the process of belief selection applied by the agent over such data (cf. 2.2). We call this procedure *Data-oriented Belief Revision (DBR)*.

More generally, data and beliefs define the two basic cognitive layers of the whole epistemic processing performed by the agent, as summarized in Figure 1. An exhaustive discussion of this general model is beyond the aim of this paper: here we will focus mainly on the treatment of data, with special reference to information update, data properties and assessment, and belief selection (cf. 2.2-2.3), since these are the features most directly involved in belief revision. However, it is important to keep in mind the overall epistemic processing, if we want to provide a formal model adequate to express belief change in cognitive agents.

In this model data are selected (or rejected) as beliefs on the basis of their properties, i.e. the possible *cognitive reasons to believe* them. DBR accounts for four distinct properties of data [6, 21]:

I.   *Relevance*: a measure of the pragmatic utility of the datum, i.e. the number and values of the (pursued) goals that depends on that datum.

II. *Credibility*: a measure of the number and values of all supporting data, contrasted with all conflicting data, down to external and internal sources;

III. *Importance*: a measure of the epistemic connectivity of the datum, i.e. the number and values of the data that the agent will have to revise, should he revise that single one;

IV. *Likeability*: a measure of the motivational appeal of the datum, i.e. the number and values of the (pursued) goals that are directly fulfilled by that datum.

The assessment of credibility is discussed in 2.3, while the assessment of importance, relevance and likeability is detailed in [21]. In DBR, credibility, importance and likeability determine the outcomes of belief selection, i.e. whether a candidate data is to be believed or not, and with which strength (cf. 2.2), while relevance is crucial in pre-selecting the sub-set of active data (focusing), i.e. determining which data in the agent's data base are useful/appropriate for the current task, and should therefore be taken in consideration as candidate beliefs (an in-depth discussion of focusing is given in [21]). While relevance and likeability depend on a comparison between data and goals, credibility and importance basically *depend on structural relations between data* [6]. In fact, in DBR data bases are highly structured domains, best conceived as *networks*: data are represented as *nodes*, interconnected through characteristic functional relations (cf. 2.3), i.e. *links* in the network.

Table 1. Data and beliefs: an overview

	Basic properties	Organization principle	Internal dynamics	Interaction principle
DATA	*Relevance, credibility, importance, likeability*	*Networks*	*Updates, propagation*	*Belief selection*
BELIEFS	*Strength*	*Ordered sets*	*Inferential reasoning*	*Data mapping*

The agent's beliefs emerge from his data base through the selection process (cf. 2.2). Beliefs are characterized by *strength*, which reflects their implicit ordering. Strength is determined by the selection process from the values of credibility, importance, and likeability of the corresponding active datum. Therefore beliefs are organized in *ordered sets*, rather than networks [14, 21].

The basic distinction between data and beliefs yields a rich picture of epistemic dynamics (Fig. 1 and Table 1). From a computational viewpoint, such distinction opens the way for *blended approaches to implementation* [21]: data structures present remarkable similarities with Bayesian networks and neural networks, while belief sets are a well-known hallmark of AGM-style belief revision [14]. Moreover, data and beliefs are here conceived as *different stages, roles, and functions in the processing of internal epistemic states*, to be accounted for in the agent architecture.

2.2 Belief Selection

Once the informational values of the active data are assessed (cf. 2.3), a selection over such data is performed, to determine the subset of reliable information (i.e. beliefs) and their degree of strength. Every time new relevant information is gathered by the agent, modifying his data network and the subset of active data, the belief selection takes place anew, possibly (but not necessarily) changing the agent's belief set.

This process of belief selection regulates the interaction from data to beliefs, determining (1) what data are to be believed, given the current informational state, and (2) which degree of strength is to be assigned to each of them. The outcome of belief selection is determined by the informational values of the candidate data (credibility, importance, likeability) and by the nature of the agent's selection process.

In DBR the agent's belief selection is represented by a mathematical system, including a *condition C*, a *threshold k*, and a *function F*. Condition C and threshold k together express the minimal informational requirements for a datum to be selected as belief. The function F assigns a value of strength to the accepted beliefs. Both C and F are mathematical functions with credibility and/or importance and/or likeability as their arguments. Given a datum ϕ, c^ϕ, i^ϕ, l^ϕ are, respectively, its credibility, importance, and likeability. Let $\boldsymbol{B}$ represents the set of the agent's beliefs, and $B^s\phi$ represents the belief ϕ with strength s. The general form of the selection process is:

$$\text{if } C(c^\phi, i^\phi, l^\phi) \leq k \qquad \text{then} \qquad B^s\phi \notin \boldsymbol{B}$$
$$\text{if } C(c^\phi, i^\phi, l^\phi) > k \qquad \text{then} \qquad B^s\phi \in \boldsymbol{B} \text{ with } s^\phi = F(c^\phi, i^\phi, r^\phi)$$

The setting of C, F and k is an individual parameter, which might vary in different agents (cf. 2.4). Examples of individual variation in belief selection are the following:

$$C: c^\phi > k \qquad\qquad k: 0.5 \qquad F: c^\phi$$
$$C: c^\phi > k \qquad\qquad k: 0.6 \qquad F: (c^\phi + i^\phi + l^\phi)/3$$
$$C: c^\phi > k \times (1 - l^\phi) \qquad k: 0.8 \qquad F: c^\phi \times (i^\phi + l^\phi)$$

All these parametrical settings assign to data credibility the main role in determining belief selection, but they do so in widely different ways. The first parametrical setting expresses a thoroughly realistic attitude towards belief selection, regardless of any considerations about importance or likeability. At the same time, the minimal threshold is set at a quite tolerant level of credibility (0.5). The threshold is slightly higher in the second parametrical setting, and the condition is identical: on the whole, this reflects a more cautious acceptance of reliable data. But once a datum is indeed accepted as belief, its strength is now calculated taking in account also importance and likeability, in contrast to the previous setting. The same happens in the third parametrical setting, although along different lines. Here the threshold is extremely high (0.8), but the condition is influenced by likeability as well: assuming that likeability ranges in the interval [0, 1], here the minimal threshold over credibility is conversely proportional to the likeability of the datum (e.g. it is 0.08 for a datum with likeability 0.9 vs. 0.72 for a datum with likeability 0.1). That expresses a systematic bias towards the acceptance of likeable (i.e. pleasant) data, in spite of their credibility. In other words, these parametrical settings define three agents with different personalities, with respect to belief selection: a *tolerant full realist* (the first), a *prudent open-minded realist* (the second), and a *wishful thinking agent* (the third).

Allowing several parametrical settings in belief selection (as well as in other features of DBR, cf. 2.4) serves to capture *individual variation in epistemic dynamics*, i.e. specifying different strategies of belief change for different agents and/or for different contexts and tasks[2]. It also shows that, although the selection process in DBR is just a mathematical simplification of the cognitive process of belief selection, it is extremely flexible and expressive, since we can manipulate and set condition, function and threshold in such a way to express different selection strategies, with an high degree of sophistication. Moreover, a mathematically straightforward treatment of individual variation will prove essential for investigating evolutionary dynamics in shaping belief revision strategies in MAS, e.g. applying genetic algorithms over population of agents with randomized internal settings (cf. 4).

2.3 Information Update and Data Assessment

Belief revision is usually triggered by *information update* either on a fact or on a source: the agent receives a new piece of information, rearranges his data structure accordingly, and possibly changes his belief set, depending on the belief selection process. Information update specifies the way in which new evidences are integrated in the agent's data structure. We define *external belief selection* the process of epistemic change triggered by information update, in contrast to *internal belief revision*, i.e. belief change due to inferring a new piece of information from old premises (on internal belief revision, see [21]).

Data structures are conceived as networks of nodes (data), linked together by characteristic relations. For the purposes of the present discussion, it will suffice to define three different types of data relations: support, contrast, and union.

---

[2] Individual variation in MAS is a major concern also for argumentation studies, e.g. as a way of framing a theory of personality in multi-agent platforms (see for instance [19]).

I.   *Support*: ϕ supports ψ ($\phi \Rightarrow \psi$) iff $c^\psi \propto c^\phi$, the credibility of ψ is directly proportional to the credibility of ϕ.
II. *Contrast*: ϕ contrasts ψ ($\phi \perp \psi$) iff $c^\psi \propto 1/c^\phi$, the credibility of ψ is conversely proportional to the credibility of ϕ.
III. *Union*: ϕ and ψ are united ($\phi \& \psi$) iff c^ψ and c^ϕ jointly (not separately) determine the credibility of another datum γ.

New external information generates not only a datum concerning its *content*, but also data concerning *source attribution* and *source reliability*, and the *structural relations* among them. More precisely, information update brings together:

I.   a datum concerning the content (object datum, *O-datum*);
II. a datum identifying the information source (*S-datum*);
III. a datum concerning the reliability of the source (*R-datum*).

These data are closely related, since the credibility of the new information depends on the jointed credibility of the other two data: i.e. the union of the S-datum and the R-datum supports the O-datum (Fig. 2). Once an agent has been told by x that ϕ holds, his confidence in ϕ will depend on the reliability he assigns to x, provided he is sure enough that the source of ϕ was indeed x. The environmental input is characterized by a content ϕ (e.g. its propositional meaning), a source x (e.g. another agent), and a noise n (affecting both source identification and content understanding)[3].

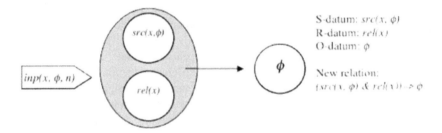

Fig. 2. Information update: integrating new external data

While pragmatic relevance, epistemic importance and motivational likeability of a datum are further discussed in [6, 21], here we focus on credibility. The credibility of a given datum depends on the credibility of its supports, weighted against the credibility of its contrasts [6, 12, 26]. Each agent must be equipped with a specific algorithm to determine such value. Although this algorithm is an individual parameter (different agents can use different heuristics), it must obey the general definition of support and contrast relations. This is an example of *credibility algorithm*[4]:

---

[3] More sophisticated models (e.g. [9]) might take in account also the degree of certainty over the content expressed by the source, allowing agents to communicate information with different shades of confidence.

[4] It is convenient to range credibility in the close interval **[0, 1]**, but of course this does not necessarily lead to probabilistic accounts of epistemic dynamics.

$$c^{\alpha} = (1 - \prod_{\mu \in s\alpha}(1 - c^{\mu})) \times \prod_{\chi \in \kappa\alpha}(1 - c^{\chi})$$

with $S\alpha$ = the set of all data supporting α

$K\alpha$ = the set of all data contrasting α

Support and contrast determine the credibility of one *relatum* in terms of the credibility of the other. Union takes in account the credibility of both *relata* at the same time, in order to assess the credibility of a third datum – either supported or contrasted. An example is given by information update (Fig. 2): the credibility of the O-datum depends on the credibility of the union of S-datum and R-datum. Therefore we need to specify a *union algorithm* for each agent [21]: i.e. a procedure to assess the credibility of $(\phi \& \psi)$, given the credibility of ϕ and ψ. For instance:

$$c^{\phi \& \psi} = min(c^{\phi}, c^{\psi})$$

Now we have enough elements to provide a quantitative description of information update, and not only a qualitative one. The credibility of the O-datum will depend on the credibility of the union of the S-datum (here with $c = 1$, assuming noiseless communication by hypothesis) and the R-datum, weighted against the credibility of all contrasting evidences (if any), according to the credibility algorithm of that particular agent. Assessment of source reliability is thoroughly discussed in [6, 12].

2.4 Principles and Parameters

The model of belief revision presented so far is based on a conceptual distinction between *principles* and *parameters*. Principles are *general* and *qualitative* in nature, defining the common features which characterize epistemic processing in every agent. Parameters, instead, are *individual* and *quantitative*, specifying in which fashion and measure each agent applies the universal principles of belief revision. The cognitive and social framework of the model is captured by its principles, while individual variation is represented through parametrical setting (as already showed in 2.2 concerning belief selection).

For instance, the overall two-steps dynamic of belief revision is a universal principle, while the mathematical nature of the selection process is an individual parameter. Credibility assessment will always be positively affected by supporting evidence and negatively affected by contrasting data, but the credibility algorithm might vary from one agent to another. All agents perform inferential deduction at the level of beliefs, but the specific axioms applied are a matter of individual variation – and so on. More details on parametrical setting are given in [21]: here we will only discuss their impact over argumentation (cf. 3.5).

3 Argumentation and Belief Revision

This section is devoted to highlight several connections between our model of belief change and argumentation theories: the impact of rhetorical arguments over the audience's beliefs (cf. 3.1), the different stages in Toulmin's model of argumentation (cf. 3.2), the treatment of defeasible reasoning (cf. 3.3), the role of contradictions in arguments (cf. 3.4), and the effects of individual parameters over argumentation strategies and outcomes (cf. 3.5). Presenting and discussing this variety of topics, we aim to verify the expressive power of our model of belief revision on several argumentation-related features of MAS (see also [10] for a similar attempt). A failure at this stage would testify the inadequacy of the formal model in dealing with argumentation – as it is the case with the AGM framework (cf. 3.2, 3.4, 4). On the contrary, the satisfactory results achieved by our model sound promising for future developments in the same direction [4]. However, it must be understood that this first survey is meant as preliminary recognition of a complex and exciting landscape, to test the chances of success (that we find quite favorable) for more ambitious and exhaustive attempts of integrating belief revision and argumentation (cf. 4).

3.1 Rhetoric and Audience's Beliefs

Aristotle's definition of rhetorical argument characterizes it as being especially focused on the *audience's beliefs*, rather than general acceptability. This definition is usually referred to in formal studies of rhetorical argumentation, e.g. [16], where the need for a model of belief revision (and more generally belief processing) is quite self-evident. However, as far as cognitive agents are concerned, even the most general and uncontroversial argument requires a process of belief revision in the mind of the audience: it is not the fact that p follows from q and q is the case which makes me believe p, but rather my beliefs that "p follows from q" and "q is the case". An integrated framework naturally emphasizes that any form of argumentation (including strictly logical ones) must be strongly focused on the audience's beliefs.

In our model, a crucial factor in determining whether a new piece of information will be accepted or rejected as belief is its *importance* [14, 21], i.e. the degree of connectivity (integration) of the new datum in the audience's data structure. An effective argument not only presents new information to the audience, but also provides the relevant connections with data already available to (and possibly believed by) that audience. Such connections vouch for the *plausibility* of the new datum [6] and are crucial in persuading the audience to accept it. In data networks, we distinguish two cases of argumentation through plausibility:

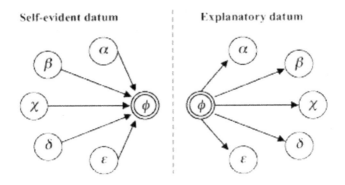

Fig. 3. Two plausibility arguments: self-evident and explanatory data

I. *Self-evident data*: the new datum is presented as following from what the audience already knew – the datum had not yet been inferred, but it might have been, and the audience is likely to remark: «Sure! Of course! Obviously!» etc.;

II. *Explanatory data*: the new datum is presented as supporting and explaining data already available – since such explanation was missing so far, it produces reactions like: «Now I see! That's why! I knew it! » etc.

This distinction is easily represented by a structured data-domain: in our model, self-evident data are data with a high number of supports, while explanatory data in turn support many other data (Fig. 3). Different degrees of self-evidence and explanatory power are expressed by epistemic importance (cf. 2.1).

3.2 Toulmin Revis(it)ed

One of the most influential account of argumentation is Toulmin's model [28], which analyzes six features of an argument: data, claim, warrant, backing, qualifier, rebuttal. *Data* are the facts (e.g. John loved his wife) which support the arguer's *claim* (e.g. John did not murder her), while the *warrant* ensures the connection between data and claim (e.g. people do not murder the ones they love), on the basis of some *backing* (e.g. murderers hate their victims); the *qualifier* specifies to what extend the warrant applies (e.g. usually), and the *rebuttal* describes special conditions which undermine the warrant (e.g. John is in bad need of money and will benefit from her insurance).

This schema is liable of immediate implementation in our model of belief revision, since it defines a specific data structure (Fig. 4). The union of data and warrant supports the claim, and the warrant is in turn supported by its backing and contrasted by the rebuttal, i.e. supports to the rebuttal make the warrant less reliable. The qualifier is represented by the degree of credibility assigned to the claim by this data structure – while more sophisticated models of source integration also distinguish between the claim's credibility and the confidence expressed by the arguer [12].

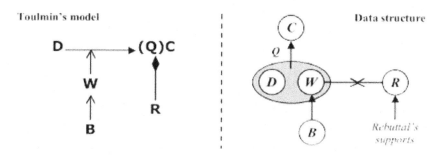

Fig. 4. Toulmin's model in data structure

This convergence is not surprising, since our model is built over the intuition that epistemic processing requires "reasons to believe" [6], and indeed argumentation is mainly concerned with the manipulation of reasons in order to change the audience's beliefs. However, it is worth noticing that other theories of belief revision fail to incorporate Toulmin's model: e.g., the AGM approach has no way to capture similar argumentative structures, without undertaking major modification of the model.

3.3 Defeasible Reasoning in Data Networks

Argumentation is often modeled in the formal framework of defeasible reasoning [2, 26], distinguishing between two kinds of defeaters (i.e. possible counterarguments against a reason-schema): *rebutting* vs. *undercutting defeaters*. Applying the terminology proposed in [28], a rebutting defeater is any reason which directly denies the claim of the argument, while an undercutting defeater is a reason which undermine the validity of the relevant warrant.

In our model, different defeaters target different nodes in the data network (Fig. 5): rebutting defeaters are data which contrast the claim-node (e.g. John has been seen shooting his wife), while undercutting defeaters are data contrasting the warrant-node (e.g. jealousy can make you kill the ones you love most). Moreover, a third category of defeaters can be expressed: *premise defeaters*, i.e. reasons which contrast the data-node (e.g. John did not love his wife). Undercutting and premise defeaters have similar function but different targets: the former attack the connection between data and claim, while the latter question the statement of fact supporting the conclusion[5].

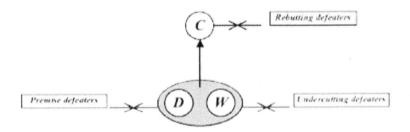

Fig. 5. Defeasible reasoning in data structure

3.4 Revising Contradictions in Argumentation

AGM-style approaches to belief revision exclude contradictions in principle, assuming belief states to be fully consistent – an untenable assumption, as far as

---

[5] Here we follow the terminology used in [26], but actually the expression 'rebutting defeater' is quite misleading, when compared with Toulmin's model. The rebuttal, as defined in [28], specifies the conditions which undermine the validity of the warrant, not of the claim – i.e. rebuttals are in fact undercutting defeaters. So the expression *direct defeaters* would be less ambiguous, to indicate defeaters which directly affect the claim.

cognitive agents are concerned. On the contrary, argumentation theories have been quite successful in handling inconsistency and conflicts [2, 7, 26, 28, 30], since the very idea of defeating an argument implies that such argument can be showed to be inconsistent with respect to a better one. Moreover, the AGM paradigm assumes belief states to be deductively closed, therefore infinite. This is not only a computational problem, but also a conceptual mistake: cognitive agents do not derive all the consequences from available data not only because they are resource-bounded [1, 21, 31], but mainly because they have no need to derive irrelevant consequences from accepted claims.

In our model, epistemic states are both finite and deductively open, and there is no universal insurance against contradictions. Instead, we are able to capture two relevant distinction concerning inconsistency: *implicit* vs. *explicit contradictions*, and *data contrasts* vs. *beliefs contradictions*. Agents are likely to entertain a certain number of implicitly contradictory beliefs, i.e. beliefs from which a contradiction could be derived, although the agent has not yet done so. As long as the contradiction remains implicit, the agent has no problem in handling it – just by ignoring it altogether! In fact, one of the most common strategy in argumentation consists in confronting the audience with their own contradictions, i.e. forcing them to draw contradictory conclusions from what they already believe.

In data structures, contrast relations capture 'contradictions' between data (cf. 2.3). However, these are not contradictions in the proper sense, since the contrasting data are not necessarily believed by the agent, and not necessarily at the same time: they are just information on mutually excluding states of the world. Moreover, contrasts among data are actually beneficial to the agent, since they provide him with crucial information on the credibility of both *relata*: information on ~p are useful to assess the credibility of p exactly because a contrast relation is defined between p and ~p, in the form $(p \perp \sim p)$. Without such relation, negative evidence would not be evidence at all, and the efficiency of our epistemic processing would be severely impaired[6].

In other terms, *contradictions need to be solved only if they arises at the level of beliefs*, i.e. if the selection process (cf. 2.2) accepts two contrasting data as beliefs. This is rare, since credibility plays a crucial role in belief selection, and the credibility of contrasting data is conversely proportional (cf. 2.3). However, under specific circumstances (e.g. a selection which emphasizes importance and likeability over credibility) it might happen that an agent is confronted with contradictory beliefs. In this case, the contradiction is solved through reasoning, e.g. applying an axiom to reject one of the contradictory beliefs, or both.

Here we are faced with an intriguing parallel between epistemic and motivational dynamics. In BDI models of agency it has been correctly postulated that an important difference between the level of mere Desires (or wishes) and the level of Intentions, i.e. goals actually directing the agent's behavior, is that while Desires can be

---

[6] We agree with Aristotle that the human mind refuses contradiction – the point is, what is a contradiction, and under which conditions contradictions arise? Contrasting data *per se* do not generate contradictions, since the agent is not yet committed to their propositional content. Hence data bases are expected to be typically inconsistent, without bothering in the least the agent. Being informed of p and ~p, e.g. by being exposed to conflicting sources of information, is not a contradiction: only *believing at the same time both contrasting claims* would produce a contradiction in the agent mind and require a solution at the level of beliefs.

subjectively contradictory and the subject can entertain them as such before being obliged to choose, on the contrary Intentions – i.e. what one has decided to pursue and to do – must be subjectively non contradictory. In other words, conflicts between possible/candidate goals must have been solved at the deliberation stage. Exactly the same happens between data and beliefs: after the selection process, inconsistency cannot be tolerated anymore and contradictions have to be solved (Fig. 6). This parallel between the processing of epistemic and motivational representations yields a convincing picture of human mind as a *coherence-seeking device*.

Contradiction management is further discussed in [21]. Here we only want to emphasize that rational agents are not preserved from contradictions for some benevolent 'law of nature': they are rather equipped *to handle contradictions efficiently* both in the epistemic and motivational processing, e.g. exploiting the informational value of contrasting evidences and balancing conflicting desires. If we fail to acknowledge inconsistency in belief change, we miss the core of argumentation: weighting against each other contradictory claims.

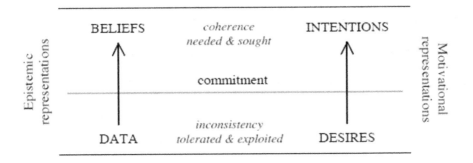

Fig. 6. The mind as a coherence-seeking device

3.5 Parameters and Argumentation

In DBR, parameters (cf. 2.2 and 2.4) provides a computational description of individual variation [21]. They also have consequences over the treatment of argumentation, capturing the relevant distinction between *local* and *global persuasion*, and the *multi-layered nature of argumentative strategies*.

An argument can either aims to change single beliefs in the mind of the audience (local persuasion), or it might address the basic processes which define the outcome of belief revision for that audience (global persuasion). Whenever persuasive argumentation is a major issue (e.g. political campaigns, advertising, religious events), global persuasion is the key feature: it is not enough to change some specific beliefs, the arguer is basically trying *to make the audience accept a different way of thinking* – i.e. different revision procedures, to be applied autonomously from now on.

Local and global strategies are grounded in our model, respectively, in *argumentation over data network* and *argumentation over parameters*. The examples discussed in 3.1-3.4 are instances of local persuasion, which attack or support nodes in the data structure. On the contrary, global persuasion questions the validity of individual parameters concerning belief revision, e.g. the selection process («You should not pay so much attention to explanatory power, otherwise you are prone to wishful thinking! »), the assessment of data values («Do not underestimate contrasting evidences, or you will be biased toward confirmation! »), the reliability assigned to new sources («Why do you trust so much somebody you does not know? ») [21].

Perhaps the most famous instance of the interplay between belief revision parameters, argumentation and global persuasion is from the Gospels: that is, the incredulity of St Thomas. When Jesus, after his resurrection, appeared for the first time to the apostles, Thomas was not there. Once he had been told of the miracle by his companions, he refused to believe in their account, claiming that "unless I see in his hands the print of the nails, and place my finger in the mark of the nails, and place my hand in his side, I will not believe" (St John, 20: 25). This bold statement was challenged when Jesus appeared again, and explicitly insisted that Thomas should probe Jesus' wounds with his incredulous finger. After that, the apostle was convinced and repentant, but Jesus was after a global persuasion, rather than a local one. Hence his final comment: "Have you believed because you have seen me? Blessed are those who have not seen and yet believe" (St John, 20: 29).

In this episode a whole attitude (skepticism) is stigmatized as inadequate within a given context (matters of faith)[7], and the misbehaving agent is required for the future to apply different parameters to his processes of belief selection and change. The positive counterpart of Thomas is exemplified by Mary Magdalene, who immediately believed in the resurrection of Jesus once she was told by him, although she was not able to distinguish his features and his voice. Nevertheless, the testimony of a stranger standing next to the sepulcher of Jesus was enough for her to believe in the miracle. Both these attitudes can be captured (in a simplified form) within the framework of DBR, as the computational analogous of Mary Magdalene and St Thomas summarized in Table 2 (for details on each parameter listed in the table, see [21]). In the MAS counterpart of the biblical episode, the argumentative strategy applied by Jesus would aim to make Thomas shift his parameters towards the ones of Mary, i.e. developing a more trustful epistemic attitude through several minor changes: e.g. a less pessimistic assessment of credibility value (the first two parameters), more refined processes to evaluate importance (the third, fourth and fifth parameter), a less realistic process of belief selection (the sixth, seventh and eighth parameter), and more reliance in new sources of information (the last parameter in Table 2).

---

[7] The episode serves also to illustrate *the relevance of context* in defining whether a given belief revision strategy is adaptive or not. In fact, Thomas' skepticism is inadequate only with respect to the situation portrayed here, i.e. the faith of a disciple towards his religious leader. In other contexts, the skeptical attitude embodied by Thomas would indeed constitute the only sensible strategy to use: this is exactly the reason why the mistreated Thomas became, starting from the Renaissance, an icon of scientific inquiry and human curiosity.

Table 2. Parameters in DBR and argumentation: Mary Magdalene vs. St Thomas

parameters	Trustful (Mary Magdalene)	Skeptic (St Thomas)
Credibility alg.	$c^\alpha = (1 - \prod_{\sigma \in S\alpha}(1 - c^\sigma)) \times \prod_{\varepsilon \in K\alpha}(1 - c^\varepsilon)$	$c^\sigma = pr^\sigma \times \prod_{\varepsilon \in K\sigma}(1 - pr^\varepsilon)$ with $\sigma \in S$ $c^\alpha = 1 - \prod_{\sigma \in S\alpha}(1 - c^\sigma)$ with $\alpha \notin S$
Union algorithm	$c^{\alpha \& \beta} = min(c^\alpha, c^\beta)$	$c^{\alpha \& \beta} = c^\alpha \times c^\beta$
Importance alg.	$\mu < 5, \ i^\phi = \mu/5 \times (1 - \prod_{\psi \in N\phi}(1 - c^\psi))$ $\mu \geq 5, \ i^\phi = 1 - \prod_{\psi \in N\phi}(1 - c^\psi)$	$\mu < 5, \ i^\phi = \mu/5 \times (1 - \prod_{\psi \in N\phi}(1 - c^\psi))$ $\mu \geq 5, \ i^\phi = 1 - \prod_{\psi \in N\phi}(1 - c^\psi)$
Depth λ	2	1
Consid. thres. w	0.3	0.6
Condition C	$c^\phi / (1 - i^\phi)$	c^ϕ
Accept. thres. k	0.6	0.8
Function F	$c^\phi + i^\phi - (c^\phi \times i^\phi)$	c^ϕ
Reliability default	0.7	0.3

Finally and more generally, it is worth noticing that parameters play a crucial role in any instance of argumentation, since the arguer is required to understand, at least partially, the parameters governing belief revision in his audience. This reflects the multi-layered nature of argumentation: for the arguer to be effective, it is not enough to figure out the audience's beliefs (the data structure and the resulting belief set), but also the way in which beliefs are processed (the audience's parameters on belief revision, e.g. how they assess data values, how they select beliefs from data, etc.). Factual evidences are useless, if the audience do not care for credibility in belief selection; on the other hand, alluring picture of highly desirable states of things does not work with matter-of-fact types – and so on. Formal models of belief change which fail to account for individual variation are implying that every audience will have identical reactions to the same base of data: an untenable assumption [5, 7, 21, 28].

4   Conclusions and Future Works

The integrated framework sketched here strongly supports a general methodological claim: a model of belief revision, in order to deal effectively with argumentation in MAS, must ensure *a proper degree of structural analysis* – i.e. it must emphasizes the relational properties which characterize epistemic processing, rather than its overall principles. Ordering criteria over propositions or sets, like in AGM-style approaches, are not expressive enough to model argumentation – nor belief revision.

Therefore, the main implication of this preliminary proposal is to initiate a systematic effort of integrating research areas necessarily connected with each other, i.e. argumentation studies and belief revisions, but that only rarely have been so far modeled within the same framework [10, 26]. Even more important, the DBR theory presented here constitutes a first step towards formal and computational models of epistemic change (both intra- and inter-agents) to express the complex socio-cognitive dynamics involved in belief revision in MAS, in contrast with the idealistic approach which dominated this field so far (see analogous considerations in [6, 21, 26, 27]).

In our future work we intend to refine the DBR model of belief revision (e.g. extending the computational treatment of data properties to motivational and emotional features, i.e. relevance and likeability [6, 11, 21]), to provide more systematic connections with argumentation theories [2, 4, 16, 17, 28, 30], especially within the MAS community [3, 19, 20, 22, 23], to explore the interaction between TMS-based belief revision and argumentation models [8, 18], and to move towards implementation in agent-based cognitive and social simulation (preliminary work in this direction is being developed within the AKIRA framework [24]), exploiting random parametrical variation to study evolutionary dynamics in belief revision and argumentation development. As a starting point, we plan to use argumentation tasks as testing ground for belief revision algorithms, and vice versa – building on the general results discussed here. Finally, we also aim to investigate the more radical idea of modeling the whole process of epistemic change as a form of *internal argumentation* [4, 21], as long ago suggested in developmental psychology by Jean Piaget [25] and Lev Vygotsky [29].

References

1. Alechina, N., Logan, B.: Ascribing Beliefs to Resource Bounded Agents. Proceedings of AAMAS'02 (2002)
2. Amgoud, L., Cayrol, C.: Inferring from Inconsistency in Preference-Based Argumentation Frameworks. Journal of Automated Reasoning 29 (2002) 125-169
3. Amgoud, L., Parsons, S., Maudet, N.: Arguments, Dialogue and Negotiation. Proceedings of ECAI 2000, Berlin (2000)
4. van Benthem, J., van Eemeren, F. H., Grootendorst, R., Veltman, F. (eds.): Logic and Argumentation. North-Holland, Amsterdam (1996)
5. Castelfranchi, C.: Guarantees for Autonomy in Cognitive Agent Architecture. Proceedings ECAI 1994 Workshop on Agent Theories, Architectures, and Languages, Springer, Berlin (1995) 56-70
6. Castelfranchi, C.: Reasons: Belief Support and Goal Dynamics". Mathware & Soft Computing 3 (1996) 233-247
7. De Rosis, F., Grasso, F., Castelfranchi, C., Poggi, I.: Modeling Conflict-Resolution Dialogues. J. H. Müller, R. Dieng (eds.): Computational Conflicts. Springer, Berlin (2000) 41-62
8. Doyle, J.: Reason Maintenance and Belief Revision: Foundations vs. Coherence Theories. P. Gärdenfors (ed.): Belief Revision. Cambridge University Press, Cambridge (1992) 29-51
9. Dragoni, A. F., Giorgini, P.: Distributed Belief Revision. Autonomous Agents and Multi-Agent Systems 6 (2003) 115-143
10. Falappa, M. A., Kern-Isberner, G., Simari, G. R.: Explanations, Belief Revision and Defeasible Reasoning. Artificial Intelligence 141 (2002) 1-28
11. Frijda, N. H., Manstead, A., Bem, S. (eds.): Emotions and Beliefs: How Feelings Influence Thoughts. Cambridge University Press, Cambridge (2000)
12. Fullam, K.: An Expressive Belief Revision Framework Based on Information Valuation. MS thesis, University of Texas at Austin (2003)
13. 13.Galliers, J. R.: Autonomous Belief Revision and Communication. P. Gärdenfors (ed.): Belief Revision. Cambridge University Press, Cambridge (1992) 220-246
14. 14.Gärdenfors, P.: Knowledge in Flux: Modeling the Dynamics of Epistemic States. The MIT Press, Cambridge (1988)

15. Gillies, A. S.: Two More Dogmas of Belief Revision: Justification and Justified Belief Change. Working paper, Harvard University (2003) consulted on May 2004, available at: http://www.people.fas.Harvard.edu/~gillies/dogmas.pdf

16. 16.Grasso, F.: A Mental Model for a Rhetorical Arguer. Proceedings of EuroCogsci 03, LEA (2003)

17. Guerini, M., Stock, O., Zancanaro, M.: Persuasion Models for Intelligent Interfaces. Proceedings of IJCAI Workshop on Computational Models of Natural Argument (2003)

18. Huns, M. N., Bridgeland, D. M.: Multiagent Truth Maintenance. IEEE Transactions on Systems, Man, and Cybernetics 21 (1991) 1437-1445

19. Kakas, A., MoraÔtis, P.: Argumentation Based Decision Making for Autonomous Agents. Proceedings of AAMAS 2003, Melbourne (2003), 883-890

20. McBurney, P., Parsons, S., Wooldridge, M.: Desiderata for Agent Argumentation Protocols. Proceedings of AAMAS 2002, Bologna (2002)

21. Paglieri, F.: Data-oriented Belief Revision: Towards a Unified Theory of Epistemic Processing. Proceeding of STAIRS 2004, Valencia, IOS Press (2004)

22. Parsons, S., Petterson, O., Saffiotti, A., Wooldridge, M.: Intention Reconsideration in Theory and Practice. Proceedings of ECAI 2000, Berlin (2000)

23. Parsons, S., Wooldridge, M., Amgoud, L.: Properties and Complexity of Some Formal Inter-agent Dialogues. Journal of Logic and Computation 13 (2003) 347-376

24. Pezzulo, G., Calvi, G.: AKIRA: a Framework for Multi-Agent Based Simulation. Proceedings of MAMABS 2004 (2004)

25. Piaget, J.: The Language and Thought of the Child. Kegan Paul, Trench, Trubner (1926)

26. 26.Pollock, J. L., Gillies, A. S.: Belief Revision and Epistemology. Synthese 122 (2000) 69-92

27. Segerberg, K.: Two Traditions in the Logic of Belief: Bringing Them Together. H. J. Ohlbach, U. Reyle (eds.): Logic, Language and Reasoning. Kluwer, Dordrecht (1999) 135-147

28. 28.Toulmin, S.: The Uses of Argument. Cambridge University Press, Cambridge (updated edition 2003, orig. ed. 1958)

29. Vygotsky, L. S.: Thought and Language. The MIT Press, Cambridge MA (1962)

30. Walton, D. N.: Argumentation Schemes for Presumptive Reasoning. LEA, Mahwah (1996)

31. 31.Wassermann, R.: Resource-Bounded Belief Revision. ILLC dissertation series DS-2000-01, Amsterdam (2000)

An Argument-Based Framework to Model an Agent's Beliefs in a Dynamic Environment

Marcela Capobianco[1], Carlos I. Chesñevar[1,2], and Guillermo R. Simari[1]

[1] Artificial Intelligence Research and Development Laboratory,
Department of Computer Science and Engineering,
Universidad Nacional del Sur – Av. Alem 1253,
(8000) Bahía Blanca, Argentina
{mc, grs}@cs.uns.edu.ar

[2] Artificial Intelligence Research Group – Departament of Computer Science,
Universitat de Lleida – Campus Cappont – C/Jaume II,
69 – E-25001 Lleida, Spain
cic@eps.udl.es

Abstract. One of the most difficult problems in multiagent systems involves representing knowledge and beliefs of agents in dynamic environments. New perceptions modify an agent's current knowledge about the world, and consequently its beliefs. Such revision and updating process should be performed efficiently by the agent, particularly in the context of real time constraints.

This paper introduces an argument-based logic programming language called *Observation-based Defeasible Logic Programming* (ODeLP). An ODeLP program is used to represent an agent's knowledge in the context of a multiagent system. The beliefs of the agent are modeled with warranted goals computed on the basis of the agent's program. New perceptions from the environment result in changes in the agent's knowledge handled by a simple but effective updating strategy. The process of computing beliefs in a changing environment is made computationally attractive by integrating a "dialectical database" with the agent's program, providing precompiled information about inferences. We present algorithms for creation and use of dialectical databases.

1 Introduction

Knowledge representation issues play a major role in practically all areas of Artificial Intelligence, and MAS is not an exception. Well-known problems in MAS involve the need of complex abilities for reasoning, planning and acting in dynamic environments ([1]). In the last years, argumentation has gained wide acceptance in the multiagent systems (MAS) community by providing tools for designing and implementing different features which characterize interaction among rational agents.

Logic programming approaches to argumentation [2, 3] have proven to be suitable formalization tools in the context of MAS, as they combine the powerful

I. Rahwan et al. (Eds.): ArgMAS 2004, LNAI 3366, pp. 95–110, 2005.

features provided by logic programming for knowledge representation together with the ability to model complex, argument-based inference procedures in unified, integrated frameworks.

Most MAS approaches based on logic programming rely on *extended logic programming* (ELP) ([4]) as underlying formalism. Thus, the agent's knowledge is codified in terms of an ELP program and the well-founded semantics of the program represents the agent's beliefs. Although ELP is expressive enough to capture different kinds of negation (strict and default negation), it has limitations for modeling incomplete and potentially contradictory information. In a MAS context it is common that agents require such capabilities, as they interact with the environment and among themselves, processing new inputs, changing dynamically their beliefs and intentions, etc. Clearly, in such a setting, the argumentation formalism underlying such MAS should be able to incorporate new information into the knowledge base of the agent and reason accordingly.

In this paper we present (ODeLP) (*Observation based Defeasible Logic Programming*), an argument-based formalism for agents reasoning in dynamic environments. Some of the basic notions of ODeLP come from *Defeasible Logic Programming* [5] (DeLP). As in DeLP, the ODeLP formalism uses a knowledge representation language in the style of logic programming and inference is based on argumentation.

To provide the agents with the ability to sense the changes in the world and integrate them into its existing beliefs, in ODeLP we have adapted the knowledge representation system to handle perceptions. Real time issues also play an important role when modeling agent interaction. In an argument-based MAS setting, a timely interaction is particularly hard to achieve, as the inference process involved is complex and computationally expensive. To solve this issue, we will enhance the behavior of ODeLP by incorporating *dialectical databases*, that is, data structures for storing precompiled knowledge. These structures can be used to speed up the inference process when answering future queries.

The remainder of this paper is organized as follows. Section 2 summarizes the main features of the ODeLP formalism. Section 3 reviews briefly previous work on truth maintenance systems, which provided the basis for our notion of dialectical databases, and introduces the notion of dialectical databases, discussing its role as a tool to speed up inference in the ODeLP formalism. Section 4 presents a worked example. Finally, section 5 summarizes the conclusions that have been obtained.

2   ODeLP: Observation-Based DeLP

Defeasible Logic Programming (DeLP) [5] provides a language for knowledge representation and reasoning that uses *defeasible argumentation* to decide between contradictory conclusions through a *dialectical analysis*. Codifying the knowledge base of the agent by means of a DeLP program provides a good trade-off between expressivity and implementability. Extensions of DeLP that integrate possibilistic logic and vague knowledge along with an argument-based framework have also been proposed [6]. Recent research has shown that DeLP provides a suitable framework for building real-world applications (e.g. clustering algorithms [7], intelligent web search [8] and critiquing systems [9]) that deal with incomplete and potentially contradictory information.

In such applications, DeLP is intended to model the behavior of a single intelligent agent in a *static* scenario. DeLP lacks the appropriate mechanisms to represent knowledge in dynamic environments, where agents must be able to perceive the changes in the world and integrate them into its existing beliefs [10]. The ODeLP framework aims at solving this problem by modeling perception as new facts to be added to the agent's knowledge base. Since adding such new facts may result in inconsistencies, an associated updating process is used to solve them. The definitions that follow summarize the main features of ODeLP.

2.1 Language

The language of ODeLP is based on the language of logic programming. In what follows we use concepts like signature, alphabet and atoms with their usual meaning. Literals are atoms that may be preceded by the symbol "~" denoting *strict* negation, as in ELP. ODeLP programs are formed by *observations* and *defeasible rules*. Observations correspond to facts in the context of logic programming, and represent the knowledge an agent has about the world. *Defeasible rules* provide a way of performing tentative reasoning as in other argumentation formalisms [11, 12].

Definition 1. [Observation]–[Defeasible Rule] *An* observation *is a ground literal L representing some fact about the world, obtained through the perception mechanism, that the agent believes to be correct. A* defeasible rule *has the form $L_0 \prec L_1, L_2, \ldots, L_k$, where L_0 is a literal and $L_1, L_2, \ldots, L_k$ is a non-empty finite set of literals.*

Definition 2. [ODeLP Program] *An* ODeLP program *is a pair $\langle \Psi, \Delta \rangle$, where Ψ is a finite set of observations and Δ is a finite set of defeasible rules. In a program $\mathcal{P}$, the set Ψ must be* non-contradictory *(i.e., it is not the case that $Q \in \Psi$ and $\sim Q \in \Psi$, for any literal Q).*

Example 1. Fig. 1 shows an ODeLP program for assessing the status of employees in a given company. Observations describe that John has a poor performance at his job, John is currently sick, Peter also has a poor performance and Rose is an applicant that demands a high salary. Defeasible rules express that the company prefers to hire employees that require a low salary. An employee that demands a high salary is usually not hired, but in the exceptional case where he/she has good references it is recommended to hire the applicant. The remaining rules deal with the evaluation of the employees' performance, according with their responsibility in the job.

2.2 Inference Mechanism

Given an ODeLP program $\mathcal{P}$, a query posed to $\mathcal{P}$ corresponds to a ground literal Q which must be supported by an *argument* [11, 5]. Arguments are built on

---

```
poor_performance(john).
sick(john).
good_performance(peter).
unruly(peter).
high_salary(rose).
applicant(rose).
good_references(rose).
hire(X) ⤙ ~high_salary(X), applicant(X).
~hire(X) ⤙ high_salary(X), applicant(X).
hire(X) ⤙ high_salary(X), applicant(X), good_references(X).
suspend(X) ⤙ ~responsible(X).
suspend(X) ⤙ unruly(X).
~suspend(X) ⤙ responsible(X).
~responsible(X) ⤙ poor_performance(X).
responsible(X) ⤙ good_performance(X).
responsible(X) ⤙ poor_performance(X),sick(X).
```

Fig. 1. An ODeLP program for assessing the status of employees in a company

the basis of a *defeasible derivation* computed by backward chaining applying the usual SLD inference procedure used in logic programming. Observations play the role of facts and defeasible rules function as inference rules. In addition to provide a proof supporting a ground literal, such a proof must be non-contradictory and minimal for being considered as an argument in ODeLP. Formally:

Definition 3. [Argument – Sub-argument] *Given a ODeLP program $\mathcal{P}$, an argument $\mathcal{A}$ for a ground literal Q, also denoted $\langle \mathcal{A}, Q \rangle$, is a subset of ground instances of the defeasible rules in $\mathcal{P}$ such that:*

1. *there exists a defeasible derivation for Q from $\Psi \cup \mathcal{A}$,*
2. *$\Psi \cup \mathcal{A}$ is non-contradictory,*
3. *$\mathcal{A}$ is minimal with respect to set inclusion in satisfying (1) and (2).*

Given two arguments $\langle \mathcal{A}_1, Q_1 \rangle$ and $\langle \mathcal{A}_2, Q_2 \rangle$, we will say that $\langle \mathcal{A}_1, Q_1 \rangle$ is a sub-argument of $\langle \mathcal{A}_2, Q_2 \rangle$ iff $\mathcal{A}_1 \subseteq \mathcal{A}_2$.

Note that to use defeasible rules in arguments we must first obtain their *ground instances*, changing variables for ground terms, such that variables with the same name are replaced for the same term.

As in most argumentation frameworks, arguments in ODeLP can attack each other. This situation is captured by the notion of *counterargument*. Defeat among arguments is defined combining the counterargument relation and a preference criterion (partial order) "$\preceq$". Specificity [13, 11, 14] is the syntactic-based preference criterion used by default in ODeLP, although other alternative criteria can be easily used. Specificity favors those arguments which are *more direct* or *more informed* (i.e., contain more specific information).

Definition 4. [Counter-argument] *An argument* $\langle \mathcal{A}_1, Q_1 \rangle$ *counter-argues an argument* $\langle \mathcal{A}_2, Q_2 \rangle$ *at a literal* Q *if and only if there is a sub-argument* $\langle \mathcal{A}, Q \rangle$ *of* $\langle \mathcal{A}_2, Q_2 \rangle$ *such that* Q_1 *and* Q *are complementary literals.*

Definition 5. [Defeater] *An argument* $\langle \mathcal{A}_1, Q_1 \rangle$ *defeats* $\langle \mathcal{A}_2, Q_2 \rangle$ *at a literal* Q *if and only if there exists a sub-argument* $\langle \mathcal{A}, Q \rangle$ *of* $\langle \mathcal{A}_2, Q_2 \rangle$ *such that* $\langle \mathcal{A}_1, Q_1 \rangle$ *counter-argues* $\langle \mathcal{A}_2, Q_2 \rangle$ *at* Q, *and either:*

1. $\langle \mathcal{A}_1, Q_1 \rangle$ *is strictly preferred over* $\langle \mathcal{A}, Q \rangle$ *according to the preference criterion* "$\preceq$" *(then* $\langle \mathcal{A}_1, Q_1 \rangle$ *is a* proper defeater *of* $\langle \mathcal{A}_2, Q_2 \rangle$), *or*
2. $\langle \mathcal{A}_1, Q_1 \rangle$ *is unrelated to* $\langle \mathcal{A}, Q \rangle$ *by* "$\preceq$" *(then* $\langle \mathcal{A}_1, Q_1 \rangle$ *is a* blocking defeater *of* $\langle \mathcal{A}_2, Q_2 \rangle$).

Defeaters are arguments and may in turn be defeated. Thus, a complete dialectical analysis is required to determine which arguments are ultimately accepted. Such analysis results in a tree structure called *dialectical tree*, in which arguments are nodes labeled as undefeated (**U-nodes**) or defeated (**D-nodes**) according to a marking procedure. Formally:

Definition 6. [Dialectical Tree] *The* dialectical tree *for an argument* $\langle \mathcal{A}, Q \rangle$, *denoted* $\mathcal{T}_{\langle \mathcal{A}, Q \rangle}$, *is recursively defined as follows:*

1. *A single node labeled with an argument* $\langle \mathcal{A}, Q \rangle$ *with no defeaters (proper or blocking) is by itself the dialectical tree for* $\langle \mathcal{A}, Q \rangle$.
2. *Let* $\langle \mathcal{A}_1, Q_1 \rangle, \langle \mathcal{A}_2, Q_2 \rangle, \ldots, \langle \mathcal{A}_n, Q_n \rangle$ *be all the defeaters (proper or blocking) for* $\langle \mathcal{A}, Q \rangle$. *The dialectical tree for* $\langle \mathcal{A}, Q \rangle$, $\mathcal{T}_{\langle \mathcal{A}, Q \rangle}$, *is obtained by labeling the root node with* $\langle \mathcal{A}, Q \rangle$, *and making this node the parent of the root nodes for the dialectical trees of* $\langle \mathcal{A}_1, Q_1 \rangle, \langle \mathcal{A}_2, Q_2 \rangle, \ldots, \langle \mathcal{A}_n, Q_n \rangle$

Definition 7. [Marking of the Dialectical Tree] *Let* $\langle \mathcal{A}_1, Q_1 \rangle$ *be an argument and* $\mathcal{T}_{\langle \mathcal{A}_1, Q_1 \rangle}$ *its dialectical tree, then:*

1. *All the leaves in* $\mathcal{T}_{\langle \mathcal{A}_1, Q_1 \rangle}$ *are marked as a* **U-node**.
2. *Let* $\langle \mathcal{A}_2, Q_2 \rangle$ *be an inner node of* $\mathcal{T}_{\langle \mathcal{A}_1, Q_1 \rangle}$. *Then* $\langle \mathcal{A}_2, Q_2 \rangle$ *is marked as* **U-node** *iff every child of* $\langle \mathcal{A}_2, Q_2 \rangle$ *is marked as a* **D-node**. *The node* $\langle \mathcal{A}_2, Q_2 \rangle$ *is marked as a* **D-node** *if and only if it has at least a child marked as* **U-node**.

Dialectical analysis may in some situations give rise to *fallacious argumentation* [15]. In ODeLP dialectical trees are ensured to be free of fallacies [14] by applying additional constraints when building *argumentation lines* (the different possible paths in a dialectical tree). A detailed analysis of these issues is outside the scope of this paper.

Given a query Q and an ODeLP program $\mathcal{P}$, we will say that Q is *warranted* wrt $\mathcal{P}$ iff there exists an argument $\mathcal{T}_{\langle \mathcal{A}, Q \rangle}$ such that the root of its associated dialectical tree $\mathcal{T}_{\langle \mathcal{A}, Q \rangle}$ is marked as a U-node.

Definition 8. [Warrant] *Let* $\mathcal{A}$ *be an argument for a literal* Q, *and let* $\mathcal{T}_{\langle \mathcal{A}, Q \rangle}$ *be its associated dialectical tree.* $\mathcal{A}$ *is a* warrant *for* Q *if and only if the root of* $\mathcal{T}_{\langle \mathcal{A}, Q \rangle}$ *is marked as a* **U-node**.

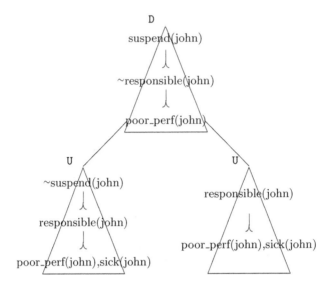

Fig. 2. Dialectical tree from Example 2

Solving a query Q in ODeLP accounts for trying to find a warrant for Q, as shown in the following example.

Example 2. Consider the program shown in Example 1, and let suspend(john) be a query wrt that program. The search for a warrant for suspend(john) will result in an argument $\langle \mathcal{A}, \text{suspend(john)} \rangle$ with two defeaters $\langle \mathcal{B}, \sim\text{suspend(john)} \rangle$ and $\langle \mathcal{C}, \text{responsible(john)} \rangle$, where

- $\mathcal{A} = \{\text{suspend(john)} \prec \sim\text{responsible(john)};$
  $\sim\text{responsible(john)} \prec \text{poor\_performance(john)}\}$.
- $\mathcal{B} = \{\sim\text{suspend(john)} \prec \text{responsible(john)};$
  $\text{responsible(john)} \prec \text{poor\_performance(john)},\text{sick(john)}\}$.
- $\mathcal{C} = \{\text{responsible(john)} \prec \text{poor\_performance(john)},\text{sick(john)}\}$.

Using specificity as the preference criterion, $\langle \mathcal{B}, \sim\text{suspend(john)} \rangle$ is a blocking defeater for $\langle \mathcal{A}, \text{suspend(john)} \rangle$, and $\langle \mathcal{C}, \text{responsible(john)} \rangle$ is a proper defeater for $\langle \mathcal{A}, \text{suspend(john)} \rangle$. The associated dialectical tree is shown in Fig.2. The marking procedure determines that the root node $\langle \mathcal{A}, \text{suspend(john)} \rangle$ is a D-node and hence suspend(john) is not warranted.

2.3 Modeling Beliefs and Perceptions in ODeLP

ODeLP models the beliefs of an agent in a simple way: given a program $\mathcal{P}$ representing an agent's knowledge, a literal Q is believed by the agent iff Q is warranted. In particular, different doxastic attitudes are distinguished wrt a given literal Q:

- Believe that Q is *true* whenever Q is warranted;
- Believe that Q is *false* (*i.e.*, believe $\sim Q$) whenever $\sim Q$ is warranted; and
- Believe that Q is *undecided* whenever none of the above cases apply.

Consistency is a basic property for agent's beliefs, in the sense that it is not possible to believe simultaneously in a literal Q and its complement $\sim Q$ [16]. Agents using ODeLP naturally satisfy this requirement. [1]

In ODeLP, the mechanism for updating the knowledge base of an agent is simple but effective. We assume that perception is carried out by devices that detect changes in the world and report them as new facts (literals). The actual devices used will depend on the particular application domain, and their characterization is outside the scope of this paper. We also make the assumption that the perception mechanism is flawless, and new perceptions always supersede old ones. Any perception will be reported as a new fact α to be added to the set of observations Ψ. If this new perception α is contradictory with Ψ, then necessarily $\sim\alpha \in \Psi$. In such a case, we use a simple update function [17] that computes a new observation set Ψ' as $\Psi\backslash\{\sim\alpha\} \cup \alpha$. Thus new perceptions are always preferred: with a flawless perception mechanism the source of the conflict must be a change in the state of world.

3   Precompiling Knowledge in ODeLP

In *truth maintenance systems* (TMS) the use of precompiled knowledge helps improve the performance of problem solvers. A similar technique will be used in ODeLP to address the real time constrains required in a MAS setting. Next we give a brief overview of TMS and then we describe the mechanism used for precompiling knowledge in ODeLP.

3.1   Truth Maintenance Systems: A Brief Overview

Truth Maintenance Systems (TMS) were defined by Doyle in [18] as support tools for problems solvers. The function of a TMS is to record and maintain the reasons for an agent's beliefs. Doyle describes a series of procedures that determine the current set of beliefs and update it in accord with new incoming reasons. Under this view, *rational thought* is deemed as the process of finding reasons for attitudes [18]. Some attitude (such as belief, desire, etc.) is rational if it is supported by some acceptable explanation.

TMS have two basic data structures: *nodes*, which represent beliefs, and *justifications* which model reasons for the nodes. The TMS believes in a node if it has a justification for the node and believes in the nodes involved in it. Although this may seem circular, there are assumptions (a special type of justifications) which involve no other nodes. Justifications for nodes may be added or retracted, and this accounts for a *truth maintenance procedure* [18], to make

---

[1] For a full discussion of ODeLP properties and their proof the interested reader can consult [14].

any necessary revisions in the set of beliefs. An interesting feature of TMS is the use of a particular type of justifications, called *non-monotonic*, to make tentative guesses. A non-monotonic justification bases an argument for a node not only on current beliefs in certain nodes, but also on lack of beliefs in other nodes. Any node supported by a non-monotonic justification is called an *assumption.*

TMS solve part of the belief revision problem in general problem solvers and provide a mechanism for making non-monotonic assumptions. As Doyle mentions in [18] performance is also significantly improved, even though the overhead required to record justifications for every program belief might seem excessive, we must consider the expense of not keeping these records. When information about derivations is discarded, the same information must be continually re-derived, even when only irrelevant assumptions have changed.

3.2   Dialectical Databases in ODeLP

Based on the existing work in TMS, our goal is to integrate precompiled knowledge into an agent framework based on ODeLP in order to address real-time constraints in a MAS setting. To do so, we want an ODeLP-based agent to be able to answer queries efficiently, by avoiding recomputing arguments which were already computed before.

Note that there are different options for integrating precompiled knowledge with an ODeLP program $\mathcal{P}$. A simple approach would be recording every argument that has been computed so far. However, a large number of arguments can be obtained from a relatively small program, resulting thus in a large database. On the other hand, many arguments are obtained using *different* instances of the *same* defeasible rules. Recording every generated argument could result in storing many arguments which are structurally identical, only differing in the constant names being used to build the corresponding derivations.

Another important problem arises with perceptions. Note that the set of arguments that can be built from a program $\mathcal{P} = \langle \Psi, \Delta \rangle$ also depends on the observation set Ψ. When Ψ is updated with new perceptions, arguments which were previously derivable from $\mathcal{P}$ may no longer be so. If precompiled knowledge depends on Ψ, it should be updated as new perceptions appear. Clearly such an alternative is not suitable, as new perceptions are frequent in dynamic environments. As a consequence, precompiled knowledge should be managed independently from the set of observations Ψ.

Based on the previous analysis we will define a database structure called *dialectical database*, which will keep a record of all possible *potential arguments* in an ODeLP program $\mathcal{P}$ as well as their defeat relationships among them. Potential arguments are formed by non-grounded defeasible rules, depending thus only on the set of rules Δ in $\mathcal{P}$. As we will discuss later, attack relationships among potential arguments can be also captured. Potential arguments and the defeat relationships among them will be stored in the dialectical database. Next we introduce some formal definitions:

Definition 9. [Instance for a set of defeasible rules] *Let A be a set of defeasible rules. A set B formed by ground instances of the defeasible rules in A is an instance of A iff every instance of a defeasible rule in B is an instance of a defeasible rule in A.*

Example 3. If $A = \{$ `s(X)` $\prec$ `~r(X)`; `~r(X)` $\prec$ `p(X)` $\}$ then $B = \{$ `s(t)` $\prec$ `~r(t)`; `~r(a)` $\prec$ `p(a)` $\}$ is an instance of A.

Definition 10. [Potential argument] *Let Δ be a set of defeasible rules. A subset A of Δ is a* potential argument *for a literal Q, noted as $\langle\!\langle A, Q \rangle\!\rangle$ if there exists a non-contradictory set of literals Φ and an instance B of the rules in A such that $\langle B, Q \rangle$ is an argument wrt $\langle \Phi, \Delta \rangle$.*

In the definition above the set Φ stands for a state of the world (set of observations) in which we can obtain the instance B from the set A of defeasible rules such that $\langle B, Q \rangle$ is an argument (as defined in Def.3). Note that the set Φ must necessarily be non-contradictory to model a coherent scenario.

Precompiled knowledge associated with an ODeLP program $\mathcal{P} = \langle \Psi, \Delta \rangle$ will involve the set of all potential arguments that can be built from $\mathcal{P}$ as well as the defeat relationships among them.

- **Potential Arguments:** to obtain and record every potential argument of $\mathcal{P}$ we have devised an algorithm that efficiently identifies all potential arguments as distinguished subsets of the rules in Δ.[2] Potential arguments will save time in computing arguments when solving queries. Instead of computing a query for a given ground literal Q, the ODeLP interpreter will search for a potential argument A for Q such that a particular instance B of A is an argument for Q wrt $\mathcal{P}$.

- **Defeat Relationships Among Potential Arguments:** Recording information about defeat relationships among potential arguments is also useful as it helps to speed up the construction of dialectical trees when solving queries, as we will see later. To do this, we extend the concepts of counterargument and defeat for potential arguments. A potential argument $\langle\!\langle A_1, Q_1 \rangle\!\rangle$ *counter-argues* $\langle\!\langle A_2, Q_2 \rangle\!\rangle$ at a literal Q if and only if there is a potential sub-argument $\langle\!\langle A, Q \rangle\!\rangle$ of $\langle\!\langle A_2, Q_2 \rangle\!\rangle$ such that Q_1 and Q are contradictory literals.[3] Note that potential counter-arguments may or may not result in a real conflict between the instances (arguments) associated with the corresponding potential arguments. In some cases instances of these arguments cannot co-exist in any scenario (*e.g.*, consider two potential arguments based on contradictory observations).

The notion of defeat is also extended to potential arguments. Since specificity is a syntactic-based criterion, a particular version of specificity [14] is

---

[2] For space reasons this algorithm is not detailed in this paper. The interested reader is referred to [14].

[3] Note that $P(X)$ and $\sim P(X)$ are contradictory literals although they are non-grounded. The same idea is applied to identify contradiction in potential arguments.

applicable to potential arguments, determining when a potential argument is more informed or more direct than another.

Using potential arguments and their associated defeat relation we can formally define the notion of *dialectical databases* associated with a given ODeLP program $\mathcal{P}$.

Definition 11. [Dialectical Database] *Let* $\mathcal{P} = \langle \Psi, \Delta \rangle$ *be an ODeLP program. The* dialectical database *of* $\mathcal{P}$, *denoted as* $\mathcal{DB}_\Delta$, *is a 3-tuple* $(\mathrm{PotArg}(\Delta), D_p, D_b)$ *such that:*

1. $\mathrm{PotArg}(\Delta)$ *is the set* $\{\langle\!\langle A_1, Q_1 \rangle\!\rangle, \ldots, \langle\!\langle A_k, Q_k \rangle\!\rangle\}$ *of all the potential arguments that can be built from* Δ.
2. D_p *and* D_b *are relations over the elements of* $\mathrm{PotArg}(\Delta)$ *such that for every pair* $(\langle\!\langle A_1, Q_1 \rangle\!\rangle, \langle\!\langle A_2, Q_2 \rangle\!\rangle)$ *in* D_p *(respectively* D_b*) it holds that* $\langle\!\langle A_2, Q_2 \rangle\!\rangle$ *is a proper (respectively blocking) defeater of* $\langle\!\langle A_1, Q_1 \rangle\!\rangle$.

Example 4. Consider the program in example 1. The dialectical database of $\mathcal{P}$ is composed by the following potential arguments:

- $\langle\!\langle A_1, \texttt{hire(X)} \rangle\!\rangle$,
  where $A_1 = \{\texttt{hire(X)} \prec \texttt{\textasciitilde high\_salary(X)}, \texttt{applicant(X)}\}$.
- $\langle\!\langle A_2, \texttt{\textasciitilde hire(X)} \rangle\!\rangle$,
  where $A_2 = \{\texttt{\textasciitilde hire(X)} \prec \texttt{high\_salary(X)}, \texttt{applicant(X)}\}$.
- $\langle\!\langle A_3, \texttt{hire(X)} \rangle\!\rangle$,
  where $A_3 = \{\texttt{hire(X)} \prec \texttt{high\_salary(X)}, \texttt{applicant(X)},$
  $\texttt{good\_references(X)}\}$.
- $\langle\!\langle B_1, \texttt{suspend(X)} \rangle\!\rangle$,
  where $B_1 = \{\texttt{suspend(X)} \prec \texttt{\textasciitilde responsible(X)}\}$.
- $\langle\!\langle B_2, \texttt{suspend(X)} \rangle\!\rangle$,
  where $B_2 = \{\texttt{suspend(X)} \prec \texttt{\textasciitilde responsible(X)};$
  $\texttt{\textasciitilde responsible(X)} \prec \texttt{poor\_performance(X)}\}$.
- $\langle\!\langle B_3, \texttt{\textasciitilde suspend(X)} \rangle\!\rangle$,
  where $B_3 = \{\texttt{\textasciitilde suspend(X)} \prec \texttt{responsible(X)}\}$.
- $\langle\!\langle B_4, \texttt{\textasciitilde suspend(X)} \rangle\!\rangle$,
  where $B_4 = \{\texttt{\textasciitilde suspend(X)} \prec \texttt{responsible(X)};$
  $\texttt{responsible(X)} \prec \texttt{good\_performance(X)}\}$.
- $\langle\!\langle B_5, \texttt{\textasciitilde suspend(X)} \rangle\!\rangle$,
  where $B_5 = \{\texttt{\textasciitilde suspend(X)} \prec \texttt{responsible(X)};$
  $\texttt{responsible(X)} \prec \texttt{poor\_performance(X)}, \texttt{sick(X)}\}$.
- $\langle\!\langle B_6, \texttt{suspend(X)} \rangle\!\rangle$,
  where $B_6 = \{\texttt{suspend(X)} \prec \texttt{unruly(X)}\}$.
- $\langle\!\langle C_1, \texttt{responsible(X)} \rangle\!\rangle$,
  where $C_1 = \{\texttt{responsible(X)} \prec \texttt{good\_performance(X)}\}$.
- $\langle\!\langle C_2, \texttt{\textasciitilde responsible(X)} \rangle\!\rangle$,
  where $C_2 = \{\texttt{\textasciitilde responsible(X)} \prec \texttt{poor\_performance(X)}\}$.
- $\langle\!\langle C_3, \texttt{responsible(X)} \rangle\!\rangle$,
  where $C_3 = \{\texttt{responsible(X)} \prec \texttt{poor\_performance(X)}, \texttt{sick(X)}\}$.

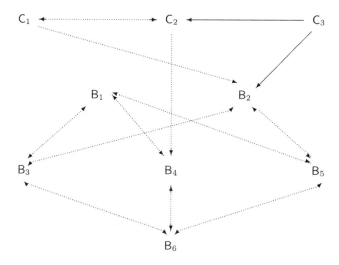

Fig. 3. Dialectical database corresponding to Example 4

and the defeat relations:

- $D_p = \{(A_3, A_2), (C_3, C_2), (C_3, B_2)\}$
- $D_b = \{(A_1, A_2), (A_2, A_1), (C_1, C_2), (C_2, C_1), (C_1, B_2), (C_2, B_4), (B_1, B_3),$
  $(B_1, B_4), (B_3, B_1), (B_4, B_1), (B_1, B_5), (B_5, B_1), (B_2, B_5), (B_5, B_2), (B_2, B_3),$
  $(B_3, B_2), (B_3, B_6), (B_6, B_3), (B_4, B_6), (B_6, B_4), (B_5, B_6), (B_6, B_5)\}.$

The relations are also depicted in figure 3, where A_1 properly defeats A_2 is indicated with an arrow from A_1 to A_2 and blocking defeat is distinguished with a dotted arrow.

3.3   Speeding Up Inference in ODeLP with Dialectical Databases

Given a ODeLP program $\mathcal{P}$, its dialectical database $\mathcal{DB}_\Delta$ can be understood as a graph from which *all* possible dialectical trees computable from $\mathcal{P}$ can be obtained. In the original ODeLP framework (as detailed in Section 2), solving a query Q wrt a given program $\mathcal{P} = \langle \Psi, \Delta \rangle$ accounted for obtaining a warranted argument $\langle \mathcal{A}, Q \rangle$. As already discussed, computing warrant involves many intermediate steps which are computationally expensive (computing arguments, detecting defeaters, building a dialectical tree, etc.).

Using the dialectical database we can speed up the inference process in ODeLP by keeping track of all possible potential arguments and the defeat relationshisp among them. Given a query Q, the extended ODeLP framework (i.e. including a dialectical database) will select first a potential argument $\langle\!\langle A, S \rangle\!\rangle$ (such that Q is a ground instance of S) that can be instantiated into $\langle \mathcal{A}, Q \rangle$, supporting Q. ¿From the D_p and D_b relationships in $\mathcal{DB}_\Delta$ the potential defeaters for $\langle\!\langle A, Q \rangle\!\rangle$ can be identified, and also instantiated.

To describe how the inference process is assisted by dialectical databases we present algorithm 1. It obtains a warrant for a query Q from a program $\mathcal{P} = \langle \Psi, \Delta \rangle$. To do this, the algorithm considers the potential arguments $\langle\!\langle A, S \rangle\!\rangle$ such that Q is an instance of S, an tries to find an instance $\langle \mathcal{B}, Q \rangle$ of $\langle\!\langle A, S \rangle\!\rangle$ that is also an argument with respect to $\mathcal{P}$, according to definition 9. This is done in function **argument** which in case such instance exists returns it in the parameter $\langle \mathcal{B}, Q \rangle$. Next, $\langle \mathcal{B}, Q \rangle$ is analyzed to see whether it is a warrant for Q. To do this, the relations D_p and D_b are used to find the defeaters of $\langle \mathcal{B}, Q \rangle$. Once the system finds an instance of the potential defeaters that is in conflict with $\langle \mathcal{B}, Q \rangle$, the function **acceptable** checks if they are arguments with respect to $\mathcal{P}$. Then the **state** function (see algorithm 2) determines the marking of these defeaters (*i.e.*, if they are marked as U-nodes or D-nodes) and finally this information is used to compute the state of $\langle \mathcal{B}, Q \rangle$.

Algorithm 1 Inference process

input: $\mathcal{P} = \langle \Psi, \Delta \rangle$, Q
output: $\langle \mathcal{B}, Q \rangle$ *(a warrant for Q, if any)*

For every $\langle\!\langle A, S \rangle\!\rangle$ in $PotArg(\Delta)$ such that argument($\langle\!\langle A, S \rangle\!\rangle$,$Q$,$\mathcal{P}$,$\langle \mathcal{B}, Q \rangle$)
   //*Looks for instances of the potential arguments that support Q*
      state := undefeated
      For every $\langle\!\langle A_2, X \rangle\!\rangle$ in $PotArg(\Delta)$ such that $(A_2, A_1) \in D_p$ or $(A_2, A_1) \in D_p$
      //*and then determines the state of their defeaters*
            For every instance $\langle \mathcal{C}, R \rangle$ of $\langle\!\langle A_2, X \rangle\!\rangle$ such that $\langle \mathcal{C}, R \rangle$ defeats $\langle \mathcal{B}, Q \rangle$
            and acceptable($\langle \mathcal{C}, R \rangle$,$\mathcal{P}$)
                  if state($\langle \mathcal{C}, R \rangle$, $\mathcal{P}$, $\emptyset$, $\{\langle \mathcal{B}, Q \rangle\}$) = undefeated
                        then state := defeated
                        //*Sets the state of the main argument according to its defeaters*
      if state = undefeated
            then return($\langle \mathcal{B}, Q \rangle$)
            //*If any of the instances remains undefeated it is a warrant*

The **state** algorithm used in the inference process takes as input an ODeLP program $\mathcal{P}$, an argument $\langle \mathcal{B}, Q \rangle$ based on it, and the *interference* and *support* argumentative lines up to this point, respectively denoted as IL and SL. Simply put, IL represents the set of arguments with an even level in the actual path of the tree under construction, and SL the arguments with an odd level. Then the **state** algorithm works like algorithm 1, analyzing the defeaters of $\mathcal{B}$ to define its state. However, one extra condition must be met: defeaters must also comply with the rules established for avoiding fallacies [14]. This test is performed by the function **valid**.

Algorithm 2 State
input: $\langle \mathcal{B}, Q \rangle$, $\mathcal{P}$, IL, SL
output:state

state := undefeated
For every pair $(\mathsf{A}_1, \mathsf{A}_2) \in D_p$ or D_b such that $\langle \mathcal{B}, Q \rangle$ is an instance of A_1
//Uses the stored defeat relation to find the defeaters of $\langle \mathcal{B}, Q \rangle$
    For every instance $\langle \mathcal{C}, S \rangle$ of A_2 such that acceptable($\langle \mathcal{C}, S \rangle$,$\mathcal{P}$) and
    valid($\langle \mathcal{C}, S \rangle$,IL,SL)
    //Then checks for every defeater whether it gives raise to fallacies.
    if $\langle \mathcal{B}, Q \rangle$ is in SL and state($\langle \mathcal{C}, S \rangle$,$\mathcal{P}$,IL,SL $\cup \{\mathcal{B}\}$) = undefeated
        then state := defeated
    if $\langle \mathcal{B}, Q \rangle$ is in IL and state($\langle \mathcal{C}, S \rangle$,$\mathcal{P}$,IL $\cup \{\mathcal{B}\}$,SL) = undefeated
        then state := defeated
    //The recursive call does the same for the defeaters of $\langle \mathcal{C}, S \rangle$
return(state)

To conclude, figure 4 summarizes the main elements of the ODeLP-based agent architecture. The agent's knowledge is represented by an ODeLP program $\mathcal{P}$. Perceptions from the environment result in changes in the set of observations in $\mathcal{P}$, handled by an appropriate updating mechanism as discussed previously. In order to solve queries from other agents, the agent relies on the ODeLP inference engine. Queries are speeded up by first searching on the potential arguments stored in the dialectical database, applying the algorithms discussed before. The final answer to a given query will be *yes*, *no* or *undecided*, according to the warrant status of the query with respect to $\mathcal{P}$.

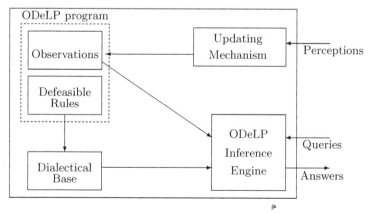

Fig. 4. Agent architecture using ODeLP as underlying framework

4   A Worked Example

In this section we present a toy example to illustrate the use of a dialectical database to speed up inference in ODeLP. Let us consider the program $\mathcal{P}$ in Example 1 as an agent's knowledge to model the status of different employees in a company. The associated dialectical database $\mathcal{DB}_\Delta$ is shown in Example 4.

Suppose that the agent has to decide whether John should be suspended or not, considering the query suspend(john). As shown in Example 2, solving this query wrt $\mathcal{P}$ involved a dialectical tree with three arguments (see Figure 2). Let us analyze now how the agent would proceed to perform the same inference using the dialectical database $\mathcal{DB}_\Delta$. Following Algorithm 1, the potential argument $\langle\!\langle B_2, Q \rangle\!\rangle$ will be instantiated resulting in the argument $\langle \mathcal{A}, Q \rangle$, with

$\mathcal{A} = \{\sim$suspend(john) $\prec$ responsible(john);
  responsible(john) $\prec$ poor_performance(john),sick(john)$\}$

From the dialectical database $\mathcal{DB}_\Delta$ it follows that $\langle\!\langle B_2, Q \rangle\!\rangle$ has defeaters $\langle\!\langle B_3, Q_3 \rangle\!\rangle$ and $\langle\!\langle B_5, Q_5 \rangle\!\rangle$ (see the list of pairs in D_b in Example 4), which are respectively instantiated to $\langle \mathcal{B}, \sim suspend(john) \rangle$ and $\langle \mathcal{C}, responsible(john) \rangle$, with:

$\mathcal{B} = \{\sim$suspend(john) $\prec$ responsible(john);
  responsible(john) $\prec$ poor_performance(john),sick(john)

$\mathcal{C} = \{$responsible(john) $\prec$ poor_performance(john),sick(john)$\}$

Note that from the information in $\mathcal{DB}_\Delta$ associated with $\langle\!\langle B_3, Q_3 \rangle\!\rangle$ and $\langle\!\langle B_5, Q_5 \rangle\!\rangle$ there are no more pairs in D_p or D_b to consider (i.e, there are no more links in the graph to new defeaters for these potential arguments that can be instanciated to defeat $\mathcal{B}$ or $\mathcal{C}$). As a consequence, a dialectical tree identical to the one shown in Figure 2 has been computed on the basis of the potential arguments present in the dialectical database and their associated defeat relationships. There are no more possible potential arguments supporting suspend(john). Therefore there is no warrant for suspend(john).

Consider now a different situation for the same sample program $\mathcal{P}$. Suppose that the facts applicant(susan) and high_salary(susan) are added as new observations to Ψ. In order to solve the query ~hire(susan) wrt to $\mathcal{P}$ the same dialectical database $\mathcal{DB}_\Delta$ can be used but relying on different potential arguments as those used above. Now other instances can be obtained relying on the new perceived facts. In this case, the potential argument $\langle\!\langle A_2, Q_2 \rangle\!\rangle$ is instantiated to $\langle \mathcal{D}, \sim hire(susan) \rangle$, with

$\mathcal{D} = \{\sim$hire(susan) $\prec$ high_salary(susan), applicant(susan)$\}$

From the information available in $\mathcal{DB}_\Delta$ a defeater for $\langle\!\langle A_2, Q_2 \rangle\!\rangle$ is detected, namely $\langle\!\langle A_1, Q_1 \rangle\!\rangle$. However there is no argument which can be obtained as an instance of $\langle\!\langle A_1, Q_1 \rangle\!\rangle$ wrt the current set Ψ, and hence there is no defeater for $\langle \mathcal{D}, \sim hire(susan) \rangle$. Therefore ~hire(susan) is warranted (as it is supported by an argument $\langle \mathcal{D}, \sim hire(susan) \rangle$ with no defeaters).

The applicant Susan may ask now for a lower salary, given that she wants to get the job. This results in a new perception for the agent, updating Ψ by adding ~`high_salary(susan)` and consequently removing `high_salary(susan)`. As in the previous situations, no change is performed on the existing dialectical database. Nevertheless, the set of beliefs of the agent changes: ~`hire(susan)` is no longer believed, since no argument supporting ~`hire(susan)` can be built as an instance of a potential argument in $\mathcal{DB}_\Delta$. On the contrary, `hire(susan)` is now in the set of beliefs as it is warranted by a tree with a single node: argument $\mathcal{E} = \{$`hire(susan)` $\prec$ ~`high_salary(susan)`, `applicant(susan)`$\}$.

5   Conclusions and Future Work

Solid theoretical foundations for agent design should be based on proper formalisms for knowledge representation and reasoning [19]. Thus, we have defined a framework for representing knowledge and beliefs of agents in dynamic environments, where new perceptions can modify the agent's view about its world.

To comply with real time issues when modeling agent interaction in a MAS setting we have proposed the notion of dialectical databases. We have discussed the main issues in the integration of this component into ODeLP, such as building the dialectical database, adapting the specificity criterion for potential arguments and modifying the inference process to take advantage of the new component. Based on this, we can affirm that the use of precompiled knowledge can improve the performance of argument-based systems in the same way Truth Maintenance Systems assist general problem solvers. We believe that this technique can also be applied to other argumentative frameworks, allowing its use in a new set of applications.

Part of our current work involves extending the analysis of ODeLP properties presented in [14] in the context of multiagent systems. We are also working on a complexity analisis of ODeLP that considers the construction and use of dialectical databases, and confirms the results obtained empirically.

Acknowledgements

This research was partially supported by Projects TIC2001-1577-C03-01 and TIC2003-00950, by Ramón y Cajal Program (*Ministerio de Ciencia y Tecnología*, Spain), by CONICET (Argentina), by CIC (Argentina), by the *Secretaría General de Ciencia y Tecnología de la Universidad Nacional del Sur* and by *Agencia Nacional de Promoción Científica y Tecnológica* (PICT 2002 No. 13096). The authors would like to thank anonymous reviewers for providing helpful comments to improve the final version of this paper.

References

1. Wooldridge., M.J.: Introduction to Multiagent Systems. John Wiley and Sons (2002)

2. Chesñevar, C.I., Maguitman, A., Loui, R.: Logical Models of Argument. ACM Computing Surveys **32** (2000) 337–383

3. Prakken, H., Vreeswijk, G.: Logical systems for defeasible argumentation. In Gabbay, D., ed.: Handbook of Philosophical Logic. Volume 4. Kluwer Academic Publisher (2002) 219–318

4. Gelfond, M., Lifschitz, V.: Classical negation in logic programs and disjunctive databases. New Generation Computing (1991) 365–385

5. García, A., Simari, G.: Defeasible Logic Programming: An Argumentative Approach. Theory and Practice of Logic Programming **4** (2004) 95–138

6. Chesñevar, C., Simari, G., Alsinet, T., Godo, L.: A logic programming framework for possibilistic argumentation with vague knowledge. In: Proc. of Uncertainty in Artificial Intelligence Conference (UAI 2004), Banff, Canada (to appear). (2004)

7. Gomez, S., Chesñevar, C.: A Hybrid Approach to Pattern Classification Using Neural Networks and Defeasible Argumentation. In: Proc. of Intl. 17th FLAIRS Conference. Palm Beach, FL, USA, AAAI (2004) 393–398

8. Chesñevar, C., Maguitman, A.:ARGUENET: An Argument-Based Recommender System for Solving Web Search Queries. In: Proc. of Intl. IEEE Conference on Intelligent Systems IS-2004. Varna, Bulgaria (to appear). (2004)

9. Chesñevar, C., Maguitman, A.: An argumentative approach to assesing natural language usage based on the web corpus. In: Proc. of European Conference on Artificial Intelligence (ECAI 2004). Valencia, Spain (to appear), ECCAI (2004)

10. Pollock, J.L.: Taking Perception Seriously. In: Proceedings of the 1st International Conference on Autonomous Agents. (1997) 526–527

11. Simari, G.R., Loui, R.P.: A Mathematical Treatment of Defeasible Reasoning and its Implementation. Artificial Intelligence **53** (1992) 125–157

12. Prakken, H., Sartor, G.: Argument-based extended logic programming with defeasible priorities. Journal of Applied Non-classical Logics **7** (1997) 25–752

13. Poole, D.L.: On the Comparison of Theories: Preferring the Most Specific Explanation. In: Proceedings of the Ninth International Joint Conference on Artificial Intelligence, IJCAI (1985) 144–147

14. Capobianco, M.: Argumentación rebatible en entornos dinámicos. PhD thesis, Universidad Nacional del Sur, Bahía Blanca, Argentina (2003)

15. Simari, G.R., Chesñevar, C.I., García, A.J.: The Role of Dialectics in Defeasible Argumentation. In: Proceedings of the XIV Conferencia Internacional de la Sociedad Chilena para Ciencias de la Computación. (1994) 111–121 http://cs.uns.edu.ar/giia.html.

16. Alferes, J.J., Pereira, L.M.: On logic program semantics with two kinds of negation. In: Proceedings of Joint International Conference and Symposium on Logic Programm, Washington, USA (1992) 574–588

17. Katsuno, H., Mendelzon, A.: On the difference between updating a knowledge base and revising it. In P.Gardenfors, ed.: Belief Revision. Cambridge University Press (1992) 183–203

18. Doyle, J.: A Truth Maintenance System. Artificial Intelligence **12** (1979) 231–272

19. Baral, C., Gelfond, M.: Reasoning Agents in Dynamic Domains. In Minker, J., ed.: Workshop on Logic-Based Artificial Intelligence, College Park, Maryland, Computer Science Department, University of Maryland (1999)

Argumentation in Bayesian Belief Networks

Gerard A.W. Vreeswijk

Utrecht University, Dept. of Computer Science, The Netherlands
gv@cs.uu.nl

Abstract. This paper establishes an explicit connection between formal argumentation and Bayesian inference by introducing a notion of argument and a notion of defeat among arguments in Bayesian networks.

First, the two approaches are compared and it is argued that argumentation in Bayesian belief networks is a typical multi-agent affair.

Since in theories of formal argumentation the so-called admissibility semantics is an important criterion of argument validity, this paper finally proposes an algorithm to decide efficiently whether a particular node is supported by an admissible argument. The proposed algorithm is then slightly extended to an algorithm that returns the top-k of strongest admissible arguments at each node. This extension is particularly interesting from a Bayesian inference point of view, because it offers a computationally tractable alternative to the NP^{PP}-complete decision problem k-MPE (finding the top-k most probable explanations in a Bayesian network).

1 Introduction

Bayesian inference and formal argumentation are two important forms of reasoning. Both address the problem of how to reason with uncertain information, and both have developed into major and mature research disciplines. Bayesian inference and argumentation also have strong application areas. Argumentation is slightly biased towards legal applications and Bayesian inference has a tendency towards applications in the medical domain.

Both disciplines share a common goal, but they start from different research hypotheses. The most famous technical difference is that Bayesian inference assumes the availability of a large number of numerical probabilities, while argumentation assumes the opposite, namely, that information on rules and evidence is scarce and qualitative. Besides the technical differences, there is also some sort of cultural gap. On the one hand, proponents of argument systems indicate that realistic problems are often under-specified and ill-formulated. For such problems almost all information is expressed in qualitative terms—provided such information is available at all. Accordingly, proponents of formal argumentation systems argue that argument systems are the best logical means to cope with such problems. On the other hand, proponents of probabilistic reasoning often emphasize that Bayesian inference is the only mathematically correct way to reason with

I. Rahwan et al. (Eds.): ArgMAS 2004, LNAI 3366, pp. 111–129, 2005.

uncertain information. Of course both camps are right, it is just that they start from different principles.

Several initiatives have been undertaken to combine Bayesian inference and argumentation [6, 7, 10, 17, 25]. Some of these initiatives use Pearl's probabilistic propagation algorithm as the fundamental notion of support. Other approaches such as [17] propose argumentation features *on top* of Bayesian networks. Finally, there is a recent paper in which an attempt is made to combine Toulmin's argument structures with Bayesian belief networks [1, 20]. However, as far as I know no attempt has been made to import dialectic notions to Bayesian networks, and run true argumentation algorithms on them. This is not done yet, perhaps because argumentation often thwarts probability.

In this paper I try to bridge a part of the gap rather than trying to extend existing formalisms. This means that there is no new theory but rather a proposal to look at Bayesian belief networks from the perspective of argumentation. More specifically, I propose an algorithm that enables users to start an argumentation process within the context of an existing Bayesian belief network. The algorithm possesses a component that is responsible for finding arguments and a component that is responsible for comparing and selecting among the various competing arguments it finds. The corresponding computer program is able to read input files of existing BBN tools (such as Genie) and argue with them in a sensible way.

With the help of the algorithm, I illustrate how one can argue according to conventional argumentation concepts in a Bayesian network, and still be faithful to fundamental probabilistic and dialectic principles.

The algorithm proposed is not a solution to the problem how to translate a defeasible knowledge base into a Bayesian belief network. This is the other direction and will not be discussed here. This paper takes care of the "easy" half of the translation.

The rest of the paper is organized as follows. First some relevant aspects of Bayesian inference and argumentation are reviewed, partially with the help of a simple running example. Then notions of argument and defeat are proposed that have meaning in the context of Bayesian belief networks. Finally, these notions are applied in an algorithm. This algorithm is demonstrated with the help of the earlier example.

2   Bayesian Inference

Bayesian inference is a complex area. This section does not aim to cover this area but discusses only those issues that are relevant here.

Bayesian inference is reasoning within a Bayesian belief network. A Bayesian belief network (BBN) is a finite and directed acyclic graph (DAG) where nodes represent random variables and edges represent probabilistic dependencies among those variables. Most Bayesian belief networks are discrete, in the sense that all random variables can assume only a finite number of states.

2.1   An Example Network

Some of the ideas presented in this paper can best be presented with the help of an example. I have chosen to use a Bayesian network that is made by Gerardina Hernandez in a class homework exercise at the University of Pittsburgh. This network is meant to assess the credit worthiness of an individual (Fig. 2.1). The network is for demonstrational purposes only and is unlikely to be used in real credit assessments. (At least in its present form.)

Fig. 2.1 does not display a general BBN, but a specific case in which there is evidence on Assets, Profession, and Age (bold nodes in the figure). Thus, for this situation we might imagine an applicant of which we only know that his (or her) assets are on the average, that he has a medium-income profession, and that he is aged 28. The dashed node indicates a so-called query node. A query node is simply a node that we are interested in. Here, the query node indicates that we are interested in the credit worthiness of this particular applicant, based on the evidence that we have at hand.

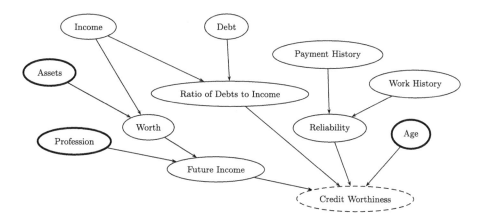

Fig. 1. A sample Bayesian belief network: loan assessment

In other cases, i.e., with other applicants, the evidence may be with other nodes. Sometimes, evidence is complete, in the sense that all prior (i.e., non-conditional) probabilities are overridden by evidence. A simple example of complete evidence is when all leaf nodes are clamped to a particular state. But evidence can also be placed at internal nodes in the network. To exclude trivial cases it is often assumed the set of evidence nodes and the set of query nodes are disjoint.

2.2   Conditional Probability Tables

Probabilistic dependencies among variables is encoded in so-called *conditional probability tables* (CPTs). Each node possesses such a CPT. The CPT of leaf

Table 1. Conditional probability table for future income in decision tree format

High:	Medium:	Low:
High income:	High income:	High income:
Promising: 0.99	Promising: 0.85	Promising: 0.8
Not promising: 0.01	Not promising: 0.15	Not promising: 0.2
Low income:	Low income:	Low income:
Promising: 0.6	Promising: 0.4	Promising: 0.01
Not promising: 0.4	Not promising: 0.6	Not promising: 0.99
Medium income:	Medium income:	Medium income:
Promising: 0.8	Promising: 0.6	Promising: 0.4
Not promising: 0.2	Not promising: 0.4	Not promising: 0.6

nodes are in fact ordinary probability tables (PTs), since such tables encode prior probabilities.

To save space, it is convenient to represent a CPT in a decision tree format (Table 1). In this table, future income can take one of two values: "promising" and "not promising". These two values depend on parent nodes "profession," which takes values "high income," "low income," and "medium income", and "worth" which assumes values "high," "medium," and "low". From the last entry, for instance, we can read that

$$P(\text{ Future income} = \text{Promising} \mid$$
$$\text{Worth} = \text{Low} \wedge \text{Profession} = \text{Medium Income }) = 0.4$$

While CPTs are responsible for representing explicit conditional dependencies, the topology of a BBN itself represents a number of conditional *independencies*. One of the consequences of this assumption is that the so-called *joint probabilitiy* of all nodes of a BBN can easily be computed by means of the formula

$$P(x_1, \ldots, x_n) = \Pi_{i=1}^{n} P(x_i \mid \pi(x_i)) \tag{1}$$

where $x_1, \ldots, x_n$ are all nodes of the network in topological order, and where $\pi(x_i)$ are the parents of node x_i.

Although (1) is a well-known and basic result in BBN-theory, the joint probability is generally considered uninteresting, because it chops the probability space into the useless little pieces. For example, to compute $P(x_1)$ in a network with five nodes that each have two states (e.g., true and false), we have to add $2^5/2 = 2^4 = 16$ probabilities, which is a computationally intensive task, at least in the general case. There are algorithms to tackle this task, however, such as the variable elimination algorithm [24].

The reason why joint probabilities are mentioned nevertheless is that they play an important role in the definition of argument strength when arguments are formed in BBNs.

2.3   Evidence Nodes and Query Nodes

In a nutshell, evidence is where reasoning begins and query nodes is where reasoning ends. Evidence is the ultimate stopping place–the things that we think we know, while the query nodes are one or more nodes that we are interested in and from which we want to know their probabilities.

In probabilistic reasoning, a random variable is considered evidence if we know its state. In argumentation, a proposition is considered evidence if it is true. In an argumentation context, evidence is often indicated as a "set of current facts," a "base set" or a "knowledge base".

Thus, each BBN possesses the following node classification.

1. A set of of evidence nodes E. These are nodes that are clamped to a particular state.
2. A set of query nodes X. Often, $|X| = 1$.
3. A set of leaf nodes with a priori probabilities.
4. A set of internal nodes of which the probabilities depend on the node's CPT and the node's parents.

This classification is important because Algorithm 1 below is based on it.

2.4   Bayesian Inference

A recurring task in BBNs is to compute the probability of a collection of query nodes X, given the probabilities that are encoded in the the network by means of CPTs, and given exact values of some observed evidence variables E. The aim of this section is give a brief overview of the complexity of this task.

There are two types of BNN inference tasks: belief updating and belief revision [8]. Many belief updating algorithms can be used for belief revision with just minor modifications, and vice versa.

Belief updating is also called probabilistic inference, or PR. The objective of PR is to compute $P(X|E)$, that is, the posterior probability of query nodes X given evidence E. A simple form of it results when X is a single node. PR typically involves a marginalization operation over query nodes.

The task of belief revision amounts to finding the most probable configuration of some hypothesis variables X, given evidence E. The resulting output is an optimal list of instantiations of X. Almost always $X \cap E = \emptyset$, and in this case the problem is known as computing the Most Probable Explanation, or MPE. A variant of MPE, known as k-MPE, is finding the top-k highest explanations [11]. In the cases when X is a proper subset of all non-evidence nodes, the task is called finding the Maximum a Posteriori Hypothesis, or MAP [3, 11, 18].

Computing PR, MPE and MAP are all NP-hard [3]. However, they still belong to different complexity classes. MPE is a combinatorial optimization problem of which its decision version is NP-complete. PR is harder. It is a counting problem and its complexity is #P-complete [11]. Its decision version is PP-complete. MAP combines both counting and optimization and it is NP^{PP}-complete.

Several algorithms have been proposed to compute the posterior probabilities of query nodes. In the light of the above discussion it should come as no surprise that these algorithms are intrinsically complex. The proposed algorithms have no problems with trees and collections of trees (called polytrees) but if the underlying graph contains multiple paths then some tricks have to be pulled of in order to be able to apply the original algorithm. One of the first Bayesian inference algorithms is Pearl's message passing algorithm [8, 12]. Today, the most commercial tools (such as Genie or Hugin) work with Spiegelhalter junction tree algorithm [4, 9]. For educational purposes the so-called variable elimination method is often used [24].

3   Argumentation

As opposed to Bayesian network theory, the research paradigm of argumentation is less clearly defined. There exist various theories of argumentation and various semantics to interpret a constellation of competing arguments [2, 16].

Nonetheless, a generally accepted view on formal argumentation is Phan Minh Dung's notion of an argument system [5]. Dung's system is an abstract framework that is often used as a stepping stone to define more elaborate systems of argumentation. On the other hand, it is general enough to function as a common divisor of different views on argumentation.

Definition 1 (Argument system, after Dung). *An* argument system *is a directed graph in which the nodes represent arguments, and the arcs between the nodes represent an attack relation among arguments. If a and b are two arguments and $a \leftarrow b$, we say that a is attacked by b.*

Note that the definition says nothing about finiteness of the graph and the absence of cycles or loops (1-cycles).

To design a full-blown argument system, it suffices to specify what an argument looks like and when one argument attacks another argument. Once these two concepts are defined, the argumentation system is defined in its entirety. (We will actually do that in Sec. 5.)

On a more abstract level, Dung's argument system leaves open which arguments we consider valid. (Recall from above that argumentation does not possess a uniform semantics.) One popular and generally accepted notion of argument validity is that of *admissibility*. A set of arguments A is called *admissible* if it satisfies two conditions:

1. *Consistency.* No two arguments in A attack each other.
2. *Self-defence.* Every attacker of an argument in A is attacked itself by an argument in A.

Further, an argument is admissible if it is in at least one admissible set. In this way, an admissible argument might be seen as an argument that belongs to a consistent and complete (read: self-defending) world-view (read: constellation of admissible arguments).[1] Another view on admissibility is to see it as victory in the competition with other arguments.

Currently, admissibility is the state-of-the-art semantics in theories of formal argumentation.

3.1   An Algorithm to Decide Admissibility

Since the purpose of this work is to present an algorithm to argue in a Bayesian network, I will conclude this section by indicating how a set of admissible arguments can be computed. This information will be used when we define an argumentation algorithm for Bayesian networks.

An algorithm to decide whether an argument a is admissible is relatively simple. It comes down to maintaining a list of arguments L, initially equal to $[a]$, together with an index $1 \leq i \leq \text{length}(L)$, initially set to 0, that indicates up to which index arguments in L are defended by other arguments in L. If a is admissible, then an admissible set can be constructed around a recursively. The algorithm can with one or two modifications in the code (i.e., extremely easily) be cast into a dialectic form, with PRO defending the main thesis and CON trying to hinder PRO's attempt to establish the main thesis [22].

For Dung-type argument systems in which the underlying graph is a-cyclic (most if not all practical systems), the situation is somewhat simpler.

Definition 2 (Defeat). *In a-cyclic and finite argument systems, an argument is* defeated *if it is attacked by an undefeated argument. An argument is* undefeated *if it is not defeated.*

Note that this definition only makes sense in a sub-class of Dung-type argument systems, viz. those argument systems that are a-cyclic and finite.

Since it follows from this definition that arguments without attackers are undefeated, Def. 2 can easily be translated into a simple recursive algorithm. Further, it is a well-known result in the theory of nonmonotonic reasoning and formal argumentation that various different semantics (such as admissibility) reduce to Def. 2 in case the attack graph is a-cyclic. Since BBNs are a-cyclic this is a strong indication for the fact that BBN-type argument systems are a-cyclic (we still have to verify this, of course). Therefore it is reasonable to expect on the basis of the above observations that admissibility in a BBN-type argument systems boils down to Def. 2.

4   Differences

This section lists a number of differences between Bayesian inference and argumentation. Since the two approaches are technically as well as culturally rather

---

[1] Actually, there exist two versions of admissibility. viz. credulous and skeptical admissibility. An argument is credulously admissible iff it is contained in at least one admissible set. An argument is skeptically admissible iff it is contained in all admissible sets.

different, there are of course a lot of differences to be mentioned. Therefore, this listing is not meant to be exhaustive but instead tries to highlight the differences that are relevant to the algorithm that is going to be proposed.

The most important difference in the light of the forthcoming argumentation algorithm is that BBNs are, what I call, *antecedent-complete* (AC). This means that all evidence for and against every network variable is present in the CPT of the parents of that variable. (Note the words "all" and "every".) Thus, if for example $P(\neg A|\neg B, C)$ is known, then antecedent-completeness guarantees that $P(\neg A|B, C)$, or $P(A|\neg B, C)$ are also known. AC has even more impact if nodes have more than two states (as in the example is the case).

Antecedent-completeness lies at the root of many differences between the two approaches. First, their is the phenomenon of synergy and anti-synergy among parent nodes. There is synergy among two nodes if we can deduce from the knowledge representation that they reinforce each other's support of the child node. For example, two independent witness testimonies typically reinforce the support of the claim that they underpin. Similarly, there is anti-synergy among two nodes if we can deduce from the knowledge representation that they weaken each other's support of the child node. For example, drug A may be a good medication to disease D, drug B may be a good medication to disease D, but their combination may be a less favorable medication to disease D. The fact that BBNs are complete in their antecedents makes them deal correctly with synergy and anti-synergy among parent nodes [12]. This phenomenon is less well mastered in argumentation, where it is called accrual of reasons, or accrual of arguments [15, 21]. There, the question is whether, or under what conditions, reasons should accrue, and if there are general principles behind the accrual of reasons. I maintain that accrual of reasons cannot be modelled in argumentation, because rule bases of argumentation systems are typically antecedent-*in*complete and therefore contain insufficient information as to decide whether there should be synergy or anti-synergy among rules that share consequents.

Another relevant difference between the two approaches is that they have a different view on dealing with new information. A major goal of Bayesian inference is to recompute the probability of all query nodes if evidence is entered into the network. This is a holistic goal, without interest for identifying connections within the network that span multiple nodes. At least Bayesian inference is not interested in explicating such connections. Argumentation, on the other hand, *is* interested in making such connections explicit. The approach of argumentation is to build a case, a "train of reasoning" in support of a claim. This case will do until someone else with other interests builds a case to the contrary.

The latter brings us to another important difference. Within BBNs all evidence is present before an inference is performed. With argumentation, evidence is often produced or retrieved on demand during the argumentation process.

Finally, Bayesian inference often is a one-agent affair. Argumentation, on the other hand, is best performed in a dialogical setting. Arguments are formed not because new evidence comes in (information push) but because parties that have interest in forming arguments on pain of losing their position in a dispute (information pull).

In conventional argument systems, the question is whether a propositions is defensible, so that a dispute more or less automatically involves two parties, viz. one agent that is trying to defend a claim, and one agent that is trying to punch holes in the defence. In Bayesian networks the situation is somewhat different. There, random variables typically have more than two states so that a scenario is thinkable in which every state (of the same node) is defended by a different agent. Agents do not have to be probabilistically omniscient. CPTs and variables can easily be synchronized along with the queries and query-updates that are sent. In some way this distribution of tasks seems to be remarkably natural, and thus it appears as if argumentation in BBNs is more amenable to multi-agent processing.

5   Argumentation in a Bayesian Belief Network

In this section we will try to interpret elements of BBNs in argumentation-theoretic terms, so as to be able to run an argumentation algorithm on a BBN.

5.1   Arguments

To start with, the CPTs of a BBN contain information that must somehow be reflected in a corresponding argumentation system. Conversely, an argumentation system assumes at the very least a set of rules of inference, because with rules of inference arguments can be formed. A rule of inference can have different forms [13, 14, 16, 19] but with some imagination, the CPTs of the above Bayesian network can be translated into the rule-base and evidence that is displayed in Fig. 2. In this translation, a priori nodes are represented as rules to distinguish them from evidence.

Rule-base = {

$$\text{Income(s0-30000)} \leftarrow(0.33)- \text{a-priori}$$
$$\text{Income(s30001-70000)} \leftarrow(0.33)- \text{a-priori}$$
$$\text{Income(s70001-more)} \leftarrow(0.33)- \text{a-priori}$$
$$\text{Debt(a0-11100)} \leftarrow(0.33)- \text{a-priori}$$
$$\cdots$$
$$\text{Ratio(favorable)} \leftarrow(0.5)- \text{Income(s0-30000)} \wedge \text{Debt(a0-11100)}$$
$$\text{Ratio(favorable)} \leftarrow(0.001)- \text{Income(s0-30000)} \wedge \text{Debt(a11101-25900)}$$
$$\cdots$$
$$\text{Ratio(unfavorable)} \leftarrow(0.9)- \text{Income(s30001-70000)} \wedge \text{Debt(a25901-up)}$$
$$\cdots$$
$$\text{Worthiness(positive)} \leftarrow(0.9)- \text{Reliability(reliable)} \wedge \text{Ratio(favorable)} \wedge$$
$$\text{FutureIncome(promising)} \wedge \text{Age(a16-21)} \}$$

Evidence = { Assets(average), Profession(Medium-income-profession), Age(a16-21)}

Fig. 2. Rule-base and evidence corresponding to the loan assessment example

The translation from CPTs to a rule base is conceptually simple and is in fact performed by a small script that rips the CPTs according to the convention that conditional probabilities in XDSL are enumerated such that the rightmost index of the parent state vector runs fastest.

A next step towards argumentation is to chain rules into arguments. In this way, arguments become trees of rules such that roots of trees are query nodes and leaves of trees are evidence or else coincide with the leaves of the network. For example, an argument for the creditworthiness of this particular applicant is

CreditWorthiness(positive) ←(0.80)–
    Reliability(reliable) ←(0.99)–
        PaymentHistory(excellent) ←(0.25)– a-priori
        WorkHistory(stable) ←(0.25)– a-priori
    RatioDebInc(favorable) ←(0.80)–
        Debt(a0-11100) ←(0.33)– a-priori
        Income(s30001-70000) ←(0.33)– a-priori
    FutureIncome(not-promising) ←(0.60)–
        Worth(low) ←(0.70)–
            Income(s0-30000) ←(0.33)– a-priori
        Assets(average)
        Profession(Medium-income-profession)
    Age(a22-65)

Numbers indicate conditional probabilities, taken directly from a BBN's CPTs. Evidence, such as "Assets(average)" is incorporated as unconditional premises of an argument. Similarly, other arguments may be constructed.

The next definition is needed for Def. 4 [attack].

Definition 3 (Sub-argument). *We say that argument a' is a* sub-argument *of argument a if a' is a sub-tree of a such that all leaves of a' are leaves of a.*

One way of looking at sub-arguments is to see them as snapshots of earlier phases in the creation of arguments bottom-up. In particular all premises of an argument a are sub-arguments of a.

5.2   Attack

What remains to be done to obtain a full-fledged argument system, is to define an attack relation between pairs of arguments. To this end, I choose to define the notion of attack on the basis of two notions that are more elementary and (therefore) fall beyond the scope of a Dung-type argument system, viz. the notion of *counterargument* and the notion of *strength* of an argument. First I will discuss counter-arguments, and then I will discuss argument strength.

A Definition of Counter-Argument. In argumentation, the idea is that counter-arguments deny the conclusion of the argument they oppose. In this case, any argument that ends in "¬CreditWorthiness(positive)" would be a counter-argument for the above argument for "CreditWorthiness(positive)". Since nodes

in a BBN are not negated, this is not possible. However, nodes do have different states so we might consider every argument for "CreditWorthiness(x)" with
$x \neq$ "positive" as an argument against "CreditWorthiness(positive)".

A Definition of Argument Strength. Sometimes, argumentation is described
as "making your case," and this is precisely what happens when one constructs
an argument. Thus, an argument might be seen as a description of a concrete
case.

To assess the strength of an argument, we will have to look at the likelihood
of the entire case supporting the claim in question. This is the joint probability
of all argument nodes, except the conclusion. The conclusion is excluded because
the degree of belief of the conclusion (the joint probability of the entire argument,
including the conclusion) may be close to zero, which indicates a strong argument
against that conclusion. Such an argument is of informational use only (e.g., can
be presented to the user) and will in particular not play a role as a counter-
argument in the further defeat among arguments, as such an argument will
most likely not be selected as sub-arguments of larger arguments.

In the case that is made in support of "CreditWorthiness(positive)" (cf. the
above argument), we end up with a support of 0.00076. This seems to be a dispro-
portional small number. However, the strength of an argument is the probability
that the entire case as described by the argument by means of variable instantiation, is realized. This probability is often very small indeed. But since all
arguments by definition model specific cases, the competition among arguments
remains fair.

A Definition of Attack. On the basis of the notions of counter-argument and
argument strength, it is now possible to define a binary attack relation among
arguments. The definition that we are going to give is common in the literature
of defeasible argumentation [2, 16].

Definition 4 (Attack). *We say that argument a is* attacked *by argument b,
written $a \leftarrow b$, if it satisfies the following two conditions:*

1. *Argument b is a counterargument of a sub-argument a' of a.*
2. *Argument b is stronger than argument a'.*

The present notion of attack is defined in terms of counter-argument and
argument strength and can thus be implemented in an algorithm.

5.3   Towards an Algorithm

This section discusses the ideas behind the algorithm and utilizes the result that
admissibility reduces to defeat in BBN-type argument systems (Sec. 3).

In Sec. 3 it was indicated that there exists a simple algorithm to decide
whether an argument is admissible. This suggests that a subroutine to enumerate all arguments for a particular conclusion (preferably in descending order of
strength) would suffice to conduct an argumentation process in Bayesian belief

networks. With such a subroutine all arguments and all attackers of all arguments can be found and, once found, conveyed to the algorithm that computes admissible sets. From an argumentation-theoretic point of view, this would be the most logical approach.

The problem with an alternating approach, however, is that such an approach turns out to be extremely wasteful, because BBNs are antecedent-complete (Sec. 4). Antecedent-complete rule-sets make it pointless to search arguments and counter-arguments in separate processes. An approach that better respects the antecedent-completeness of BBNs is to combine the search for arguments and counter-arguments, rather than to conduct search in separate processes. In non-Bayesian argumentation scenario's the latter approach would be intuitive and defensible, but here it is a waste of resources.

The following proposition utilizes the fact that BBNs are a-cyclic and shows that searching for arguments and counter-arguments in parallel still yields admissible arguments. Hence the simpler criterion of Def. 2 can be applied safely.

Proposition 1. *In BBN-type argument systems, an argument a is admissible if and only if*

1. *All immediate sub-arguments of a (i.e., all top-subarguments of a) are undefeated.*
2. *Argument a is the strongest argument for its conclusion node (modulo states) such that (1) holds.*

Proof. First we prove that BBN-type argument systems are are finite and a-cyclic. Finiteness follows from the finiteness of the corresponding BBN. Suppose that there exists an argument system with a cycle $a_1 \leftarrow a_2 \leftarrow \ldots a_n \leftarrow a_1$. If this were the case, then $a_1 \leq a_1' < a_2 \leq a_2' < \ldots < a_n \leq a_{n-1}' < a_1$, where a_i' are the sub-arguments of a_i that are countered by a_{i+1} "$<$" and means "stronger than". This clearly is impossible. The upshot is that we may change the word "admissible" by the word "undefeated," since BBNs are finite and a-cyclic, and from Def. 4 it then follows that argument systems derived from BBNs are finite and a-cyclic.

To prove the proposition, first suppose a is undefeated. We will have to prove that it (1) and (2) hold. To prove the first condition, suppose a' is an immediate sub-argument of an undefeated argument a. [We use a reductio ad absurdum argument because defeat is defined in terms of the existence of defeating arguments.] If a' were defeated, there would be an undefeated argument b against a sub-argument a'' of a'. But in this case b would be a defeater of a as well, which contradicts our earlier assumption. The claim for non-immediate sub-arguments now follows with a simple induction argument. To prove the second condition, suppose that b would be an argument that satisfies (1) but is stronger than a. Then b would fulfill all conditions of being an attacker. Further, since all sub-arguments of b are undefeated, and b is the strongest argument for the conclusion of a (modulo states), b is undefeated. But this would mean that a is defeated by b, which contradicts our earlier assumption.

Conversely, suppose that a is an argument satisfying (1) and (2). We will have to prove that a is undefeated. To this end, let us assume the contrary. Since we may assume that all sub-arguments of a are undefeated by induction, a's defeater must be a counter-argument of a itself. This would imply that this defeater is stronger than a (modulo states). But this would contradict (2).   □

The proposition ensures that searching admissible arguments in a BBN amounts to searching for arguments and counter-arguments in parallel, and then simply selecting the strongest argument found.

6   Algorithm

This section explains the algorithm, and finally the algorithm is listed in pseudo-code.

The routine is called recursively at line 4. In order to form the Cartesian product of all sub-arguments, all $A_1, \ldots, A_p$ must be known before the iteration can start at line 6. This implies a considerable memory-overhead. On the other hand, the iteration itself can be executed in an on-demand fashion by means of lazy evaluation. This is what actually has been done in the implementation.

The original algorithm is obtained if $k = 1$ (Alg. 1, line 12). In fact, the algorithm then performs a so-called beam search with beam width $k = 1$. An interesting variation on the original algorithm is obtained if $k > 1$. In that case, the k strongest arguments for each node survive and may act as sub-arguments of possibly larger arguments. The thus obtained variant is an interesting alternative problem statement to the k-MPE problem of finding the top-k most probable explanations in a Bayesian network, because the corresponding decision problem is known to be NP^{PP}-complete [3, 8].

In this context, it is interesting to determine the time complexity of our argumentation algorithm. We will now do this.

Proposition 2. *The time complexity of Algorithm 1 is $\mathcal{O}(nsk^p)$.*

Proof. First, choose a fixed $k \geq 1$. From this point on we may assume that, for every node, at most k arguments are selected as the top-k of undefeated-arguments-for that node. Suppose a BBN possesses n nodes, and that each node possesses maximally s states and p parents. Let N be a fixed node. At this node the Cartesian product $A_1, \ldots, A_p$ contains at most k^p elements. Since N itself possesses at most s states, at most sk^p arguments need to be considered to determine the top-k of undefeated-arguments-for N. Thus, at worst the strength of at most nsk^p arguments need to considered overall. Since arguments are compared with respect to their strength at every node, and since argument strength is computed once for every argument, the complexity of the entire algorithm is $\mathcal{O}(nsk^p)$.   □

Thus, the complexity of Algorithm 1 depends linearly on all graph attributes, except on p. In other words, the complexity of Algorithm 1 is acceptable as long as

---

Algorithm 1 computing the top-k of undefeated-arguments-for(N)

Require: A node N, a desired state d of N, and an agent X that is interested in strong arguments for $N = d$

1: **if** N is clamped to $s_{\text{evidence}} \in \text{states}(N)$ **then**
2:     $R :=$ the singleton set consisting of
                Argument.new(
                    conclusion $\to N$,
                    conclusion-state $\to s_{\text{evidence}}$,
                    degree-of-belief $\to 1.0$,
                    degree-of-support $\to 1.0$,
                    sub-arguments $\to \emptyset$,
                    stakeholder $\to$ party
)
3: **else**
4:     $A_1, \ldots, A_p = \{$ Undefeated-arguments-for(P) $\mid P$ is a parent of $N \}$
5:     $R := \emptyset$
6:     **for** each argument-vector $(a_1, \ldots, a_p) \in A_1 \times \ldots \times A_p$ **do**
7:         DOS $:= \Pi_{i=1}^{p}$ degree-of-belief(a_i)
8:         parent-states $:= \{ s_i \mid s_i$ is the state of the conclusion of $a_i \}$
9:         **for** each state s of N **do**
10:            DOB $:=$ DOS $\times$ CPT$_N(s_1, \ldots, s_p, s)$
11:            $a =$ Argument.new(
                        conclusion $\to N$,
                        conclusion-state $\to s$,
                        degree-of-belief $\to$ DOB,
                        degree-of-support $\to$ DOS,
                        sub-arguments $\to (a_1, \ldots, a_p)$,
                        stakeholder $\to$ party
)
12:            Extend R with a, removing R's weakest, or one of R's weakest arguments, if $|R| > k$
13:        **end for**
14:    **end for**
15: **end if**
16: **return** R

---

we maintain an upper bound on the number of parents. In practice this is always the case, since the number of entries in a CPT also exponentially depends on p.

Based on the above observations, I think it it safe to claim that the above algorithm is useable for all practical BBNs.

7   Experiments and Results

This section describes how existing case files from the Bayesian network domain are processed. Then, one such file will be run through the argumentation program and the results will be displayed and discussed. Finally, some observations of a more general nature will be made.

```
<?xml version="1.0" encoding="ISO-8859-1"?>
<smile version="1.0" id="Credit assesssment" numsamples="1000">
    <nodes>
        <cpt id="PaymentHistory">
            <state id="Excellent" />
            <state id="Aceptable" />
            <state id="NoAceptable" />
            <state id="Without_Reference" />
            <probabilities>0.25 0.25 0.25 0.25</probabilities>
        </cpt>
        <cpt id="Reliability">
            <state id="Reliable" />
            <state id="Unreliable" />
            <parents>PaymentHistory WorkHistory</parents>
            <probabilities>
                0.99 0.01 0.7 0.3 0.7 0.3 0.5 0.5 0.7 0.3 0.55 0.45 0.6
                0.4 0.4 0.6 0.196429 0.803571 0.01 0.99 0.1 0.9 0.01
                0.99 0.7 0.3 0.3 0.7 0.5 0.5 0.2 0.8
            </probabilities>
        </cpt>
    ...
```

Fig. 3. Start of an XDSL input file

The algorithm has been implemented in Ruby 1.8.2, which is an object-oriented scripting language particularly suitable for rapid prototyping. The resulting program has been extended with an XML interface to import Genie 2.0 XDSL files. Genie is a leading software package to create and manipulate decision theoretic models using a graphical user interface. Genie 2.0 stores its networks in a dedicated XML format, named XDSL (Fig. 3).

Besides the network itself (Fig. 3) the argumentation program needs to know which nodes are considered as evidence, and it needs to know the states to which these evidence nodes are clamped. This is specified in the program as an associative array, but we can read this of from Fig. 2. Further, a query node must be specified. This is a node tied to a particular state. In our case the query node is "CreditWorthiness(positive)".

When this program is run on the input as displayed in Fig. 3, we obtain an output as displayed in Fig. 4. From this output, we see that evidence nodes create only one argument, while leaf nodes generate as many arguments as there are states for that node. Since $k = 3$, the algorithm proceeds with at most three strongest arguments at every node and eventually ends up with three arguments in all. The strongest argument supports conclusion "CreditWorthiness(positive)" with sttrength 0.00077 and degree of belief 0.00062. The second strongest argument supports an opposite conclusion with equal support but with less DOB. The second argument is relevant to the main claim but will typically not be used as a sub-argument in further reasoning (if that would happen—here the second argument one of the top arguments).

```
Parsing 'Credit.xdsl' ... done

  1. Searching evidence for CreditWorthiness=Positive
  2. | Searching evidence on both sides for Reliability
  3. | | Searching evidence on both sides for PaymentHistory
  4. | | Search for PaymentHistory=ALL, returns 3 argument(s):
     . . PaymentHistory(excellent) 0.25 1

     . . PaymentHistory(aceptable) 0.25 1

     . . PaymentHistory(noaceptable) 0.25 1

     [snip -- rest of search omitted]

 26. Search for CreditWorthiness=Positive, returns 3 argument(s):
     CreditWorthiness(positive) 0.00062 0.00077
     . Reliability(reliable) 0.062 0.063
     . . PaymentHistory(excellent) 0.25 1
     . . WorkHistory(stable) 0.25 1
     . RatioDebInc(favorable) 0.089 0.11
     . . Debt(a0_11100) 0.33 1
     . . Income(s30001_70000) 0.33 1
     . FutureIncome(not_promissing) 0.14 0.23
     . . Worth(low) 0.23 0.33
     . . . Income(s0_30000) 0.33 1
     . . . Assets(average) 1 1
     . . Profession(medium_income_profession) 1 1
     . Age(a22_65) 1 1

     CreditWorthiness(negative) 0.00015 0.00077
     . Reliability(reliable) 0.062 0.063

     [snip -- rest of argument in output omitted]

     CreditWorthiness(positive) 0.00043 0.00054
     . Reliability(reliable) 0.044 0.063

     [snip -- rest of argument in output omitted]

 27. Ended with 3 arguments.
```

Fig. 4. Output

8   Related Work

Related work falls apart in two categories: probabilistic argumentation systems, such as PAS and hybrid argumentation, and approaches that try to convey dialectic concepts to Bayesian belief networks.

J. Kohlas *et al.* (Fribourg U. Switzerland) work on Probabilistic argumentation systems (PASs). According to their creators, PASs are a form of assumption-based reasoning for obtaining arguments that support hypotheses [7, 6]. PASs are obtained from propositional logic by considering two disjoint sets $P = \{p_1, \ldots, p_n\}$ and $A = \{a_1, \ldots, a_m\}$ of propositions. The elements of A are called assumptions. $L_{A \cup P}$ denotes the corresponding propositional language. If η is a propositional sentence in $L_{A \cup P}$, then a triple $\mathcal{AS} = (\eta, P, A)$ is called propositional argumentation system and η is called the knowledge base of $\mathcal{AS}$. The knowledge base η is often given as a conjunctive set $\Sigma = \varphi_1, \ldots, \varphi_r$ of clauses $\varphi_i \in \mathcal{D}_{A \cup P}$, where $\mathcal{D}_{A \cup P}$ represents the set of all possible clauses over $A \cup P$. The authors claim that PASs are applicable public-key cryptography and so-called webs of trust, which are essentially holistic and cyclic. Unlike BBNs, the Kohlas *et al.* claim that PASs are able to deal with such cyclic graphs, which is for example essential in the domain of public-key cryptography.

Between 1997-2000, work has been reported on the NAG ("The Nice Argument Generator"), Monash U. Australia [25, 10]. The NAG is an architecture to enable the generation of natural language arguments from BBNs, so that users can argue with the NAG about the implications of various BBN scenario's. Because the NAG is not only concerned with logics but also with user interaction, it consists of several components, such as an argument generator, a strategist, an analyzer, a presenter, an attentional mechanism and an interface. Since the formation of arguments takes place within the NAG's analyzer, only this part of the NAG seems to be relevant within the context of the present paper. Work in which the NAG is reported is not very detailed about the argument formation algorithm. It is mentioned that "the Analyzer performs BN propagation on the portions of the normative and user models which correspond to the Argument Graph and are connected to the goal". Further on in [25], it is mentioned that the NAG applies a Pearl-type propagation algorithm [12]. In [10] a "Generation-Analysis Algorithm" is given in rather detailed terms, but not detailed enough to see how it exploits Pearl's propagation algorithm.

The NAG is partially influenced by Vreeswijk's interactive argumentation system IACAS [23]. Like IACAS, the NAG allows the user to manipulate underlying scenarios. In addition, the NAG is also able to model attentional focus and tailor its arguments to the user in the course of a dialogue.

Finally, there is recent work on modelling argumentation with belief networks, in which an attempt is made to convey Toulmin's argument structures (claim, datum, reason, warrant, backing) to BBNs [1, 20]. This work still is in its preliminary stages but the initial results look promising and demand further research.

9   Conclusion

We have introduced an algorithm with which it is possible to conduct an argumentation process within existing Bayesian belief networks.

The extended algorithm with bean size k is particularly interesting from a Bayesian inference point of view, because it offers a computationally tractable alternative to the $\mathrm{NP}^{\mathrm{PP}}$-complete decision problem k-MPE.

Acknowledgement. This research was supported in part by a European Commission STReP grant ASPIC IST-FP6-002307. This project aims to develop re-usable software components for argumentation-based interactions between autonomous agents.

References

1. V. Carofiglio. Modelling argumentation with belief networks. In F. Grasso, Chris Reed, and Giuseppe Carenini, editors, *Proc. of the 4th Workshop on Computational Models of Natural Argument (CMNA-2004)*, 2004.
2. C.I. Chesñevar, A.G. Maguitman, and R.P. Loui. Logical models of argument. *ACM Comput. Surv.*, 32(4):337–383, 2000.
3. G.F. Cooper. The computational complexity of probabilistic inference using bayesian belief networks. *Artificial Intelligence*, 42:393–405, 1990.
4. R.G. Cowell, A.P. Dawid, S.L. Lauritzen, and D.J. Spiegelhalter. *Probabilistic Networks and Expert Systems*. Springer-Verlag, 1999.
5. Phan Minh Dung. On the acceptability of arguments and its fundamental role in nonmonotonic reasoning, logic programming, and n-person games. *Artificial Intelligence*, 77(2):321–357, 1995.
6. Jürgen Kohlas. Probabilistic argumentation systems a new way to combine logic with probability. *Journal of Applied Logic*, 1(3-4):225–253, 2003.
7. Jürgen Kohlas and Rolf Haenni. Assumption-based reasoning and probabilistic argumentation systems. In Jürgen Kohlas and S. Moral, editors, *Defeasible Reasoning and Uncertainty Management Systems: Algorithms*. Oxford University Press, 1996.
8. Kevin B. Korb and Ann E. Nicholson. *Bayesian Artificial Intelligence*. Chapman and Hall/CRC Computer Science and Data Analysis, 2003.
9. S.L. Lauritzen and D.J. Spiegelhalter. Local computations with probabilities on graphical structures and their applications to expert systems. *Journal of the Royal Statistical Society, B*, 50:157–224, 1988.
10. Richard McConachy, Kevin B. Korb, and Ingrid Zuckerman. A Bayesian approach to automating argumentation. In David M. W. Powers, editor, *Proc. of the Joint Conf. on New Methods in Language Processing and Computational Natural Language Learning: NeMLaP3/CoNLL98*, pages 91–100. Association for Computational Linguistics, Somerset, New Jersey, 1998.
11. J. D. Park. Map complexity results and approximation methods. *Proc. of the 18th Conf. on Uncertainty in Artificial Intelligence (UAI)*, pages 388–396, 2002.
12. Judea Pearl. *Probabilistic Reasoning in Intelligent Systems: Networks of Plausible Inference*. Morgan Kaufmann, Inc., Palo Alto CA, 2 edition, 1994.
13. John L. Pollock. *Cognitive Carpentry. A Blueprint for How to Build a Person*. MIT Press, Cambridge, MA, 1995.
14. John L. Pollock. Implementing defeasible reasoning. Presented at the Computational Dialectics Workshop, at FAPR'96, June 3-7, 1996, Bonn. Cf. http://nathan.gmd.de/ projects/zeno/fapr/programme.html., 1996.
15. John L. Pollock. Defeasible reasoning with variable degrees of justification. *Artificial Intelligence Journal*, 133(1-2):233–282, 2001.
16. H. Prakken and Gerard A.W. Vreeswijk. Logics for defeasible argumentation. In D.M. Gabbay et al., editors, *Handbook of Philosophical Logic*, pages 219–318. Kluwer Academic Publishers, Dordrecht, 2002.

17. S. Saha and S. Sen. A bayes net approach to argumentation based negotiation. In *Proc. of the AAMAS-2004 workshop on Argumentation in Multi-Agent Systems (ArgMAS-2004)*, 2004.

18. S. E. Shimony. Finding maps for belief networks is np-hard. *Artificial Intelligence*, 68:399–410, 1994.

19. G.R. Simari and R.P. Loui. A mathematical treatment of defeasible argumentation and its implementation. *Artificial Intelligence*, 53:125–157, 1992.

20. Stephen Toulmin. *The Uses of Argument*. Cambridge University Press, 1985.

21. H. Bart Verheij. Accrual of arguments in defeasible argumentation. In C. Witteveen, W. van der Hoek, J.-J. Ch. Meyer, and B. van Linder, editors, *Proc. of the 2nd Dutch/German Workshop on Nonmonotonic Reasoning*, pages 217–224, Utrecht, 1995.

22. G. Vreeswijk and Prakken H. Credulous and sceptical argument games for preferred semantics. In M. Ojeda-Aciego, I.P. de Guzman, G. Brewka, and L.M. Pereira, editors, *Proceedings of the 7th European Workshop on Logics in Artificial Inteligence (JELIA 2000)*, volume 1919 of *Lecture Notes in Artificial Intelligence*, pages 239–253. Springer-Verlag, Heidelberg, 2000.

23. Gerard A.W. Vreeswijk. IACAS: An implementation of Chisholm's principles of knowledge. In C. Witteveen, W. van der Hoek, J.-J. Ch. Meyer, and B. van Linder, editors, *The Proc. of the 2nd Dutch/German Workshop on Nonmonotonic Reasoning*, pages 225–234, Utrecht, 1995. Delft University of Technology, University of Utrecht.

24. Nevin Lianwen Zhang and David Poole. Exploiting causal independence in bayesian network inference. *Journal of Artificial Intelligence Research*, 5:301–328, 1996.

25. I. Zukerman, R. McConachy, K. B. Korb, and D. Pickett. Exploratory interaction with a bayesian argumentation system. In T. Dean, editor, *Proc. of the 16th Int. Joint Conf. on Artificial Intelligence (IJCAI-99)*, pages 1294–1299. Morgan Kaufmann, 1999.

Specifying and Implementing a Persuasion Dialogue Game Using Commitments and Arguments

Jamal Bentahar[1], Bernard Moulin[1,2], and Brahim Chaib-draa[1]

[1] Laval University, Computer Science and Software Engineering Department,
Ste Foy, QC, G1K 7P4, Canada
jamal.bentahar.1@ulav1.ca
{bernard.moulin, brahim.chaib-draa}@ift.ulaval.ca
[2] Geomatica Research Centre,
Ste Foy, QC, G1K 7P4, Canada

Abstract. In this paper we propose a new persuasion dialogue game for agent communication. We show how this dialogue game is modeled by a framework based on social commitments and arguments. Called Commitment and Argument Network (CAN), this framework allows us to model communication dynamics in terms of actions that agents apply to commitments and in terms of argumentation relations. This dialogue game is specified by indicating its entry conditions, its dynamics and its exit conditions. In order to solve the problem of the acceptance of arguments, the protocol integrates the concept of agents' trustworthiness in its specification. The paper proposes a set of algorithms for the implementation of the persuasion protocol and discusses their termination, complexity and correctness.

1 Introduction

Research in agent communication languages and protocols has received much attention during the last years. Protocols describe the allowed communicative acts that agents can perform when conversing. These protocols specify the rules governing a dialogue between agents in multi-agent systems (MAS).

Traditionally, protocols are specified as finite state machines or Petri nets without taking into account the agents' autonomy. Therefore, these protocols are not flexible enough to be used in open MAS [13]. To solve this problem, several researchers proposed protocols using dialogue games (DGs) [9, 10, 13, 14]. DGs are interactions between players, in which each player moves by performing utterances according to a pre-defined set of roles [14].

The protocols described in the literature are often specified by pre/post conditions. These protocols often neglected the decision-making process that allows agents to accept or to refuse an utterance. The protocols based on formal dialectics [2, 15, 23] use the argumentation as a way of expressing decision-making. However, the sole argumentation does not make it possible to solve a decision-making problem. We think that other social elements such as agents' trustworthiness must be taken into account.

I. Rahwan et al. (Eds.): ArgMAS 2004, LNAI 3366, pp. 130–148, 2005.

The contribution of this paper is the proposition of a formal specification and an implementation of a new persuasion dialogue game for agent communication using a unified framework based on social commitments and on arguments. Our protocol is presented in the context of this framework called Commitment and Argument Network (CAN) [5, 6]. This protocol is characterized by the fact that it integrates the agents' trustworthiness as a component of the decision-making process.

The rest of this paper is organized as follows. In Section 2 we present our approach based on commitments and arguments. In Section 3 we introduce the CAN formalism. In Section 4 we present the specification of our dialogue game and we highlight the importance of agents' trustworthiness. In Section 5 we present our model of trustworthiness. In Section 6 we describe some issues of the implementation. In Section 7 we discuss some characteristics of our algorithms. In Sections 8 and 9 we compare our protocol to related work and we conclude the paper.

2   Approach Based on Commitments and Arguments

2.1   Social Commitment

In the domain of agent communication, it is largely recognized that social commitments are a powerful representation for modeling multi-agent interactions [4, 5, 8, 12, 13, 25]. In opposition to the BDI (beliefs, desires and intentions) approach, the commitment-based approach stresses the importance of conventions and the public and social aspects of dialogue. It is based on social commitments that are thought of as social and deontic notions. As a social notion, commitments are a base for a normative framework that makes it possible to model the agents' behavior. Indeed, considering their deontic nature, these commitments define constraints on this behavior. The agent must behave in accordance to its commitments. For example, by committing towards other agents that a certain fact is true, the agent is compelled not to contradict itself during the conversation. It must also be able to explain, argue, justify and defend itself if another participant contradicts it. A speaker is committed to a statement when he made this statement or when he agreed with this statement made by another participant. In fact, we do not speak here about the expression of a belief, but rather about a particular relationship between a participant and a statement.

A Social commitment *SC* is a commitment made by an agent (called the *debtor*), that some fact is true. This commitment is directed to a set of agents (called *creditors*) [8]. In order to model the dynamics of conversations, we interpret a speech act *SA* as an *action* performed on a commitment or on its content (we refer to this as "take position on a commitment"). A speech act is an abstract act that an agent, the speaker, performs when producing an utterance *U* and addressing it to another agent, the addressee [24]. The actions that an agent can perform on a commitment are: *Act∈{Create, Withdraw}*. The actions performed on the content of a commitment are: *Act-content∈ {Accept, Refuse, Challenge}*. Thus, a speech act is defined as an action on a commitment when the speaker is the debtor, or as an action on a commitment content when the speaker is the debtor or the creditor. Formally:

Definition 1. $SA(Ag_1, Ag_2, U) =_{def}$
$Act(Ag_1, SC(Ag_1, Ag_2, p))$
$| Act\text{-}content(Ag_k, SC(Ag_i, Ag_j, p))$

where $i, j \in \{1, 2\}$ and $(k=i$ or $k=j)$, $=_{def}$ means "is interpreted by definition as", p the commitment content. This definition allows us to model agent interaction using actions that agents perform on commitments and on their contents.

2.2 Argumentation and Social Commitments

An argumentation system essentially includes a logical language L, a definition of the argument concept, a definition of the attack relation between arguments and finally a definition of acceptability. Several definitions were also proposed for the argument concept [19, 28]. In our model, we adopt the following definitions from [11]. Here Γ indicates a possibly inconsistent knowledge base with no deductive closure. $\vdash$ Stands for classical inference and $\equiv$ for logical equivalence.

Definition 2. *An argument is a pair (H, h) where h is a formula of L and H a sub-set of Γ such that : i) H is consistent, ii) $H \vdash h$ and iii) H is minimal, so no subset of H satisfying both i and ii exists. H is called the support of the argument and h its conclusion.*

Definition 3. *Let (H_1, h_1), (H_2, h_2) be two arguments. (H_1, h_1) attack (H_2, h_2) iff*
$h_1 \equiv \neg h_2.$
The *defense* relation is defined as a dual relation of *attack*.

Argumentation is based on the construction of arguments and counter-arguments, the comparison of these various arguments and finally the selection of the arguments that are considered to be acceptable. In our approach, agents must reason on their own mental states in order to build arguments in favor of their future commitments, as well as on other agents' commitment in order to be able to take position with respect to the contents of these commitments.

In fact, before committing to some fact h being true (i.e. before creating a commitment whose content is h), the speaker agent must use its argumentation system to build an argument (H, h). On the other side, the addressee agent must use its own argumentation system to select the answer it will give (i.e. to decide about the appropriate manipulation of the content of an existing commitment). For example, an agent Ag_1 accepts the commitment content h proposed by another agent Ag_2 if Ag_1 has an argument for h. If Ag_1 has an argument neither for h, nor for $\neg h$, then it must ask for an explanation. Thus, we claim that an agent's argument must support an action performed by this agent on a given commitment or on its content. The semantics of our commitment and argument approach is described in [6]. Surely, an argumentation system is essential to help agents to act on commitments and on their contents. However, reasoning on other social attitudes should be taken into account in order to explain the agents' decisions. In our persuasion protocol we highlight the importance of agents' trustworthiness to decide, in some cases, about the acceptance of arguments.

3 The CAN Formalism

So far, we presented our framework of commitments and arguments. Thus, agents can participate in conversations by manipulating commitments and by producing arguments. In this section, we show how a conversation can be modeled using the CAN formalism on the basis of this framework. In this paper we use a simplified version of the CAN which is sufficient to specify our persuasion DG. The complete version is described in [5]. A CAN is a mathematical structure which we define formally as follows:

Definition 4: *A CAN is a 7-uple: <A, E, SC(Ag₁, Ag₂, p), Ω, Σ, Δ, α> where:*

- *A: a finite set of agents. A= {Ag₁, ..., Agₙ}.*
- *E: a finite set of commitments. E= {SC(Ag₁, Ag₂, p), SC(Ag₂, Ag₁, q),...}.*
- *SC(Ag₁, Ag₂, p): a distinguished element of E: the initial commitment.*
- *Ω: a finite set of creation and positioning actions. Ω={Create, Accept, Refuse, Challenge, Withdraw}.*
- *Σ: a finite set of argumentation relations.*
  Σ= {Defend, Attack, Justify}.
- *Δ: a partial function relating a commitment to another commitment using one argumentation relation.*
  Δ: E×E→Σ
- *α: a partial function relating an agent to a commitment using a creation and a positioning action.*
  α: A×E→Ω

The function Δ allows us to define the argumentation relation that can exist between two commitments, i.e. a defense, an attack or a justification relation. For example:

Δ(SC(Ag₁, Ag₂, p), SC(Ag₁, Ag₂, q))=Defend.

This means that the commitment *SC(Ag₁, Ag₂, p)* (called *source* of the defense relation) defends the commitment *SC(Ag₁, Ag₂, q)* (called *target* of the defense relation).

The function α allows us to define creation and positioning actions (acceptance, refusal, etc.) performed by an agent on a commitment content. For example:

α(Ag₁, SC(Ag₂, Ag₁, p))=Accept

This reflects the acceptance of the content of *SC(Ag₁, Ag₂, p)*. *Ag₁* belongs to the debtors set associated with this commitment.

4 Specification of a Persuasion Dialogue Game Based on the CAN Formalism

In this section, we propose a new protocol for persuasion dialogues modeled as *actions* that agents apply to commitments. In this protocol, the persuasion is captured by the argument agents use to support their actions. The semantics of these actions is defined in a dynamic logic and that of the argumentation relations is defined in an extension of CTL* [6]. Our purpose is to show that the CAN framework can be successfully used to represent a persuasion dialogue game. At a theoretical level, this framework can represent all the elements that constitute the persuasion dynamics. This framework offers a language to represent the dynamics more expressive than the simple pre/post conditions traditionally used as a specification of dialogue games. The differences between our protocol and other protocols proposed in the agent literature are discussed in Section 8.

4.1 General Form

According to the classification of Walton and Krabbe [29], each type of dialogue has an initial situation and the goal of the dialogue is to change this situation in a particular way. Fig. 1 illustrates the initial situation as well as the goal of the persuasion dialogue.

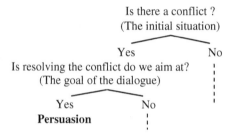

Fig. 1. Goal and initial situation of the persuasion dialogue

In the same context, Vanderveken [27] proposed a *logic of discourse* in which there are only four possible discursive goals speakers can attempt to achieve by conversing. These goals are: descriptive, deliberative, declaratory and expressive goals. Persuasion dialogue is a sub-type of the dialogue types having a descriptive goal. In his typology, Vanderveken argued that each dialogue type with a discursive goal has a mode of achievement of the discursive goal and preparatory conditions. The mode of achievement imposes a certain sequence of speech acts. For a persuasion dialogue, a certain sequence of defense utterances, questions and answers is needed for the successful implementation of such a dialogue. Preparatory conditions determine a structured set of presuppositions related to the discursive goal. The persuasion dialogue has the preparatory conditions that there is a conflict between the agents' points of view and that each agent has the capacity to defend its point of view.

In addition, in the domain of artificial intelligence and law, many computational and logical models of argument and debate, and of reasoning with conflicting information have been proposed [3, 17, 18]. In [18], Prakken and Sartor introduced a dialectical proof theory for an argumentation framework. A proof of a formula takes the form of a dialogue tree, in which each branch of the tree is a dialogue and the root of the tree is an argument for the formula. The idea is that every move in a dialogue consists of an argument based on the input theory, where each stated argument attacks the last move of the opponent in a way that meets the player's burden of proof.

Our persuasion protocol is defined by specifying its entry conditions, its exit conditions and its dynamics. Entry conditions correspond to the initial situation of the dialogue and to the preparatory conditions. Exit conditions correspond to the final situation that makes it possible to determine if the dialogue goal is achieved or not. Dynamics results in the different types of actions that can be performed by agents so that each agent can achieve its goal. The dynamics correspond to the mode of achievement of the discursive goal. It also corresponds to the dialectical proof theory where the root is the persuasion subject. Dynamics is reflected by a set of initiative/reactive DGs. An initiative game is captured by creating a new commitment. A reactive game is captured by taking position on an existing commitment (acceptance, refusal, challenge, defense, etc.).

4.1.1   Entry Conditions

As illustrated by Fig. 1, the entry condition of the persuasion protocol is a conflict of point of view. This is translated in the CAN formalism by the creation of a commitment $SC(p)$ by an agent Ag_1 and the refusal of this commitment by an agent Ag_2. Formally, the initial situation is reflected as follows:

$\alpha(Ag_1, SC(Ag_1, Ag_2, p))=Create,\ \alpha(Ag_2\ SC(Ag_1, Ag_2, p))=Refuse$
$\alpha(Ag_2, SC(Ag_2, Ag_1, \neg p))=Create.$

4.1.2   Dynamics

Generally, the persuasion dialogue takes the form of a sequence of attacks and defenses where each agent tries to defend its point of view or attack the point of view of its partner. This dialogue can also contain questions and answers (dialogue game of information seeking). In the CAN formalism, this results in the creation of a commitment that defends or attacks the initial commitment and other commitments and argumentation relations. The dialogue games of information seeking can be represented by challenge actions and argumentation relations. Formally, the dialogue dynamics can be expressed by a combination of the following functions:

$\alpha(Ag_1, SC(Ag_1, Ag_2, q))=Create,\ \Delta(SC(Ag_1, Ag_2, q),\ SC(Ag_1, Ag_2, p))=Defend,$
$\alpha(Ag_2, PC(Ag_2, Ag_1, r))=Create,\ \Delta(SC(Ag_2, Ag_1, r),\ SC(Ag_1, Ag_2, p))=Attack,$
where p, q, r are propositional formulas.

Information seeking can be, for example, represented by:

$\alpha(Ag_2, SC(Ag_1, Ag_2, q))=Challenge$
$\alpha(Ag_1, SC(Ag_1, Ag_2, r))=Create$
$\Delta(SC(Ag_1, Ag_2, r),\ SC(Ag_1, Ag_2, q))=Justify.$

4.1.3   Exit Conditions

The persuasion dialogue terminates either if the conflict is solved, or with a situation in which each agent does not accept the argument of the other. In this case the protocol terminates with an unsolved conflict. The conflict is solved when one of the two agents adopts the point of view of its partner. In the CAN formalism, this results in the acceptance of the initial commitment $SC(Ag_1, Ag_2, p)$ (respectively $SC(Ag_2, Ag_1, \neg p)$) by Ag_2 (respectively Ag_1). This implies the cancellation of all commitments attacked $SC(Ag_1, Ag_2, p)$ (respectively $SC(Ag_2, Ag_1, \neg p)$). Formally, if Ag_2 accepts $SC(p)$, the final situation is described as follows:

$\alpha(Ag_2, SC(Ag_1, Ag_2, p))=Accept\Rightarrow$
$[\forall q: \Delta(SC(Ag_2, Ag_1, q), SC(Ag_1, Ag_2, p))=Attack\Rightarrow$
$\alpha(Ag_2, SC(Ag_2, Ag_1, q)):=Withdraw]$

When the two agents mutually refuse the argument of the other, the protocol stops because the conflict cannot be solved.

4.2   Algorithms of the Persuasion Dialogue Game

The general algorithm representing our persuasion dialogue game is given by Algorithm 1. Part A of Algorithm 1 specifies the entry conditions. Part B indicates the exit conditions. The persuasion dynamics (i.e. the sequence of utterances) is given by the function *Dynamics*. The specification of this function is given by Algorithms 2, 3, 4, 5 and 6. In these algorithms S_{Ag1} indicates the set of arguments of agent Ag_1 (i.e. its knowledge base). S'_{Ag1} indicates the set of arguments that Ag_1 used in the current dialogue. The set S'_{Ag1} allows us to avoid the use of same arguments several times. These algorithms specify the different DGs of our dialogue as *if then* roles. These DGs are: *acceptance, refusal, challenge, justification, attack* and *defense*.

{ If $\alpha(Ag_1, SC(Ag_1, Ag_2, p)) = Create$
   And $\alpha(Ag_2, SC(Ag_1, Ag_2, p)) = Refuse$ ⎫ Part A
   Then ⎭
      { Conflict := 0 ;
      Dynamics;
      If Conflict = 1 Then
         « The conflict is solved » ⎫ Part B
      Else « The conflict is not solved » ⎭
      }}

Algorithm 1

Algorithm 2 deals with the acceptance and the refusal cases. The acceptance of $SC(Ag_1, Ag_2, p)$ makes it possible to solve the conflict and to stop the algorithm. In the refusal case, if Ag_1 finds an argument (r, q) not yet used for its commitment $SC(Ag_1, Ag_2, q)$, then this agent creates a new commitment $SC(Ag_1, Ag_2, r)$ to defend $SC(Ag_1, Ag_2, q)$. Ag_1 updates the set S'_{Ag1} by adding the argument (r, q). Ag_1 informs Ag_2 about its action using the *Send* primitive. The *Send* primitive has the form *Send(Destination, Action)*. If Ag_1 does not have arguments to defend its commitment, then the conflict cannot be solved because each agent refuses the arguments of the other and the algorithm stops.

Algorithm 3 deals with the challenge case. Ag_1 justifies its commitment if it finds an argument not yet used. As for the refusal case, Ag_1 updates S'_{Ag1} and informs Ag_2 about its action. If Ag_1 does not find such an argument, then it indicates to Ag_2 that the content of the challenged commitment is a knowledge that Ag_1 believes true by justifying it by itself. The formal definition of the *justification* relation is the same as the *defense* relation.

> If $\alpha(Ag_2, SC(Ag_1, Ag_2, p)) = Accept$ Then {
>   Conflict := 1; Return Conflict; }
> If $\alpha(Ag_2, SC(Ag_1, Ag_2, q)) = Refuse$ Then {
>   If $(r, q) \in S_{Ag1} / S'_{Ag1}$ Then {
> $\alpha(Ag_1, SC(Ag_1, Ag_2, r)) :=$ Create;
> $\Delta(SC(Ag_1, Ag_2, r), SC(Ag_1, Ag_2, q)) :=$ Defend;
> $S'_{Ag1} := S'_{Ag1} \cup \{(r, q)\}$;
>   Send($Ag_2, \Delta(SC(Ag_1, Ag_2, r), SC(Ag_1, Ag_2, q))$); }
>   Else { Conflict : = -1; Return Conflict; }}

Algorithm 2

> If $\alpha(Ag_2, PC(Ag_1, Ag_2, q)) = Challenge$ Then {
>   If $(r, q) \in S_{Ag1} / S'_{Ag1}$ Then {
> $\alpha(Ag_1, SC(Ag_1, Ag_2, r)) : =$ Create;
> $\Delta(SC(Ag_1, Ag_2, r), SC(Ag_1, Ag_2, q)) :=$ Justify;
> $S'_{Ag1} = S'_{Ag1} \cup \{(r, q)\}$;
>   Send($Ag_2, \Delta(SC(Ag_1, Ag_2, r), SC(Ag_1, Ag_2, q))$); }
>   Else { $\Delta(SC(Ag_1, Ag_2, q), SC(Ag_1, Ag_2, q)) :=$ Justify;
>   Send($Ag_2, \Delta(SC(Ag_1, Ag_2, q), SC(Ag_1, Ag_2, q))$);}}

Algorithm 3

Algorithm 4 deals with the case of Ag_1 reaction if Ag_2 justifies the content of its commitment by itself. *Trustworthy(Ag_2)* is a Boolean function that enables Ag_1 to determine if Ag_2 is trustworthy or not. If according to Ag_1, Ag_2 is trustworthy, then Ag_1 accepts Ag_2's commitment. If not, Ag_1 refuses Ag_2's commitment. In the following section we propose a probabilistic model of trustworthiness to determine the value of *Trustworthy(Ag_2)* function.

> If $\Delta(SC(Ag_2, Ag_1, q), SC(Ag_2, Ag_1, q)) = Justify$ Then {
>   If Trustworthy(Ag_2)
>   Then $\alpha(Ag_1, SC(Ag_2, Ag_1, q)) :=$ Accept
>   Else $\alpha(Ag_1, SC(Ag_2, Ag_1, q)) :=$ Refuse
>   Send($Ag_2, \alpha(Ag_1, SC(Ag_2, Ag_1, q))$);
> }

Algorithm 4

Algorithm 5 deals with the case where Ag_2 attacks the support of Ag_1's argument. Ag_1 attacks Ag_2's argument if it has an against-argument or it defends its argument if it has an argument or it accepts Ag_2's argument if it has an argument. If Ag_1 has no arguments nor against-arguments, then it challenges Ag_2's argument.

If $\Delta(SC(Ag_2, Ag_1, q), SC(Ag_1, Ag_2, r)) = Attack$ Then {
   If $(s, \neg q) \in S_{Ag1} / S'_{Ag1}$ Then {
      $\alpha(Ag_1, SC(Ag_1, Ag_2, s)) := Create;$
      $\Delta(SC(Ag_1, Ag_2, s), SC(Ag_2, Ag_1, q)) := Attack;$
      $S'_{Ag1} := S'_{Ag1} \cup \{(s, \neg q)\};$
      Send($Ag_2, \Delta(SC(Ag_1, Ag_2, s), SC(Ag_2, Ag_1, q))$)); }
   Else If $(s, r) \in S_{Ag1} / S'_{Ag1}$ Then {
      $\alpha(Ag_1, SC(Ag_1, Ag_2, s)) := Create;$
      $\Delta(SC(Ag_1, Ag_2, s), SC(Ag_1, Ag_2, r)) := Defend;$
      $S'_{Ag1} = S'_{Ag1} \cup \{(s, r)\};$
      Send($Ag_2, \Delta(SC(Ag_1, Ag_2, s), SC(Ag_1, Ag_2, r))$));}
   Else {
      If $(s, q) \in S_{Ag1} / S'_{Ag1}$ Then
         $\alpha(Ag_1, SC(Ag_2, Ag_1, q)):=Accept;$
      Else $\alpha(Ag_1, SC(Ag_2, Ag_1, q)):=Challenge;$
      Send($Ag_2, \alpha(Ag_1, SC(Ag_2, Ag_1, q))$));}}

Algorithm 5

Algorithm 6 deals with the case in which the reactive game of Ag_2 is a defense of its argument. Thus, Ag_1 can attack the support of the Ag_2's argument or its conclusion according to Ag_1's arguments. As in Algorithm 5, Ag_1 accepts or challenges the support of Ag_2's argument in the opposite case.

5 Trustworthiness Model

Several models of trustworthiness have been developed in the context of MAS [20, 22, 31]. However, their formulations do not take into account the elements we use in our approach. For this reason, we propose a model that is more appropriate for our protocol. This model has the advantage of being simple and rigorous.

In our model, an agent's trustworthiness is a probability function defined as follows: *TRUST : $A \times A \times D \rightarrow [0, 1]$*. This function associates to each agent a probability measure representing its trustworthiness in the domain D according to another agent. Let X be a random variable representing an agent's trustworthiness. To evaluate the trustworthiness of an agent Ag_b, an agent Ag_a uses the records of its interactions with Ag_b. Formula 1 indicates how to calculate this trustworthiness as a probability measure (number of successful outcomes / total number of possible outcomes).

$$TRUST(Ag_b)_{Aga} = \frac{Nb\_arg(Ag_b)_{Aga} + Nb\_SC(Ag_b)_{Aga}}{T\_Nb\_arg(Ag_b)_{Aga} + T\_Nb\_SC(Ag_b)_{Aga}} \ . \tag{1}$$

If $\Delta(PC(Ag_2, Ag_1, q), PC(Ag_2, Ag_1, r)) = Defend$ Then {
    If $(s, \neg q) \in S_{Ag1} / S'_{Ag1}$ Then {
        $\alpha(Ag_1, SC(Ag_1, Ag_2, s)) := Create;$
        $\Delta(SC(Ag_1, Ag_2, s), SC(Ag_2, Ag_1, q)) := Attack;$
        $S'_{Ag1} := S'_{Ag1} \cup \{(s, \neg q)\};$
        $Send(Ag_2, \Delta(SC(Ag_1, Ag_2, s), SC(Ag_2, Ag_1, q)));\}$
    Else If $(s, \neg r) \in S_{Ag1} / S'_{Ag1}$ Then {
        $\alpha(Ag_1, SC(Ag_1, Ag_2, s)) := Create;$
        $\Delta(SC(Ag_1, Ag_2, s), SC(Ag_2, Ag_1, r)) := Attack;$
        $S'_{Ag1} := S'_{Ag1} \cup \{(s, \neg r)\};$
        $Send(Ag_2, \Delta(SC(Ag_1, Ag_2, s), SC(Ag_2, Ag_1, r)));\}$
    Else {
        If $(s, q) \in S_{Ag1} / S'_{Ag1}$ Then
            $\alpha(Ag_1, SC(Ag_2, Ag_1, q)) := Accept;$
        Else $\alpha(Ag_1, SC(Ag_2, Ag_1, q)) := Challenge;$
        $Send(Ag_2, \alpha(Ag_1, SC(Ag_2, Ag_1, q)));\}\}$

Algorithm 6

$Nb\_arg(Ag_b)_{Aga}$ is the number of Ag_bs' arguments that are accepted by Ag_a.
$Nb\_SC(Ag_b)_{Aga}$ is the number of satisfied commitments whose Ag_b is the debtor and Ag_a is the creditor.
$T\_Nb\_arg(Ag_b)_{Aga}$ is the total number of Ag_bs' arguments towards Ag_a.
$T\_Nb\_SC(Ag_b)_{Aga}$ is the total number of commitments whose Ag_b is the debtor and Ag_a is the creditor.

All these commitments and arguments are related to the domain D. The basic idea is that the trust degree of an agent can be induced according to how much information acquired from it has been accepted as belief in the past. Because all the factors of equation 1 are related to the past, this information number is finite.

$TRUST(Ag_b)_{Aga}$ is the trustworthiness of Ag_b according to Ag_a's point of view. This trustworthiness is a dynamic value that changes according to the interactions taking place between Ag_a and Ag_b. This supposes that Ag_a knows Ag_b. If not, or if the number of interactions is not sufficient to determine this trustworthiness, the consultation of other agents becomes necessary.

As proposed in [1, 31], each agent has two kinds of beliefs when evaluating the trustworthiness of another agent: local beliefs and total beliefs. Local beliefs are based on the direct interactions between agents. Total beliefs are based on the combination of the different testimonies of other agents called *witnesses*. In our model, local beliefs are given by Formula 1. Total beliefs require studying how different probability measures offered by witnesses can be combined. We deal with this aspect in the following section.

5.1 Estimating Agent's Trustworthiness

Let us suppose that an agent Ag_a wants to evaluate the trustworthiness of an agent Ag_b with which it never (or not enough) interacted before. This agent must consult agents that it knows to be trustworthy (*confidence agents*). A trustworthiness threshold w must be fixed. Thus, Ag_b will be considered trustworthy for Ag_a iff $TRUST(Ag_b)_{Aga}$ is higher or equal to w. Ag_a attributes a trustworthiness measure to each confidence agent Ag_i. When it is consulted by Ag_a, each confidence agent Ag_i provides a trustworthiness value for Ag_b if Ag_i knows Ag_b. Confidence agents use their local beliefs to calculate this value (Formula 1). Thus, the problem consists in evaluating Ag_b's trustworthiness using the trustworthiness values transmitted by confidence agents.

We notice that this problem cannot be formulated as a problem of conditional probability. Consequently, it is not possible to use *Bayes' theorem* or *total probability theorem*. The reason is that events in our problem are not mutually exclusive, whereas this condition is necessary for these two theorems. Probability values offered by confidence agents are not mutually exclusive since they are provided simultaneously.

To solve this problem we must study the distribution of the random variable X. Since X takes only two values: 0 (the agent is not trustworthy) or 1 (the agent is trustworthy), variable X follows a Bernoulli distribution $\beta(1, p)$. According to this distribution, we have:

$$E(X) = p . \tag{2}$$

where $E(X)$ is the expectation of the random variable X *and* p is the probability that the agent is trustworthy. Thus, p is the probability that we seek. Therefore, *it is enough to calculate the expectation $E(X)$ to find $TRUST(Ag_b)_{Aga}$*. However, this expectation is a theoretical mean that we must estimate. To this end, we can use the *Central Limit Theorem* (CLT) and the *law of large numbers*. The CLT states that whenever a random sample of size n $(X_1,...X_n)$ is taken from any distribution with mean μ, then the sample mean $(X_1 + ... +X_n) / n$ will be approximately normally distributed with mean μ. As an application of this theorem, the arithmetic mean (average) $(X_1+...+ X_n)/n$ approaches a normal distribution of mean μ, the expectation Generally, and according to the law of large numbers, the expectation can be estimated by the weighted arithmetic mean.

Our random variable X is the weighted average of n independent random variables X_i that correspond to Ag_b's trustworthiness according to the point of view of confidence agents Ag_i. These random variables follow the same distribution: the Bernoulli distribution. They are also independent because the probability that Ag_b is trustworthy according to an agent Ag_t is independent of the probability that this agent (Ag_b) is trustworthy according to another agent Ag_r. Consequently, the random variable X follows a normal distribution whose average is the weighted average of the expectations of the independent random variables X_i. The estimation of expectation $E(X)$ is given by Formula 3.

$$M = \frac{\sum_{i=1}^{n} TRUST(Ag_i)_{Aga} N(Ag_i)_{Agb} TRUST(Ag_b)_{Agi}}{\sum_{i=1}^{n} TRUST(Ag_i)_{Aga} N(Ag_i)_{Agb}}. \tag{3}$$

The value M represents an estimation of $TRUST(Ag_b)_{Aga}$ where $N(Ag_i)_{Agb}$ indicates the number of interactions between a confidence agent Ag_i and Ag_b. This number can be identified by the total number of Ag_b's commitments and arguments. This formula shows how trust can be obtained by merging the trustworthiness values transmitted by some mediators. This merging method takes into account the proportional relevance of each trustworthiness value, rather than treating them equally. This formula gives us a good estimation of $TRUST(Ag_b)_{Aga}$ that takes into account the three most important factors: (1) the trustworthiness of confidence agents according to the point of view of Ag_a (2) the Ag_b's trustworthiness according to the point of view of confidence agents (3) the number of interactions between confidence agents and Ag_b. This number is an important factor because it makes it possible to favor information coming from agents knowing more Ag_b. The function $Trustworthy(Ag_y)$ can be specified as follows:

If $M > w$ Then Return true Else return false.

According to (3), we have :

$$\forall i, TRUST(Ag_b)_{Agi} < w \Rightarrow M < w. \frac{\sum_{i=1}^{n} TRUST(Ag_i)_{Aga} N(Ag_i)_{Agb}}{\sum_{i=1}^{n} TRUST(Ag_i)_{Aga} N(Ag_i)_{Agb}}$$

$$\Rightarrow M < w$$

Consequently, the well-known *lottery paradox* of Kyburg can never happen. If all trustworthiness values transmitted by the mediators are below the threshold w, then Ag_a will not trust Ag_b.

To calculate M, we need the trustworthiness of other agents. A practical solution consists in building a *trust graph* like the *TrustNet* proposed by [31].

6   Implementation

The algorithms and the trustworthiness model presented in this paper are implemented using *Jack^{TM}* technology. *Jack^{TM}* is an agent-oriented language offering a framework for MAS development. It is built on top of and fully integrated with Java programming language. The implemented prototype enabled us to verify the correctness of our algorithms and that the persuasion dynamics terminates because it converges to an acceptance or a refusal of the conversation subject. An agent accepts the conversation subject presented by $SC(p)$ or $SC(\neg p)$ if it accepts the last argument presented by its interlocutor using its argumentation system or because this interlocutor is trustworthy.

Agents' knowledge are implemented using *Jack^{TM}* data structures called *beliefsets*. The argumentation systems are implemented as Java modules using a logical programming paradigm. These modules use agents' beliefsets to build arguments for or against certain propositional formulas. The actions that agents perform on commitments or on their contents (presented by the functions α *and* Δ) are programmed as *events*. When an agent receives such an event, it seeks a *plan* to handle it. These plans are the algorithms presented in the paper.

The trustworthiness model is implemented using the same principle (events + plans). The requests sent by an agent about the trustworthiness of another agent are events and the calculations are programmed in plans. The trust graph is implemented as a Java data structure (oriented graph). Fig. 2 illustrates an example generated by our prototype of the process allowing an agent Ag_1 to measure the trustworthiness of another agent Ag_7 in a given domain.

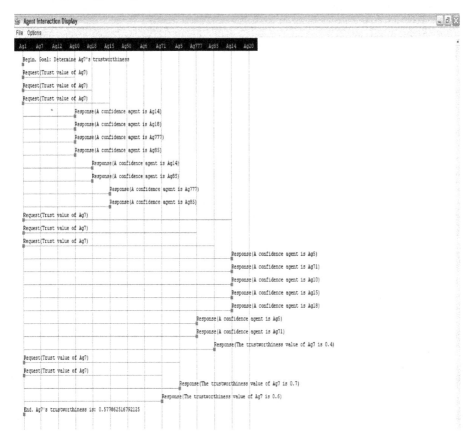

Fig. 2. Example of process of trustworthiness measure

Fig. 3 illustrates an abstract example of the persuasion dynamics. In this figure an argument is denoted (*[Support], Conclusion*).

7   Discussion

In this section we discuss three fundamental characteristics of our algorithms: termination, complexity and correctness.

1. Termination. To prove the termination of Algorithm 1, it is enough to prove that the protocol dynamics always converges to a final acceptance or a final refusal.

According to the Algorithms 2, 3, 4 ,5 and 6, the protocol chaining can have one of the following possibilities:

Fig. 3. Example of persuasion dynamics

1- Agent Ag_2 accepts all the supports of the initial commitment $SC(Ag_1, Ag_2\ p)$. Therefore, we have: $\alpha(Ag_2, SC(Ag_1, Ag_2, p)) = Accept$.

2- Agent Ag_2 refuses one of the supports of $SC(Ag_1, Ag_2, p)$, and Ag_1 does not find an argument to defend this support. Thus, we have: $\alpha(Ag_2, SC(Ag_1, Ag_2, p)) = Refuse$.

3- The two agents attack each other about a part of the last arguments.

4- Agent Ag_2 challenges a part of the arguments presented by Ag_1.

Possibilities 1 and 2 converge to a final acceptance and a final refusal. Possibility 3 converges to a situation where an agent finds an argument (H, h) to attack the support of the interlocutor's argument, but this argument was already used $((H, h) \in S'_{Ag})$. The reason is that the agents' knowledge bases are finite. In this case, this agent refuses the interlocutor's argument (Algorithm 2). Thus, possibility 3 converges to a final refusal. For the same reason, possibility 4 converges to the situation in which Ag_1 justifies a support by itself. In this situation, Ag_2 can play only an acceptance move if Ag_1 is trustworthy or a refusal move if not (Algorithm 4). Thus, possibility 4 converges to a final acceptance or a final refusal.

2. Complexity. The purpose of Algorithm 1 is to resolve the initial conflict or to decide after a finite number of moves that the conflict can not be resolved. Every move is based on the state of S_{Ag} and S'_{Ag} because agents must seek arguments or counter-arguments in S_{Ag} and S'_{Ag}. If we do not take into account the trustworthiness part of the algorithm, and since $|S_{Ag}| < |S'_{Ag}|$, the time complexity of algorithm 1 is $O(max(|S_{Ag1}|, |S_{Ag2}|))$. Thus the complexity is linear in the size of the knowledge bases of the agents. Before dealing with the complexity of the trustworthiness part, we introduce the following definition of the trust graph.

Definition 5. *A trust graph is a directed and weighted graph. The nodes are agents and an edge (Ag_i, Ag_j) means that agent Ag_i knows agent Ag_j. The weight of the edge (Ag_i, Ag_j) is a pair (x, y) where x is the Ag_j' trust according to the point of view of Ag_i and y is the interaction number between Ag_i and Ag_j. The weight of a node is the agent trust according to the point of view of the source agent.*

According to this definition, in order to determine the trustworthiness of the target agent Ag_b, it is necessary to find the weight of the node representing this agent in the graph. The algorithm is based on the construction of the graph and on a recursive call to assess the weight of all the nodes. Since each node is visited exactly once, there are n recursive calls, where n is the number of nodes in the graph. To assess the weight of a node we need the weights of its neighboring nodes and the weights of the input edges. Thus, the algorithm takes a time in $O(n)$ for the recursive calls and a time in $O(a)$ to assess the agents' trust where a is the number of edges. The run time of the trustworthiness algorithm is therefore in $O(max(a, n))$ i.e. linear in the size of the graph. In total, Algorithm 1 takes a time in $O(max(|S_{Ag1}|, |S_{Ag2}|) + max(a, n)) = O(max(|S_{Ag1}|, |S_{Ag2}|, a, n))$.

3. Correctness. We formalize the correctness problem of our algorithms as follows: Algorithm 1 is correct iff the protocol description based on this algorithm satisfies the protocol specification (i.e. what the protocol must do). The specification can be formalized as a set of claims or properties. The idea is to describe the protocol by a formal model M using a Kripke structure, and to express the specification as a logical formula ψ using our DCTL*$_{CAN}$ logic [6]. This formalization enables us to deal with the correctness problem as a model-checking problem, i.e. whether $M \models \psi$ or not. For this reason, it is possible to use the well-known model-checking technique for the CTL* fragment of our logic. However, resolving this problem for the all DCTL*$_{CAN}$ logic needs to develop a new model-checking technique for dynamic and temporal properties. The solution we are investigating as a future work is to use a combination of an automata-theoretic approach and a tableau-based approach [7].

8 Related Work

Smith et al [26] developed protocols having the advantage of being based on a logical theory (the theory of joint intention) that suggests how protocols can be linked together to form more complex interactions. However, these protocols do not take into account how different strategies can be chosen. Because our protocol uses DGs, it is possible to combine it with other protocols (information seeking, negotiation, ...). Semantically, the protocols proposed by Smith et al. are based on private attitudes whereas we use a public and argumentative semantics.

Yolum and Singh [30] developed an approach for specifying protocols in which actions' content is captured through agents' commitments [25]. They provide operations and reasoning rules to capture the evolution of commitments. Using these rules, agents can reason about their actions. In a similar way, Fornara and Colombetti [12] proposed a method to define interaction protocols. This method is based on the specification of an interaction diagram (ID) specifying which actions can be performed under given conditions. The advantage of these approaches is to be verifiable because they are based on public notions. They also allow us to represent the interaction dynamics through the allowed operations. Our protocol is comparable to these protocols because it is also based on commitments. However, it is different in the following respects. The choice of the various operations is explicitly dealt with in our protocol by using argumentation and trustworthiness. The CAN formalism used to represent the protocol enables us to distinguish the various operations applied to commitments and to their contents as well as the argumentation relations. In addition, our protocol uses a specification based on philosophical foundations that allow us to specify the interaction dynamics.

To tackle the problem of the lack of flexibility in protocols, Reed [21], Dastani et al. [9], Maudet and Chaib-draa [13], and Dignum et al. [10] proposed protocols based on DGs. These protocols can be composed of various operations: sequencing, chaining, etc. Our protocol belongs to this family of protocols. However, our approach based on commitments and arguments makes our protocol different in terms of the allowed actions and in terms of the specification that our protocol has. In addition, our protocol clearly indicates how agents can choose a strategy using argumentative and social notions.

Parsons et al. [16], Amgoud et al. [2], McBurney [15], Sadri et al. [23] proposed protocols based on an argumentative approach. These protocols are based on Walton and Krabbe's classification and on formal dialectics. In these protocols, agents can argue about the truth of propositions. Agents can communicate both propositional statements and arguments about these statements. These protocols have the advantage of taking into account the capacity of agents to reason as well as their attitudes (confident, careful,....). Semantically, these protocols are specified by defining pre/post conditions for each locution. The difference between these protocols and ours is that our protocol deals with the social aspects of the interaction in its specification by integrating the notion of trustworthiness. In addition, we use a hybrid approach based on commitments and arguments. Our protocol is specified not by pre/post conditions, but by algorithms specifying the entry conditions, the exit conditions and the dynamics. Particularly, there are other differences between our protocol and that of Parsons et al.: 1. From the theoretical point of view, Parsons et al.'s protocol uses moves from formal dialectics, whereas our protocol uses actions that agents apply on commitments. These actions capture the speech acts that agents perform when conversing (see Definition 1). The advantage of using these actions is that they enable us to better represent the persuasion dynamics considering that their semantics can be defined in an unambiguous way in a dynamic logic. 2. Parsons et al.'s protocol uses only three moves: assertion, acceptance and challenge, whereas our protocol uses, over and above creation, acceptance, refusal and challenge actions, attack and defense actions in an explicit way. These argumentation relations allow us to directly illustrate the concept of dispute in this type of protocols. 3. Parsons et al. use an acceptance criterion directly related to the argumentation system, whereas we use an acceptance criteria for the agents (supports of arguments and trustworthiness). This makes it possible to decrease the computational complexity of the protocol for agent communication.

9   Conclusion and Future Work

In this paper we proposed a new persuasion protocol based on DGs. This protocol is presented within a social and argumentative approach. Using our CAN formalism, this protocol is specified by indicating its entry conditions, exit conditions and dynamics. This protocol is characterized by the fact that it integrates trustworthiness as a component of the decision-making process. We described the implementation of this protocol using an agent platform.

As future work, we intend to specify other protocols according to Walton and Krabbe's classification and Vanderveken's typology. Another objective of this research is to verify some formal properties of these protocols (termination, soundness, ...) using model-checking techniques. The idea we are investigating is to use a tableau method and an automata theoretic approach to branching time model checking. Thus, to prove that our protocol M verifies some properties ψ, we have to verify that $M \models \psi$ which is a model-checking problem.

Acknowledgments

We would like to thank John-Jules Ch. Meyer for his valuable suggestions. We would also like to thank the two anonymous referees. Their detailed and very interesting comments allowed us to improve the quality of this paper.

References

1. Abdul-Rahman, A. and Hailes. S. Supporting Trust in Virtual Communities. In Proc. Of the 33rd Hawaii Int. Conf. On Systems Science (2000) .
2. Amgoud, L., Maudet, N., and Parsons, N. Modelling dialogues using argumentation. In Proc. of the 4th Int. Conf. on MAS (2000) 31-38.

3. Bench-Capon, T.J.M., Freeman J.B., Hohmann, H., and Prakken, H. Computational models, argumentation theories and legal practice. In Reed, C. and Norman, T.J. (eds.). Argumentation Machines. New Frontiers in Argument and Computation. Kluwer Argumentation Library (2003) 85-120.
4. Bentahar, J., Moulin, B., and Chaib-draa, B. Vers une approche à base d'engagements et d'arguments pour la modélisation du dialogue. In Modèles Formels de l'Interaction, Cépaduès (2003) 19-28.
5. Bentahar, J., Moulin, B., and Chaib-draa, B. Commitment and argument network: a new formalism for agent communication. Dignum, F. (ed.). Advances in Agent Communication. Lecture Notes in Artificial Intelligence, vol. 2922. Springer-Verlag, (2003) 146-165.
6. Bentahar, J., Moulin, B., Meyer, J-J, Ch., and Chaib-draa, B. A logical model for commitment and argument network (extended abstract). In Proc. Of the 3rd Int. J. Conf. On AAMAS (2004) 792-799.
7. Bhat, G., Cleaveland, R., and Groce, A. Efficient model checking via Büchi tableau automata. In Berry, G., Comon, H., and Finkel, A. (eds). Computer-Aided Verification, Lecture Notes in Computer Scuence, vol. 2102. Springer-Verlag, (2001) 38-52.
8. Castelfranchi, C. Commitments: from individual intentions to groups and organizations. In Proc. of the Int. Conf. on Multi-Agent Systems (1995) 41-48.
9. Dastani, M., Hulstijn, J. and der Torre, L. V. Negotiation protocols and dialogue games. In Proc. of the Belgium/Dutch AI Conf. (2000) 13-20.
10. Dignum, F., Dunin-Keplicz, and Verbugge, R., Creation collective intention through dialogue. Logic Journal of the IGPL, 9(2) (2001) 305-319.
11. Elvang-Goransson, M., Fox, J., and Krause, P. Dialectic reasoning with inconsistent information. In Proc. of the 9th Conf. on Uncertainty in AI. (1993) 114-121.
12. Fornara, N. and Colombetti, M. Defining protocols using a commitment-based agent communication language. In Proc. Of the 2nd Int. J. Conf. On AAMAS (2003) 520-527.
13. Maudet, N. and Chaib-draa, B. Commitment-based and dialogue-game based protocols, new trends in agent communication languages. Knowledge Engineering Review, 17(2), Cambridge Univ. Press (2002) 157-179.
14. McBurney, P. and Parsons, S. Games that agents play: A formal framework for dialogues between autonomous agents. Journal of Logic, Language, and Information, 11(3) (2002) 1-22.
15. McBurney, P. Rational Interaction. Thesis of Univ. of Liverpool (2002).
16. Parsons, S., Wooldridge, M., and Amgoud, L. On the outcomes of formal inter-agent Dialogues. In Proc. Of the 2nd Int. J. Conf. On AAMAS (2003) 616-623.
17. Prakken, H. Logical Tools for Modelling legal argument. A study of defeasible reasoning in law. Kluwer Law and Philosophy Library (1997).
18. Prakken, H. and Sartor, G. Modelling reasoning with precedents in a formal dialogue game. Artificial Intelligence and Law, vol.6 (1998) 231-287.
19. Prakken, H. and Vreeswijk, G. Logics for defeasible argumentation. Gabbay, D., (ed.), Handbook of Philosophical Logic, Kluwer (2000) 218-319.
20. Ramchurn, S.D., Sierra, C., Jennings, N.R., and Godo L. A computational trust model for multi-agent interactions based on confidence and reputation. In Proc. of 6th Int. Workshop of Deception, Fraud and Trust in Agent Societies (2003) 69-75.
21. Reed, C. Dialogue frames in agent communication. In Proc. of the 3rd Int. Conf. on MAS. (1998) 246-253.
22. Sabater, J. and Sierra, C. Reputation and social network analysis in multi-agent systems. In Proc. Of the 1st Int. J. Conf. On AAMAS (2002) 475-482.
23. Sadri, F., Toni, F., Torroni, P. Logic agents, dialogues and negotiation: an abductive approach. In Proc. of Symposium on Information Agents for E-Commerce (2001).

24. Searle, J.R. Speech acts: an essay in the philosophy of language. Cambridge University Press, England (1969).
25. Singh, M.P. Agent communication languages: rethinking the principles, IEEE Computer (1998) 40-47.
26. Smith, I.A., Cohen, P.R., Bradshaw, J.M., Greaves, M., and Holmback, H. Designing conversation policies using joint intention theory. In Proc. of the 3rd Int. Conf on MAS (1998) 269-276.
27. Vanderveken, D., Illocutionary logic and discourse typology. Searle with his Replies of Revue Internat. de Philosophie. 2001.
28. Vreeswijk, G.A.W. Abstract argumentation systems. Artificial Intelligence, 90 (1-2), 1997, 225-279.
29. Walton, D.N. and Krabbe, E.C.W. Commitment in dialogue: basic concepts of interpersonal reasoning. State Univ. of New York Press, Albany, NY (1995).
30. Yolum, P. and Singh, M.P. Flexible protocol specification and execution: applying event calculus planning using commitments. In Proc. of Int. J. Conf. On AAMAS (2002) 527-534.
31. Yu, B. and Singh, M. An evidential model of distributed reputation management. In Proc. Of the 1st Int. J. Conf. On AAMAS (2002) 294-301.

A Dialogue Game Protocol for Multi-agent Argument over Proposals for Action

Katie Atkinson, Trevor Bench-Capon, and Peter McBurney

Department of Computer Science,
University of Liverpool,
Liverpool L69 7ZF UK
{k.m.atkinson, tbc,p.j.mcburney}@csc.liv.ac.uk

Abstract. We present the syntax and semantics for a multi-agent dialogue game protocol which permits argument over proposals for action. The protocol, called the *PARMA Protocol*, embodies an earlier theory by the authors of persuasion over action which enables participants to rationally propose, attack, and defend, an action or course of actions (or inaction). We present an outline of both an axiomatic and a denotational semantics, and discuss an implementation of the protocol for two human agents.

1   Introduction

Developers of real-world software agent systems typically desire either the system as a whole or the agents within it to effect changes in the state of the world external to the system. Whether the software agents represent human bidders in an online auction or the system collectively manages some resource, such as a utility network, the agents and/or the system usually need to initiate, maintain or terminate actions in the world [12]. Agent interaction protocols, therefore, must be concerned with argument over actions: agents in such systems may not be concerned with sharing and reconciling one another's beliefs, except insofar as these assist in sharing and coordinating their actions.

Philosophers of argumentation, however, have mostly concentrated their attention on beliefs, and not on actions.[1] Computer scientists, also, have typically not distinguished between justifications for beliefs and for actions. Attempting to fill this gap, we have previously articulated a theory of persuasion over actions, in which a proponent of a proposed action can seek to persuade another party (a human or software agent) to endorse it [5]. By classifying all the possible attacks on a proposal for action, our theory permits dialogue participants to represent, to attack and to defend a proposal for action in a systematic manner. We now extend this work by presenting a novel dialogue game protocol, which we call the *PARMA* (for Persuasive ARgument for Multiple Agents) *Action Persuasion Protocol*, in which proposals for action may be presented, and these attacks and defences may occur.

---

[1] Stephen Toulmin's book entitled *"Knowing and Acting"* [20], for example, has 18 chapters on beliefs, and 1 on actions.

I. Rahwan et al. (Eds.): ArgMAS 2004, LNAI 3366, pp. 149–161, 2005.

The paper is structured as follows: Section 2 reprises our general theory of persuasion over action, and indicates the possible attacks of a proposal for action. Section 3 presents the syntax and an axiomatic semantics for the *PARMA Action Persuasion Protocol* while Section 4 outlines a denotational semantics for dialogues under the protocol. Section 5 then describes an implementation we have undertaken of the protocol, and Section 6 concludes with a discussion of some of the issues raised and possible future work.

It is important to note that dialogues under our protocol are Persuasion dialogues, in the influential terminology of Walton and Krabbe [22].[2] Both Negotiation dialogues (which concern the division of some scarce resource) and Deliberation dialogues (which concern what action to take in some circumstance) in this terminology also concern dialogues over action. A key difference between Negotiation and Deliberation dialogues, on the one hand, and Persuasion dialogues, on the other, is that Persuasion dialogues commence with at least one participant supporting the proposal for action under discussion (a proposal which may involve not acting). This is not necessarily the case with Negotiation dialogues or Deliberations, both of which may commence without any endorsement by a participant to any proposed action (or inaction), or, indeed, commence without any proposal for action before the participants.

2   A Theory of Persuasion over Action

Our focus is on rational interactions between agents engaged in joint practical reasoning, that is, seeking to agree an action or course of action. We use the word *rational* in the sense of argumentation theory, where it is understood as the giving and receiving of reasons for beliefs or actions [9]. In these interactions, we assume that one agent endorses a particular action, and seeks to have another agent do the same. This type of dialogue is a Persuasion dialogue, and our theory permits actions to be proposed, to be attacked, and to be defended by agents engaged in a Persuasion interaction. For such an interaction, we first define what it means to propose an action (Section 2.1), then consider rational attacks on it (Section 2.2), and then rational counter-attacks and resolution (Section 2.3).

2.1   Stating a Position

We give the following as the general argument schema (called *AS1*)for a rational position proposing an action:

> *Argument Schema AS1:*
> In the Current Circumstances R
> we should perform Action A
> to achieve New Circumstances S
> which will realize some goal G
> which will promote some value V.

For current purposes, we need recognize no difference between resolving on a future action and justifying a past action. Moreover, an action may achieve multiple goals, and

---

[2] Although not Persuasion dialogues in the revised typology of [21].

each goal may promote multiple values. For simplicity, we assume that the proponent of an action articulates an argument in the form of schema *AS1* for each goal realized and value promoted. We assume the existence of:

- A finite set of distinct actions, denoted *Acts*, with elements, A, B, C, etc.
- A finite set of propositions, denoted *Props*, with elements, p, q, r, etc.
- A finite set of states, denoted *States*, with elements, R, S, T, etc. Each element of *States* is an assignment of truth values $\{T, F\}$ to every element of *Props*.
- A finite set of propositional formulae called goals, denoted *Goals*, with elements G, H, etc.
- A finite set of values, denoted *Values*, with elements v, w, etc.
- A function *value* mapping each element of *Goals* to a pair $< v, sign >$, where $v \in$ *Values* and $sign \in \{+, =, -\}$.
- A ternary relation *apply* on *Acts* $\times$ *States* $\times$ *States*, with *apply(A, R, S)* to be read as: *"Performing action A in state R results in state S."*

The argument schema *AS1* contains a number of problematic notions which are not readily formalized in classical logic. We can, however, see that there are four classical statements which must hold if the argument represented by schema AS1 is to be valid:

> **Statement 1:** R is the case.
> **Statement 2:** $apply(A, R, S) \in apply$.
> **Statement 3:** $S \models G$. ("G is true in state S.")
> **Statement 4:** $value(G) =< v, + >$.

We can represent a position expressed according to *AS1* in the following diagrammatic form:

$$R \xrightarrow{A} S \models G \uparrow v.$$

The possible attacks on a position presented in the next sub-section may be viewed as attacking one or more elements of this representation, or the connections between them.

2.2   Attacking a Position

A position proposing an action may be attacked in a number of ways, and we have identified what we believe is a comprehensive list of rational attacks. In Table 1 we summarize these attacks, and indicate the number of variants for each. The fourth column of this table indicates the basis for resolution of any disagreement, which we discuss in the next subsection. Some attacks (Attacks 1–4) deny the truth or validity of elements of a position, such as the validity of the inference that $S \models G$, for a state S and goals G. A second group of attacks (Attacks 5–7) argue that the same effects can be achieved by a different action. A third group (Attacks 8–9, 11) argue against the action proposed because of its undesirable side effects or because of interference with other, preferred, actions. Attack 10 agrees with the action proposed, but offers different reasons from those stated in the position. Such an attack may be important in domains, such as legal reasoning, where the reasons given for actions act as precedents for future decisions. Finally, the last group of attacks (Attacks 12–15) argue that elements of the stated position are invalid or impossible, as, for example, when the attacker disagrees that the proposed action is possible.

The variants on these attacks follow a pattern. An attacker may simply express disagreement with some aspect of a position, as when an attacker denies that R is the current state of the world. Beyond this minimalist attack, an attacker may also state an alternative position to that proposed, for example, expressing not only that R is not the current state of the world, but also that T is the current state. A full list and description of the attacks and their variants are given in [1, 5].

Table 1. Attacks on a Proposal for Action

Attack	Variants	Description	Basis of Resolution
1	2	Disagree with the description of the current situation	Empirical investigation
2·	7	Disagree with the consequences of the proposed action	Causal theory
3	6	Disagree that the desired features are part of the consequences	Logical theory
4	4	Disagree that these features promote the desired value	Social theory
5	1	Believe the consequences can be realized by some alternative action	Preferences over actions
6	1	Believe the desired features can be realized through some alternative action	Preferences over actions
7	1	Believe that an alternative action realizes the desired value	Preferences over actions
8	1	Believe the action has undesirable side effects which demote the desired value	Causal theory
9	1	Believe the action has undesirable side effects which demote some other value	Preferences over values
10	2	Agree that the action should be performed, but for different reasons	Judgment
11	3	Believe the action will preclude some more desirable action	Preferences over actions
12	1	Believe the action is impossible	Empirical investigation
13	2	Believe the circumstances or consequences as described are not possible	Empirical investigation
14	1	Believe the desired features cannot be realized	Social theory
15	1	Disagree that the desired value is worth promoting	Preferences over values

2.3   Responding to an Attack and Resolution

How a proponent of a proposal for action responds to an attack depends upon the nature of the attack. For those attacks which explicitly state an alternative position, the original proponent is able to counter-attack with some subset of the attacks listed in Table 1. For example, if a proponent argues for an action on the grounds that this will promote some value v, and an attacker argues in response that the proposed action will also demote some other value w, then the proponent may respond to this attack by arguing that the action does not have this effect on w (Attack 4), or that an alternative action can promote w, or that w is not worth promoting (Attack 15), etc.

Whether or not two participants may ultimately reach agreement on a proposed action will depend on the participants and on the precise nature of the disagreement. A basis for any resolution between participants for each type of attack is shown in the fourth column of Table 1. If the disagreement concerns the nature of the current world-state (Attack 1), for example, then some process of agreed empirical investigation may resolve this difference between the participants. Alternatively, if the participants disagree over which value should be promoted by the action (Attacks 9 or 15), then resolution will require agreement between them on a preference ordering over values. Such resolution may require other types of dialogue, and some of these interactions have received considerable attention from philosophers, for example [6, 16, 17]. We leave this topic for another occasion.

3   The *PARMA Protocol*

In this section we present the syntax of the *PARMA Action Persuasion Protocol* together with an outline of an axiomatic semantics for the protocol. We assume, as in recent work in agent communications languages [11], that the language syntax comprises two layers: an inner layer in which the topics of conversation are represented formally, and an outer, wrapper, layer comprising locutions which express the illocutionary force of the inner content.

Table 2. Locutions to Control the Dialogue

Locution	Pre-conditions	Post-conditions
Enter dialogue	Speaker has not already uttered enter dialogue	Speaker has entered dialogue
Leave dialogue	Speaker has uttered enter dialogue	Speaker has left dialogue
Turn finished	Speaker has finished making their move	Speaker and hearer switch roles so new speaker can now make a move
Accept denial	Hearer has made an attack on an element of speaker's position	Speaker committed to the negation of the element that was denied by the hearer
Reject denial	Hearer has made an attack on an element of speaker's position	Disagreement reached

The locutions of the *PARMA Protocol* are shown in the left-most columns of Tables 2–6. These tables also present the pre-conditions necessary for the legal utterance of each locution under the Protocol, and any post-conditions arising from their legal utterance. Thus, Tables 2–6 present an outline of an axiomatic semantics for the PARMA Protocol [19], and imply the rules governing the combination of locutions under the protocol [13]. We further assume, following [7] and in accordance with recent work in agent communications, that a *Commitment Store* is associated with each participant, which stores, in a manner which all participants may read, the commitments made by that participant in the course of a dialogue. The post-conditions of utterances shown in Tables 2–6 include any commitments incurred by the speaker of each utterance while the pre-conditions indicate any prior commitments required before an utterance can be legally made. Commitments in this protocol are dialogical — ie, statements which an agent must defend if attacked, and may bear no relation to the agent's real beliefs or intentions [7].

Table 3. Locutions to Propose an Action

Locution	Pre-conditions	Post-conditions
State circumstances(R)	Speaker has uttered enter dialogue	Speaker committed to R
		Speaker committed to R $\in$ States
State action(A)	Speaker has uttered enter dialogue	Speaker committed to A
	Speaker committed to R	Speaker committed to A $\in$ Acts
	Speaker committed to R $\in$ States	
State consequences(A,R,S)	Speaker has uttered enter dialogue	Speaker committed to
	Speaker committed to R	apply(A,R,S) $\in$ apply
	Speaker committed to R $\in$ States	Speaker committed to S $\in$ States
	Speaker committed to A	
	Speaker committed to A $\in$ Acts	
State logical consequences(S,G)	Speaker has uttered enter dialogue	Speaker committed to S $\models$ G
	Speaker committed to R	Speaker committed to G $\in$ Goals
	Speaker committed to R $\in$ States	
	Speaker committed to A	
	Speaker committed to A $\in$ Acts	
	Speaker committed to apply(A,R,S) $\in$ apply	
	Speaker committed to S $\in$ States	
State purpose(G,V,D)	Speaker has uttered enter dialogue	Speaker committed to (G,V,D)
	Speaker committed to R	Speaker committed to V $\in$ Values
	Speaker committed to R $\in$ States	
	Speaker committed to A	
	Speaker committed to A $\in$ Acts	
	Speaker committed to apply(A,R,S) $\in$ apply	
	Speaker committed to S $\in$ States	
	Speaker committed to S $\models$ G	
	Speaker committed to G $\in$ Goals	

4   A Denotational Semantics

We now outline a denotational semantics for the *PARMA* protocol, that is a semantics which maps statements in the syntax to mathematical entities [19]. Our approach draws

Table 4. Locutions to ask about an Agent's Position

Locution	Pre-conditions	Post-conditions
Ask circumstances(R)	Hearer has uttered enter dialogue Speaker has uttered enter dialogue Speaker not committed to circumstances(R) about topic in question	Hearer must reply with state circumstances(R) or don't know(R)
Ask action(A)	Hearer has uttered enter dialogue Speaker has uttered enter dialogue Speaker not committed to action(A) about topic in question	Hearer must reply with state action(A) or don't know(A)
Ask consequences(A,R,S)	Hearer has uttered enter dialogue Speaker has uttered enter dialogue Speaker not committed to consequences(A,R,S) about topic in question	Hearer must reply with state consequences(A,R,S) or don't know(A,R,S)
Ask logical consequences(S,G)	Hearer has uttered enter dialogue Speaker has uttered enter dialogue Speaker not committed to logical consequences(S,G) about topic in question	Hearer must reply with state logical consequences(S,G) or don't know(S,G)
Ask purpose(G,V,D)	Hearer has uttered enter dialogue Speaker has uttered enter dialogue Speaker not committed to purpose(G,V,D) about topic in question	Hearer must reply with state purpose(G,V,D) or don't know(G,V,D)

on the semantics proposed by Charles Hamblin for imperative statements [8], which itself may be viewed as a process theory of causality. The main proponent of such theories has been Wesley Salmon, whose theory of causal processes *"identifies causal connections with physical processes that transmit causal influence from one spacetime location to another"* [18, p. 191]. Our approach draws on elements of category theory, namely topos theory. Our reason for using this, rather than (say) a Kripkean possible worlds framework or a labelled transition system, is that topos theory enables a natural representation of logical consequence $(S \models G)$ in the same formalism as mappings between spaces $(R \xrightarrow{A} S$ and $G \uparrow v)$. To our knowledge, no other non-categorical denotational semantics currently proposed for action formalisms permits this.

We begin by representing proposals for action. We assume, as in Section 2.1, finite sets of Acts, Propositions, States, Goals, and Values, and various mappings. For simplicity, we assume there are n propositions. Each State may be considered as being equivalent to the set of propositions which are true in that State, and so there are 2^n States. We consider the space $\mathcal{C}$ of these States, with some additional structure to enable the representation of actions and truth-values. We consider values as mappings from Goals to some space of evaluations, called $\mathcal{S}$. This need not be the three-valued set $Sign = \{+, =, -\}$ we assumed in Section 2.1, although we assume that $\mathcal{S}$ admits at least one partial order. The structures we assume on $\mathcal{C}$, $\mathcal{S}$ and between them is intended to enable us to demonstrate that these are categorical entities [3]. We begin by listing the mathematical entities, along with informal definitions.

Table 5. Locutions to Attack Elements of a Position

Locution	Pre-conditions	Post-conditions
Deny circumstances(R)	Speaker has uttered enter dialogue Hearer has uttered enter dialogue Hearer committed to R Hearer committed to R ∈ States	Speaker committed to deny circumstances(R)
Deny consequences(A,R,S)	Speaker has uttered enter dialogue Hearer has uttered enter dialogue Hearer committed to R Hearer committed to R ∈ States Hearer committed to A Hearer committed to A ∈ Acts Hearer committed to apply(A,R,S) ∈ apply Hearer committed to S ∈ States	Speaker committed to deny consequences(A,R,S) ∈ apply
Deny logical consequences(S,G)	Speaker has uttered enter dialogue Hearer has uttered enter dialogue Hearer committed to R Hearer committed to R ∈ States Hearer committed to A Hearer committed to A ∈ Acts Hearer committed to apply(A,R,S) ∈ apply Hearer committed to S ∈ States Hearer committed to S ⊨ G Hearer committed to G ∈ Goals	Speaker committed to deny logical consequences(S,G) S ⊨ G
Deny purpose(G,V,D)	Speaker has uttered enter dialogue Hearer has uttered enter dialogue Hearer committed to R Hearer committed to R ∈ States Hearer committed to A Hearer committed to A ∈ Acts Hearer committed to apply(A,R,S) ∈ apply Hearer committed to S ∈ States Hearer committed to S ⊨ G Hearer committed to G ∈ Goals Hearer committed to (G,V,D) Hearer committed to V ∈ Values	Speaker committed to deny purpose(G,V,D)

- The space $\mathcal{C}$ comprises a finite collection $\mathcal{C}_0$ of objects and a finite collection $\mathcal{C}_1$ of arrows between objects.
- $\mathcal{C}_0$ includes 2^n objects, each of which may be considered as representing a State. We denote these objects by the lower-case Greek letters, $\alpha, \beta, \gamma, \ldots$, and refer to them collectively as *state objects* or *states*. We may consider each state to be equivalent (in some sense) to the set of propositions which are true in the state.

Table 6. Locutions to Attack Validity of Elements

Locution	Pre-conditions	Post-conditions
Deny initial circumstances exist(R)	Speaker has uttered enter dialogue Hearer has uttered enter dialogue Hearer committed to R ∈ States	Speaker committed to deny initial circumstances exist(R)
Deny action exists(A)	Speaker has uttered enter dialogue Hearer has uttered enter dialogue Hearer committed to R Hearer committed to R ∈ States Hearer committed to A ∈ Acts	Speaker committed to deny action exists(A)
Deny resultant state exists(S)	Speaker has uttered enter dialogue Hearer has uttered enter dialogue Hearer committed to R Hearer committed to R ∈ States Hearer committed to A ∈ Acts Hearer committed to S ∈ States	Speaker committed to deny resultant state exists(S)
Deny goal exists(G)	Speaker has uttered enter dialogue Hearer has uttered enter dialogue Hearer committed to R Hearer committed to R ∈ States Hearer committed to A ∈ Acts Hearer committed to S ∈ States Hearer committed to G ∈ Goals	Speaker committed to deny goal exists(G)
Deny value exists(V)	Speaker has uttered enter dialogue Hearer has uttered enter dialogue Hearer committed to R Hearer committed to R ∈ States Hearer committed to A ∈ Acts Hearer committed to S ∈ States Hearer committed to G ∈ Goals Hearer committed to V ∈ Values	Speaker committed to deny value exists(V)

- $\mathcal{C}_1$ includes arrows between state objects, denoted by lower case Roman letters, $f, g, h, \ldots$. If f is an arrow from object α to object $beta$, we also write $f : \alpha \rightarrow \beta$. Some arrows between the state objects may be considered as representing actions leading from one state to another, while other arrows are causal processes (not actions of the dialogue participants) which take the world from one state to another. There may be any number of arrows between the same two objects: zero, one, or more than one.

- Associated with every object $\alpha \in \mathcal{C}_0$, there is an arrow $1_\alpha \in \mathcal{C}_1$ from α to α, called the identity at α. In the case where α is a state object, this arrow may be considered as that action (or possibly inaction) which preserves the status quo at a state α.

- If $f : \alpha \rightarrow \beta$ and $g : \beta \rightarrow \gamma$ are both arrows in $\mathcal{C}_1$, then we assume there is an arrow $h : \alpha \rightarrow \gamma$. We denote this arrow h by $g \circ f$ ("g composed with f"). In other words, actions and causal processes may be concatenated.

- We assume that $\mathcal{C}_0$ includes a special object *Prop*, which represents the finite set of all propositions. We further assume that for every object $\alpha \in \mathcal{C}_0$ there is a monic arrow $f_\alpha : \alpha \to Prop$. Essentially, a monic arrow is an injective (one-to-one) mapping.
- We assume that $\mathcal{C}_0$ has a terminal object, **1**, ie, an object such that for every object $\alpha \in \mathcal{C}_0$, there is precisely one arrow $\alpha \to \mathbf{1}$.
- We assume that $\mathcal{C}$ has a special object Ω, and an arrow $true : \mathbf{1} \to \Omega$, called a *sub-object classifier*. The object Ω may be understood as the set comprising $\{True, False\}$.
- We assume that $\mathcal{S}$ is space of objects over which there is a partial order $<_i$ corresponding to each participant in the dialogue. Such a space may be viewed as a category, with an arrow between two objects α and β whenever $\alpha <_i \beta$. For each participant, we further assume the existence of one or more mappings v between $\mathcal{C}$ and $\mathcal{S}$, which takes objects to objects, and arrows to arrows. We denote the collection of all these mappings by $\mathcal{V}$.

The assumptions we have made here enable us to show that $\mathcal{C}$ is a category [3], and we can thus represent the statement $R \xrightarrow{A} S$, for states R and S, and action A. Moreover, the presence of a sub-object classifier structure enables us to represent statements of the form $S \models G$, for state S and goal G, inside the same category $\mathcal{C}$. This structure we have defined for $\mathcal{C}$ creates some of the properties needed for $\mathcal{C}$ to be a topos [3]. Finally, each space $\mathcal{S}$ with partial order $<_i$ is also a category, and the mappings v are functors (structure-preserving mappings) between $\mathcal{C}$ and $\mathcal{S}$. This then permits us to represent statements of the form $G \uparrow v$, for goal G and value v.

We define a denotational semantics for the *PARMA* Protocol by associating dialogues conducted according to the Protocol with mathematical structures of the type defined above. Thus, the statement of a proposal for action by a participant in a dialogue

$$R \xrightarrow{A} S \models G \uparrow v$$

is understood semantically as the assertion of the existence of objects representing R and S in $\mathcal{C}$, the existence of an arrow representing A between them, the existence of an arrow with certain properties[3] between *Prop* and Ω, and the existence of a functor $v \in \mathcal{V}$ from $\mathcal{C}$ to $\mathcal{S}$. Attacks on this position then may be understood semantically as denials of the existence of one or more of these elements, and possibly also, if the attack is sufficiently strong, the assertion of the existence of other objects, arrows or functors.

Thus, our denotational semantics for a dialogue conducted according to the *PARMA* Protocol is defined as a countable sequence of triples,

$$\langle \mathcal{C}_1, \mathcal{S}_1, \mathcal{V}_1 \rangle, \langle \mathcal{C}_2, \mathcal{S}_2, \mathcal{V}_2 \rangle, \langle \mathcal{C}_3, \mathcal{S}_3, \mathcal{V}_3 \rangle, \ldots,$$

where the k-th triple is created from the k-th utterance in the dialogue according to the representation rules just described. Then, our denotational semantics for the *PARMA* Protocol itself is defined as the collection of all such countable sequences of triples for valid

---

[3] This arrow is the characteristic function for the object representing G, and the properties are that a certain diagram commutes in $\mathcal{C}$.

dialogues conducted under *PARMA*. This approach views the semantics of the protocol as a space of mathematical objects, which are created incrementally and jointly by the participants in the course of their dialogue together. The approach derives from the constructive view of human language semantics of Discourse Representation Theory [10], and is similar in spirit to the denotational semantics, called a *trace semantics*, defined for deliberation dialogues in [14], and the *dialectical graph* recording the statements of the participants in the Pleadings Game of Thomas Gordon [4]. We are currently engaged in specifying formally this denotational semantics in accordance with the outline presented here.

5   Implementation of the Dialogue Game

We have also implemented the *PARMA Action Persuasion Protocol* in the form of a Java program. The program implements the protocol so that dialogues between two human participants can be undertaken under the protocol, with each participant taking turns to propose and attack positions uttering the locutions specified above. The program checks the legality of the participants' chosen moves by verifying that all pre-conditions for the move hold. Thus, the participants are able to state and attack each other's positions with the program verifying that the dialogue always complies with the protocol. If a participant attempts to make an illegal move then they are informed about this and given the opportunity to chose an alternative move. After a move has been legally uttered, the commitment store of the participant who made the move is updated to contain any new commitments created by the utterance. All moves, whether legal or illegal, are entered into the history, which records which moves were made by which participant and the legality of the move chosen. After a move has been legally made, the commitment store of the player who made the move is printed to the screen to show all previous commitments and any new ones that have consequently been added. By publicly displaying the commitment stores in this way each participant is able to see their own and each other's commitments. Thus, participants can determine which of their commitments overlap with those of the other participant, and thereby identify points of agreement. Conversely, this also allows each participant to identify any commitments of the other participant in conflict with their own, and thus which commitments are susceptible to an attack.

Dialogues undertaken via the program can terminate in a number of ways. A participant can decide to leave the game by exiting at any time, thereby terminating the dialogue. A dialogue can also terminate if disagreement about a position is reached. This occurs when a participant states an element of a position which is is consequently attacked by the other participant, and the first participant disagrees with the attack. If the first participant refuses to accept the reasons for the attack then disagreement has been identified and the dialogue terminates. Dialogues may also reach a natural end with agreement between the two participants on a course of action. If this occurs, both players may choose to exit the dialogue.

When a dialogue terminates, whether in agreement or disagreement, the history and commitment stores of both players are printed on screen and also to a file. The dialogue may then be analyzed, for example to see which attacks occurred, or how often or how successful they were. Such analysis may be useful for a study of appropriate strategies for dialogue conducted under the protocol. Further details of the implementation can be found in [2].

6 Conclusions

This paper has presented the syntax and semantics for a novel agent dialogue game protocol for argument over proposals for action. The protocol, called the *PARMA Action Persuasion Protocol*, implements our previous theory of persuasion over actions, which presents a general argument schema for the advocacy and justification of actions, and so supports rational discourse over proposed courses of actions. The protocol enables such persuasive dialogues to be undertaken by autonomous software agents.

There are several avenues we hope to explore in future work. Firstly, we plan to articulate in detail the axiomatic and denotational semantics we have presented in outline here. These should be straightforward, if somewhat tedious, exercises. Secondly, we note that formalisms of actions and their effects have received a great deal of attention in AI, for example, the situation calculus [15]. We hope to explore the connections between these formalisms and our approach. Thirdly, we have initially excluded from this schema any consideration of: time and temporal factors; uncertainty of consequences; or obligations and moral arguments. We hope to consider these issues in future development of the *PARMA* protocol.

References

1. K. Atkinson, T. Bench-Capon, and P. McBurney. Computational representation of persuasive argument. Technical Report ULCS-04-006, Department of Computer Science, University of Liverpool, UK, 2004.
2. K. Atkinson, T. Bench-Capon, and P. McBurney. Implementation of a dialogue game for persuasion over action. Technical Report ULCS-04-005, Department of Computer Science, University of Liverpool, UK, 2004.
3. R. Goldblatt. *Topoi: The Categorial Analysis of Logic*. North-Holland, Amsterdam, The Netherlands, 1979.
4. T. F. Gordon. The Pleadings Game: An exercise in computational dialectics. *Artificial Intelligence and Law*, 2:239–292, 1994.
5. K. Greenwood, T. Bench-Capon, and P. McBurney. Towards a computational account of persuasion in law. In *Proc. Ninth Intern. Conf. AI and Law (ICAIL-2003)*, pages 22–31, New York, NY, USA, 2003. ACM Press.
6. J. Habermas. *Between Facts and Norms: Contributions to a Discourse Theory of Law and Democracy*. MIT Press, Cambridge, MA, USA, 1996. (Translation by W. Rehg).
7. C. L. Hamblin. *Fallacies*. Methuen, London, UK, 1970.
8. C. L. Hamblin. *Imperatives*. Basil Blackwell, Oxford, UK, 1987.
9. R. Johnson. *Manifest Rationality: A Pragmatic Theory of Argument*. Lawrence Erlbaum Associates, Mahwah, NJ, USA, 2000.
10. H. Kamp and U. Reyle. *From Discourse to Logic: Introduction to Modeltheoretic Semantics of Natural Language, Formal Logic and Discourse Representation Theory*. Kluwer Academic, Dordrecht, The Netherlands, 1993. Two Volumes.

11. Y. Labrou, T. Finin, and Y. Peng. Agent communication languages: The current landscape. *IEEE Intelligent Systems*, 14(2):45–52, 1999.

12. M. Luck, P. McBurney, and C. Preist. *Agent Technology: Enabling Next Generation Computing. A Roadmap for Agent Based Computing*. AgentLink II, Southampton, UK, 2003.

13. P. McBurney and S. Parsons. Games that agents play: A formal framework for dialogues between autonomous agents. *J. Logic, Language and Information*, 11(3):315–334, 2002.

14. P. McBurney and S. Parsons. A denotational semantics for deliberation dialogues. In N. R. Jennings, C. Sierra, E. Sonenberg, and M. Tambe, editors, *Proc.Third Intern. Joint Conf. Autonomous Agents and Multi-Agent Systems (AAMAS 2004)*, 2004.

15. J. McCarthy and P. J. Hayes. Some philosophical problems from the standpoint of artificial intelligence. In B. Melzer and D. Michie, editors, *Machine Intelligence 4*, pages 463–502. Edinburgh University Press, 1969.

16. C. Perelman and L. Olbrechts-Tyteca. *The New Rhetoric: A Treatise on Argumentation*. University of Notre Dame Press, Notre Dame, IN, USA, 1969.

17. H. S. Richardson. *Practical Reasoning about Final Ends*. Cambridge University Press, Cambridge, UK, 1994.

18. W. C. Salmon. *Causality and Explanation*. Oxford University Press, New York, NY, USA, 1998.

19. R. D. Tennent. *Semantics of Programming Languages*. Prentice-Hall, Hemel Hempstead, UK, 1991.

20. S. E. Toulmin. *Knowing and Acting: An Invitation to Philosophy*. Macmillan, New York, NY, USA, 1976.

21. D. N. Walton. *The New Dialectic: Conversational Contexts of Argument*. University of Toronto Press, Toronto, Ontario, Canada, 1998.

22. D. N. Walton and E. C. W. Krabbe. *Commitment in Dialogue: Basic Concepts of Interpersonal Reasoning*. SUNY Press, Albany, NY, USA, 1995.

A Denotational Semantics for Deliberation Dialogues

Peter McBurney[1] and Simon Parsons[2]

[1] Department of Computer Science,
University of Liverpool,
Liverpool L69 7ZF, UK
p.j.mcburney@csc.liv.ac.uk
[2] Department of Computer and Information Science,
Brooklyn College,
City University of New York,
Brooklyn NY 11210, USA
parsons@sci.brooklyn.cuny.edu

Abstract. We present a denotational semantics for agent deliberation dialogues, i.e., dialogues over proposed actions, conducted under a broad class of interaction protocols. The semantics uses category-theoretic entities to represent deals proposed by agents and the preferences they articulate between these. The semantics is constructed jointly and incrementally by the participating agents in the course of the dialogue, and evolves with the dialogue. We consider properties of the semantics relating to deals and dialogue termination.

1 Introduction

Over the last two decades, considerable attention has been given to the design of agent communications languages and interaction protocols, and their semantics. Most of this attention has focused on the semantics of utterances in agent dialogues, rather than on the semantics of dialogues or the semantics of dialogue protocols. Speech act theory, for example, has been used to provide a semantics for individual utterances in the FIPA Agent Communications Language, FIPA ACL [10]. However, such fixed, pre-defined utterance-level semantics does not allow for the meaning of utterances to change with the context of utterance, or for the meaning of utterances to be created by the participants in the course of dialogue together. Both of these are features of human dialogues [20]. While it is possible that the semantics of dialogues and dialogue protocols are compositional, it is not obvious that this is a property of every type of dialogue or protocol.

The contribution of this paper is to present the first formal, denotational semantics for a particular class of dialogues, namely deliberations. We call this semantics a *trace semantics*. In the influential typology of human dialogues proposed by Walton and Krabbe [29], deliberation dialogues involve two or more participants seeking to agree upon an action or a course of action, actions which may or may not be undertaken by the participants. Negotiation dialogues, in the Walton and Krabbe typology, are a special case of deliberations, when the action(s) under discussion involve(s) the division of some scarce resource. Both deliberations and negotiations are distinguished from dialogues over beliefs, such as Information-Seeking dialogues and Mutual Inquiries.

I. Rahwan et al. (Eds.): ArgMAS 2004, LNAI 3366, pp. 162–175, 2005.

A deliberation dialogue arises with a need for action in some circumstance. In general human discourse, this need may be initially expressed in governing questions which are quite open-ended, as in, *What shall we do for dinner this evening?* or *How should we respond to the prospect of global warming?* Proposals for actions to address the expressed need may only arise late in a dialogue, after discussion of the governing question, and discussion of what considerations are relevant to its resolution. When possible courses of action are proposed, they may be evaluated on a large number of attributes, including: their direct or indirect costs and benefits; their opportunity cost; their consequences; their practical feasibility; their ethical, moral or legal implications; their resourcing implications; their likelihood of realization or success; their conformance with other goals or strategies; their timing or duration; etc.

Given such complexity and multi-dimensionality, it would be possible to develop quite complex models for deliberation dialogues, such as those in [11, 15]. Our approach will be simpler than these. We will assume that the parties to the dialogue are willing participants, and that resolution of the dialogue requires all parties to agree to a proposed course of action. We further assume that the participants co-operate sufficiently to commence a dialogue together to achieve this joint agreement, although they may have mutually-incompatible objectives for the content of the agreement. Each agent may also withdraw at any time. We will then define (in Section 2) two broad classes of protocols for deliberation dialogues; our results will apply to any dialogue conducted under any protocol in the respective class. As will be seen, these results cover many deliberation and negotiation interactions.

Following the definition of the classes of deliberation protocols, we give in Section 3 some examples of them. Section 4 then presents a denotational semantics for these protocols. In the theory of programming semantics (e.g., [12]), a denotational semantics for a programming language assigns an object in a mathematical space to each well-formed statement in the language syntax. For example, the well-known possible-worlds (or Kripke) semantics defines a class of relational structures for logical languages containing modal operators. Because mathematics provides us with tools to reason about mathematical objects, such an assignment can enable us to reason about programming languages, to study the properties of languages, and to compare one language with another. In this paper, we define a denotational semantics for deliberation dialogues using the mathematics of category theory. Our formalism attempts to make precise some intuitions about agent interactions presented graphically and informally in recent work on agent negotiations, for example, [4, 16]. Section 5 will follow the semantics with an exploration of deal properties, and the paper concludes with a discussion in Section 6.

Why use category theory? Our long-term objective is a formal theory of interaction protocols which incorporates the protocols and languages studied in the agent communications community, e.g., [3], and the interaction mechanisms studied in mathematical economics, e.g., [14]. Existing semantic frameworks do not provide this single theory of all types of deliberations. For example, as mentioned above, speech act semantics provides a semantic understanding of individual utterances, but not necessarily of dialogues or protocols. The real-valued mathematical spaces studied in mathematical economics, on the other hand, do not apply to negotiation or deliberation interactions over more general domains, or where the consequences of outcomes can not be readily quantified. Because category theory is an abstraction of mathematics itself [21], it is a plausible candidate to provide the basis for a single, unified framework for these various forms of deliberation interaction. Such a unified framework would aid understanding of the differences between protocols and potentially permit the generalization of results about specific protocols in both agent communications and mathematical economics.

2   Deliberation Protocols

We begin by defining a general class of protocols for deliberation dialogues. We assume that time is continuous, and isomorphic to the positive real numbers, but that utterances occur only at integer values, with precisely one utterance made at each integer time-point. We further assume that these protocols are specified as dialogue games, in accordance with current research in agent communications protocols, e.g., [23, 25]. In this approach, the syntax of legal utterances comprises two layers, with the lower, content layer being wrapped in a higher, speech-act locution.[1] We denote participating agents by P_i, for $i \in \mathcal{I}$ a positive integer for some finite set $\mathcal{I}$, and locution contents by lower-case letters of the Greek alphabet. We let $\mathcal{L} = \{\alpha, \beta, \ldots\}$ denote this collection of locution contents, and each of these represents an action or plan of action to be undertaken following agreement by the dialogue participants.[2] Although not strictly necessary, for ease of presentation, we assume the first field in the content of utterances is the integer time t of the utterance, and the second field in the content is an identifier P_i of the agent uttering the locution.

Definition 1: Class $\mathcal{D}$: General Deliberation Dialogue Protocols
An agent interaction protocol is a member of the class of General Deliberation Dialogue Protocols (denoted $\mathcal{D}$) if it satisfies these five conditions:

Condition 1: General Locutions
The protocol contains locutions for participants to initiate, enter and withdraw from the protocol, such as those defined in other recent dialogue game protocols, e.g., [22]. We assume the syntax of the withdrawal illocution is *WITHDRAW(t, P_i)*.

Condition 2: Specific Locutions
The protocol contains three locutions of the following form:

2.1 *PROPOSE(t, P_i, α)*, which enables the speaker, agent P_i, to propose the deal α. We further assume that utterance of *PROPOSE(t, P_i, α)* by a speaker expresses a willingness of the speaker P_i to accept the proposal α at the time t of utterance.
2.2 *ACCEPT(t, P_i, α)*, which indicates to the hearer that the speaker, agent P_i, wishes to accept the deal α, which has been the subject of a prior *PROPOSE(s, P_j, α)* locution by some agent P_j (possibly P_i), and with $s < t$.

---

[1] The FIPA ACL uses the same two-layer syntax [10].
[2] For example, the contents in $\mathcal{L}$ may represent commitments, as in [27].

2.3 *PREFER(t, P_i, α, β)*, which indicates to any hearers that the speaker, agent P_i, prefers proposal β to proposal α.[3]

Condition 3: Combination Rules
The three locutions listed in Condition 2 are subject to the following combination rules:

3.1: The instantiated locution *ACCEPT(t, P_i, α)* can only be legally uttered if there has been a prior utterance of *PROPOSE(s, P_j, α)* by some agent P_j at some time $s < t$.

3.2: The instantiated locution *PREFER(t, P_i, α, β)* may only be legally uttered if there have been prior utterances of *PROPOSE(s_1, P_j, α)* and *PROPOSE(s_2, P_k, α)* by some agents P_j and P_k at some times s_1, $s_2 < t$.

3.3 The protocol has a voting rule indicating when an agreement is reached on an action, and this results in the termination of the dialogue and execution of the action, called *the deal*. For example, for unanimous agreement, the rule could be as follows: If there is a proposal α such that all participants P_i have uttered either *PROPOSE(t, P_i, α)* or *ACCEPT(t, P_i, α)*, then the dialogue ends immediately, with the participants agreeing to execute the action or action plan represented by the deal α.

Condition 4: Transitivity of Preferences
Expressed participant preferences are transitive, i.e. utterance of the following two locutions at any times t and $t + k$ in a dialogue
>   *PREFER(t, P_i, α, β)*
>   *PREFER(t + k, P_i, β, γ)*

entitles a hearer to infer the following relationship:
>   *PREFER(t + k, P_i, α, γ)*.

Condition 5: Reflexivity of Preferences
Participant preferences are reflexive, i.e. for every deal α, every speaker P_i is able to utter:
>   *PREFER(t, P_i, α, α)*.   □

In the remainder of this paper, we will assume that unanimous agreement (Condition 3.3) is required for a deal. Conditions 4 and 5 are required for the resulting mathematical structure to be a category. Note that we do not assume that every participant is able to express a preference between any two proposals. At any given time, a participant may prefer one proposal to a second, or may prefer the second to the first, or may be indifferent between them, or may not yet have determined its preference between them.

Definition 2: Class $\mathcal{D}_M$: Monotonic Deliberation Dialogue Protocols
We also define a sub-class of class $\mathcal{D}$, called Class $\mathcal{D}_M$, Monotonic Deliberation Dialogue Protocols, which satisfy all five conditions above, in addition to:

---

[3] Note that preference is not the same as private welfare: an agent may prefer one outcome to another even though the first outcome makes the agent personally worse off. In other words, an agent's preferences may incorporate social aspects of its utility.

Condition 6: Monotonicity of Proposals

Assume $\alpha \neq \beta$ are two non-identical proposals. If participant P_i utters the locution *PROPOSE(s, P_i, α)* in a dialogue, and, later in the same dialogue, utters the locution *PROPOSE(t, P_i, β)*, hearers are entitled to infer that participant P_i prefers proposal α to proposal β. In other words, for integers $s < t$, the sequence

$$PROPOSE(s, P_i, \alpha)$$

$$\vdots$$

$$PROPOSE(t, P_i, \beta)$$

is equivalent to the sequence:

$$PROPOSE(s, P_i, \alpha)$$

$$\vdots$$

$$PROPOSE(t, P_i, \beta)$$
$$PREFER(t + 1, P_i, \beta, \alpha). \qquad \square$$

Dialogues undertaken using protocols from Class $\mathcal{D}_M$ require that agents utter new proposals that are less preferred by themselves than any of their own previous proposals.

3 Examples

In this section we present some examples of common deliberation interactions expressed in the syntax of Section 2.

***Example 1: Open-Cry Dutch Auction**. A Dutch auction has a single potential seller of an item interacting with multiple potential buyers. The seller (or an auctioneer, acting on the seller's behalf) shouts successively decreasing selling prices until a buyer indicates a willingness to purchase the item at the most-recently quoted price. Using the illocutions given in Definition 1, a dialogue for a Dutch auction would have the following general form, where each successive proposed price,* price-p, *is lower than the one before it,* price-(p-1):

    PROPOSE(1, seller, sell-item-at-price-1)
    PROPOSE(2, seller, sell-item-at-price-2)

    ⋮

    PROPOSE(s, seller, sell-item-at-price-s)
    ACCEPT(s+1, buyer-k, sell-item-at-price-s).

The dialogue then terminates, with buyer-k *executing a transaction with* seller *at price-s.* $\qquad \square$

Because proposed prices are descending, this is an example of a monotonic protocol. Provided the other conditions are satisfied (i.e., Conditions 1, 3–5), then the Dutch Auction protocol would be a member of Class $\mathcal{D}_M$. Note that the syntax presented here is similar to the specification given by FIPA for these auctions [9].

Example 2: Open-Cry English Auction. In an English auction a single potential seller of an item interacts with multiple potential buyers. The seller (or an auctioneer) shouts successively increasing prices, and buyers indicate their willingness to accept these. As prices rise, fewer buyers indicate acceptance. The item is sold to the last-remaining buyer for the most recent price. Using the illocutions given in Definition 1, a dialogue for an English auction would have the following general form, where each successive proposed price, price-p, *is higher than the one before it,* price-(p-1):

> PROPOSE(1, seller, sell-item-at-price-1)
>> ACCEPT(2, buyer-h, sell-item-at-price-1)
>> ACCEPT(3, buyer-i, sell-item-at-price-1)
>>
>> $\vdots$
>>
>> ACCEPT(n1, buyer-j, sell-item-at-price-1)
> PROPOSE(n1+1, seller, sell-item-at-price-2)
>
> $\vdots$
>
> PROPOSE(s, seller, sell-item-at-price-s)
>> ACCEPT(s+1, buyer-k, sell-item-at-price-s).

The dialogue then terminates, with buyer-k *executing a transaction with* seller *at* price-s.   □

The English auction protocol is not monotonic in the sense of Definition 2, but is in class $\mathcal{D}$ if Conditions 1, 3–5 hold.

Example 3: Monotonic Concession Protocol (MCP) Zeuthen [26, 32] described a negotiation process in which two parties each make successive proposals to one another. At each proposal, the other party can either accept the proposal, or make a counter-proposal, or withdraw. For each participant, every subsequent proposal after its first must concede something to the opponent. Thus, relative to the most recent proposal made by a participant, the next proposal made by that same participant could be no more attractive to that participant and no less attractive to the other participant.   □

If we assume we can map "attractiveness" onto preferences in the obvious way, then the MCP is an example of a protocol in class $\mathcal{D}_M$, provided Conditions 1, 3–5 hold.

4   Trace Semantics

We now define a denotational semantics, which we call a *trace semantics*, for dialogues conducted using protocols in Class $\mathcal{D}$, using concepts from Category Theory [21]. Assume $G \in \mathcal{D}$ is a deliberation protocol in $\mathcal{D}$. Let $\mathcal{P} = \{P_1, \ldots, P_n\}$ be a finite set of n distinct agents, engaged in a deliberation dialogue conducted in accordance with protocol G, with $\mathcal{L} = \{\alpha, \beta, \ldots\}$ the topics of the dialogues (i.e., the contents of locutions). We let $g_1, g_2, \ldots$ denote dialogues — sequences of instantiated locutions — conducted by $\mathcal{P}$ under protocol G. We denote the agent index set $\{1, \ldots, n\}$ by $\mathcal{I}$. For each agent $P_i, i \in \mathcal{I}$, we assume there exists two sequences of mathematical categories:[4]

---

[4] We use the letter $\mathcal{C}$ for the public stores, since these are inspired by the Commitment Stores of dialogue games [29]; we use $\mathcal{M}$ for the private stores, since these embody mentalistic notions.

- Each $\mathcal{C}_i^t$, with t a non-negative integer, is called the *public proposal store* of agent P_i at time t, and contains objects corresponding to the proposals presented by agent P_i up to and including time t in the dialogue.
- Each $\mathcal{M}_i^t$, with t a non-negative real number, is called the *private proposal store* of agent P_i at time t. Agent P_i is assumed to commence the deliberation dialogue with private proposal store $\mathcal{M}_i^0$, which may be empty. This store contains proposals which agent P_i is considering at time t, but may not yet have revealed to the dialogue.

These categories are constructed by the following trace-semantics rules, linking dialogue statements to objects and arrows in the appropriate categories. In all categories, we label those objects corresponding to proposed deals with lower-case Greek letters, while certain other objects have mnemonic labels; arrows are labelled with lower-case Roman letters. An object labelled θ^k may be understood as the action (or course of action) θ to be agreed and executed at time k. Arrows are used to indicate preferences, with the arrow pointing to the more-preferred object. Time-stamping in this way allows us to model an agent's preferences between the same action agreed at different times. We first list the rules for the public stores:

TS1: Each agent P_i begins the dialogue with a public proposal store $\mathcal{C}_i^0$ which is empty.

TS2: An utterance of the locution *PROPOSE(t, P_i, α)* by an agent P_i at integer time t results in an object labelled α^t, corresponding to the execution of α at time t, being inserted into the public proposal store $\mathcal{C}_i^t$ of P_i.

TS3: An utterance of the locution *ACCEPT(t, P_j, α)* by an agent P_j at integer time t results in an object labelled α^t, corresponding to the execution of α at time t, being inserted in the public proposal store $\mathcal{C}_j^t$ of P_j.

TS4: For each agent P_i and for all times $t \geq 0$, every object θ^k in the public proposal store $\mathcal{C}_i^t$ of P_i has associated to it an identity arrow $id_{\theta^k} : \theta^k \rightarrow \theta^k$. This rule encodes Condition 5.

TS5: An utterance of the locution *PREFER(t, P_i, α, β)* by an agent P_i at integer time t results in an arrow from the object corresponding to α^t to the object corresponding to β^t being inserted into the public proposal store $\mathcal{C}_i^t$ of P_i.

TS6: An utterance of the locution *PREFER(s, P_i, α, β)* by an agent P_i at integer time s following at a later integer time t by an utterance of the locution *PREFER(t, P_i, β, γ)* results in an arrow from the object corresponding to α^s to the object corresponding to γ^t being inserted into the public proposal store $\mathcal{C}_i^t$ of P_i. This rule encodes Condition 4.

TS7: For protocols in class $\mathcal{D}_M$, the utterance by an agent P_i of the two locutions *PROPOSE(s, P_i, α)* and *PROPOSE(t, P_i, β)*, with integer times $s < t$, creates an arrow in the public proposal store $\mathcal{C}_i^t$ of P_i from every object corresponding to β^t to the object corresponding to α^s. This rule encodes Condition 6.

TS8: An object inserted at time s in a public proposal store remains in the store for all times $t \geq s$. An arrow a from object α to object β inserted at time s in a public proposal store remains in the store for all times $t \geq s$ unless and until an arrow b is inserted from object β to object α. The presence of an arrow $a : \alpha \rightarrow \beta$ between two distinct objects α and β in a public proposal store means there is no arrow $b : \beta \rightarrow \alpha$ in that store.

We now list the rules for the private stores:

TS9: Each agent P_i begins the dialogue with a private proposal store $\mathcal{M}_i^0$ (which may be empty).

TS10: An utterance of the locution *PROPOSE(t, P_i, α)* by an agent P_i at integer time t means that there exists $\epsilon > 0$ such that an object corresponding to α^t is in the private proposal store $\mathcal{M}_i^{t-\epsilon}$ of P_i at time $t - \epsilon$.

TS11: An utterance of the locution *PROPOSE(t, P_i, α)* by an agent P_i at integer time t results in an object corresponding to α^t being inserted in the private proposal store $\mathcal{M}_j^t$ of agent P_j, for every $j \neq i$.

TS12: For each agent P_i and each time $t \geq 0$, every object θ^k in the private proposal stores $\mathcal{M}_i^t$ of P_i has associated to it an identity arrow $id_{\theta^k} : \theta^k \rightarrow \theta^k$.

TS13: For every agent P_i and every time $t > 0$, the private proposal store $\mathcal{M}_i^t$ has a distinguished object, called ND_i^t, intended to represent *"No Deal"*.

TS14: For every agent P_i and every time $t > 0$, the private proposal store $\mathcal{M}_i^t$ has a distinguished object, called FP_i^t, an abbreviation for *"Future Prospects at t"*, intended to represent the valuation at time t by agent P_i of all possible future deals, allowing for the estimation by the agent of any uncertainty in their achievement.[5]

TS15: An utterance of the locution *PREFER(t, P_i, α, β)* by an agent P_i at integer time t means that there exists $\epsilon > 0$ such that there is an arrow from the object corresponding to α^t to the object corresponding to β^t in the private proposal store $\mathcal{M}_i^{t-\epsilon}$ of P_i at time $t - \epsilon$.

TS16: An utterance of the locution *PREFER(s, P_i, α, β)* by an agent P_i at integer time s following at a later integer time t by an utterance of the locution *PREFER(t, P_i, β, γ)* means that there exists $\epsilon > 0$ such that there is an arrow from the object corresponding to α^t to the object corresponding to γ^t in the private proposal store $\mathcal{M}_i^{t-\epsilon}$ of P_i at time $t - \epsilon$.

TS17: For every agent P_i and every time $t \geq 0$, whenever there are arrows $a : \alpha \rightarrow \beta$ and $b : \beta \rightarrow \gamma$ in the private proposal stores $\mathcal{M}_i^t$ then there is also an arrow $c : \alpha \rightarrow \gamma$ in $\mathcal{M}_i^t$.

TS18: For protocols in class $\mathcal{D}_M$, the utterance by an agent P_i of the two locutions *PROPOSE(s, P_i, α)* and *PROPOSE(t, P_i, β)*, with integer times $s < t$ means that there exists $\epsilon > 0$ such that there is an arrow from the object corresponding to β^t to the object corresponding to α^s in the private proposal store $\mathcal{M}_i^{t-\epsilon}$ of P_i at time $t - \epsilon$.

TS19: The presence of an arrow $a : \alpha \rightarrow \beta$ between two distinct objects α and β in a private proposal store means there is no arrow $b : \beta \rightarrow \alpha$ in that store.

The rules for the private stores (TS9–TS19) create a mathematical model of the private states of the participating agents. It is important to note that agents may not necessarily conform to this model in their actual decision processes when engaged in deliberation dialogues. In any case, such conformance would be in general unverifiable [30]. Rule TS17 corresponds to an assumption that the private preferences of each agent are

---

[5] Thus, for an agent engaged in utility-maximizing behavior, FP_i^t would represent its estimated maximum expected utility, evaluated at t, of all future deals believed possible by the agent P_i.

transitive. Note that we make no assumption that an agent's preferences are fixed or pre-determined. Thus, objects may enter and leave the private proposal stores of the participants throughout a dialogue, and arrows likewise may change. In other words, there is no assumed relationship between $\mathcal{M}_i^s$ and $\mathcal{M}_i^t$, for $s \neq t$. We believe this captures nicely the notion that agents may have resource-constraints on their processing powers, and so they may not consider all options at all times throughout an interaction.

Using these rules, we now define a denotational semantics for dialogues conducted under protocols in class $\mathcal{D}$:

Definition 3: Given a finite set of agents $\mathcal{P}$, a collection of locution contents $\mathcal{L}$, and a deliberation dialogue protocol $G \in \mathcal{D}$, we define the *Deliberation Trace Semantics*, or *Trace Semantics*, of a dialogue g undertaken by $\mathcal{P}$ about topics in $\mathcal{L}$ according to protocol G by the pair:

$$\langle \mathcal{C}, \mathcal{M} \rangle$$

where $\mathcal{C} = \{\mathcal{C}_i^t \mid i \in \mathcal{I}, \ t \in \mathbb{Z}^+ \cup \{0\}\}$ is a collection of public proposal stores for each agent in the dialogue, created according to rules TS1–TS8, and $\mathcal{M} = \{\mathcal{M}_i^t \mid i \in \mathcal{I}, \ t \in \mathbb{R}^+ \cup \{0\}\}$ is a collection of private proposal stores for each agent in the dialogue, created according to Rules TS9–TS19. We also call $\langle \mathcal{M}, \mathcal{C} \rangle$ a *deliberation trace* of $\mathcal{P}, \mathcal{L}$ and G, denoted:

$$\langle \mathcal{C}, \mathcal{M} \rangle \models (\mathcal{P}, \mathcal{L}, G). \qquad \square$$

Proposition 1: *Each element of $\mathcal{C}$ and $\mathcal{M}$ is a category.*

Proof. A category contains zero or more objects and zero or more arrows between objects, subject to two conditions: (a) from each object to the same object there is an identity arrow; and (b) if there exists an arrow between objects α and β and between objects β and γ, then there exists an arrow between objects α and γ [21]. These conditions are guaranteed by Rules TS4 and TS6 respectively, in the case of elements of $\mathcal{C}$, and Rules TS12 and TS16 respectively, in the case of elements of $\mathcal{M}$. $\qquad \square$

It is easy matter to demonstrate consistency of the trace semantics with respect to deliberation dialogues in $\mathcal{D}$.

Proposition 2: (Consistency) *For any finite set of agents $\mathcal{P}$, any collection of locutions $\mathcal{L}$ and any dialogue protocol $G \in \mathcal{D}$, there is a trace semantics $\langle \mathcal{C}, \mathcal{M} \rangle$ such that $\langle \mathcal{C}, \mathcal{M} \rangle \models (\mathcal{P}, \mathcal{L}, G)$.*

Proof. This is straightforward from the rules of construction above. $\qquad \square$

We can also demonstrate completeness of the trace semantics with respect to deliberation dialogues in $\mathcal{D}$. For this, we must confine attention to collections of categories satisfying the properties implied by rules TS1–TS19.

Proposition 3: (Completeness) *Suppose the two collections of categories $\langle \mathcal{C}, \mathcal{M} \rangle$, with $\mathcal{C} = \{\mathcal{C}_i^t \mid i \in \mathcal{I}, \ t \in \mathbb{Z}^+ \cup \{0\}\}$ and $\mathcal{M} = \{\mathcal{M}_i^t \mid i \in \mathcal{I}, \ t \in \mathbb{R}^+ \cup \{0\}\}$, have the following properties:*
(a) $\mathcal{I}$ is finite.

(b) $C_i^0 = \emptyset$, $\forall i \in \mathcal{I}$.

(c) Each C_i^t is isomorphic to a subcategory of $\mathcal{M}_i^t$, $\forall i \in \mathcal{I}$ and $\forall t \in \mathbb{Z}^+ \cup \{0\}$.

(d) Each category $\mathcal{M}_i^t$ has at most a countable number of objects, $\forall i \in \mathcal{I}$ and $\forall t \in \mathbb{R}^+ \cup \{0\}$.

(e) Every object and arrow of C_i^s is also an object and arrow of C_i^t, $\forall s \leq t$ integers and $\forall i \in \mathcal{I}$.

(f) There is at most one arrow between any two distinct objects in each category in the two collections $\langle C, \mathcal{M} \rangle$.

(g) The total combined number of objects and arrows in the union of categories $\bigcup_\mathcal{I} C_i^t$ is at most t, $\forall t \in \mathbb{Z}^+ \cup \{0\}$.

Then there is a dialogue g undertaken by a finite set of agents $\mathcal{P}$, about a collection of topics $\mathcal{L}$ according to a dialogue protocol $G \in \mathcal{D}$, for which $\langle C, \mathcal{M} \rangle$ is the trace semantics of $(\mathcal{P}, \mathcal{L}, G)$.

Proof. [Outline] Assign a distinct agent identifier P_i to each $i \in \mathcal{I}$. Starting with $t = 1$, and then for each successive integer value of t, label the objects and arrows of $\bigcup_\mathcal{I} C_i^t$ as follows: $\alpha(1)_i^t, \alpha(2)_i^t, \ldots$ and $a(1)_i^t, a(2)_i^t, \ldots$ etc. Do this only for objects and arrows on their first appearance in each sequence, i.e., for the smallest value of t in which the object or arrow appears. Thus the objects and arrows are indexed both by a count (in parentheses) and by the category C_i^t in which they first appear. It is then possible to construct a dialogue between the agents using the illocutions of Definition 1, instantiated with these labels. One can readily show that this dialogue is conducted according to the rules of a protocol which is a member of class $\mathcal{D}$.   □

5   Deals

In this section we consider some of the circumstances of deal agreement. Throughout, we are assuming a finite set of agents $\mathcal{P}$, a collection of locution contents $\mathcal{L}$, and a deliberation dialogue protocol $G \in \mathcal{D}$, for the class $\mathcal{D}$ defined earlier. For simplicity, when agents are willing to accept a proposal, we ignore the time taken for each of them to express this acceptance. Since some properties depend on the nature of the participants, we first need to define a class of agents.

Definition 4: A *serious* agent P_i has the following three properties:

S1: P_i utters *WITHDRAW(s, P_i)* iff
$\forall t > s, \forall \beta^t \in \mathcal{M}_i^s$, and $\forall \alpha^s \in \mathcal{M}_i^s$, there exist arrows $\alpha^s \to ND^s$ and $\beta^t \to ND^s$ in $\mathcal{M}_i^s$.

S2: P_i utters *PROPOSE(s, P_i, α)* iff
$\exists \alpha^s \in \mathcal{M}_i^s$, such that
(i) $\mathcal{M}_i^s$ has an arrow $ND^s \to \alpha^s$, OR
(ii) $\exists t > s$ and $\beta^t \in \mathcal{M}_i^s$ with arrows $\alpha^s \to \beta^t$ and $ND^s \to \beta^t$.

S3: P_i utters *ACCEPT(s, P_i, α)* iff
$\exists \alpha^s \in \mathcal{M}_i^s$, such that $\forall t > s$ and $\forall \beta^t \in \mathcal{M}_i^s$ there are arrows $ND^s \to \alpha^s, \beta^t \to \alpha^s$ and $\beta^t \to ND^s$ in $\mathcal{M}_i^s$.   □

We intend these conditions to permit agents to be insincere, i.e., to propose deals they do not wish to accept, but not to be capricious or whimsical. Condition S2(ii), for example, permits an agent to propose a deal α^s at time s with the strategic intention of agreeing a more preferred deal β^t at some future time t in the dialogue. This property enables the two following results, whose proofs are straightforward from Definitions 1, 3 and 4.

Proposition 4: *Let α^u be a deal agreed at time u, according to the voting rule of Condition 3.3. Suppose all participating agents are serious. Then $\forall i \in \mathcal{I}, \exists t_i < u$ such that $\alpha^u \in \mathcal{M}_i^{t_i}$ and $\exists s$ with $max_{\mathcal{I}}\{t_i\} \leq s \leq u$ such that $\forall i \in \mathcal{I}\alpha^u \in \mathcal{C}_i^s$.* □

Proposition 5: *Let α^u be a deal agreed at time u, according to the voting rule of Condition 3.3. Suppose all participating agents are serious. Then, $\forall i \in \mathcal{I}, \exists s_i \leq u$ such that $\forall t \in (s_i, u]$, there is no arrow $\alpha^u \to ND_i^u$ in $\mathcal{M}_i^t$ and, $\forall v > u$ and $\forall \beta^v \in \mathcal{M}_i^t$, for β^v possibly the same as α^v, there is no arrow $\alpha^u \to \beta^v$.* □

Proposition 4 says that, for serious agents, deals must have been considered prior to proposal or acceptance, and must appear in the public stores of all agents before a deal is reached. Proposition 5 says that, again for serious agents, a proposal cannot become a deal at some time point if an agent prefers no deal to that proposal, or prefers some future proposal to that deal. We now define a notion of Pareto-Optimality in our semantic framework.

Definition 5: A proposal α^t is said to be *Pareto-Optimal at time t* iff $\forall \beta^t \in \bigcup_{\mathcal{I}} \mathcal{C}_i^t$, with $\beta^t \neq \alpha^t$, $\exists j \in \mathcal{I}$ such that it is not the case that there is an arrow $\alpha^t \to \beta^t$ in $\mathcal{C}_j^t$. □

In other words, a proposal is *Pareto-Optimal at time t* precisely when, for every alternative proposal presented by this time, there is at least one participant who has not yet described the alternative proposal as preferred. Thus, the definition only concerns publicly-known proposals, and only those which have been uttered up to the time of consideration. Definition 5 is therefore a constructive definition of Pareto-Optimality. We are able to demonstrate the following result regarding deliberations between two parties using a monotonic deliberation protocol:

Proposition 6: *Let $\mathcal{I} = \{1, 2\}$ index two serious agents engaged in a deliberation dialogue using a monotonic protocol $G \in \mathcal{D}_M$. Suppose that the rules of G require that an agent P_i may only utter $\text{ACCEPT}(t, P_i, \alpha)$ for the most recent proposal of agent $P_j, j \neq i$. Let α be a deal agreed at time t. Then the following are equivalent:*

- *α is Pareto-Optimal at time t.*
- *If $\beta \in \mathcal{C}_1^t \bigcup \mathcal{C}_1^t$ is any other proposal, distinct from α, then if $\exists s_1 \leq t$ with the arrow $\alpha \to \beta$ contained in $\mathcal{M}_i^{s_1}$, then $\exists s_2 \leq t$ with the arrow $\beta \to \alpha$ contained in $\mathcal{M}_j^{s_2}$, for $i \neq j$, and $i, j \in \mathcal{I}$.*

Proof. ($\Longrightarrow$) The result follows, with some care, from Definitions 2, 4 and 5. ($\Longleftarrow$) Straightforward from Definition 5. □

We may use Proposition 6 to generate a corollary regarding Zeuthen's Monotonic Concession Protocol (Example 3 in Section 3), provided that we can map "attractiveness" onto preferences in the obvious manner.

Proposition 7: *Suppose α is a deal agreed at time t by two serious agents using the MCP. Then, α is Pareto-Optimal at t.*

Proof. Straightforward from Proposition 6 and Definition 4.   □

This proposition generalizes a result of Harsanyi [13] regarding the MCP. Our definitions of agent strategies (i.e., that agents are serious, Definition 4), of the protocol (Definition 2) and its semantics (Definition 3), and of Pareto-Optimality (Definition 5) are all more general than has usually been the case in economics. We conjecture that a version of Proposition 6 also holds with more than two participants; however, we have not yet identified the conditions under which this conjecture is true.

6   Discussion

The research reported here is original. The only previous work relating category theory with argumentation was Ambler's categorical semantics for static, monolectical (one-party) argument over beliefs [2]; in contrast, our work concerns dynamic, dialectical (multi-party) argument over possible actions. Within economics, the study of negotiation mechanisms has a long history; however, mathematical economics, even when undertaken by mathematicians, has not sought to find the most general mathematical representation for these mechanisms, but confined attention to real spaces, e.g. [5, 14]. Even in the one publication known to us where category theory was applied in mathematical economics [28], categorical methods were used to prove a result about real spaces. Our semantics is not confined to real-valued proposals, nor to those denominated in prices. In any case, the problem of defining semantics for interaction mechanisms — a very important problem for computer science — has not been considered in economics.

Within theoretical computer science, category theory has been applied to the development of game semantics for interaction, e.g., [1]. That work views interactions more abstractly than the specific deliberation dialogues of interest to us, and has not treated semantic structures as objects created and manipulated by participants in an interaction. Moreover, it has only considered very simple sets of illocutions, such as questions and answers. Finally, within category theory itself, little attention appears to have been given to sequences of categories indexed by time. The only such structures known to us are the Memory Evolutive Systems of [7], designed to model emergent phenomena in complex adaptive systems, such as ecologies; these structures are monotonic over time, which is not true in our case.

An obvious question in response to this paper is: *Why not Kripke semantics?* Our reason for proposing a categorical rather than Kripkean semantic framework is that our focus in deliberation is on preferences between alternative outcomes, rather than on the outcomes themselves. For example, a rational agent choosing between: (a) accepting a proposal; (b) suggesting an alternative proposal; or (c) withdrawing from the dialogue; would make its decision on the basis of its preferences between these options. Category theory, because it emphasizes arrows not objects, is better suited to a formalization of such preference relationships.[6] In addition, categories provide greater scope for generalization than do Kripke frames, and have available a richer and more sophisticated mathematical theory. In particular, the category-theoretic treatment of the differential calculus [19] potentially means that a single categorical theory of agent interactions could model both argumentation interactions and economic transactions.

This paper has revealed a garden we believe to be profuse with interesting flora. Much work remains to study and exploit these delights, however. In future work we plan to explore, firstly, categorical definitions of other dialogue properties, such as other types of outcomes [8]. Secondly, we aim to consider the similarity of protocols. Our long-term objective is a formal, semantic classification of protocols to complement the preliminary classifications in [18, 24]. This should help to better understand protocol properties, such as the computational complexity of dialogues under specific protocols [6, 31]. Finally, we plan to re-visit Condition 4, the assumption of transitivity of preferences. It may be possible to do without this assumption if we map non-transitive preferences to one or more arrows representing "illegal" compositions, as in [17].

Acknowledgments

An earlier version of this paper was presented at AAMAS 2004 in New York City, and we are grateful for comments received from the anonymous referees, and from the AAMAS audience. We also thank Michael Wooldridge for his comments on an earlier draft.

References

1. S. Abramsky and R. Jagadeesan. Games and full completeness for multiplicative linear logic. *J. Symbolic Logic*, 59(2):543–574, 1994.
2. S. J. Ambler. A categorical approach to the semantics of argumentation. *Mathematical Structures in Computer Science*, 6:167–188, 1996.
3. L. Amgoud, S. Parsons, and N. Maudet. Arguments, dialogue, and negotiation. In W. Horn, editor, *Proc. ECAI 2000*, pages 338–342, Berlin, 2000. IOS Press.
4. M. Bratu, J. M. Andreoli, O. Boissier, and S. Castellani. A software infrastructure for negotiation within inter-organisational alliances. In J. Padget *et al.*, editor, *Agent-Mediated Electronic Commerce IV*, LNAI 2531, pages 161–179. Springer, Berlin, 2002.
5. W. D. A. Bryant. *Information, Adjustment and the Stability of Equilibrium*. Macquarie Economics Research Paper 6/2000, Macquarie University, Sydney, Australia, 2000.
6. P. E. Dunne and P. McBurney. Optimal utterances in dialogue protocols. In J. S. Rosenschein *et al.*, editor, *Proc. AAMAS 2003*, pages 608–615, New York, 2003. ACM Press.
7. A. C. Ehresmann and J-P. Vanbremeersch. Hierarchical evolutive systems: a mathematical model for complex systems. *Bulletin of Mathematical Biology*, 49(1):13–50, 1987.
8. U. Endriss and N. Maudet. Welfare engineering in multiagent systems. In A. Omicini *et al.*, editor, *Engineering Societies in the Agents World (ESAW-2003)*, LNAI, 2004.
9. FIPA. *Dutch Auction Interaction Protocol Specification*. Experimental Standard XC00032F, FIPA, 2001.
10. FIPA. *Communicative Act Library Specification*. Standard SC00037J, Foundation for Intelligent Physical Agents, 2002.

---

[6] Indeed, it is possible to define categories entirely in terms of arrows, without any objects.

11. K. Greenwood, T. Bench-Capon, and P. McBurney. Towards a computational account of persuasion in law. In *Proc. Ninth Intern. Conf. on AI and Law (ICAIL-03)*, pages 22–31, New York, 2003. ACM Press.

12. C. A. Gunter. *Semantics of Programming Languages: Structures and Techniques*. MIT Press, Cambridge, MA, 1992.

13. J. C. Harsanyi. Approaches to the bargaining problem before and after the theory of games: a critical discussion of Zeuthen's, Hicks' and Nash's theories. *Econometrica*, 24:144–157, 1956.

14. P. J-J. Herings. Universally converging adjustment processes — a unifying approach. *J. Mathematical Economics*, 38:341–370, 2002.

15. D. Hitchcock, P. McBurney, and S. Parsons. A framework for deliberation dialogues. In H. V. Hansen *et al.*, editor, *Proc. Fourth Biennial Conf. Ontario Society for the Study of Argumentation (OSSA 2001)*, Windsor, Ontario, Canada, 2001.

16. N. R. Jennings, P. Faratin, A. R. Lomuscio, S. Parsons, M. Wooldridge, and C. Sierra. Automated negotiation: prospects, methods and challenges. *Group Decision and Negotiation*, 10(2):199–215, 2001.

17. M. W. Johnson. *On Pointed Enrichments and Illegal Compositions*. Technical Report ULCS-03-010, Department of Computer Science, University of Liverpool, UK, 2003.

18. M. W. Johnson, P. McBurney, and S. Parsons. When are two protocols the same? In M-P. Huget, editor, *Communication in Multi-Agent Systems*, LNAI 2650, pages 253–268. Springer, Berlin, 2003.

19. A. Kock. *Synthetic Differential Geometry*. Cambridge University Press, Cambridge, UK, 1981.

20. S. C. Levinson. *Pragmatics*. Cambridge University Press, Cambridge, UK, 1983.

21. S. Mac Lane. *Categories for the Working Mathematician*. Springer, New York, NY, USA, 1971.

22. P. McBurney, R. M. van Eijk, S. Parsons, and L. Amgoud. A dialogue-game protocol for agent purchase negotiations. *J. Auton. Agents & Multi-Agent Systems*, 7(3):235–273, 2003.

23. P. McBurney and S. Parsons. Games that agents play: A formal framework for dialogues between autonomous agents. *J. Logic, Language and Information*, 11(3):315–334, 2002.

24. S. Parsons, P. McBurney, and M. J. Wooldridge. The mechanics of some formal inter-agent dialogues. In F. Dignum, editor, *Advances in Agent Communication*, LNAI 2922. Springer, Berlin, 2004.

25. S. Parsons, M. Wooldridge, and L. Amgoud. On the outcomes of formal inter-agent dialogues. In J. S. Rosenschein *et al.*, editor, *Proc. AAMAS 2003*, pages 616–623, New York, 2003. ACM Press.

26. J. S. Rosenschein and G. Zlotkin. *Rules of Encounter: Designing Conventions for Automated Negotiation among Computers*. MIT Press, Cambridge, MA, 1994.

27. M. P. Singh. An ontology for commitments in multiagent systems: toward a unification of normative concepts. *Artificial Intelligence and Law*, 7:97–113, 1999.

28. H. Sonnenschein. An axiomatic characterization of the price mechanism. *Econometrica*, 42(3):425–434, 1974.

29. D. N. Walton and E. C. W. Krabbe. *Commitment in Dialogue: Basic Concepts of Interpersonal Reasoning*. SUNY Press, Albany, NY, 1995.

30. M. J. Wooldridge. Semantic issues in the verification of agent communication languages. *J. Autonomous Agents & Multi-Agent Systems*, 3(1):9–31, 2000.

31. M. J. Wooldridge and S. Parsons. Languages for negotiation. In W. Horn, editor, *Proc. 14th ECAI 2000*, pages 393–397, Berlin, Germany, 2000. IOS Press.

32. F. Zeuthen. *Problems of Monopoly and Economic Warfare*. Routledge and Sons, London, UK, 1930.

Bargaining and Argument-Based Negotiation: *Some Preliminary Comparisons*

Iyad Rahwan[1], Liz Sonenberg[1], and Peter McBurney[2]

[1] Department of Information Systems, University of Melbourne,
Parkville, VIC 3010, Australia
i.rahwan@pgrad.unimelb.edu.au, l.sonenberg@unimelb.edu.au
http://www.dis.unimelb.edu.au/agent/
[2] Department of Computer Science, University of Liverpool,
Liverpool L69 7ZF, UK
p.j.mcburney@csc.liv.ac.uk

Abstract. Argumentation-based techniques are being increasingly used to construct frameworks for flexible negotiation among computational agents. Despite the advancements made to date, the relationship between argument-based negotiation and bargaining frameworks has been rather informal. This paper presents a preliminary investigation into understanding this relationship. To this end, we present a set of negotiation concepts through which we analyse both bargaining and argumentation-based methods. We demonstrate that if agents have false beliefs, then they may make decisions during negotiation that lead them to suboptimal deals. We then describe different ways in which argument-based communication can cause changes in an agent's beliefs and, consequently, its preferences over contracts. This enables us to demonstrate how the argumentation-based approach can improve both the likelihood and quality of deals.

1   Introduction

Negotiation is a form of interaction in which a group of agents, with conflicting interests and a desire to cooperate, try to come to a mutually acceptable division/exchange of scarce resources [22]. Resources can be commodities, services, time, etc.; in short, anything that is needed to achieve something. Resources are "scarce" in the sense that not all competing claims over them can be simultaneously satisfied.

Frameworks for automated negotiation have been studied analytically using game-theoretic techniques [19] as well as experimentally [4, 6, 10]. Most such negotiation frameworks are focused on *bargaining*, in which the main form of interaction is the exchange of potential deals, i.e., potential allocations of the resources in question.

Recently, it has been proposed that mechanisms for *argumentation* can be used to facilitate negotiation among computational agents. These mechanisms attempt to overcome some of the limitations of bargaining-based frameworks by allowing agents to exchange additional information, or to "argue" about their beliefs and other internal characteristics, during the negotiation process. This process of argumentation allows an agent to *justify* its negotiation stance; and/or *influence* another agent's negotiation stance [9].

I. Rahwan et al. (Eds.): ArgMAS 2004, LNAI 3366, pp. 176–191, 2005.

Existing literature on argumentation-based negotiation can be roughly classified into two major strands: (i) attempts to adapt dialectical logics for defeasible argumentation by embedding negotiation concepts within these [1, 15, 20]; and (ii) attempts to extend bargaining-based frameworks by allowing agents to exchange rhetorical arguments, such as promises and threats [11, 18].[1]

Despite the advances made to date, the relationship between argument-based negotiation and bargaining frameworks has been rather informal [9]. This paper presents a preliminary investigation into understanding this relationship. To this end, we present a set of negotiation concepts through which we analyse both bargaining and argument-based methods. We demonstrate that if agents have false beliefs, then they may make decisions during negotiation that lead them to suboptimal deals. We then describe different ways in which argument-based communication can cause changes in an agent's beliefs and, consequently, its preferences over contracts. This enables us to demonstrate how the argumentation-based approach can improve both the likelihood and quality of deals.

The paper advances the state of the art in two ways. First, it provides a step towards a more systematic comparison of argument-based and bargaining-based negotiation frameworks. Second, by making the link between belief change and preference change more explicit, we pave the way for the study of negotiation strategies within argument-based frameworks.

The paper is organised as follows. In the next section, we provide a conceptual framework which enables us to capture key negotiation concepts. We use these concepts in section 3 to show how bargaining works and demonstrate how it can lead to suboptimal outcomes. In section 4, we present an abstraction of a class of argument-based negotiation frameworks. We show different ways in which preferences can change due to changes in beliefs, and draw some comparisons with bargaining. We then conclude in section 5.

2   A Conceptual Framework for Negotiation

In this section, we set up the scene for the rest of the paper by formalising the main concepts involved in negotiation.

2.1   Agents and Plans

We have two autonomous agents A and B sharing the same world, which is in some initial state $s \in S$, where S is the set of all possible world states. Each agents might, however, believe it is in a different state from s, which can influence its decisions.

To get from one state s_1 to another s_2, agents execute actions. An action $\alpha \in \mathcal{A}$, where $\mathcal{A}$ is the set of all possible actions, moves the world from one state to another; hence it is a function $\alpha : S \rightarrow S$. We assume that actions are deterministic, and that the world changes only as a result of agents executing actions.[2]

---

[1] For a comprehensive review, the reader may refer to the forthcoming review article [17].

[2] We concede that this treatment of actions is rather simplistic. We made this choice deliberately in order to simplify the analysis.

Definition 1. (Plan) *A one-agent plan or simply plan P to move the world from state s_1 to s_2 is a finite list $[\alpha_1, \ldots, \alpha_n]$ of actions such that $s_2 = \alpha_n(\alpha_{n-1}(\ldots \alpha_1(s_1) \ldots))$*

We denote by $\mathcal{P}$ the set of all possible plans. And we denote by $s_1 \models [P]s_2$ that if the world is in state s_1, then executing plan P moves the world to state s_2.

What we have just defined is the *objective* action operators specification, i.e., how the world actually changes as a result of executing actions. Agents, however, might have possibly incomplete or incorrect beliefs about how the world changes as a result of executing actions. We therefore assume each agent i has its own mapping $\alpha^i : \mathcal{S} \cup \{?\} \rightarrow \mathcal{S} \cup \{?\}$ for each action, such that always $\alpha^i(?) =?$. If $\alpha_x^i(s_1) =?$, then we say that agent i does not know what state action α_x results in if executed in state s_1. The expression $s_1 \models^i [P]s_2$ means that agent i believes executing plan P in state s_1 results in state s_2. Moreover, the expression $s_1 \models^i [P]?$ means that agent i does not know what state results from executing plan P in state s_1.

Agents can evaluate actions and plans based on their costs.

Definition 2. (Cost of Action) *The* cost of action α for agent $i \in \{A, B\}$ is defined *using an action cost function $Cost : \{A, B\} \times \mathcal{A} \rightarrow \mathbb{R}^+$, which assigns a number to each action.*

Definition 3. (Cost of Plan) *The* cost of plan $P \in \mathcal{P}$ to agent i is defined using a plan *cost function*

$$Cost : \{A, B\} \times \mathcal{P} \rightarrow \mathbb{R}^+ \text{ such that } Cost(i, P) = \sum_{\alpha \in P} Cost(i, \alpha)$$

Unlike the case with action operators, where agents can have incorrect beliefs about the results of actions, we assume each agent has accurate knowledge about how much each action costs him/her. However, an agent may not know how much an action would cost another agent (i.e., we only assume each agent i knows accurately what $Cost(i, \alpha)$ is for each α).

Each agent $i \in \{A, B\}$ has a set of desires $\mathcal{D}^i \subseteq \mathcal{D}$, where $\mathcal{D}$ is the set of all possible desires. These desires are formulae in propositional logic or closed formulae in first-order logic (i.e., with no free variables). We say that a world state s satisfies a desire d if $s \models d$, where $\models$ is an appropriate semantic entailment relation.

Definition 4. (Worth of Desire) *The* worth of desire d for agent i is defined using a *desire worth function $Worth : \{A, B\} \times \mathcal{D} \rightarrow \mathbb{R}^+$, which assigns a number to each desire.*

Definition 5. (Worth of State) *The* worth of state $s \in \mathcal{S}$ to agent i is defined using a *state worth function*

$$Worth : \{A, B\} \times \mathcal{S} \rightarrow \mathbb{R}^+ \text{ such that } Worth(i, s) = \sum_{s \models d} Worth(i, d)$$

As with costs, each agent knows precisely what each desire is worth to him/her. Also, an agent may not know how much a desire is worth to another agent (i.e., we only assume each agent i knows accurately what $Worth(i, s)$ is).

We can now define the *utility* of a plan for an agent given it is in a particular state. We distinguish between the *objective* and *perceived* utility. The objective utility denotes the 'actual' gain achieved by the agent based on the actual resulting state (i.e., according to the objective action operators definition). The perceived utility, on the other hand, is the utility the agent 'thinks' it would achieve from that plan, based on what it believes the resulting state is.

Definition 6. (Utility of Plan) *The* utility of plan P *for agent i from state s_1 is defined as:*

$$Utility(i, P, s_1) = Worth(i, s_2) - Cost(i, P) \text{ where } s_1 \models [P]s_2$$

Definition 7. (Perceived Utility of Plan) *The* perceived utility of plan P *for agent i from state s_1 is defined as:*

$$Utility^i(i, P, s_1) = Worth(i, s_2) - Cost(i, P) \text{ where } s_1 \models^i [P]s_2$$

Definition 8. (Best Plan) *The* best plan *for agent i from state s_1 is a plan $P = BestP(i, s_1)$ such that $Utility(i, P, s_1) \geq Utility(i, P', s_1)$ for all $P' \neq P$*

Definition 9. (Perceived Best Plan) *The* perceived best plan *for agent i from state s_1 is a plan $P = BestP^i(i, s_1)$ such that $Utility^i(i, P, s_1) \geq Utility^i(i, P', s_1)$ for all $P' \neq P$.*

2.2   Contracts and Deals

So far, we have outlined how an agent can individually achieve its desires through the execution of plans. An agent might also be able to achieve its desires by contracting certain actions to other agents. Since agents are self-interested, they would only perform actions for one another if they receive something in return (i.e., if they get actions done for them, resulting in achieving their own desires). A specification of the terms of such exchange of services is a *contract*.

Definition 10. (Contract) *A contract Ω between agents A and B is a pair (P_A, P_B) of plans, and a schedule, such that P_i, $i \in \{A, B\}$ is the part of the contract to be executed by agent i according to the schedule.*

A schedule is a total order over the union of actions in the two one-agent plans. As with one-agent plans, we denote by $s_1 \models [\Omega]s_2$ that if the world is in state s_1, then executing the contract Ω moves the world to state s_2. Similarly, the perceived result of the contract by agent i is denoted by $s_1 \models^i [\Omega]s_2$. We denote by $\mathcal{C}$ the set of all possible contracts. We now define the cost of a contract to an agent.

Definition 11. (Cost of Contract) *The* cost of contract $\Omega = (P_A, P_B)$ *for agent $i \in \{A, B\}$ is the cost of i's part in that contract; i.e., $Cost(i, \Omega) = Cost(i, P_i)$.*

We define the contract's objective and perceived utilities, denoted $Utility(i, \Omega, s_1)$ and $Utility^i(i, \Omega, s_1)$, and the best contract and best perceived contract, denoted $BestC(i, s_1)$ and $BestC^i(i, s_1)$, analogously to plans above.

We can now define the set of contracts acceptable to an agent.

Definition 12. (Individual Rational Contract) *A contract* $\Omega = (P_A, P_B)$ *is* individual rational, *or simply* acceptable, *for agent* i *in state* s *if and only if* $Utility(i, \Omega, s) \geq Utility(i, BestP(i, s), s)$.

A *perceived individual rational contracts* is defined similarly using perceived utilities.

A rational agent[3] should only accept contracts that are individual rational. We denote by $IRC(i)$ the set of individual rational contracts for agent i, and by $IRC^i(i)$ the set of perceived individual rational contracts. On this basis, each agent can classify each possible contract into two sets: *acceptable*, *unacceptable*, and *suspended* contracts. Suspended contracts are contracts for which the agent does not know the result (i.e., for which $s_1 \models^i [\Omega]?$), and is hence unable to assess the utilities. If $IRC(i) = \emptyset$, then it makes no sense for agent i to negotiate; i.e., an agent better do things individually.

If agents do not change their beliefs, then the set $IRC^i(i) \cap IRC^j(j)$ is the set of possible deals: contracts that are individual rational from the points of view of both agents. Possible deals are those contracts that make both agents (as far as they know) better off than they would be working individually. If $IRC^i(i) \cap IRC^j(j) = \emptyset$, then agents will never reach a deal unless they change their preferences. Figure 1 exemplifies two cases. Each oval shows the set of individual rational contracts for an agent. If these sets intersect, then a deal is possible.

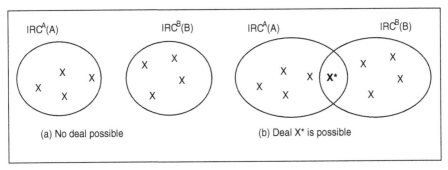

Fig. 1. Possible and impossible deals

3   Searching for Deals Through Bargaining

In the previous section, we outlined the main concepts involved in the stage prior to negotiation. The questions that raises itself now is the following: *given two agents, each with a set of individual rational contracts, how can agents decide on a particular deal, if such deal is possible?* One way is to search for a deal by suggesting contracts to one another.

3.1   Elements of Bargaining

Negotiation can be seen as a process of joint search through the space of all contracts (i.e., through the set C), in an attempt to find a mutually acceptable contract (i.e., one

---

[3] I.e., rational in the economic sense, attempting to maximise expected utility.

that belongs to $IRC^i(i) \cap IRC^j(j)$). Furthermore, agents may wish to find a contract that also satisfies some kind of 'optimality' criteria. For example, agents may attempt to find a contract that is Pareto optimal, or one that maximises the sum or product of their individual utilities.[4]

One of the most widely studied mechanisms for searching for a deal is *bargaining* [12]. In bargaining, agents exchange *offers* – or *proposals*: contracts that represent potential deals. Of course, it would only make sense for each agent to propose contracts that are acceptable to it.

Definition 13. (Offer) *An offer is a tuple* $\langle i, \Omega \rangle$, *where* $i \in \{A, B\}$ *and* $\Omega \in C$, *and represents an announcement by agent i that* $\Omega \in IRC^i(i)$.

During negotiation, each agent may make multiple offers until agreement is reached. At any particular point in time, the offers made constitute the negotiation *position* of the agent: those contracts the agent has announced it is willing to accept as deals. We denote by $\mathcal{O}$ the set of all possible offers (by all agents).[5]

Definition 14. (Position) *The* position *of agent i, denoted $Position(i)$, is a set of contracts i has offered so far, such that at any time, we have $Position(i) \subseteq IRC^i(i)$.*

Note that while the set $IRC^i(i)$ is static during bargaining, the set $Position(i)$ is dynamic, since it expands, within the confines of $IRC(i)$, as the agent makes new offers.

A question that raises itself now is: *how does an agent expand its position?* In other words, *given a set of offers made so far, what should an agent offer next?* The answer to this question is what constitutes the agent's bargaining strategy.

Definition 15. (Bargaining Strategy) *A bargaining strategy for agent i, denoted Δ^i is a function that takes the history of all proposals made so far, and returns a proposal to make next. Formally:* $\Delta^i : 2^{\mathcal{O}} \to \mathcal{O}$, *where* $2^{\mathcal{O}}$ *is the power set of the set of all possible offers* $\mathcal{O}$.

One of the key factors in influencing an agent's negotiation strategy is its preferences over contracts. It would make sense for an agent to begin by offering contracts most preferable to itself, then progressively 'concede' to less preferred contracts if needed.[6] Preference, however, is not the only factor that guides strategy. For example, an agent might have time constraints, making it wish to reach agreement quickly even if such agreement is not optimal. To reach a deal faster, the agent might make bigger concessions than it would otherwise. This issue becomes particularly relevant if the number of possible contracts is very large.

A variety of bargaining strategies have been studied in the literature. Such strategies might be specified in terms of a preprogrammed, fixed sequence of offers [3] or be dependent on factors observed during negotiation itself, such as the offers made by the counterpart [2, 5, 23], or changes in the availability of resources [4]. A thorough

---

[4] For more on outcome evaluation, refer to the book by Rosenschein and Zlotkin [19].
[5] Note that $\mathcal{O}$ is different from C. While the latter denotes the set of all possible contracts, the former denotes the set of all possible agent/contract pairs.
[6] This is commonly known as the monotonic concession bargaining strategy.

examination of these strategies is outside the scope of this study. We note, however, that strategies are highly dependent on the interaction protocol and on the information agents have. For example, following a risk-dependent strategy under the monotonic concession protocol when agents have complete information can be guaranteed to lead to a Pareto-optimal agreement [8]. Such result could not be guaranteed if agents do not know each other's preferences.

3.2   Limitations of Bargaining

One of the main limitations of bargaining frameworks is that they usually assume agents have complete and accurate information about the current world state and the results of actions, and are consequently capable of providing a complete and accurate ranking of all possible contracts. If these assumptions are not satisfied, serious problems start to arise. In particular, bargaining could not be guaranteed to lead to agreements that truly maximise the participants' utilities.

To clarify the above point, consider the following example. Suppose a customer intending to purchase a car assigns a higher preference to Volvos than Toyotas because of his[7] perceived safety of Volvos. Suppose also that this holds despite the customer's belief that Toyotas have cheaper spare parts, because safety is more important to him. If this information is false –for example if Toyota's actually perform as good as Volvos on safety tests–, then the actual utility received by purchasing a Volvo is not maximal. This example is formalised below.

Example 1. Suppose buyer agent B trying to purchase a car from seller A, such that:

- B believes they are in s_1
- $\mathcal{D}^B = \{safety, cheapParts\}$
- $Worth(B, safety) = 18$, $Worth(B, cheapParts) = 12$
- $s_1 \models^B [do_A(give\,Volvo), do_B(pay\$10K)]s_2$ where $s_2 \models safety$
- $s_1 \models^B [do_A(give\,Toyota), do_B(pay\$10K)]s_2'$ where $s_2' \models cheapParts$
- $Cost(B, pay\$10K) = 10$

Then B will assign the following utilities:

- $Utility^B(B, [do_A(give\,Volvo), do_B(pay\$10K)], s_1) = 18 - 10 = 8$
- $Utility^B(B, [do_A(give\,Toyota), do_B(pay\$10K)], s_1) = 12 - 10 = 2$

Consequently, B will attempt to purchase a Volvo. However, suppose that the truth is that:

- $s_1 \models [do_A(give\,Toyota), do_B(pay\$10K)]s_2''$ where $s_2'' \models cheapParts \wedge safety$

In this case, the actual utility of the Toyota contract would be:

- $Utility(B, [do_A(give\,Toyota), do_B(pay\$10K)], s_1) = 12 + 18 - 10 = 20$

Hence, this lack in B's knowledge can lead to negotiation towards a suboptimal deal.

---

[7] To avoid ambiguity, we shall refer to the seller using she/her and to the buyer using he/his.

Another case based on the example above is when B does not know about the safety features of cars of make Honda. In this case, B would assign value '?' to Honda contracts, and would be unable to relate it preferentially to Toyotas and Volvos. If Honda's where indeed cheaper, and offer both safety and good spare part prices, agent B would be missing out, again.

What we have just demonstrated is that if agent preferences remain fixed during negotiation and their beliefs are inaccurate, then they may fail to reach deals that maximise their utility. We can generalise this to the following result.

Proposition 1. *In bargaining between agents i and j, the actual best reachable deal is the best deal acceptable to both agents according to their perceived preferences.*

Proof. Let us denote the actual best deal by $BEST(i, j)$. This deal lies in the set $IRC(i) \cap IRC(j)$. But since agents make their decisions based on their perceived contract utilities, each contract $\Omega \notin IRC^i(i) \cap IRC^j(j)$ is unacceptable for at least one agent, and hence will never be selected as a deal. This means that the actual best reachable deal through bargaining is in the set:

$$IRC^i(i) \cap IRC^j(j) \cap IRC(i) \cap IRC(j)$$

Now, if

$$BEST(i, j) \in ((IRC(i) \cap IRC(j)) \setminus (IRC^i(i) \cap IRC^j(j)))$$

then the agents will never reach $BEST(i, j)$. The same thing may apply for the actual second best deal, and so on, until we reach a deal that is within $IRC^i(i) \cap IRC^j(j)$.

This straightforward result demonstrates clearly that as long as agent preferences are inaccurate, they might miss out on better deals. Note, however, that this does not give us an indication of how good or bad the best perceived deal is.

4   Argument-Based Negotiation

In the previous section, we explored how bargaining can be used to search for a deal on the basis of fixed agents preferences over contracts. We showed that there are circumstances in which bargaining fails to achieve a deal, or leads to a suboptimal deal. In this section, we explore argument-based approaches to negotiation and relate it to bargaining.

As mentioned earlier, if $IRC^i(i) \cap IRC^j(j) = \emptyset$, then agents will never reach a deal unless at least one of them changes its perceived individually rational contracts. Figure 2 shows two cases where initially no deal was possible because the agents' individual rational contract sets did not intersect, but a deal is enabled by changes in the set of individual rational contracts. In figure 2(a), a deal is enabled when agent B's perceived IRC set changes such that contract X^* becomes acceptable. In figure 2(b), both agents IRCs change, making deal X^{**} (which initially was not acceptable to either agents) mutually acceptable. Changing $IRC^i(i)$ requires changing agent i's preferences, which in fact requires change in i's beliefs. *Argumentation* is a way to enable agents to rationally influence such beliefs through rational dialogues.

The benefit of argumentation is apparent in human negotiations. Humans form their preferences based on information available to them. As a result, they acquire and modify

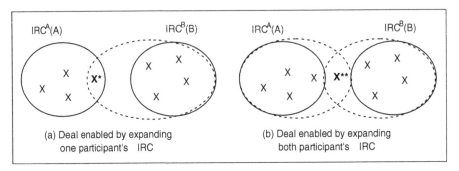

Fig. 2. Changes in perceived individual rational contracts

their preferences as a result of interaction with the environment and other consumers [13]. Advertising capitalises on this idea, and can be seen a process of argumentation in which marketers attempt to persuade consumers to change their preferences over products [21]. In negotiation, participants are encouraged to argue with one another and discuss each other's interests. This enables them to jointly discover new possibilities and correct misconceptions, which increases both the likelihood and quality of agreement [7]. Computational agents may realise a similar benefit if they are able to conduct dialogues over interests during negotiation.

4.1   Elements of ABN

Argument-based negotiation (ABN) extends bargaining-based protocols. Therefore, concepts such as offers and positions are also part of ABN. In addition, agents can exchange information in order to influence each others' beliefs. As a result, they influence each others' negotiation positions and set of acceptable contracts. The first step towards understanding how preferences over contracts change is, therefore, to understand the different ways influence on beliefs may take place, and how such influence affects the utility an agent assigns to a contract.

Recall that the utility of contracts and plans are calculated by agent i based on the following definition, which merges the definitions of plan and contract utility.

Definition 16. (Utility of Plan or Contract) *The utility of contract or plan X for agent i from state s_1 is defined as:* $Utility^i(i, X, s_1) = Worth(i, s_2) - Cost(i, X)$ *where* $s_1 \models^i [X]s_2$.

From the definition, it is clear that the utility of a contract or plan (a) increases as the the perceived worth of the resulting state increases, and (b) decreases as the perceived cost of carrying out that contract or plan increases. Since we assume that perceived costs are subjective, and are hence accurate, we concentrate on how changes in perceived worth of state s_2 affect the utility. According to definition 5, the worth of state s_2 depends on the set of desires from $\mathcal{D}^i$ that are satisfied in s_2.

Based on this understanding, we can now enumerate how changes in beliefs can influence the perceived utility of a contract or plan. We dub these changes **C1**, **C2**, etc.

C1 *Learn that in s_1, X results in a state other than s_2:*

Description: Agent i learns that $s_1 \models^i [P]s_2'$ where $s_2' \neq s_2$.

Effect: This may trigger a change in the worth of X's result, which then influences the utility of X, as follows:

1. If $\textit{Worth}(i, s_2') = \textit{Worth}^i(s_2)$, then the utility of X remains the same;
2. If $\textit{Worth}(i, s_2') \geq \textit{Worth}(i, s_2)$, then the utility of X increases;
3. If $\textit{Worth}(i, s_2') \leq \textit{Worth}(i, s_2)$, then the utility of X decreases;

Example: A traveller who knew it was possible to travel to Sydney by train learns that by doing so, he also gets free accommodation with the booking. As a result, his preference for train travel increases. Hence, this is an example of the second effect described above.

C2 *Learn that it is in a different state:*

Description: The agent learns that it is not in state s_1 as initially thought, but rather in state s_1', where $s_1' \neq s_1$.

Effect: Two things might happen:

1. If the agent believes that in this new state, X has the same result, i.e. that $s_1' \models^i [X]s_2'$, then the perceived utility of X remains the same.
2. If the agent believes X now results in a different state, i.e. that $s_1' \models^i [X]s_2$ where $s_2' \neq s_2$, then the utility of X changes as in the three cases described in **C1** above.

Example: A traveller who was planning a conference trip learns that the conference has been cancelled. Now, flying to Sydney will no longer achieve his desire to present a research paper.

C3 *Learn a new plan:*

Description: Agent i, which did not know what plan X results in, i.e., $s_1 \models^i [X]?$, now learns that $s_1 \models^i [X]s_2$.

Effect: X moves from being suspended to having a precise utility. If X is a contract, it gets classified as either acceptable or unacceptable.

Example: A car buyer did not know whether a car of make Honda has airbags. After learning that they do, he can now calculate the utility of this car.

C4 *Unlearn an existing plan:*

Description: Agent i discovers that some X actually does not achieve the expected resulting state, i.e., that $s_1 \models^i [X]?$.

Effect: The utility of X becomes undefined, and X becomes suspended.

Example: A traveller might find out that merely booking a ticket does not achieve the state of being in Sydney.

As a result of a perceived utility change, the relative preferences among various plans and contracts *may* change. Preference change may not take place if the agent's perceived utilities of contracts does not change at all, or if utilities do not change enough to cause a reordering of preferences.

Note that what we described above is the effect of a belief change on the utility of a single contract. In fact, each belief change may trigger changes in the utilities of a large number of contracts, resulting in quite complex changes in the agent's preference relation. This adds a significant complexity to strategic reasoning in ABN.

4.2   Embedded Dialogues as Means for Utility Change

One might ask: *on what basis could the above changes in belief and perceived utilities take place during negotiation?* A rational agent should only change its preferences in light of new information. One way to receive such information is through perception of the environment. Another way is through communication with others. Our focus here is on the latter and in particular on situations where belief change happens during the negotiation dialogue itself. In this context, the idea of *embedding* one dialogue in another is relevant. Walton and Krabbe [22, pp. 66] provide a classification of main dialogue types, namely: *persuasion, negotiation, inquiry, deliberation, information seeking*, and *eristic* dialogues. Embedding is one type of dialectical shift –moving from one dialogue to another [22, pp. 100–102]. During negotiation between two participants, the following shifts to embedded dialogues may take place:

- *Information seeking in negotiation*: one participant seeks information from its counterpart in order to find out more (e.g., a customer asks a car seller about the safety record of a particular vehicle make);
- *Persuasion in negotiation*: one participant enters a persuasion dialogue in an attempt to change the counterpart's beliefs (e.g., a car salesperson tries to persuade a customer of the value of airbags for safety);
- *Inquiry in negotiation*: both participants initiate an inquiry dialogue in order to find out whether a particular statement is true, or in order to establish the utility of a particular contract; a precondition to enquiry is that neither agent knows the answer a priori (e.g., a customer and car seller jointly attempt to establish whether a particular car meets the customer's safety criteria);
- *Deliberation in negotiation*: both participants enter a deliberation dialogue in order to establish the best course of individual or joint action (i.e., the best plan or joint plan), potentially changing their initial preferences (e.g., a customer and car seller jointly attempt to find out the best way to achieve the customer's safety and budget requirements);

Note that in order to enable the above types of dialogue shifts during negotiation, a protocol that allows dialogue embedding is needed. One such framework was presented by McBurney and Parsons [14].

4.3   Some ABN Examples

We now list a number of examples, building on example 1, which demonstrate some ways in which preference can change as a result of belief change.

Example 2. Car selling agent A initiates the following persuasion dialogue in order to get the buyer B to choose the Toyota:

A: Don't you know that Toyotas actually perform as good as Volvos on major road safety tests?
B: Oh really? And it costs the same right?
A: True.
B: Well, I would rather purchase the Toyota then!

As a result of argumentation, B now believes that

$$s_1 \models^B [do_A(give\,Toyota), do_B(pay\$10K)]s_2'' \text{ where } s_2'' \models cheapParts \wedge safety$$

As we discussed in example 1, this leads to a more accurate preference. Note that this example involves a belief change of type **C1**, where B changes his expectation about the result of the Toyota contract.

Example 3. Suppose B did not initially know about the safety features of cars of make Honda. In this case, B would have the following belief:

$$s_1 \models^B [do_A(give\,Honda), do_B(pay\$10K)]?$$

As a result, B would be unable to relate it preferentially to Toyotas and Volvos. Suppose B then initiates the information seeking dialogue:

B: How about that Honda over there?
A: Actually Hondas satisfy both your criteria. They are safe, and also have cheap parts. In fact, this one is available for $8K.
B: Seems better than both. I'll go for the Honda then!

If we have $Cost(B, pay\$8K) = 8$, then as a result of the above dialogue, B can now give a utility valuation for contract $[do_A(give\,Honda), do_B(pay\$8K)]$. This will be $12 + 18 - 8 = 22$, which will rank the Honda higher than both Toyotas and Volvos. Note that this example involves a belief change of type **C3** for the Honda contract.

Example 4. Suppose that the seller would still rather sell the Toyota than the Honda, because she wants to get rid of the old Toyota stock. Consider the following dialogue:

B: From what you said, I like this Honda. It offers the same features as the Toyota, but is cheaper.
A: But did you consider its registration cost?
B: It's the same for all cars, so I think it's irrelevant.
A: Actually, the government recently introduced a new tax cut of $3K for purchasing locally manufactured cars. This is aimed at encouraging national industry.
B: Wow! This would indirectly reduce the cost of Toyotas because they are manufactured in Australia. This does not apply to the imported Hondas.
A: That's correct.
B: Aha! Toyota is definitely the way to go then.

Before the dialogue, B knew that if there was a tax cut for local cars, i.e., if it is in $s_1' \models^i localTaxCut$, then purchasing a Toyota results in an additional worth of 3, i.e., that:

$$s_1' \models^i [do_A(give\,Toyota), do_B(pay\$10K)]cheapParts \wedge safety \wedge get\$3K$$

But because B initially thought that there is no such tax cut, i.e., that it is in $s_1 \models^i \neg localTaxCut$, the resulting state was not thought to contain $get\$3K$. During the dialogue B finds out that it is in s_1' rather than s_1. As a result, the utility of the Toyota contract becomes $12+18+3-10 = 23$, whereas the utility of the Honda remains $12+18-8 = 22$. Note that this dialogue involves a belief change of type **C2**.

4.4   Position and Negotiation Set Dynamics

The examples presented in the previous subsection demonstrate how preferences can change during negotiation as a result of belief and utility changes. Now, the question is: *how can such preference change influence the likelihood and quality of agreement?*

Proposition 2. *Argumentation can influence a negotiator i's set of individually rational contracts.*

This is because changes in utilities may cause existing contracts to leave the set $IRC^i(i)$, or new contracts to enter this set.

Recall from Proposition 1 that the quality of reachable deals depends on the contents of the sets $IRC^i(i)$ (or more specifically, on their intersection) and how they differ from their actual counterparts $IRC(i)$. Hence, changes to $IRC^i(i)$ caused by argumentation could influence the quality of reachable deals. Moreover, argumentation can enable a deal in an otherwise failed negotiation. This happens when the sets of individual rational contracts did not initially intersect.

Proposition 3. *Argumentation can improve the actual quality of the deal reached.*

Proof. Let A and B be two agents negotiating over two mutually acceptable contracts, Ω and Ω'. And suppose that for each agent $i \in \{A, B\}$, the perceived utilities are such that $Utility^i(i, \Omega, s_1^i) \geq Utility^i(i, \Omega', s_1^i)$ whereas actual utilities are such that $Utility(i, \Omega, s_1^i) \leq Utility(i, \Omega', s_1^i)$. This means that contract Ω Pareto dominates[8] Ω' from the point of view of both agents, whereas based on the actual objective utilities, Ω' Pareto dominates Ω. If the agents were bargaining, they would choose Ω. Through argumentation, the beliefs of participants may change such that the perceived utility of Ω' becomes higher than that of Ω for both agents. In this case, Ω' would be chosen, resulting in an objectively better outcome.

A popular example that demonstrates the above proposition has been presented by Parsons et al [15]. The example concerns two home-improvement agents – one trying to hang a mirror, the other trying to hang a painting. They each have some but not all of the resources needed. Even though a deal was possible, the agents could not reach a deal because one agent knew only one way to achieve his goals. By engaging in argument, that agent was able to learn that he could achieve his goals in a different way, by using a different set of resources. Thus, the information exchanged in the course of the interaction resulted in that agent learning a new way to achieve his goal (i.e., learning some new beliefs), and so changed his preferences across the set of possible contracts.

As much as the above result seems promising, there is a flip side to things.

Proposition 4. *Agents can be worse off as a result of argumentation.*

Proof. Similar to Proposition 3 above, except that the agents begin correctly *preferring Ω', and end up preferring Ω.*

Argumentation can lead to worse outcomes if the resulting preference ordering is more different from the objective ordering than it initially was. Whether and how this happens would depend on the efficiency of the agents' argumentative abilities, their reasoning capabilities and any time constraints, and whether or not they attempt to deceive each other.

---

[8] I.e., makes one agent better off without making the other worse off.

5   Conclusions

In this paper, we initiated an investigation into understanding the relationship between bargaining and argumentation-based negotiation frameworks. We described both types of frameworks using a uniform "vocabulary", and made some intuitions more precise. In particular, we provided a precise account of how argumentation can influence preferences over contracts. We then showed how the ability to exchange such arguments can help overcome some problems with bargaining. In particular, we have demonstrated that:

- Rational agents *may* change their preferences in the light of new information;
- Rational agents should *only* change their preferences in the light of new information;
- Negotiation involving the exchange of arguments provides the capability for agents to change their preferences;
- Such negotiations could increase the likelihood and quality of a deal, compared to bargaining, particularly in situations where agents have incomplete and/or inaccurate beliefs;
- Such negotiations could also lead to worse outcomes compared to bargaining;

We are now extending our framework in order to capture richer types of argument-based influences. For example, we are investigating allowing agents to influence each others' desire set itself. In this case, we must distinguish between perceived and actual state worths. The same could be done to plan costs.

Our study also paves the way for a more systematic study of strategies in argument-based negotiation [16]. Understanding the possible effects of different types of embedded dialogues can help an agent make decisions about how to argue during negotiation. This also enables studying more complex strategies that result in multiple related changes in utility. For example, a car seller may first attempt to persuade a customer of adopting a new desire towards safety, then attempt to convince him that his current preferred contract does not achieve this desire.

Acknowledgements

Iyad Rahwan is grateful for the support of a Melbourne University Research Scholarship; Iyad thanks Andrew Clausen for many interesting chats, and Frank Dignum and Rogier van Eijk for their valuable input on the relationship between bargaining and negotiation dialogues, especially to a formalisation which is the subject of current related work. Peter McBurney is grateful for partial support from the European Commission, through Project ASPIC (IST-FP6-002307). The authors thank the anonymous reviewers for their valuable comments.

References

1. L. Amgoud, S. Parsons, and N. Maudet. Arguments, dialogue, and negotiation. In W. Horn, editor, *Proceedings of the European Conference on Artificial Intelligence (ECAI 2000)*, pages 338–342, Amsterdam, Netherlands, 2000. IOS Press.
2. R. Axelrod. *The Evolution of Cooperation*. Basic Books, Inc. Publishers, New York NY, USA, 1984.

3. A. Chavez and P. Maes. Kasbah: An agent marketplace for buying and selling goods. In *First International Conference on the Practical Appication of Intelligent Agents and Multi-Agent Technology*, 1996.
4. P. Faratin. *Automated Service Negotiation Between Autonomous Computational Agents*. PhD thesis, University of London, Queen Mary and Westfield College, Department of Electronic Engineering, 2000.
5. P. Faratin, C. Sierra, and N. R. Jennings. Using similarity criteria to make trade-offs in automated negotiations. *Artificial Intelligence*, 142(2):205–237, 2002.
6. S. Fatima, M. J. Wooldridge, and N. R. Jennings. Multi-issue negotiation under time constraints. In C. Castelfranchi and L. Johnson, editors, *Proceedings of the 1st International Joint Conference on Autonomous Agents and Multiagent Systems (AAMAS-2002)*, pages 143–150, New York, USA, 2002. ACM Press.
7. R. Fisher, W. Ury, and B. Patton. *Getting to Yes: Negotiating Agreement Without Giving In*. Penguin Books, New York, USA, second edition, 1991.
8. J. C. Harsanyi. Approaches to the bargaining problem before and after the theory of games: a critical discussion of Zeuthen's, Hicks', and Nash's theories. *Econometrica*, 24:144–157, 1956.
9. N. R. Jennings, S. Parsons, P. Noriega, and C. Sierra. On argumentation-based negotiation. In *Proceedings of the International Workshop on Multi-Agent Systems*, pages 1–7, Boston, USA, 1998.
10. S. Kraus. *Strategic Negotiation in Multi-Agent Environments*. MIT Press, Cambridge MA, USA, 2001.
11. S. Kraus, K. Sycara, and A. Evenchik. Reaching agreements through argumentation: A logical model and implementation. *Artificial Intelligence*, 104(1–2):1–69, 1998.
12. K. Larson and T. Sandholm. An alternating offers bargaining model for computationally limited agents. In C. Castelfranchi and L. Johnson, editors, *Proceedings of the 1st International Joint Conference on Autonomous Agents and Multi-Agent Systems (AAMAS-2002)*, pages 135–142, 2002.
13. G. L. Lilien, P. Kotler, and S. K. Moorthy. *Marketing Models*. Prentice-Hall Press, USA, 1992.
14. P. McBurney and S. Parsons. Games that agents play: A formal framework for dialogues between autonomous agents. *Journal of Logic, Language and Information*, 11(3):315–334, 2002.
15. S. Parsons, C. Sierra, and N. Jennings. Agents that reason and negotiate by arguing. *Journal of Logic and Computation*, 8(3):261–292, 1998.
16. I. Rahwan, P. McBurney, and L. Sonenberg. Towards a theory of negotiation strategy (a preliminary report). In S. Parsons and P. Gmytrasiewicz, editors, *Proceedings of the 5th Workshop on Game Theoretic and Decision Theoretic Agents (GTDT-2003)*, pages 73–80, 2003.
17. I. Rahwan, S. D. Ramchurn, N. R. Jennings, P. McBurney, S. Parsons, and L. Sonenberg (2003). Argumentation-Based Negotiation. *The Knowledge Engineering Review*, Volume 18, No. 4, 2003, pages 343-375.
18. S. D. Ramchurn, N. R. Jennings, and C. Sierra. Persuasive negotiation for autonomous agents: a rhetorical approach. In C. Reed, F. Grasso, and G. Carenini, editors, *Proceedings of the IJCAI Workshop on Computational Models of Natural Argument*, pages 9–17. AAAI Press, 2003.
19. J. Rosenschein and G. Zlotkin. *Rules of Encounter: Designing Conventions for Automated Negotiation among Computers*. MIT Press, Cambridge MA, USA, 1994.
20. S. V. Rueda, A. J. García, and G. R. Simari. Argument-based negotiation among BDI agents. *Computer Science & Technology*, 2(7), 2002.

21. C. Slade. Reasons to buy: The logic of advertisements. *Argumentation*, 16:157–178, 2002.
22. D. N. Walton and E. C. W. Krabbe. *Commitment in Dialogue: Basic Concepts of Interpersonal Reasoning*. SUNY Press, Albany NY, USA, 1995.
23. F. L. B. Zeuthen. *Problems of Monopoly and Economic Warfare*. Routledge and Sons, London, UK, 1930.

On the Generation of Bipolar Goals in Argumentation-Based Negotiation

Leila Amgoud[1] and Souhila Kaci[2]

[1]Institut de Recherche en Informatique de Toulouse (I.R.I.T.),
Université Paul Sabatier,
118, route de Narbonne 31062 Toulouse, France
amgoud@irit.fr
[2]Centre de Recherche en Informatique de Lens (C.R.I.L.),
IUT de Lens,
Rue de l'Université SP 16 62307 Lens, France
kaci@cril.univ-artois.fr

Abstract. The notion of agent's goals is crucial in negotiation dialogues. In fact, during a negotiation, each agent tries to make and to accept the offers which satisfy its own *goals*. Works on negotiation suppose that an agent has a set of fixed goals to pursue. However, it is not shown how these goals are computed and chosen by the agent. Moreover, these works handle one kind of goals: the ones that an agent wants to achieve.

Recent studies on psychology claim that goals are bipolar and there are at least two kinds of goals: the *positive goals* representing what the agent wants to achieve and the *negative goals* representing what the agent rejects. In this paper, we present an argumentation-based framework which generates the goals of an agent. The framework returns three categories of goals: the *positive* goals, the *negative* ones and finally the goals in *abeyance*.

Keywords: Negotiation, Argumentation.

1 Introduction

In most agent applications, the autonomous components need to interact with one another because of the inherent interdependencies which exist between them, and negotiation is the predominant mechanism for achieving this by means of an exchange of offers. The purpose of negotiation is to make a deal and each agent aims to maximize its profit. In fact, an agent makes and accepts only offers that satisfy its *goals*.

Works in multi-agents negotiation can be roughly divided into two categories. The first one has mainly focused on the numerical computation of trade-offs in terms of utilities, and the search for concessions which still preserve the possibility of reaching preferred states of affairs e.g.[10, 15]. These works suppose that each agent has a set of fixed goals that it should pursue.

Recently, a second line of research [2, 9, 13] has focused on the necessity of supporting offers by arguments during a negotiation. Indeed, an offer supported by a good argument has a better chance to be accepted by an agent and may lead an agent to *revise*

I. Rahwan et al. (Eds.): ArgMAS 2004, LNAI 3366, pp. 192–207, 2005.

its goals. However, in these works, it is not clear how the goals are handled and updated if necessary.

In sum, in all these approaches, it is not shown how the goals are computed and chosen by the agent and how they can be revised. Moreover, in all the above approaches, only one kind of goals is considered: the ones that an agent wants to achieve. However, in [3] the authors argued that when an agent expresses its goals, it usually does that in a *bipolar* way. On one hand, it expresses what it really wants, what it considers as really satisfactory. These are *positive goals.* They will represent the goals which will be pursued by the agent and each offer satisfying these goals is *rewarded.* On the other hand, it expresses what it definitely rejects, what it considers as unacceptable. These are *negative goals.* They represent the goals which will not be pursued by the agent. This category of goals is very important in a negotiation since each offer satisfying a negative goal will automatically be rejected by the agent. Indeed, reasoning on both what an agent likes and what it rejects, enriches the negotiation process since an offer can be evaluated w.r.t. both kinds of goals. For example an agent may consider an offer better than another if both falsify all its positive goal but the first one does not satisfy any negative goal (i.e., it is not rejected) while the second one satisfies at least one negative goal (i.e., it is rejected).

Beware that positive goals do not just mirror what is not rejected since a goal which is not rejected is not necessarily pursued. This category of goals which are neither negative nor positive are said to be *in abeyance.* Note however that positive and negative goals are related by a coherence condition which says that what is pursued should be among what is not rejected.

This distinction between positive and negative goals is supported by recent studies in cognitive psychology which have shown that these two types of goals are independent and processed separately in the mind [5, 6, 12, 4].

This paper focuses on the computation of goals. It particularly answers the following questions: what is a goal? what is its origin? what is its nature? what are the different kinds of arguments supporting it? and how it is computed or obtained?

We present an argumentation-based framework which returns the three categories of goals, namely *positive goals*, *negative goals* and *goals in abeyance.*

The paper is organized as follows: section 2 studies the nature of a goal. Section 3 introduces two different types of arguments supporting a goal: *explanatory arguments* and *instrumental arguments.* Section 4 presents an argumentation framework which evaluates the explanatory arguments and section 5 presents another framework which evaluates the instrumental arguments. Section 6 computes the positive and the negative goals of an agent. Section 7 shows through an example how the positive and negative goals of an agent may change in a negotiation dialogue.

2   The Nature of a Goal

In this section, we will discuss the nature of a goal according to three different criteria: *subjectivity* which has been already discussed in [11], *bipolarity* and finally the *origin.*

2.1   The Subjective Nature

As it has already been mentioned in [11] goals are considered as *motivational* attitudes of an agent and they are therefore by nature intrinsic to an agent. Indeed, one cannot say, as for beliefs, that a given goal of an agent is correct or incorrect. But, we can attempt to establish that a goal seems unachievable, not useful or unsupported. Let's take the following dialogues between two agents:

Example 1.
P: I would like to fly to Algiers with Algerian Airlines because it is not expensive.
C: But flying with Algeria Airlines means changing your flight arrangements is not flexible.
P: I know that.

In this case even if the argument given by **C** seems *acceptable* and in some sense defeats the argument supporting the goal *to fly with Algerian Airlines*, **P** maintains its goal.

Example 2.
P: I would like to fly to Algiers with Algerian Airlines because it is not expensive.
C: Actually flying with Algeria Airlines can be quite expensive because it is the holiday season.
P: I didn't know that.

In this case, if the agent **P** does not find another company which is cheaper than Algerian Airlines, then we can also imagine that the agent keeps its goal.

2.2   A Bipolar Nature

As we said in the introduction, an original representation of goals called bipolar goals [3] has been proposed. Indeed, we distinguish two independent types of goals: positive goals describing the goals pursued by the agent and negative goals describing the goals rejected, not pursued by the agent. The goals which are neither negative nor positive are called goals in abeyance. In example 1, we can imagine that the flexibility arrangements of a flight is not very important for the agent.

Goals are matter of degrees. Thus an agent expresses its goals by means of two different bases. A base representing what is more or less rejected by the agent and another base representing what is more or less satisfactory for him.

To illustrate the idea of bipolar goals, let us consider the following example (introduced in [8]) of an agent who goes to an agency in order to buy a house or an apartment. It gives the following positive and negative goals to the seller.

Example 3. The agent does not want a house or an apartment with a small surface and which is expensive. This negative goal is encoded as ($small \land expensive$). Another negative goal is that it does not accept a house without a garden ($house \land \neg garden$). However, the agent has some positive goals which are: an apartment with a large surface ($\neg house \land large$)[1] and a house with a medium surface and a garden ($house \land medium \land garden$).

---

[1] where $\neg house$ encodes an apartment.

Note that none of positive goals is rejected. Also the goal to have a medium and cheap apartment without garden is neither a negative goal nor a positive one. This is a goal in abeyance.

2.3   The Origins of the Goals

Agent's goals come generally from two different sources:

- from beliefs that justify their existence. So, the agent believes that the world is in a state that warrants the existence of its goals. These goals are called the *initial* ones or also *conditional* goals. They are conditional because they depend on the beliefs.
- an agent can adopt a goal because it allows him to achieve an initial goal. These are called *sub-goals* or *adopted goals*.

Example 4 (Trip to Central Africa).
Let's consider an agent who wants to go to Central Africa because there is a conference there. The goal jca is derived from the belief $Conference$.
The agent believes that to go to Central Africa, it should get tickets (t) and to be vaccinated (vac). To get tickets, the agent can either pass to an agency (ag) or ask a friend of him to get them (fr). Similarly, to be vaccinated, the agent has the choice between *going to a doctor* (dr) or *going to the hospital* (hop). Thus, t, vac, ag, fr, dr and hop become sub-goals of that agent.

3   Arguing About Goals

As mentioned above, there are two kinds of goals: the *initial/conditional* goals and the *adopted* ones called also *sub-goals*. These goals are justified or supported by two different kinds of arguments: *explanatory arguments* and *instrumental arguments*.

Before presenting formally these two types of arguments, we will start by presenting the logical language which will be used throughout this paper. In what follows, $\mathcal{L}$ will denote a propositional language. $\vdash$ denotes classical inference and $\equiv$ denotes logical equivalence.

Definition 1 (Conditional Rules).
A conditional rule *is an expression of the form*

$$R : \phi_1 \wedge \ldots \wedge \phi_n \Rightarrow \phi$$

where R is the name *of the rule and each ϕ_i and ϕ are* literals *of $\mathcal{L}$. The conjunction at the left of the arrow is the* antecedent *and the literal at the right is its* consequent.

A conditional rule expresses the fact that if $\phi_1 \ldots \phi_n$ are true then the agent will have the goal ϕ. Similarly, we will define the planning rules.

Definition 2 (Planning Rules).
A planning rule *is an expression of the form*

$$P : \varphi_1 \wedge \ldots \wedge \varphi_n \mapsto \varphi$$

where P is the name *of the rule and each φ_i and φ are* literals *of $\mathcal{L}$. The conjunction at the left of the arrow is the* antecedent *and the literal at the right is its* consequent.

Such a formulae means that the agent believes that if he realizes $\varphi_1, \ldots, \varphi_n$ then he will be able to achieve φ.

Remark 1. Note that the implications used to define both conditional rules and planning rules are not the material implication.

In what follows, we suppose that the agent's beliefs are more or less certain and that its conditional goals or planning rules may not have equal priority.

Definition 3. *An agent is equipped with three bases* $<\mathcal{B}, \mathcal{B}_c, \mathcal{B}_p>$ *such that:*

- $\mathcal{B} = \{(\alpha_i, a_i) : i = 1, \ldots, n\}$ *with* α_i *is a propositional formulae of the language* $\mathcal{L}$ *and* a_i *its certainty degree. This base contains the basic beliefs of the agent.*
- $\mathcal{B}_c = \{(R_j, b_j) : j = 1, \ldots, m\}$ *where* R_j *is a conditional rule and* b_j *represents the* priority degree *of the consequent of* R_j.
- $\mathcal{B}_p = \{(P_k, c_k) : k = 1, \ldots, l\}$ *where* P_k *is a planning rule and* c_k *represents the* priority degree *of this rule.*

In what follows, we suppose that a_i, b_i and c_i belong to the interval $(0, 1]$. Moreover, we shall denote by $\mathcal{B}^*$, $\mathcal{B}_c^*$ and $\mathcal{B}_p^*$ the corresponding sets when the weights are ignored i.e.

- $\mathcal{B}^* = \{\alpha_i : (\alpha_i, a_i) \in \mathcal{B}, i = 1, \ldots, n\}$
- $\mathcal{B}_c^* = \{R_j : (R_j, b_j) \in \mathcal{B}_c, j = 1, \ldots, m\}$
- $\mathcal{B}_p^* = \{P_k : (P_k, c_k) \in \mathcal{B}_p, k = 1, \ldots, l\}$

Once the language is introduced, we are now able to define formally the *potential initial goals* and the *sub-goals*.

Definition 4 (Initial goal — Sub-goal).
Let an agent be equipped with $<\mathcal{B}, \mathcal{B}_c, \mathcal{B}_p>$.

- $\mathcal{IG} = \{\phi \text{ s.t } \exists \phi_1 \wedge \ldots \wedge \phi_n \Rightarrow \phi \in \mathcal{B}_c^*\}$ *is the set of potential* initial goals *of the agent.*
- *SubG is the set of potential* sub-goals *of the agent: A literal* $\varphi' \in SubG$ *iff there exists a rule* $\varphi_1 \wedge \varphi' \ldots \wedge \varphi_n \mapsto \varphi \in \mathcal{B}_p^*$ *with* $\varphi \in \mathcal{IG}$ *or* $\varphi \in SubG$. *In that case,* φ' *is a sub-goal of* φ.

Remark 2. Note that in the above definition, we speak about potential initial goals of the agent. The reason is that we are not sure that the antecedents of the corresponding rules are true. Consequently, if a potential goal is not adopted by the agent (the antecedents are not true), then it is not useful for the agent to realize its plan.

Example 5 (Trip to Central Africa).
Let us consider an agent who has the two following goals:

1. To go on a journey to central Africa if there is a Conference there. (jca)
2. To finish a publication before going on a journey. (fp)

Thus, $\mathcal{B}_c = \{(conf \Rightarrow jca, 0.6), (\Rightarrow fp, 0.8)\}$.

In addition to the goals, the agent is supposed to have beliefs on the way of achieving a given goal (we suppose that all the rules have equal priority):

$$\mathcal{B}_p^* = \begin{cases} t \wedge vac \mapsto jca \\ w \quad \mapsto fp \\ ag \quad \mapsto t \\ fr \quad \mapsto t \\ hop \quad \mapsto vac \\ dr \quad \mapsto vac \end{cases}$$

and $\mathcal{B} = \{(w \rightarrow \neg ag, 0.8), (w \rightarrow \neg dr, 0.8), (conf, 0.8), (can, 0.4), (can \rightarrow \neg conf, 1)\}$.
with: conf = "a conference", can = "to be canceled", t = "to get the tickets", vac = "to be vaccinated", w = "to work", ag = "to go to the agency", fr = "to have a friend who may bring the tickets", hop = "to go to the hospital", dr = "to go to a doctor".
In this example, $\mathcal{IG} = \{jca, fp\}$ and $Sub\mathcal{G} = \{t, vac, ag, fr, dr, hop, w\}$.

4   Explanatory Arguments

Explanatory arguments are used to explain / to give a reason of adopting a given goal. They are also used to give reasons for and against beliefs. In this section, we will propose an argumentation system which constructs explanatory arguments from the different bases of an agent and which evaluates them.

4.1   Basic Definitions

Definition 5 (Explanatory argument).
An explanatory argument is a pair $<H, h>$ such that:

- $H \subseteq \mathcal{B}^* \cup \mathcal{B}_c^*$.
- $H \vdash h$.
- *H is consistent and minimal (for set inclusion).*

$\mathcal{A}_g$ *denotes the set of all arguments such that $h \in \mathcal{IG}$. In other terms, it gathers all the arguments supporting initial goals. $\mathcal{A}_b$ gathers all the arguments supporting beliefs (i.e $h \notin \mathcal{IG}$). Finally, $\mathcal{A} = \mathcal{A}_g \cup \mathcal{A}_b$.*

Definition 6 (Sub-argument).
Let $<H, h>, <H', h'> \in \mathcal{A}. <H, h>$ is a sub-argument of $<H', h'>$ iff $H \subseteq H'$.

Example 6 (Trip to Central Africa).
The arguments $<\{conf, conf \Rightarrow jca\}, jca>$ and $<\{\Rightarrow fp\}, fp> \in \mathcal{A}_g$. However, the argument $<\{can, can \rightarrow \neg conf\}, \neg conf> \in \mathcal{A}_b$.

Remark 3. Note that the implication used in conditional rules is not material and it has no contrapositive. So, for example the set $\{x, x \rightarrow \neg y, g \Rightarrow y\}$ does not infer $\neg g$. Consequently, $<\{x, x \rightarrow \neg y, g \Rightarrow y\}, \neg g>$ is not an explanatory argument.

4.2   The Strength of Explanatory Arguments

As mentioned before, each of the three bases $<\mathcal{B}, \mathcal{B}_c, \mathcal{B}_p>$ is pervaded with certainty or priority. From the certainty degrees, we define the certainty level of an argument.

Definition 7 (Certainty level of an explanatory argument).
Let $A = <H, h> \in \mathcal{A}$. The certainty level of $<H, h>$, denoted by $level(A) = min\{a_i | \varphi_i \in H \cap \mathcal{B}^* \text{ and } (\varphi_i, a_i) \in \mathcal{B}\}$. If $H \cap \mathcal{B}^* = \emptyset$ then $level(A) = 1$.

Remark 4. Note that the priority degree of a given conditional goal is not taken into account in the definition of the strength of its supporting argument. In fact, the intuition behind a conditional goal is that: "the agent will adopt the goal, with its associated priority degree, if the condition is satisfied". So even if the goal is very desired by the agent, if the conditions are not satisfied, then that goal will not be pursued.

The certainty level of the arguments makes it possible to compare different arguments as follows:

Definition 8 (Preference relation).
Let A_1 and A_2 be two arguments in $\mathcal{A}$. A_1 is preferred to A_2, denoted by $A_1 \succ A_2$, iff $level(A_1) > level(A_2)$.

Example 7 (Trip to Central Africa).
In the above example, the certainty level of the argument $<\{conf, conf \Rightarrow jca\}, jca>$ is 0.8. Whereas, the certainty level of the argument $<\{can, can \rightarrow \neg conf\}, \neg conf>$ is 0.4. The certainty level of the argument $<\{\Rightarrow fp\}, fp>$ is 1. Thus, $<\{\Rightarrow fp\}, fp> \succ <\{conf, conf \Rightarrow jca\}, jca> \succ <\{can, can \rightarrow \neg conf\}, \neg conf>$.

4.3   Conflicts Between Explanatory Arguments

An explanatory argument can be defeated either on one of its beliefs or one of its conditional goals. For example, the argument supporting the goal of going to Central Africa because there is a conference can be defeated by another argument stating that the conference has actually been canceled. This kind of defeat is modeled by the relation of "undercut" defined as follows:

Definition 9 (Undercut relation).
Let $<H, h>, <H', h'> \in \mathcal{A}$. $<H, h>$ undercuts $<H', h'>$ iff $\exists h'' \in H' \cap \mathcal{B}$ such that $h \equiv \neg h''$.

A conditional goal can also be defeated. For instance, the argument of going to Central Africa can be defeated by an argument stating that there is no money and if there is no money then the agent cannot go to Central Africa $< \{NoMoney, NoMoney \rightarrow \neg jca\}, \neg jca >$. This kind of defeat is modeled by the following relation of "rebut".

Definition 10 (Rebut relation).
Let $<H, h>, <H', h'> \in \mathcal{A}$. $<H, h>$ rebuts $<H', h'>$ iff $h' \in \mathcal{IG}$ and $h \equiv \neg h'$.

The two relations of conflicts are brought together in a unique relation called *attack*:

Definition 11 (Attack relation).
Let $<H, h>$ and $<H', h'> \in \mathcal{A}$. $<H, h>$ attacks $<H', h'>$ iff:

- $<H, h>$ *undercuts* $<H', h'>$ *and not($<H', h'> \succ <H, h>$) or*
- $<H, h>$ *rebuts* $<H', h'>$ *and not($<H', h'> \succ <H, h>$) or*
- $<H, h>$ *rebuts a sub-argument of* $<H', h'>$ *and not($<H', h'> \succ <H, h>$).*

4.4 The Acceptability of Explanatory Arguments

We can now define the argumentation system we will use to evaluate our arguments:

Definition 12 (Argumentation system).
An argumentation system *(AS) is a pair $\langle \mathcal{A}, Attack \rangle$ such that $\mathcal{A}$ is the set of all explanatory arguments built from $\mathcal{B} \cup \mathcal{B}_c$.*

This system will return three categories of explanatory arguments:

- The class $\underline{S}$ of *acceptable* explanatory arguments. Goals supported by such arguments are really justified and they may be the "positive goals" that an agent will pursue, if they are achievable.
- The class $\underline{R}$ of *rejected* arguments. An argument is rejected if it is attacked by an acceptable one. Goals supported only by such arguments will be rejected by the agent even if they can be achieved. They will represent the negative goals of the agent.
- The class $\underline{C}$ of arguments *in abeyance*. Such arguments are neither acceptable nor rejected. $\underline{C} = \mathcal{A} \setminus (\underline{S} \cup \underline{R})$.

In what follows, we will define the class of acceptable arguments. For that purpose, we will start by presenting the notion of defence introduced in [7].

Definition 13 (Defence).
Let A, B be two arguments of $\mathcal{A}$ and $S \subseteq \mathcal{A}$. S defends A iff for every argument B where B attacks A, there is some argument in S which attacks B.

Henceforth, the set C_{Attack} will gather all non-attacked arguments. We can show that the set $\underline{S}$ of acceptable arguments of the argumentation system $\langle \mathcal{A}, Attack \rangle$ is the least fixpoint of a function $\mathcal{F}$:

$$S \subseteq \mathcal{A},$$
$$\mathcal{F}(S) = \{(H, h) \in \mathcal{A}(\Sigma) | (H, h) \text{ is defended by } S\}.$$

Proposition 1. *Let $\langle \mathcal{A}, Attack \rangle$ be an an argumentation system. The set of its acceptable arguments is:*

$$\underline{S} = \bigcup \mathcal{F}_{i \geq 0}(\emptyset) = C_{Attack} \cup [\bigcup \mathcal{F}_{i \geq 1}(C_{Attack})].$$

Example 8 (Trip to Central Africa).
In this example, the argument $<\{\Rightarrow fp\}, fp>$ is not attacked then it is acceptable. The argument $<\{conf, conf \Rightarrow jca\}, jca>$ is preferred to its unique undercutting argument $<\{can, can \rightarrow \neg conf\}, \neg conf>$. Then it is not attacked and consequently it is also acceptable.

Let T be a set of arguments. The function $Supp(T) = \cup H_i$ such that $<H_i, h_i> \in T$. In other terms, the function $Supp$ returns the union of all the supports of arguments of T. We can show the following result:

Proposition 2. *Let $\langle \mathcal{A}, Attack \rangle$ be an argumentation framework and $\underline{S}$ its set of acceptable arguments. Then $Supp(\underline{S})$ is consistent.*

Property 1. Let $A \in \mathcal{A}$. If A is acceptable then each sub-argument B of A is also acceptable.

5   Instrumental Arguments

An agent may have another kind of goals. These last are not derived from the current beliefs of the agent, but from the plans to achieve the initial goals. In fact, they are justified by the fact that they will contribute to the achievement of initial goals. They are thus considered as sub-goals of the initial goals.

In [1], an argumentation framework which handles conflicting goals has been developed. This framework takes as input a set of initial goals, a belief base and a base of planning rules and returns the goals which can be achieved together, as well as the appropriate plans (i.e. the sub-goals). In this section, we will present an extended version of that framework which takes into account the priorities of the goals.

5.1   Basic Definitions

An agent may have one or several ways to achieve a given goal. We bring the two notions together in a new notion of *partial plan.*

Definition 14 (Partial plan).
A partial plan is a pair $a = <H, h>$ such that:

- h *is an initial goal or a sub-goal.*
- $H = \{\varphi_1, \ldots, \varphi_n\}$ *if there exists a rule $\varphi_1 \wedge \ldots \wedge \varphi_n \mapsto h \in \mathcal{B}_p^*$, $H = \emptyset$ otherwise.*

The function $Goal(a) = h$ returns the initial goal or sub-goal of a given partial plan "a" and the function $Plan(a) = H$ returns the support of the partial plan. $\aleph$ will gather all the partial plans that can be built from $<\mathcal{IG}, \mathcal{B}, \mathcal{B}_p>$.

Note that a goal may have several partial plans.

Remark 5. Let $a = <H, h>$ be a partial plan. Each element of the support H is a sub-goal of h.

Definition 15. *A partial plan* $a = <H, h>$ *is elementary iff* $H = \emptyset$.

Remark 6. If there exists an elementary partial plan for a goal h, it means that the agent knows how to achieve directly h.

A partial plan shows the actions that should be performed in order to achieve the corresponding goal (or sub-goal). However, the elements of the support of a given partial plan are considered as sub-goals that must be achieved at their turn by another partial plan. The whole way to achieve a given goal is called in [1] a *complete plan*. A *complete plan* for a given goal g is an *AND* tree. Its nodes are partial plans and its arcs represent the sub-goal relationship. The root of the tree is a partial plan for the goal g. It is an AND tree because all the sub-goals of g must be considered. When for the same goal, there are several partial plans to carry it out, only one is considered in a tree.

Definition 16 (Instrumental argument).
An instrumental argument *is a pair* $<G, g>$ *such that* $g \in \mathcal{IG}$ *and G is a finite tree such that:*

– *The root of the tree is a partial plan* $<H, g>$.
– *A node* $<\{\varphi_1, \ldots, \varphi_n\}, h'>$ *has exactly n children* $<H'_1, \varphi_1>, \ldots, <H'_n, \varphi_n>$ *where* $<H'_i, \varphi_i>$ *is a partial plan for* φ_i.
– *The leaves of the tree are elementary partial plans.*

The function $Nodes(G)$ *returns the set of all the partial plans of the tree G.* $\mathcal{A}'$ *will denote the set of all the instrumental arguments that can be built from the bases* $<\mathcal{IG}, \mathcal{B}, \mathcal{B}_p>$.

Example 9. The goal jca has four instrumental arguments: $<g_1, jca>$, $<g_2, jca>$, $<g_3, jca>$ and $<g_4, jca>$. The goal fp has only one instrumental argument $<g_5, fp>$ (see figure 1 for the trees g_i).

5.2   The Strength of Instrumental Arguments

As mentioned before, the base $\mathcal{B}_c$ is pervaded with priority. From the priority degrees, we define the weight of an instrumental argument.

Definition 17 (Weight of an instrumental argument).
Let $A = <G, g> \in \mathcal{A}'$. *The* weight *of* $<G, g>$ *is* $Weight(A) = min\{b_i\}$ *such that* $(R_i, b_i) \in \mathcal{B}_c$ *and* $R_i = \varphi_1 \wedge \ldots \wedge \varphi_n \Rightarrow g$.

In other words, the weight of an instrumental argument is exactly the degree of priority/importance of the corresponding goal. The weights make it possible to compare different arguments as follows:

Definition 18 (Preference relation).
Let A_1 *and* A_2 *be two arguments in* $\mathcal{A}'$. A_1 *is preferred to* A_2, *denoted by* $A_1 \succ A_2$, *iff* $Weight(A_1) > Weight(A_2)$.

Example 10. The weight of the four instrumental arguments $A_1 = <g_1, jca>$, $A_2 = <g_2, jca>$, $A_3 = <g_3, jca>$ and $A_4 = <g_4, jca>$ is 0.6 whereas the weight of the argument $A_5 = <g_5, fp>$ is 0.8. Hence, $<g_5, fp> \succ <g_1, jca>, <g_2, jca>, <g_3, jca>$ and $<g_4, jca>$.

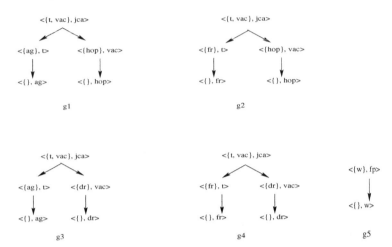

Fig. 1. Complete plans

5.3   Conflicts Between Instrumental Arguments

In [1], it has been shown that partial plans may be conflicting for several reasons. These different kinds of conflicts are brought together in a unique relation of *conflict* defined as follows:

Definition 19 (Conflict).
Let a_1 and a_2 be two partial plans of ℵ. a_1 *conflicts with* a_2 *iff:*
$$\{Goal(a_1), Goal(a_2)\} \cup Plan(a_1) \cup Plan(a_2) \cup \mathcal{B}^* \cup \mathcal{B}_p^* \vdash \perp.$$

Example 11. In example 5, $a_{11a} = <\{ag\}, t>$ conflicts with $a_2 = <\{w\}, fp>$. Indeed, $Plan(a_{11a}) \cup \mathcal{B}^* \vdash \{\neg w\}$ and $Plan(a_2) = \{w\}$.

More generally, a set of partial plans may be conflicting.

Definition 20. *Let $S \subseteq$ ℵ. S is conflicting iff*
$$\bigcup_{a \in S} (\{Goal(a)\} \cup Plan(a)) \cup \mathcal{B}^* \cup \mathcal{B}_c^* \vdash \perp.$$

Since partial plans may be conflicting, two instrumental arguments may be conflicting too.

Definition 21 (Defeat).
Let $<G_1, g_1>, <G_2, g_2> \in \mathcal{A}'$. $<G_1, g_1>$ defeats $<G_2, g_2>$ iff $\exists a_1 \in Nodes(G_1)$ and $\exists a_2 \in Nodes(G_2)$ such that a_1 conflicts with a_2 and $not(<G_2, g_2> \succ <G_1, g_1>)$.

More generally we are interested in conflict-free sets of instrumental arguments.

Definition 22 (Conflict-free).
Let $S = \{<G_i, g_i>: i = 1, \ldots, n\} \subseteq \mathcal{A}'$. S is conflict-free iff
$$[\bigcup_{<G,g> \in S} [\bigcup_{a \in Nodes(G)} (Plan(a) \cup \{Goal(a)\})] \cup \mathcal{B}^* \cup \mathcal{B}_p^* \nvdash \perp].$$
If $S = \{< G, g >\}$ then we say that the argument $< G, g >$ is conflict-free.

Proposition 3. *Let $S \subseteq \mathcal{A}'$. If S is conflict-free then $\nexists A_1$ and $\nexists A_2$ in S such that A_1 defeats A_2.*

The following example shows that we can find an instrumental argument which is not conflict-free even if it does not defeat itself.

Example 12. X is an agent equipped with the following bases:

$$\mathcal{IG} = \{d\}, \mathcal{B}^* = \{b' \wedge c' \rightarrow \neg a\} \text{ and } \mathcal{B}_p^* = \left\{ \begin{array}{ll} a' & \mapsto a \\ b' & \mapsto b \\ c' & \mapsto c \\ a \wedge b \wedge c & \mapsto d \end{array} \right.$$

There is a unique instrumental argument for d whose set of nodes is conflicting.

Obviously a goal which has no conflict-free instrumental argument will be called *un-achievable*. This means it is impossible to carry out such a goal.

5.4 Acceptability of Instrumental Arguments

From the preceding definitions, we can now present the formal system for handling instrumental arguments.

Definition 23. *Let's consider a triple $<\mathcal{B}, \mathcal{B}_c, \mathcal{B}_p>$. The pair $<\mathcal{A}', Defeat>$ will be called a system for handling instrumental arguments.*

As for explanatory arguments, this system will return three categories of instrumental arguments:

- The *acceptable* instrumental arguments. These arguments represent the *good plans* to achieve their corresponding goals.
- The class <u>R'</u> of *rejected* instrumental arguments. This class gathers the arguments which are not conflict-free and those defeated by acceptable arguments. Goals supported only by such arguments are *unachievable*.
- The class <u>C'</u> of arguments *in abeyance*. Such arguments are neither acceptable nor rejected.

Unlike the previous system, we may have here several acceptable sets. Each of them will correspond to a set of goals which can be achieved together.

Definition 24. *Let $<\mathcal{A}', Defeat>$ be a system and $S \subseteq \mathcal{A}'$. S is an* acceptable *set of arguments iff:*

- *S is conflict-free.*
- *S is maximal (for set inclusion).*

Let $\underline{S_1}, \ldots, \underline{S_n}$ be the different sets of acceptable arguments.

Example 13. In example 5, there are four instrumental arguments (A_1, A_2, A_3, A_4) for the goal "going on a journey to Central Africa" and exactly one argument A_5 for the goal "finishing the paper". Moreover, A_5 defeats A_1, A_2 and A_3. We have exactly two acceptable sets of arguments:

- $\underline{S_1} = \{A_1, A_2, A_3, A_4\}$,
- $\underline{S_2} = \{A_4, A_5\}$

The purpose of an agent is to achieve a maximal subset of $\mathcal{I}G$. Consequently, among the sets of acceptable arguments, we will choose the ones which achieve maximal sets of desires (for set inclusion). In the above example, we will choose the set $\underline{S_2}$.

6   Computing Bipolar Goals

Once we have defined the two frameworks which evaluate the different arguments supporting goals, we are now able to define among the potential initial goals and sub-goals the positive goals of the agent, the negative ones and finally the goals in abeyance.

Definition 25 (Positive goals).
Let $g \in \mathcal{I}G$. g is a positive goal *iff:*

- $\exists\, (H, g) \in \mathcal{A}_g$ *such that* $(H, g) \in \underline{S}$, *and*
- $\exists\, (G, g) \in \mathcal{A}'$ *and* $\exists\, \underline{S_i}$ *such that* $(G, g) \in \underline{S_i}$.

This means that a goal is positive if it is justified and it is achievable.
Note that the sub-goals of a positive initial goal are also considered as positive.

Definition 26 (Negative goals).
Let $g \in \mathcal{I}G$. g is a negative goal *iff:*

- $\forall\, (H, g) \in \mathcal{A}_g, (H, g) \in \underline{\mathcal{R}}$, *or*
- $\forall\, (G, g) \in \mathcal{A}', (G, g) \in \underline{\mathcal{R}'}$

Indeed, a goal is negative if it is not justified or if it is unachievable.

Definition 27 (Goals in abeyance).
Let $g \in \mathcal{I}G$. g is in abeyance *iff it is neither positive nor negative.*

Example 14 (Trip to Central Africa).
In this example, the two initial potential goals of the agent (jca, fp) become positive goals of the agent. Moreover, the sub-goals (t, vac, fr, hop, w) are also positive goals. However, the following sub-goals are in abeyance: (dr, ag).

7   Handling Bipolar Goals

Let's consider an agent P who has the following belief base: $\mathcal{B} = \{(\neg age > 40, 1),$ $(PhD, 0.5)\}$. Suppose that this agent has two potential goals: to be a president and/or to be a professor. $\mathcal{B}_c = \{(age > 40 \Rightarrow president, 1), (PhD \Rightarrow professor, 1)\}$.

To be a president, the agent knows that he should have more than 40 years old however he has less than 40 years. According to its beliefs, there is no argument in favor of this goal. Consequently, the agent will keep this goal in *abeyance*.

Concerning the goal of becoming a professor, it has the following explanatory argument: $A_1 =< \{PhD, PhD \Rightarrow professor\}, professor >$. This argument is not attacked at all, thus it is acceptable. In this example, there are no instrumental arguments. So, the goal *professor* is a *positive* one. Note that at this stage, the agent has one positive goal, one goal in abeyance an no negative goals.

Suppose that one year later, the agent has more than 40 years old then $\mathcal{B}$ is updated as follows: $\mathcal{B} = \{(age > 40, 1), (PhD, 0.5)\}$.

Using this new base, we can find an argument in favor of the goal *president*, namely: $A_2 =< \{age > 40, age > 40 \Rightarrow president\}, president >$ which is acceptable since it is not attacked. Thus, the goal *president* which was in abeyance will become a positive one. In sum, the agent has now two positive goals that it will pursue.

This agent applies for the job of president and starts a negotiation with the appropriate services. Let's imagine the following dialogue:

X: I want to become a president.
S: This entails that you will leave your actual job.
X: But I want to be a professor too. I can do both jobs.
S: It's impossible. You should not have another job.
X: Okey.

When the agent receives the new information which says that he cannot have two jobs so he pursues either the goal *president* or the goal *professor* but not both, he updates its belief base: $\mathcal{B} = \{(president \rightarrow \neg professor, 1), (age > 40, 1), (PhD, 0.5)\}$.

Due to this change of beliefs we have the following arguments: A_1, A_2 computed above and $A_3 =< \{age > 40, age > 40 \Rightarrow president, president \rightarrow \neg professor\}, \neg professor >$, $A_4 =< PhD, PhD \Rightarrow professor, president \rightarrow \neg professor\}, \neg president >$ and $A_5 =< \{age > 40, age > 40 \Rightarrow president, PhD, PhD \Rightarrow professor\}, \neg(president \rightarrow \neg professor) >$.

The certainty level of A_1, A_4 and A_5 is 0.5 and the certainty level of A_2 and A_3 is 1. Thus, A_2, $A_3 \succ A_1$, A_4 and A_5. We can check easily that A_4 rebuts A_2 but since A_2 is preferred to A_4 then A_2 is not attacked and consequently it is acceptable. The argument A_3 rebuts and defeats A_1. Moreover, A_3 is preferred to its unique undercutting argument A_5. Then A_3 is also acceptable. Consequently, A_1 is rejected. The goal of being president is supported by an acceptable argument A_2 then this goal is positive. However, the goal of being a professor is supported only by the rejected argument A_1 then it is a negative goal.

8   Conclusion

In most negotiation literature, each negotiating agent is supposed to have a set of fixed and predefined goals. It is not clear where do these goals come from and how an agent selects them. Argumentation-based negotiation makes an advance by supposing that the goals are not fixed during a negotiation and may change. However, even in these works the goals are predefined and it is not clear how they are changed. In fact, since there is no work on how goals are computed, it seems difficult to model the way in which they are updated.

The aim of this paper is twofold. First, it presents the goals in a bipolar way. In fact, an agent has positive goals that it will pursue and also negative goals that it does not want to achieve. This second category of goals is very important in negotiation since the offers that satisfy such goals will be rejected by the agent. The second aim of this paper is to present a formal framework which computes the goals of an agent. We have shown through an example how an agent may change its goals during a negotiation.

The principle of goals generation proposed in this paper is close to the one proposed in [14] in the context of planning, where an argument-based generation of goals is implicitly used. However in this latter, the author *only* generates the positive goals (called *wants*), those that the agent will pursue, from a set of initial conditional goals called *wishes*. Moreover, the set of beliefs on which initial conditional goals are based is flat (i.e., all the beliefs are equally certain) then there is no evaluation of arguments when they are conflicting.

In this paper, we have shown that a goal may be supported by two different kinds of arguments: the exaplanatory arguments and the instrumental ones. We have then presented two different systems for handling each category of arguments. An extension of our work will be to handle the two kinds of arguments in a unique framework. We are actually working in this direction. We are also planning to investigate more deeply the handling of bipolar goals in a negotiation dialogue.

Acknowledgments

This work was supported by the Commission of the European Communities under contract IST-2004-002307, ASPIC project "Argumentation Service Platform with Integrated Components".

References

1. L. Amgoud. A formal framework for handling conflicting desires. In *Proceedings of the 7th European Conference on Symbolic and Quantitative Approaches to Reasoning with Uncertainty, ECSQARU'2003*, pages 552–563, 2003.
2. L. Amgoud, S. Parsons, and N. Maudet. Arguments, dialogue, and negotiation. In *Proceedings of the 14th European Conference on Artificial Intelligence (ECAI'00)*, pages 338–342, 2000.
3. S. Benferhat, D. Dubois, S. Kaci, and H. Prade. Bipolar representation and fusion of preferences in the possibilistic logic framework. In *Proceedings of the eighth International Confenrence on Principle of Knowledge Representation and Reasoning (KR'02)*, pages 158–169, 2002.
4. J. Borod. The neuropsychology of emotion. Oxford University Press,, 2000.
5. J. Cacioppo and G. Bernston. The affect system: Architecture and operating characteristics. *Current Directions in Psychological Science*, 8, 5:133–137, 1999.
6. J. Cacioppo, W. Gardner, and G. Bernston. Beyond bipolar conceptualizations and measures: The case of attitudes and evaluative space. *Personality and Social Psychology Review*, 1, 1:3–25, 1997.
7. P. M. Dung. On the acceptability of arguments and its fundamental role in nonmonotonic reasoning, logic programming and n-person games. *Artificial Intelligence*, 77:321–357, 1995.
8. S. Kaci and H. Prade. Bipolar goals. A possibilistic logic characterization of preferred choices. In *Proceedings of Workshop on Local Computation for Logics and Uncertainty, in conjunction with ECAI'04*, 2004.

9. S. Kraus, K. Sycara, and A. Evenchik. *Reaching agreements through argumentation: a logical model and implementation*, volume 104. Journal of Artificial Intelligence, 1998.

10. X. Luo, N. Jennings, N. Shadbolt, H. fung Leung, and J. H. man Lee. A fuzzy constraint based model for bilateral, multi-issue negotiations in semi-competitive environments. In *Artificial Intelligence, 148(1-2)*, pages 53–102, 2003.

11. I. Rahwan, L. Sonenberg, and F. Dignum. Towards interest-based negotiation. In *Proceedings of the Second International Conference on Autonomous Agents and Multi-Agent Systems (AAMAS'03)*, pages 773–780, 2003.

12. E. Rolls. Precis of "brain and emotion". *Behavioral and Brain Sciences*, 23(2):177–234, 2000.

13. C. Sierra, N. Jennings, P. Noriega, and S. Parsons. A framework for argumentation-based negotiation. In *Proceedings of the fourth Workshop on Agent Theories, Architectures and Languages (ATAL'97)*, pages 167–182, 1997.

14. R. Thomason. Desires and defaults: A framework for planning with inferred goals. In *Proceedings of the seventh International Confenrence on Principle of Knowledge Representation and Reasoning (KR'00)*, pages 702–713, 2000.

15. O. Wong and R. Lau. Possibilistic reasoning for intelligent payment agents. In *Proceedings of the second Workshop on AI in Electronic Commerce AIEC*, pages 170–180, 2000.

A Bayes Net Approach to Argumentation Based Negotiation

Sabyasachi Saha and Sandip Sen

Department of Mathematical & Computer Sciences,
University of Tulsa,
Tulsa, Oklahoma, USA
{sabyasachi-saha, sandip-sen}@utulsa.edu

Abstract. Negotiation is one of the most fundamental and effective mechanism for resolving conflicts between self-interested agents and producing mutually acceptable compromises. Most existing research in negotiation presumes a fixed negotiation context which cannot be changed during the process of negotiation and that the agents have complete and correct knowledge about all aspects of the issues being negotiated. In practice, the issues being negotiated may change and the agents may have incorrect beliefs of relevant issues updated during the negotiation process. Argumentation-based negotiation approaches have therefore been proposed to capture such realistic negotiation contexts. Here we present a novel Bayesian network based argumentation and decision making framework that allows agents to utilize models of the other agents. The agents will generate effective arguments to influence the other agent's belief and produce more profit.

1 Introduction

Agents deployed for real-world applications like electronic commerce, recommender systems, and personal assistants have limited, specialized capabilities and have to depend on other agents to achieve their goals. They often interact in an open environment with other agents or humans. Agents with conflicting interests need to negotiate to improve profits. Negotiation allows agents to reach a mutually acceptable agreement.

Automated negotiation has drawn significant attention in Multiagent systems research [3, 8, 13]. Negotiation is viewed as a distributed search through a space of potential agreements [3]. Existing frameworks allow agents to propose counter offer in addition to accepting or rejecting the previous offer. Offers include attributes which belong to some pre-fixed *issues*. Agents are assumed to have correct and complete knowledge of preferences and the negotiation context as well as agents' preferences are held constant during the course of negotiation. In real-life negotiation scenarios, however, the participating individuals do not have fixed preferences. Also, at times they might have incorrect belief about the world or may not be cognizant about all pertinent attributes. In such situations,

I. Rahwan et al. (Eds.): ArgMAS 2004, LNAI 3366, pp. 208–222, 2005.

agents can influence each other by argumentation with convincing, relevant information. The existing game theoretic or heuristic based approaches do not provide a framework for argumentation-aided negotiation.

In last few years argumentation based framework for negotiation is discussed in Multiagent systems research [4, 10]. Most existing argumentation based negotiation frameworks are logic or rule-based [8, 9, 11]. While these approaches provide a formal framework with provable properties, we believe there is a need for alternative frameworks that can better capture the uncertainty and complexity of real-life negotiations. In particular, the factors influencing an agent's decisions may be incompletely known and be gradually revealed to a negotiator. Accordingly, negotiation frameworks should incorporate approximate opponent models represented in a form that can capture complex relationships between domain attributes and can be efficiently updated based on information revealed during negotiation. The specific research questions we are interested in include the following:

- When processing an offer or a counter-offer, what decision mechanisms should an agent use to decide whether to accept a proposal, argue about its last proposal, or generate a new proposal?
- How are arguments for negotiation generated/selected?
- Should an agent try to persuade the other agent by reward, threat, etc.
- How and when does an agent update its belief about the other agent or about the negotiation issues based on received arguments and offers?
- How does the agent's model of the opponent influence its argumentation and proposals?

In this paper, we present a decision architecture of the arguing agent. We propose to use a Bayesian network model [5] to represent the influences of different factors on agent decisions. An agent's knowledge of such causal factors and their relative importance is captured in the topology of the network as well as the prior and conditional probability assignments. Initial, approximate knowledge of an agent can be further refined based on actual negotiation experiences. If values of all the factors are known, then the actual decision taken by another agent given these factors can be used to update the conditional probabilities at the outcome nodes. If some of the factors values are not known, the decision taken and the values of the known factors can be used to update either the conditional probabilities at the outcome nodes or the prior probabilities of the unknown factors. In this paper we focus on the decision mechanism that allows a modeling agent to use its knowledge to determine negotiation offers and select arguments to influence the opponent to accept offers that it has turned down. The goal is to use the Bayes net model of the opponent to select and manipulate the negotiation context to increase the chance of an favorable offer being accepted by the other party.

Though the general framework of Bayesian network based argumentation can be used in peer-level or symmetric negotiation, we have focused our discussion in this paper on asymmetric scenarios where a knowledgeable domain-expert agent is negotiating with a user agent. Hence we assume that our agent has access to significant domain knowledge that can be used to argue against possibly incorrect assumptions made by the user. This asymmetry also means that the expert agent can use argumentation based on its model of the user agent to influence that agent to accept offers that are preferable to the expert agent. The Bayes net model is the key component that allows the expert agent to select initial offers, respond to counter offers with convincing arguments or with further offers that are acceptable to both parties to the negotiation.

The paper is organized as follows. Section 2 presents a few motivating examples for the types of argumentative negotiation we are interested in. Next, in Section 3, we have discussed relevant research works that have influenced the research in this field and the relationship of our work with these existing reasearch. In Section 5, we present an architecture that allows an agent to choose from and construct from a set of different classes of negotiation arguments based on a Bayesian network based opponent model. Following this, we present decision mechanisms that select arguments and offers based on the probabilistic model. We conclude with observations about the strength and applicability of such a coherent and powerful approach to argumentation-augmented negotiation.

2   Argumentation Scenarios

In this section, we use the running example of a negotiation scenario between a travel agent and a customer. Here, we have described the generation of arguments or counter proposals from the travel agent's perspective. At first, we present a conversation that shows the necessity of the argumentation in negotiation process. Then we have produced three more conversations to clarify the importance of modelling opponent's belief.

Consider the following conversation between our domain expert, a travel agent (TA), and another buyer agent (A) who has contacted TA for a ticket from Tulsa to Calcutta on the first week of February.

Conversation 1:
TA: Ticket Offer: $< \$1400, \# \text{ stop } 1, \text{ waiting hrs } = 5, \text{ Date } 2/4 >$.
A: Reject because price is high.
TA: I can offer deals as cheap as \$1200 but if you purchase the previous offer you will get a free round trip within continental USA.
A: That's cool. I accept the previous deal.

In this conversation, **TA** has influenced the preference of A by rewarding him with a free RT offer which was not in the original negotiation context. This is an example of negotiation based on arguments. To produce convincing arguments, it becomes extremely crucial to know the opponent's belief model because the same argument may not work for different opponents. Consider the following three conversations:

Conversation 2:
In response to the request for a cheaper deal by another agent **B** for the same itinerary in Conversation 1, the travel agent responds

TA: Unfortunately no ticket below $1400 is available for February 4 and if you delay the price will go up to $1600.
B: OK then give me this deal.
Conversation 3:
The travel agent tries the same "threat" as in Conversation 2 for the same itinerary with another agent **C** who responds
C: Then I am not interested.
Conversation 4:
In response to the request for a cheaper deal by another agent **D** for the same itinerary in Conversation 1, the travel agent responds
TA: I fear I can not give you any ticket below $1400 on February 4 but if you take this deal I can give you 15,000 frequent flier bonus miles.
D: OK then I will purchase the ticket.

In conversations 2 and 3 we find that the same argument can result in opposite results. The agent has missed the deal in the second conversation. For the agent B the fear that the price of the ticket may increase dominates its decision whereas agent C believes that it can get better deals. For agent C the reward offer clinches the sale. Notice that here the travel agent TA need to concede some utility in Conversation 4 to seal the deal. Which of the arguments the TA should use, will depend on available offers, local utility function for the deals and the opponent models that can be used as a predictor for offer/argument acceptance. In reality, even though it is unlikely that the TA will have an exact knowledge of the user agent's belief model, such models can be approximated from domain knowledge, interactions with other agents and previous interactions with this agent. We propose a Bayesian network based approach for opponent agent modeling.

The above-mentioned negotiations are based on a set of *issues*, e.g., *price, # stops, waiting time, departure date, destination city, departure city, etc.*. Some of these issues are negotiable and some of them are constraints and can be determined from domain knowledge. In the conversation 4, though *bonus miles* was not part of the original set of issues being negotiated, the TA may have the model that it can be used as a leverage on agent D. In other scenarios an agent may have incorrect belief about some attributes. For example, a customer agent G has a belief that airlines E has poor luggage handling record. When an offer is rejected based on this premise, the TA will need to argue to correct this misconception. This may, in turn convince G to accept the proposed deal.

3   Related Work

When we talk about negotiation process or argumentation in the negotiation process in a multiagent society, it becomes extremely important to decide upon communication language, domain language and negotiation protocols [1]. Common agent languages like FIPA ACL does not provide all the locutions which are required to capture necessary expressions in the negotiation process. So, researchers introduce explicit locutions for expressions [14]. In this paper, we concentrate on the argumentation generation in the negotiation process and handle the communication introducing some explicit terminologies.

In a recent survey [10], Rahwan *et. al.* has presented a clear current state of research in argumentation based negotiation. They have compared different existing frameworks in the light of main characteristics. Kraus *et. al.* address the problem of argumentation negotiation as a multiagent system problem and proposed a framework for persuasion [8]. In their framework, agents used threats, rewards, etc. as argumentation. They assume a prefixed set of arguments. Some research has focused on providing framework for argumentation based negotiation [4, 7]. They have mainly focused on the protocol for negotiation. Parsons et. al. design it as a finite state model [9]. Our work is quite different from these work, as unlike others we have concentrated on decision mechanism of the agents. Ramchurn et. al. proposed a fuzzy logic based approach for selecting rhetorics for persuasion [12]. They have addressed the problem of negotiation process. They evaluate different locutions based on utility and trust. Rahwan et. al. proposed a goal based approach for argumentation [11]. He argues that since preferences are adopted to fulfill some goals, the arguing agent can influence the other agent by influencing the associated or subgoals. Our work is also much different from them. In our work, we have dealt with preferences which are subject to change and use a continually updated model of the opponent. Then, we propose a novel Bayesian network based decision mechanism for arguing during negotiation. Since we use expected utility based evaluation of the proposals and arguments, the preference ordering also change during the negotiation process and always produce the proposal which is most suitable at that point of time and with the uncertainty of the domain and acquired knowledge. We believe that using our model it will be possible to address argumentation during a negotiation process in a more rich and dynamic environment. Zukerman *et. al.* have used Bayesian networks to generate arguments in natural language as part of a human-computer interaction scenario [16]. Given a goal proposition by the user, the system, NAG generates arguments to justify it. We are using argumentation to enable a neogtiating agent to strike better deals with a peer agent. As such, the problem solving and communication protocol, as well as the nature of arguments are fundamentally different.

4   Definitions

In this section we present the formal definitions of different arguments or offers. $\mathcal{A}$ is the whole set of attributes in the environment. We call $name_i$ and $state_{i,j}$ as the name and jth state, respectively of the ith attribute in the environment, $j = 1(1)n_i$. We assume that each agent will be aware of all possible values of $name_i$ and $state_{i,j}$, $j = 1..n_i$. The domain of $state_{i,j}$ may be numbers or discrete values like *high, low, good, etc.*. We now define the attributes used in negotiation

- $\mathcal{I} \subset \mathcal{A}$ to be the set of current context attributes.
- $\mathcal{E} \subset (\mathcal{A} - \mathcal{I})$ to be the set of additional attributes which are not in the current negotiation context but they can be included in $\mathcal{I}$ during the process of negotia-

tion. That means an element $a \in \mathcal{E}$ can be removed from the set $\mathcal{E}$ and included in the set $\mathcal{I}$.

- $\mathcal{P} \subset (\mathcal{A} - (\mathcal{I} \cup \mathcal{E}))$ to be the set of persuasive attributes which are used for argumentation but are non-negotiable, e.g., *reward-bonus-miles, threat-increase-future-price*, etc.
- $\mathcal{V}$ to be the collection of attributes with their name and a particular state value in the outgoing proposal. An agent constructs this set with the name state pairs of the attributes it choose for argument or offer.

We broadly categorize the *locutions* used in the conversation into following types *viz, request for proposal (or req), offer, argument, accept, reject and terminate*. Within each categorization, there are different types of locutions. Here we discuss only the important locutions.

request($\mathcal{V}$): This is asked at the beginning of the conversation where the asking agent states its basic need.

offer($\mathcal{V}$): This may be a completely new offer satisfying all constraints or it may be the one stating the opponent that if it waives one or more constraints this offer matches the other specifications and may be useful to it.

Argument: We define four different types of arguments:

conflict-argument($\mathcal{V}$): This is argument to the opponent about the conflict in belief this agent has about the attributes in the $\mathcal{V}$. It states $\langle name_i, state_i \rangle$ as its belief about the ith attribute in $\mathcal{V}$.

emphasizing-argument($\mathcal{V}$): This is argument to emphasize some additional attributes in the offer to influence the opponent to accept the previous offer. Here $\mathcal{V} \subset \mathcal{E}$.

persuasive-argument($\mathcal{V}$): This argument is used to persuade the opponent. Here $\mathcal{V} \subset \mathcal{P}$.

justification($\mathcal{V}$): This argument is used to justify a previous argument. Here $\mathcal{V} \subset (\mathcal{A} - (\mathcal{I} \cup \mathcal{E} \cup \mathcal{P}))$.

accept($\mathcal{V}$): This is used to accept any proposal from the opponent.

reject($\mathcal{V}$): This is used to reject any proposal from the opponent. $\mathcal{V}$ contains the name state pair of the attributes which are the reason for this rejection.

terminate(): used for termination of the conversation.

5   Architecture of Argumentation Based Agent

In this section, we present the architecture of our agent Ag (now onward we maintain the convention of calling the agent by Ag and the opponent agent by $OpAg$) for negotiation using arguments. Figure 5 shows the different components in the agent architecture. We will discuss the different components here.

Proposal Analysis: The opponent agent can send either a counter offer or it can simply reject previous offer made by the agent. Here we like to emphasize one thing, when an agent rejects one proposal, we assume that it gives some argument for his decision. It can also send *null* argument. This component

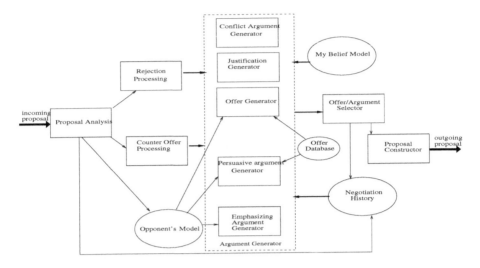

Fig. 1. Decision Architecture of the arguing agent

recognizes opponent's proposal type and update opponent's model. If opponent sent an counter offer it inform the *Counter offer processing* component and if opponent rejects previous offer with some argument it informs the *Rejection processing* component. If the other agent terminate the negotiation after updating the opponent model it terminates the process.

Rejection Processing: It interacts with the *argument generator* to generate argument or another offer to change opponent's rejection.

Counter Offer Processing: It interacts with the *argument generator* to generate argument or counter offer for the opponent agent.

Argument Generator: It has five subcomponents which are responsible to generate arguments or counter offer or rejection for the opponent. They are *Conflict Argument Generator, Justification Generator, Emphasizing Argument Generator, Persuasive Argument Generator* and *Offer Generator*. It starts working with *Conflict Argument Generator*.

Conflict Argument Generator: This subcomponent decides if the opponent agent rejects the earlier offer because of any "wrong" or conflicting belief about some attribute. Based on the negotiation history it determines whether to argue with this conflict. If it decides to argue with this conflict it informs the *Offer/Argument Selector*, which is described later in this section, to generate *conflict-argument* with the attribute(s) it finds conflict, otherwise, it relinquish the control to *Justification Generator*. For example, opponent agent may have a belief that E airlines has a poor luggage handling reputation. So, when the travel agent offer a ticket with E airlines in a reasonable price, G rejects that with an argument of ⟨*luggage handling: poor*⟩. Then travel agent needs to argue with confidence that in recent years E does not have any complain of poor luggage handling. Then opponent agent may accept this deal. And if it rejects again then this component updates the opponent model with this as a constraint.

Justification Generator: If the opponent rejects the previous offer and send name-state pair of a set of attributes, say W, as the reason. If there is no conflict in belief but the agent finds that there is one more attributes v_1 in the environment ($\notin (\mathcal{I} \cup \mathcal{E})$) which influence some attributes in W and v_1 is not under the control of any agent, then the agent asks *Offer/Argument Selector* to justify the previous proposal with v_1. For example, if an agent reiterates that the *price* is high then this agent can justify it as the ⟨ peak-season?: yes⟩. If this sumcomponent does not find any justification to make it calls the following subcomponents to take control.

Emphasizing Argument Generator: Based on the *Opponent model*, discussed later in this section, this subcomponent decides if there is any *emphasizing-argument* which can influence the opponent's decision. If it finds any such argument it send that to *Offer/Argument Selector* to form *emphasizing-argument*. Later we will discuss in detail which attributes are chosen and how. This argument may seem unnecessary as the agent could have sent all the attributes along with the attributes in $\mathcal{I}$. But in practice, an agent slowly expands the context, if possible. This gives the other agent a feeling that it is offered as a benefit. Moreover, in some real life negotiation, the number of issues that may influence it is large and uncertain. So, initially, $\mathcal{I}$ is chosen as the combination of the attributes that the other agent precisely mentioned and other dominant attributes known by this agent from the domain knowledge. Then $\mathcal{I}$ is changed during negotiation based on the interaction of the agents. For example, suppose Ag's proposal of ⟨ \$1300, # stop $= 1$, waiting hr. $= 15$ ⟩ is rejected by $OpAg$ with an argument of that ⟨ waiting hr. $=15$, problematic: yes ⟩. Now, from the belief model of $OpAg$, agent Ag knows that the notification that ⟨ hotel facilities: 5 star, accommodation: free ⟩ with the previous offer will decreasing the probability of ⟨ problematic: yes ⟩ and in turn increase the probability of acceptance of the last offer.

Persuasive Argument Generator: This subcomponent decides with the help of *Opponent model* if there is any persuasive argument which can influence the opponent to accept the previous offer. For example, suppose a reward of bonus miles has a very positive influence on the opponent. Then if you reward a reward of 10,000 bonus miles, it may accept your previous offer. Sometimes threat about rising price may cause an acceptance of the offer which the opponent previously rejected. It sends the persuasive arguments *persuasive-argument* to the *Offer/Argument Selector*.

Offer Generator: This subcomponent generates the offer which it finds best. If there is no offer that matches the conditions given by the opponent then it also finds the offers which is possible if some weak constraints are removed. It compares the best offer with the offer of the opponent, if any. It informs the *Offer/Argument Selector* which one is better and if the opponent needs to drop any attribute.

Offer Database: This is a filtered repository of all the offers relevant to the opponent. This also includes the offers with *weak* constraints. After each interaction if the agent finds some new *strict constraints* in the opponent's model it updates the *offer database*.

My Model: This is a collection of the agent's own belief about the domain attributes. Say for example, it has a knowledge of the services in the airlines, luggage handling, flight security, crew service quality, insurance facilities, etc. Belief about an attribute may be strong or weak. A weak belief may change hearing some strong counter arguments from someone whom it trusts. For a domain expert (e.g. here the travel agent) we assume that all the belief are *strong*.

Opponent Model: Opponent model consists of *Constraint information* and *Opponent's belief model*. We believe that, in any negotiation it is important to recognize which attributes are *strict* constraints and which are negotiable. If *OpAg* asks quote for tickets from JFK airport, NY to London and the travel agent offer him cheap deals from NY to Shanghai, it will be enough reason for the agent *OpAg* to terminate the conversation. But if it is difficult to find deals from JFK, NY to London it will be a reasonable suggestion to try from another airport of NY. Using the domain knowledge we initially classify the constraints. Then it is updated based on the response from the opponent. We present *Opponent's belief model* as a Bayesian network and it will be discussed in the next section.

Negotiation History: This consists of the history of offers and arguments from both the agents.

Offer/Argument evaluator: This is an implicit component of the architecture. Each of the above three argument uses this component. Based on the Opponent's belief model and the agent's own evaluations of the corresponding offer or persuasion, this component finds out the expected utility of the offers or arguments.

Offer/Argument Selector: This component chooses the offer or argument producing maximum expected utility. It compares among the offers or arguments which are sent by different argument and offer generator subcomponents. If the opponent's counter offer is the most profitable producing maximum utility then it asks the *Proposal Constructor* to accept the negotiation. If the offer/argument generated exceeds the opponent's proposal then send that to *Proposal Constructor* and if it does not receive any profitable offer from the other components it asks the *Proposal Constructor* to terminate the negotiation.

Proposal Constructor: This forms the outgoing proposal and send it to the opponent agent.

6   Bayes Net Model of Opponent's Belief

In section 5, we have briefly discussed the architecture of a negotiating agent. We have described how the decision mechanism largely depends on the agent's approximation of the opponent's model. We have discussed that, one proposal may be very quite profitable for one opponent but may be unacceptable for another opponent. This makes it necessary and desirable for the negotiating agent to model its opponent. In practice, one agent may have only approximate *a priori* estimates of the dependencies and influences of the different factors on the other agent's behavior. We propose the use of Bayesian networks to capture the causal dependencies of the different factors on the decision mechanism of the opponent. Bayesian networks can capture the inherent uncertainty in the domain. We use an augmentation of the Bayesian network to evaluate the utility of different actions of the modeling agent. The extended network is known as *influence diagram*. This mechanism will allow the modeling agent to choose the action that will produce maximum expected utility. We have shown an example of modeling the opponent's belief in Figure 2. We will discuss the details of the decision mechanism in the next section.

6.1   Bayesian Networks and Influence Diagram

A Bayesian network is a graphical method of representing causal relationships [5], i.e. dependencies and independencies among different variables that together define a real-world situation. Technically it is a Directed Acyclic Graph (DAG) with nodes as the variables and a directed edge represent a causal relationship between the corresponding nodes. In addition to its structure, a Bayesian network is also specified by a set of parameters θ, that qualify the network. The causal relationship is characterized by the corresponding conditional probability tables (CPTs).

Consider a vector X of variables and an instantiation-vector x. If the immediate parents of a variable X_i is the vector Pa_{X_i}, with its instantiation pa_{x_i}, then

$$Pr[X = x|\theta] = \prod_i Pr[X_i = x_i|Pa_{X_i} = pa_{x_i}, \theta].$$

This defines the joint distribution of the variables in X, where each variable X_i is conditionally independent of its non-descendants, given its parents. For more detailed discussion on Bayesian networks we refer [2, 5].

We use Bayesian networks for representing belief structures, for the following reasons:

- Bayesian network can readily handle incomplete data sets.
- It allows one to learn about causal relationships. This is useful to gain understanding about a problem domain. It successfully represent the non-linear causal relationships of the variables.
- It handles uncertainty in the domain efficiently.
- Bayesian networks in conjunction with Bayesian statistical techniques facilitate the combination of domain knowledge and data.
- It offers a method of updating the belief or the CPTs.

An influence diagram is a Bayesian network augmented with action variables and utility functions. There are three types of nodes in the influence diagram: *chance nodes, value nodes* and *action nodes* [6]. The action variables represent different actions of the decision maker. There exists utility function attached to the value nodes in the network. Influence diagram can be used to calculate the utilities of different values of the decision variables. In the context of negotiation, we want to use such networks to find out the conditional probability of accepting a proposal given the proposal contents listed as an attribute-value vector.

6.2   An Illustration of the Agent Belief Model

In our negotiation framework, we assume that the arguing agent has an approximation of the belief model of the opponent agent. In this paper, we model the opponent's belief as a Bayesian belief network. We have assumed that the arguing agent knows the exact structure of the network and it has an approximate idea of the conditional probability tables (CPT) from the domain and earlier interactions with the opponent agent. For the sake of simplicity we have assumed all variables to be discrete. In figure 2, we show an example of modeling opponent agent's belief. It shows the model of a customer agent $OpAg$ approximated by the travel agent Ag in our example. The agent $OpAg$ has asked for a round-trip airline ticket from Tulsa to Calcutta in the first week of February. He send the request for proposal $req(V)$ where V is collection of the attributes ⟨ from: Tulsa, To: Calcutta, Roundtrip: yes, # of stops: ≤ 2, date: 02/04/04⟩. In the network shown, the decision node represents the decision whether $OpAg$ accepts the offer or argument. The outcome is boolean, yes or no. The chance nodes, value nodes and action nodes are represented as circles, rhombus and rectangles, respectively. Double circles imply that the offer deterministically determines their values. The double circles that are joined by a solid line with their parents implies that they are initially among the set $\mathcal{I}$ of the negotiation and the double circles joined

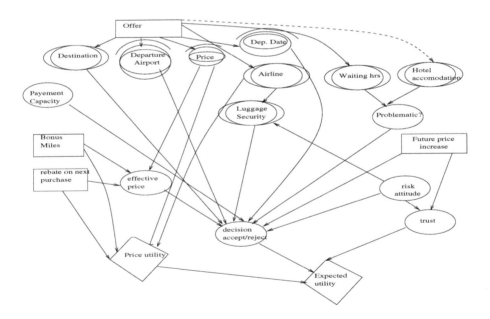

Fig. 2. Approximate belief model of the opponent

with dotted lines belong to $\mathcal{E}$ in the negotiation. An arc above some double circles qualify them as *negotiable*. The action nodes represent the actions taken by agent Ag and its influence on $OpAg$'s decision is represented by the CPT's.

Here the action *offer* by the agent Ag determines the value of different nodes like *airlines name, # of stops, date of journey, destination city, departure city, requirement for transit visa, etc.* Whereas, Ag has a belief about the value of some chance nodes for $OpAg$ like *risk attitude, payment capacity, etc.* which influence the decision of $OpAg$. We consider different offers as different possible actions for the node *offer*.

For each offer available to Ag it can find out a conditional probability of acceptance by $OpAg$ given evidences in the offer. Based on the reply of $OpAg$ to an offer or argument the CPTs are updated by the sequential update rule of Bayesian network [15].

7   Offer or Argument Selection Procedure

In section 5, we discuss the different components that influence the decision of the agent Ag. In this section, we will present an algorithm to clearly state the decision taking procedure. Also we will discuss briefly how the agent evaluates different and choose the offer or argument.

The decision procedure is presented in Algorithm 1. Now lets describe some methods of the algorithm.

• **Find-best-offer:** Each offer sets different values to the attributes. From agent's own model it will get a utility for the offer with corresponding values of the attributes. It will also get the corresponding probability that this will be accepted by the other agent from the opponent agent's belief model presented by the Bayesian network. So, for a each offer with specified values of the attributes, the agent can find the expected utility. The offer generator will choose the one producing maximum expected utility. If it is not possible to find an offer for the constraints, it will check if removing some weak constraint can yield some good deal. If so, it chooses that deal as the best offer.

• **Conflict-belief:** If the opponent agent rejects some proposal and produces some attribute which has conflict with the belief of this agent. The subcomponent *Conflict Argument Generator* generates *conflict-argument* with the belief it has about the conflicting attribute.

• **Justify-belief:** This argument is used if the opponent rejects the offer and send name-state pair of a set of attributes, say W, as the reason. If there is no conflict in belief but the agent finds that there is an attribute v_1 in the environment ($\notin (\mathcal{I} \cup \mathcal{E})$) which influence some attributes in W and v_1 is not under the control of any agent, then the agent send justify with $v_1 \in \mathcal{V}$. This is done by *Justification Generator*.

•**Find-significant-emphasizing-argument:** If the opponent agent rejects or produces counter offer the agent will emphasize on those attribute values which have significant influence on the opponent but not mentioned in the

---

Algorithm 1 Decision(proposal($\mathcal{V}$)): Decision Algorithm of the Agent

---

Update-opponent-model($\mathcal{V}$);

if proposal($\mathcal{V}$) is reject or argument **then**
    Process-Rejection-Processing($\mathcal{V}$);

else {proposal($\mathcal{V}$) is counter offer}
    Counter-Offer-Processing($\mathcal{V}$)

Process-Rejection-Processing($\mathcal{V}$):
finalarg = null;
finalarg = conflict-belief($\mathcal{V}$,myModel,NegoHistory);{This is done by *Conflict Argument Generator*}

if (finalarg==null) {there is no conflict in belief} **then**
    finalarg = Justify-belief($\mathcal{V}$,myModel,NegoHistory);{*Justification generator* controls this method}

if (finalarg==null) {no additional justification for offer} **then**
    finalarg = OfferOrPersuasiveOrEmp(m,null);{this method which option generates maximum expected utility}
    {where, m = $\langle\mathcal{V}$,myModel,OpModel,NegoHistory$\rangle$}
    {null second argument corresponds to no counter-offer from opponent}
Offer-argument-select(finalarg);{final proposal formed}

Counter-Offer-Processing($\mathcal{V}$):
finalarg = null;
finalarg = Justify-belief($\mathcal{V}$,myModel,NegoHistory);

if (finalarg==null) {no additional justification for offer} **then**
    finalarg = OfferOrPersuasiveOrEmp(m,proposal($\mathcal{V}$);

OfferOrPersuasiveOrEmp(m,proposal($\mathcal{V}$)):
$\langle u_2, arg_1\rangle$ = Find-significant-emphasizing-argument(m);{this method finds the significant emphasizing argument$\in \mathcal{E}$}
$\langle u_3, arg_2\rangle$ = Find-best-persuasive-argument(m);{this method finds out best persuasive argument and corresponding expected utility}
$\langle u_4, offer\rangle$ = Find-best-offer(m);{finds out the best offer}
u_1 = getutility(proposal($\mathcal{V}$));{Opponent's offer utility}
find out which utility, u_i is maximum.

if max u_i is positive **then**
    Offer-argument-select(finalarg) {finalarg is the generated argument or offer or opponent proposal for which the corresponding u_i is maximum}
else
    Terminate()

Offer-argument-select(finalarg):
form outgoing proposal based on finalarg.

---

negotiation. This arguments reinforce the negotiation context to make the offer more acceptable to the opponent.

So, the task is to find out significant attributes for argumentation. Now, given the evidences in the offer, we need to find out those attributes ($\in \mathcal{E}$) in the offer which has significant influence but not yet included in $\mathcal{I}$. Suppose, x_i's are the values already in $\mathcal{I}$. We need to calculate $P(acceptance|\mathcal{I}, y_{j,k})$, from the

Bayesian network of the opponent's belief,where $y_{j,k}$ is the kth value of $y_j \in \mathcal{E}$, for different j's.

Having obtained this probabilities we can test of significant of the influence of the y_j in the acceptance of the other agent. Conduct a t-test for the test of significance of individual probabilities. We consider the null hypothesis as H_{0i} : i^{th} *varianle in $\mathcal{E}$ has significant influence* against H_1 : , i^{th} *variable in $\mathcal{E}$ has no significant influence*. We choose those values, for which null hypothesis is accepted. If more than one value of a single variable has chosen to be significant take that value for which the corresponding p-value is maximum. We choose those attributes and the corresponding value and form the set $\mathcal{V}$ and the argument *emphasizing-argument*($\mathcal{V}$). If we found that no attribute has significant influence on the opponent's decision then no argument is chosen.

• **Find-best-persuasive-argument:** Each time the opponent agent rejects an offer, the agent try to find based on the opponent's belief model, if some persuasive arguments can increase the probability of accepting the offer by the opponent agent. This has a corresponding utility. persuasive argument is sent if its expected utility exceeds the expected utility of the other arguments or offers. There may be more than once persuasion the agent want to make in one *persuasive-argument*.

8   Conclusion and Future Work

In this paper, we have presented a novel architecture that allows an agent to negotiate better deals by using argumentation. We also propose the use of Bayesian network for representing the opponent's belief model and provide a framework by which such a model can be used to generate arguments that are likely to convince the opponent to accept proposed offers. The use of Bayes nets allow us to formally capture the complex interrelationships between domain issues and their influence on the opponent's decisions. Such models allow agents to efficiently arrive at profitable negotiated settlements. Such models can also be updated based on negotiation history and can serve as useful repositories for dealing with steady customers.

We have presented an asymmetric negotiation model, with a knowledgeable domain expert interacting with a user agent. We plan to extend this model for peer-to-peer level interaction scenarios. In particular we are interested in applying such techniques in P2P environments, where both the agents may have similar knowledge, for resource procurement and exchange.

Acknowledgements

This work has been supported in part by an NSF award IIS-0209208. We thank the anonymous reviewers for their valuable comments.

References

1. L. Amgoud, N. Maudet, and S. Parsons. An argumentation-based semantics for agent communication languages. In F. Van Harmelen, editor, *Proceedings of the European Conference on Artificial Intelligence (ECAI-2002)*, pages 38–42, Lyon, France, July 2002. IOS Press.

2. David Heckerman. A tutorial on learning bayesian networks. Technical Report MSR-TR-95-06, Microsoft Research, March 1995.

3. Nicholas Jennings, P. Faratin, Alessio R. Lomuscio Simon Parsons, Carles Sierra, and Michael Wooldridge. Automated negotiation: prospects, methods and challenges. *Int. Journal of Group Decision and Negotiation*, 10(2):199–215, 2001.

4. Nicholas Jennings, Simon Parsons, P. Noriega, and Carles Sierra. On argumentation-based negotiation. In *Proc. of Int. Workshop on Multi-Agent Systems*, 1998.

5. Finn Jensen. *An Introduction to bayesian Networks*. UCL Press and Springer Verlag, 1996.

6. Finn V. Jensen. Bayesian networks and influence diagrams. *Risk Management Strategies in Agriculture; Huirne et al (eds.); Mansholt Studies*, pages 199–213, 1997.

7. Antonis Kakas and Pavlos Moraitis. Argumentation based decision making for autonomous agents. In *Proceedings of AAMAS-03*, pages 883–890, 2003.

8. Sarit Kraus, Katia Sycara, and Amir Evenchik. Reaching agreements through argumentation: a logical model and implementation. *Artificial Intelligence journal*, 104(1-2):1–69, 1998.

9. Simon Parsons, Carles Sierra, and Nicholas R. Jennings. Agents that reason and negotiate by arguing. *Journal of Logic and Computation*, 8(3):261–292, 1998.

10. Iyad Rahwan, Sarvapali D. Ramchurn, Nicholas R. Jennings, Peter McBurney, Simon Parsons, and Liz Sonenberg. Argumentation-based negotiation. *Knowledge Engineering Review*, 2004.

11. Iyad Rahwan, Liz Sonenberg, and Frank Dignum. Towards interest-based negotiation. In *Proceedings of AAMAS-03*, pages 773–780, 2003.

12. Sarvapali D. Ramchurn, Nicholas R. Jennings, and Carles Sierra. Persuasive negotiation for autonomous agents: A rhetorical approach. In *Proc. IJCAI Workshop on Computational Models of Natural Argument*, pages 9–17, 2003.

13. Tuomas W. Sandholm and Victor R. Lesser. Issues in automated negotiation and electronic commerce: Extending the contract net framework. In *First International Conference on Multiagent Systems*, pages 328–335, 1995.

14. Carles Sierra, Nicholas R. Jennings, Pablo Noriega, and Simon Parsons. A framework for argumentation-based negotiation. *Intelligent Agents IV LNAI*, 1365:177–192, 1998.

15. D. J. Spiegelhalter and S. L. Lauritzen. Sequential updating of conditional probabilities on directed graphical structures. *Networks*, 20:579–605, 1990.

16. Ingrid Zukerman, Richard McConachy, and Kevin B. Korb. Bayesian reasoning in an abductive mechanism for argument generation and analysis. In *Proceedings of AAAI-98*, pages 833–838, 1998.

Negotiation Among DDeLP Agents

Fernando A. Tohmé[1] and Guillermo R. Simari[2]

[1] Department of Economics and National Research Council (CONICET),
ftohme@criba.edu.ar
[2] Artificial Intelligence Research and Development Laboratory,
Department of Computer Science and Engineering,
Universidad Nacional del Sur
Baha Blanca – Argentina
grs@cs.uns.edu.ar

Abstract. Negotiation can be conceived as the exchange of messages among self-interested agents in order to settle on an agreement over a given issue. They decide which messages to send according to their preferences and their evolving beliefs. Agents able to handle this dynamics of messages and beliefs can be represented by means of Defeasible Logic Programming augmented with utility functions. This approach to argumentation has the advantage of providing a useful platform for the representation of beliefs and the generation of messages. The interactive nature of negotiations requires an updating mechanism to be applied over the knowledge bases of the agents. The features of this mechanism are described by a *protocol* of a negotiation. Although there are many possible protocols, we concentrate on one that ensures the existence of an agreement in negotiations. The formalism of DeLP provides a very natural approach to the characterization of such a protocol.

1 Introduction and Motivation

The design of agents able to engage in negotiations is one of the main goals in the research on Multi-Agent Systems [LS01]. Justifications for the behavior of agents in negotiations have been known for a long time in disciplines related to the study of Decision-Making processes [Mye89]. Despite the efforts of many authors both in the Decision Sciences as in Multi-Agents Systems, the characterization of precise mechanisms of interaction in negotiations has shown to be a hard problem because, unlike markets and voting situations, the context of interaction varies from a negotiation to another. An abstract characterization of the conditions for mechanisms (*protocols*) that may ensure the convergence to agreements in negotiations has been presented in [Toh02]. We take up some of the ideas there, but adapted to the additional requirement of giving a precise foundation for the internal argumentation processes carried out by each individual agent.

To represent those deliberation processes we choose an alternative form of declarative programming, Defeasible Logic Programming (DeLP) [SCG94, Gar00, GS04]. This formalism combines Logic Programming with Defeasible Argumentation [Pol87, SL92, Pol95, Dun95, CML00, PV00], allowing the representation of

I. Rahwan et al. (Eds.): ArgMAS 2004, LNAI 3366, pp. 223–233, 2005.

tentative knowledge and leaving for the inference mechanism the task of finding the conclusions that the knowledge base warrants [CDSS03]. Furthermore, we introduce Decision-Theoretic tools into DeLP, in order to represent the fact that agents are self-interested. This is achieved by adding preferences to the formalism of DeLP, *i.e.* *utility* considerations [Lou90, TS04]. We call agents that reason using this Decision-theoretic enhanced Defeasible Logic Programming, *DDeLP agents*.

We consider only two-agent negotiations, since the extension to any number of agents follows basically the same pattern but is more involved in its syntax, without providing extra intuitions. In this simple kind of negotiations, one agent (by convention she is always called a_1), chooses one preferred conclusion derived from her beliefs. This conclusion represents a possible settlement for the negotiation. The other agent (a_2) treats this message as a query Q. Agent a_2 *agrees* with a_1 if he can find a warranted argument $\mathcal{A}$ for Q. Otherwise, he explores his own knowledge base in order to select a new proposal to make.

If we want to ensure the convergence of the negotiation, we may impose over the agents a protocol to guide the process of exchange of messages towards an agreement [Lou98]. As shown in [Toh02] a sufficient condition for such a protocol is its *monotonicity*. One consequence of this property is the absence of cycles, understood as the repetition of messages. Since a message cannot be repeated by either of the agents, any attempt to "convince" the other party in the negotiation is implicitly ruled out. In fact, a monotonic protocol rather forces an agent to accept the message of the other as a constraint.[1] Therefore, returning to our Decision-theoretic DeLP framework, if no warranted argument for the message of the other party is found, the agent must look for at least one rule responsible for this. From among several, she should choose the one that yields less utility and eliminate it from the knowledge base. Although there are other possible responses, this procedure represents a very cautious change of beliefs of the agent. With the corrected knowledge base, which represents the current beliefs of the agent, a message is chosen and the process repeats itself until either a query becomes warranted or there are no longer rules to be deleted from the knowledge base. In the first case the negotiation is said to end in an agreement. In the latter case, instead, it results in the breakup of the negotiation (which can be seen as a form of degenerate agreement on not pursuing further the negotiation).

The plan of the rest of this paper is as follows. In section 2 we will present the rudiments of DeLP with utilities. In section 3 we introduce the protocol and describe how it proceeds. Section 4 discusses possible extensions for this work.

2   Decision-Theoretic Defeasible Logic Programming

We consider a language with three disjoint components:

- *Facts*, which are ground literals representing atomic information (or the negation of atomic information).

---

[1] This is a requirement shared by all known models of bargaining.

- *Strict Rules* of the form $L_0 \leftarrow L_1, \ldots, L_n$, where L_0 is the *head* and $\{L_i\}_{i>0}$ is the *body*. Each L_i in the body or the head is a literal.
- *Defeasible Rules* of the form $L_0 \prec L_1, \ldots, L_n$, where L_0 is the *head* and $\{L_i\}_{i>0}$ is the *body*. Each L_i in the body or the head is a literal.

Then, a *Defeasible Logic Program* is a set of facts, strict rules, and defeasible rules. $\mathcal{P} = (\Pi, \Delta)$, where Π denotes the set of facts and strict rules, while Δ denotes the set of defeasible rules. For each query Q there are four possible answers: YES, NO, UNDECIDED or UNKNOWN.

To determine which answer is correct, we need the notion of *argument*. Given a program $\mathcal{P} = (\Pi, \Delta)$ and a literal L, $\langle \mathcal{A}, L \rangle$ is an argument structure for L. $\mathcal{A}$ is a set of defeasible rules in Δ such that:

1. there exists a *defeasible derivation* of L from $\Pi \cup \mathcal{A}$. That is, there exists a finite sequence $L_1, \ldots, L_n = h$ of ground literals, such that each L_i is either a fact in Π or there exists a rule in $\Pi \cup \mathcal{A}$ with L_i as its head, and every literal in the body B_j is such that $B_j \in \{L_k\}_{k<i}$,
2. there is no literal P such that both P and $\neg P$ have defeasible derivations from $\Pi \cup \mathcal{A}$,
3. $\mathcal{A}$ is minimal, *i.e.*, there does not exist $\mathcal{A}_1 \subseteq \mathcal{A}$ such that $\mathcal{A}_1$ satisfies (1) and (2).

This framework can be enhanced by means of *preferences*, $\Phi : \Pi \cup \Delta \rightarrow \mathbf{B}$, where $\mathbf{B}$ is an arbitrary Boolean algebra with top $\top$ and bottom $\bot$. The new elements $\Phi(\cdot)$ and $\mathbf{B}$ represent explicit preferences, in the sense that given two pieces of information $\mu_1, \mu_2 \in \Pi \cup \Delta$ if μ_1 is strictly *more preferred* than μ_2 then $\Phi(\mu_1) \succ_\mathbf{B} \Phi(\mu_2)$, where $\succeq_\mathbf{B}$ is the order of $\mathbf{B}$. The elements of $\mu \in \Pi \cup \Delta$ which are most preferred receive a label $\Phi(\mu) = \top$.

We do not assume here that Φ assigns $\top$ to all strict rules in Π, and not even that $\Phi(\mu_1) \succ_\mathbf{B} \Phi(\mu_2)$ for $\mu_1 \in \Pi$ and $\mu_2 \in \Delta$. This is because $\Phi(\cdot)$ has, unlike the distinction between *strict* and *defeasible* rules, no epistemic content. Instead, the preferences represent other kinds of rationales. In particular the cost-benefit rates of the pieces of information (since their use may preclude the use of other pieces in the reasoning process).

Whatever the reasons are for preferring elements of $\Pi \cup \Delta$, we postulate a Boolean algebra $\mathbf{B}$ over which $\Phi(\cdot)$ ranges. It can be argued that a more general ordering could be appropriate but, as we will see, the inference engine has to perform some operations over the labels of the pieces of information used in the process of argumentation. In consequence, the range of $\Phi(\cdot)$ has to be not only an ordered set but also be closed under the logic operators $\wedge$ and $\vee$. This can be easily represented by means of a Boolean algebra. In the simplest case, in which $\mathbf{B}$ is just a compact subset of real numbers with the natural order, we may say that $\Phi(\mu)$ is the *utility* of the piece of information μ.

From the preferences over $\Pi \cup \Delta$, we can find *preferential values* over defeasible derivations. A fact L, which can be seen as the head of a (strict) rule with an empty body, has a value denoted $V(L, \emptyset) = \Phi(L)$. By induction, given rule μ (strict or defeasible) with head L and body $B_1, \ldots, B_m$, if L is derived using μ its preferential value is $V(L, \mu) = \Phi(\mu) \wedge \bigwedge_{k=1}^{m} V(B_k)$. The intuition here is that a conclusion is as strongly preferred as the weakest of either its premises or the rule used in the derivation. Given a defeasible derivation from $\Pi \cup \Delta$, $\mathcal{L}_{\Pi \cup \Delta}(L) : L_1, \ldots, L_n = h$, it yields for its conclusion L a value $V(h, \mathcal{L}_{\Pi \cup \Delta}(L)) = V(L, \mu)$ where μ is the rule that yields $h = L_n$ up from some literals in $\{L_j\}_{j<n}$.

By extension, an argument structure $\langle \mathcal{A}, L \rangle$ yields a value for L, $V(L, \mathcal{A}) = \bigwedge_{\mathcal{L}_{\Pi \cup \mathcal{A}}(L)} V(L, \mathcal{L}_{\Pi \cup \mathcal{A}}(L))$. That is, it yields the lowest value among all the derivations of L by using defeasible rules in $\mathcal{A}$. Notice that, by definition of $\mathcal{A}$ there is no other set $\mathcal{A}' \subset \mathcal{A}$ that allows the derivation of L, but more than one selection of strict rules may exist in Π that allows, jointly with $\mathcal{A}$, to do that.

Let $\mathcal{F}$ the set of all literals that can have a defeasible derivation from $\Pi \cup \Delta$. Any subset $H \subseteq \mathcal{F}$ has a value $V(H) = \bigvee_{L \in H} \bigwedge_{\mathcal{L}_{\Pi \cup \Delta}(L)} V(L, \mathcal{L}_{\Pi \cup \Delta}(L))$. This means that H is as valuable as the most valuable of its elements, which in turn is as valuable as the weakest of its derivations.

With this characterization we speak of an Decision-theoretic enhanced Defeasible Logic Program or $\mathcal{P}' = (\Pi, \Delta, \Phi, \mathbf{B})$ which is intended to provide answers to queries through a process of argumentation that proceeds making comparisons among arguments. The main criterion of comparison used is *preferential specificity* [Poo85, SL92, SGCS03, TS04]. Consider a program $\mathcal{P}' = (\Pi, \Delta, \Phi, \mathbf{B})$ with Π_G the set of strict rules from Π. Let $\mathcal{F}$ the set of all literals that can have a defeasible derivation from $\Pi \cup \Delta$. Let $\langle \mathcal{A}_1, L_1 \rangle$ and $\langle \mathcal{A}_2, L_2 \rangle$ be two argument structures with $L_1, L_2 \in \mathcal{F}$. Then $\langle \mathcal{A}_1, L_1 \rangle$ is *strictly more preferentially specific than* $\langle \mathcal{A}_2, L_2 \rangle$ if:

1. For all $H \subseteq \mathcal{F}$, if there exists a defeasible derivation of L_1 from $\Pi_G \cup H \cup \mathcal{A}_1$ while $\Pi_G \cup H \nvdash L_1$, then L_2 can be defeasibly derived from $\Pi_G \cup H \cup \mathcal{A}_2$, and

2. there exists $H' \subseteq \mathcal{F}$ such that there exists a defeasible derivation of h_2 from $\Pi_G \cup H' \cup \mathcal{A}_2$ and $\Pi_G \cup H' \nvdash L_2$ but there is no defeasible derivation of L_1 from $\Pi_G \cup H' \cup \mathcal{A}_1$.

3. For every H verifying (1) and H' verifying (2), $V(H) \succeq_{\mathbf{B}} V(H')$.

Argument $\langle \mathcal{A}_1, L_1 \rangle$ *counterargues* another $\langle \mathcal{A}_2, L_2 \rangle$ at a literal L if there exists a sub-argument of $\langle \mathcal{A}_2, L_2 \rangle$, $\langle \mathcal{A}, L \rangle$, i.e., $\mathcal{A} \subseteq \mathcal{A}_2$, such that there exists a literal P verifying both $\Pi \cup \{L, L_1\} \vdash P$ and $\Pi \cup \{L, L_1\} \vdash \neg P$.

If $\langle \mathcal{A}_1, L_1 \rangle$ and $\langle \mathcal{A}_2, L_2 \rangle$ are two argument structures, $\langle \mathcal{A}_1, L_1 \rangle$ is a *proper preferential defeater* for $\langle \mathcal{A}_2, L_2 \rangle$ at literal L iff there exists a sub-argument of $\langle \mathcal{A}_2, L_2 \rangle$, $\langle \mathcal{A}, L \rangle$ such that $\langle \mathcal{A}_1, L_1 \rangle$ counterargues $\langle \mathcal{A}_2, L_2 \rangle$ at L and $\langle \mathcal{A}_1, L_1 \rangle$ is strictly more preferentially specific than $\langle \mathcal{A}, L \rangle$. Alternatively, $\langle \mathcal{A}_1, L_1 \rangle$ is a *blocking preferential defeater* for $\langle \mathcal{A}_2, L_2 \rangle$ at literal L iff there exists a sub-argument of $\langle \mathcal{A}_2, L_2 \rangle$, $\langle \mathcal{A}, L \rangle$ such that $\langle \mathcal{A}_1, L_1 \rangle$ counterargues $\langle \mathcal{A}_2, L_2 \rangle$ at L and neither $\langle \mathcal{A}_1, L_1 \rangle$ is strictly more preferentially specific than $\langle \mathcal{A}, L \rangle$ nor is $\langle \mathcal{A}, L \rangle$ strictly more preferentially specific than $\langle \mathcal{A}, L \rangle$. If $\langle \mathcal{A}_1, L_1 \rangle$ is either a proper or a blocking preferential defeater of $\langle \mathcal{A}_2, L_2 \rangle$, it is said to be a *preferential defeater* of the latter.

An *argumentation line* for an argument structure $\langle \mathcal{A}_0, L_0 \rangle$ is a sequence $\Gamma = [\langle \mathcal{A}_0, L_0 \rangle, \langle \mathcal{A}_1, L_1 \rangle, \langle \mathcal{A}_2, L_2 \rangle, \cdots]$ where for each $i > 0$ $\langle \mathcal{A}_{i+1}, L_{i+1} \rangle$ is a defeater of $\langle \mathcal{A}_i, L_i \rangle$. $\Gamma_S = [\langle \mathcal{A}_0, L_0 \rangle, \langle \mathcal{A}_2, L_2 \rangle, \langle \mathcal{A}_4, L_4 \rangle, \cdots]$ is the sequence of *supporting* argument structures of Γ, while the sequence of *interfering* ones is $\Gamma_I = [\langle \mathcal{A}_1, L_1 \rangle, \langle \mathcal{A}_3, L_3 \rangle, \langle \mathcal{A}_5, L_5 \rangle, \cdots]$.

An *acceptable* argumentation line in a defeasible program $\mathcal{P}' = (\Pi, \Delta, \Phi, \mathbf{B})$ is a finite sequence $\Gamma = [\langle \mathcal{A}_0, L_0 \rangle, \cdots, \langle \mathcal{A}_n, L_n \rangle]$ such that:

1. Both Γ_S and Γ_I are *concordant*, i.e., there is no P such that both P and $\neg P$ have defeasible derivations from $\Pi \cup \bigcup_{i=0}^{\lfloor \frac{n}{2} \rfloor} \mathcal{A}_{2i}$ and no P' with defeasible derivations for both P' and $\neg P'$ from $\Pi \cup \bigcup_{i=0}^{\lfloor \frac{n-1}{2} \rfloor} \mathcal{A}_{2i+1}$.
2. No argument $\langle \mathcal{A}_k, L_k \rangle \in \Gamma$ is a subargument of an argument $\langle \mathcal{A}_j, L_j \rangle$, i.e., $\mathcal{A}_k \not\subset \mathcal{A}_j$, for $j < k$.
3. For each $i < n$, if $\langle \mathcal{A}_i, L_i \rangle$ is a blocking preferential defeater of $\langle \mathcal{A}_{i-1}, L_{i-1} \rangle$ then $\langle \mathcal{A}_{i+1}, L_{i+1} \rangle$ is a proper preferential defeater of $\langle \mathcal{A}_i, L_i \rangle$.

To answer a query Q, the *preferential warrant procedure* builds up a candidate argument structure $\langle \mathcal{A}, Q \rangle$. Then, it associates to this argument a *preferential dialectical tree* $T_{\langle \mathcal{A}, Q \rangle}$ as follows:

1. The root of the tree is labeled, $\langle \mathcal{A}_0, Q_0 \rangle$, i.e., $\mathcal{A}_0 = \mathcal{A}$ and $Q_0 = Q$.
2. Let n be a non-root node, with label $\langle \mathcal{A}_n, Q_n \rangle$ and $\Gamma = [\langle \mathcal{A}_0, Q_0 \rangle, \cdots, \langle \mathcal{A}_n, Q_n \rangle]$ the labels in the path from the root to n. Let $\mathcal{B} = \{ \langle \mathcal{B}_1, H_1 \rangle, \cdots, \langle \mathcal{B}_k, H_k \rangle \}$ be the set of all the preferential defeaters for $\langle \mathcal{A}_n, Q_n \rangle$. For $1 \leq i \leq k$, if $\Gamma' = [\langle \mathcal{A}_0, Q_0 \rangle, \cdots, \langle \mathcal{A}_n, Q_n \rangle, \langle \mathcal{B}_i, H_i \rangle]$ is an acceptable argumentation line, n has a child n_i labeled $\langle \mathcal{B}_i, H_i \rangle$. If $\mathcal{B} = \emptyset$ or no $\langle \mathcal{B}_i, H_i \rangle \in \mathcal{B}$ is such that Γ' is acceptable, then n is a leaf of the tree.

The nodes of $T_{\langle \mathcal{A}, Q \rangle}$ can be marked, yielding a tagged tree $T^*_{\langle \mathcal{A}, Q \rangle}$ as follows:

- All leaves of $T_{\langle \mathcal{A}, Q \rangle}$ are marked U in $T^*_{\langle \mathcal{A}, Q \rangle}$.
- If $\langle \mathcal{B}, H \rangle$ is the label of a node which is not a leaf, the node will be marked U in $T^*_{\langle \mathcal{A}, Q \rangle}$ if every child is marked D. Otherwise, if at least one of its children is marked U, it is marked as D.

Then, given an argument $\langle \mathcal{A}, Q \rangle$ and its associated tagged tree $T^*_{\langle \mathcal{A}, Q \rangle}$, if the root is marked U, the literal Q is said to be *preferentially warranted*. $\mathcal{A}$ is said to be the *preferential warrant* for Q. Therefore, given a query Q the possible answers will be:

YES,   if Q is preferentially warranted;
NO,   if $\neg Q$ is preferentially warranted;
UNDECIDED,   if neither Q nor $\neg Q$ are preferentially warranted;
UNKNOWN,   if Q is not in the language of the program.

3   Negotiation

A negotiation can be seen as the exchange of messages among agents in order to reach an agreement over a given issue. The main elements in a negotiation are the following:

- The possible settlements.
- The preferences over them.
- The individual beliefs about the possible results.
- The messages that can be exchanged.

The messages are chosen according to the preferences over the class of settlements that are believed to be acceptable. Once a message is received, an agent has to decide whether to accept the implied settlement or to break up the negotiation or to explore for new possibilities. If the latter is the case, the agent has to update her beliefs and choose her message according to that.

In terms of DDeLP consider a program $\mathcal{P}' = (\Pi, \Delta, \Phi, \mathbf{B})$ where $\Phi = \Phi_1 \times \ldots \Phi_n$ with range $\mathbf{B}^n$, from which we may define the elements of a n-person negotiation as follows:

- The possible settlements are the literals L that can be defeasibly derived from $\Pi \cup \Delta$.
- The preferences over the literals are derived from Φ.
- The individual beliefs are subsets of $\Pi \cup \Delta$.
- The messages are the literals L plus two extra symbols, "yes" and "break", to indicate either agreement or the breakup of negotiations.

That is, we assume that agents consider only a certain subset of rules, from which they select some literals as both possible settlements and as messages. We consider only two agents, 1 and 2. Each agent i performs, at each stage t of the negotiation, a DDeLP program $\langle \Pi_i^t, \Delta_i^t, \Phi_i^t, \mathbf{B} \rangle$, where $\Pi_i^t \cup \Delta_i^t \subseteq \Pi \cup \Delta$ and Φ_i^t is the restriction of Φ_i over $\Pi_i^t \cup \Delta_i^t$.

At $t = 1$ agent $\mathbf{a}_1$ sends a message (a literal L^1 derived from $\Pi_1^1 \cup \Delta_1^1$) to agent $\mathbf{a}_2$. He may query his program $\Pi_2^2 \cup \Delta_2^2$ and if the answer is YES end the negotiation by accepting L and sending the message "yes". Otherwise, if the answer is UNKNOWN he may break the negotiation (because the issue has become meaningless) and send "break". In case that the answer is either NO or UNDECIDED, a new literal is chosen to be send as a message.

In general, a response to a message L^t received by agent $\mathbf{a}_i$ at round $t + 1$ of the negotiation, is a message L^{t+1} defeasibly derived from $\Pi_i^{t+1} \cup \Delta_i^{t+1}$. The exchange of messages proceeds in orderly fashion: agent $\mathbf{a}_1$ sends her messages at odd values of t (i.e. at $1, 3, \ldots$) while $\mathbf{a}_2$ sends hers at even values $(2, 4, \ldots)$.

A possibility is that L^t is either NO or UNDECIDED. Then, $\Pi_i^{t+1} \cup \Delta_i^{t+1}$ must be revised and updated according to L^t. The result of this operation of updating is $\bar{\Pi}_i^{t+1} \cup \bar{\Delta}_i^{t+1}$[2]. There are alternative characterizations of this updating opera-

---

[2] The next time agent i receives a message, $t + 3$, his knowledge base will be $\Pi_i^{t+3} \cup \Delta_i^{t+3} \equiv \bar{\Pi}_i^{t+1} \cup \bar{\Delta}_i^{t+1}$.

tion [FKIS02], but a mandatory requirement is that it must be consistent with the protocol of negotiation.

Since we assume that the goal of both agents is either to reach an agreement or break up the negotiation, any sufficient condition that ensures such result may be applied to define a protocol. In [Toh02] it is shown that such condition is *monotonicity*, in the sense of reducing disagreements. In other words, agents are allowed to exchange messages (without repetition) until either an agreement is found or the negotiation breaks up.

In this sense, if until stage t the messages that have been sent back and forth are $L^1, L^2, \ldots, L^{t-1}$, the possible messages to be send from then on are constrained by the protocol.

The following is obviously a monotonic protocol:

Protocol 31. *If an agreement nor a break up is reached, the response to a message* L^t *must be a* L^{t+1} *in* $\mathcal{L} \setminus \{L^j\}_{j=1}^t$, *where* $\mathcal{L}$ *is the set of literals that can be defeasibly derived from* $\Pi \cup \Delta$.

If such non-deterministic protocol is applied, a process of updating $\Pi_i^{t+1} \cup \Delta_i^{t+1}$ must be consistent with it. In this sense, if L^t is not preferentially warranted, no L^j for $j = 1, \ldots, t$ should be used as a message up from the resulting knowledge base $\bar{\Pi}_i^{t+1} \cup \bar{\Delta}_i^{t+1}$.

This means that, in particular, the current beliefs must be changed. The beliefs should no longer allow the messages sent in the previous rounds to be considered warranted.[3] One way to achieve this is by using the following procedure:

Procedure 31. *Consider, for a given* i, *the tagged trees* $\mathcal{T}_i^k$, *for* $k = 1, \ldots, t$. *Among those with roots marked* U, *choose the leaves* $\langle \mathcal{H}^k, H^k \rangle$ *that minimize* $V_i(H^k, \mathcal{H}^k)$, *derived from* Φ_i^{t+1}.

For each of those leaves, choose a rule that minimizes $\Phi_i^{t+1}(\mu^k)$ *over all the rules that participate in the derivation of* H^k *from* $\Pi^{t+1} \cup \mathcal{H}^k$. *Then define* $\bar{\Pi}_i^{t+1} \cup \bar{\Delta}_i^{t+1} := (\Pi_i^{t+1} \cup \Delta_i^{t+1}) \setminus \{\mu\}_k$.

This procedure, used in the following algorithm allows to find the updated beliefs and choose next message:

Algorithm 31. [Update Beliefs and Select Message]

1. *Define* $\mathcal{T}_{\langle \mathcal{A}, L^k \rangle}$ *for* $k = 1, \ldots, t$.
2. *Run Procedure 3.1.*
3. *Find* $\{\mathcal{T}_i^k\}_{k=1}^t$ *over* $\bar{\Pi}_i^{t+1} \cup \bar{\Delta}_i^{t+1}$
4. *If a root is marked* U *go to 2. Else*
   (a) *If* $\bar{\Pi}_i^{t+1} \cup \bar{\Delta}_i^{t+1} = \emptyset$, *send the message* "break".

---

[3] As said, preferences could also change, but this equivalent to replace Φ_i for Φ_i'. Although this can be easily introduced in our framework, we leave the details for an extension of this work.

    (b) Else choose L^{t+1} such that minimizes $\Phi_i^{t+1}(L)$ over those literals L that can be preferentially warranted in $\bar{\Pi}_i^{t+1} \cup \bar{\Delta}_i^{t+1}$.

It is immediate that:

Proposition 31. *Algorithm 3.1 implements Protocol 3.1.*

Proof: *Trivial. If L^t is warranted, then an agreement is reached and the selected message is "yes", else if L^t is* UNKNOWN *the negotiation breaks up. Otherwise, Algorithm 3.1 is such that if $\bar{\Pi}_i^{t+1} \cup \bar{\Delta}_i^{t+1} = \emptyset$ the negotiation breaks up, otherwise, it ensures that $L^1, \ldots, L^t$ are not preferentially warranted in $\bar{\Pi}_i^{t+1} \cup \bar{\Delta}_i^{t+1}$, therefore it chooses $L^{t+1} \in \mathcal{L} \setminus \{L^j\}_{j=1}^t$.*

Notice that Algorithm 3.1 is not the only possible implementation of Protocol 3.1, since the latter just asks for monotonicity in the messages, while the Algorithm intends to find the *best* messages for agent $\mathbf{a}_i$.

    Another result that follows is:

Proposition 32. *If both agents use Algorithm 3.1 to choose messages, the negotiation either ends in an agreement or in a break up.*

Proof: *Algorithm 3.1 implements Protocol 3.1. We denote $\mathcal{L}^t = \mathcal{L} \setminus \{L^k\}_{k=1}^t$. There are two possibilities, either there exists a T such that when one of the agents sends a message L^T the other agent responds with "yes". Alternatively, if there is no L that may result in an agreement, as a consequence of the Compactness Theorem for First-Order Logic there exists a $T' < \infty$ such that $\mathcal{L}^{T'} = \emptyset$ and leads to a response "break".*

A final consequence of using Algorithm 3.1 is that if agreements (including break ups as degenerate agreements) are *path dependent*. That is, the choices made by the agents condition further choices. Therefore, over the same knowledge base, the agents may end up agreeing on different conclusions. The following example shows this:

Example 31. *Consider the classical example in defeasible argumentation where preferences are defined for $\mathbf{B} = \{0, 1\}$, with $0 < 1$. The preferences, which for simplicity are assumed common to both agents, are indicated in parentheses next to the corresponding pieces of information:*

$\Pi = \{bird(X) \prec penguin(X)\ (1),\ penguin(tweety)\ (1),\ bird(tweety)\ (1)\}$
$\Delta = \{\neg flies(X) \prec penguin(X)\ (1),\ flies(X) \prec bird(X)\ (0.5)\}$

Agents have different beliefs:

$\Pi_1^1 = \{penguin(tweety)\ (1), bird(tweety)\ (1)\}$
$\Delta_1^1 = \{\neg flies(X) \prec penguin(X)\ (1)\}$

while

$$\Pi_2^1 = \{bird(X) \prec penguin(X) \ (1), \ penguin(tweety) \ (1),\}$$
$$\Delta_2^1 = \{flies(X) \prec bird(X) \ (0.5)\}$$

For agent a_1, there are two warranted conclusions, $penguin(tweety)$ and $\neg flies(tweety)$. Suppose that her message is $L^1 = penguin(tweety)$. Since it is also a warranted conclusion for a_2, he will respond with "yes". Otherwise, suppose that $L^1 = \neg flies(tweety)$. Since for a_1 $flies(tweety)$ is warranted he must apply Algorithm 3.1. It follows that he has to drop the rule with lowest preference, namely $flies(X) \prec bird(X)$. Then,

$$\Pi_2^2 = \{bird(X) \prec penguin(X) \ (1), \ penguin(tweety) \ (1),\}$$
$$\Delta_2^2 = \emptyset$$

The only (trivially) warranted conclusions are $penguin(tweety)$ and $bird(tweety)$. In the case that $L^2 = penguin(tweety)$, the response is "yes" and the same is true if $L^2 = bird(tweety)$.
On the other hand, assume that $\Phi(flies(X) \prec bird(X)) = 1$ while $\Phi(bird(X) \prec penguin(X)) = 0.5$. Accordingly, if $L^1 = \neg flies(tweety)$ then

$$\Pi_2^2 = \{ \ penguin(tweety) \ (1),\}$$
$$\Delta_2^2 = \{flies(X) \prec bird(X) \ (1)\}$$

Therefore, $L^2 = penguin(tweety)$, and the response is "yes".

Finally, if

$$\Pi_2^1 = \{bird(tweety) \ (1)\}$$
$$\Delta_2^1 = \{flies(X) \prec bird(X) \ (0.5)\}$$

and $L^1 = penguin(tweety)$, the response is "break".

4   Conclusions

We presented in this paper a framework of negotiation with DeLP extended with preferences. An algorithm of belief updating based on the elimination of rules ensures that agents will reach an agreement, although this agreement depends on the particular sequence of messages chosen.

A matter of further work will be to see if a negotiation still converges to an agreement if another mechanism of belief updating is used.

Acknowledgments

This research was partially supported by CONICET, by the Secretaría General de Ciencia y Tecnología de la Universidad Nacional del Sur and by Agencia Nacional de Promoción Científica y Tecnológica (PICT 2002 No. 13096). The authors would like to thank anonymous reviewers for providing helpful comments to improve the final version of this paper.

References

[CDSS03]   Carlos I. Chesñevar, Jürgen Dix, Frieder Stolzenburg, and Guillermo R. Simari. Relating defeasible and normal logic programming through transformation properties. *Theoretical Computer Science*, 290(1):499–529, Jan 2003.

[CML00]   Carlos I. Chesñevar, Ana G. Maguitman, and Ronald P. Loui. Logical Models of Argument. *ACM Computing Surveys*, 32(4), December 2000.

[Dun95]   Phan M. Dung. On the acceptability of arguments and its fundamental role in nonmonotonic reasoning and logic programming and *n*-person games. *Artificial Intelligence*, 77:321–357, 1995.

[FKIS02]   Marcelo A. Falappa, Gabrielle Kern-Isberner, and Guillermo R. Simari. Explanations, belief revision and defeasible reasoning. *Artificial Intelligence Journal*, 141(1-2):1–28, October 2002.

[Gar00]   Alejandro J. García. *Defeasible Logic Programming: Definition, Operational Semantics and Parallelism.* PhD thesis, Computer Science and Engineering Department, Universidad Nacional del Sur, Bahía Blanca, Argentina, December 2000.

[GS04]   Alejandro J. García and Guillermo R. Simari. Defeasible logic programming: An argumentative approach. *Theory and Practice of Logic Programming*, 4(1):95–138, 2004.

[KSE98]   Sarit Kraus, Katia Sycara, and Amir Evenchik. Reaching agreements through argumentation: A logical model and implementation. *Artificial Intelligence*, 104(1–2):1–69, 1998.

[Lou90]   Ronald P. Loui. Defeasible specification of utilities. In Henry Kyburg, Ronald Loui, and Greg Carlson, editors, *Knowledge Representation and Defeasible Reasoning*, pages 345–359. Kluwer Academic Publishers, Dordrecht, 1990.

[Lou98]   Ronald P. Loui. Process and policy: Resource-bounded nondemonstrative reasoning. *Computational Intelligence: An International Journal*, 14, 1998.

[LS01]   Kate Larson and Tuomas Sandholm. Bargaining with limited computation: Deliberation equilibrium. *Artificial Intelligence*, 132, 2001.

[Mye89]   Roger B. Myerson. Credible negotiation statements and coherent plans. *Journal of Economic Theory*, 48, 1989.

[Pol87]   John Pollock. Defeasible Reasoning. *Cognitive Science*, 11:481–518, 1987.

[Pol95]   John Pollock. *Cognitive Carpentry: A Blueprint for How to Build a Person.* MIT Press, 1995.

[Poo85]   David L. Poole. On the Comparison of Theories: Preferring the Most Specific Explanation. In *Proc. 9th IJCAI*, pages 144–147. IJCAI, 1985.

[PV00]   Henry Prakken and Gerard Vreeswijk. Logical systems for defeasible argumentation. In D.Gabbay, editor, *Handbook of Philosophical Logic, 2nd ed.* Kluwer Academic Pub., 2000.

[SCG94]   Guillermo R. Simari, Carlos I. Chesñevar, and Alejandro J. García. The role of dialectics in defeasible argumentation. In *XIV International Conference of the Chilenean Computer Science Society*, November 1994.

[SGCS03]   Frieder Stolzenburg, Alejandro J. García, Carlos I. Chesñevar, and Guillermo R. Simari. Computing generalized specificity. *Journal of Aplied Non-Classical Logics*, 13(1):87–113, January 2003.

[SL92]   Guillermo R. Simari and Ronald P. Loui. A Mathematical Treatment of Defeasible Reasoning and its Implementation. *Artificial Intelligence*, 53:125–157, 1992.

[Syc89]   Katia Sycara. Multi-agent compromise via negotiation. In L. Gasser and M. Huhns, editors, *Distributed Artificial Intelligence (Vol. 2)*. Morgan Kaufmann, Los Altos, CA, September 1989.

[Syc90]   Katia Sycara. Persuasive argumentation in negotiation. *Theory and Decision*, 28(3):203–242, May 1990.

[Toh02]   Fernando Tohmé. Negotiation and defeasible decision making. *Theory and Decision*, 53(4):289–311, 2002.

[TS04]   Fernando A. Tohmé and Guillermo R. Simari. Preferential defeasibility: Utility in defeasible logic programming. In *Proceedings of the 10th International Workshop on Non-Monotonic Reasoning*, pages 394–399. NMR, June 2004.

Is It Worth Arguing?

Nishan C. Karunatillake and Nicholas R. Jennings

School of Electronics and Computer Science,
University of Southampton,
Southampton, UK
{nnc02r, nrj}@ecs.soton.ac.uk

Abstract. Argumentation-based negotiation (ABN) is an effective means of resolving conflicts in a multi-agent society. However, it consumes both time and
computational resources for agents to generate, select and evaluate arguments.
Furthermore, in many cases, argumentation is not the only means of resolving
conflicts. Thus, some could be avoided either by finding an alternative means
(evading the conflict) or by modifying the intended course of action (re-planning).
Therefore, it would be advantageous for agents to identify those situations and
weigh the costs and the benefits of arguing before using it to resolve conflicts.
To this end, we present a preliminary empirical analysis to evaluate the performance of a simple ABN system, with respect to other non-arguing approaches,
in a particular task allocation scenario. In our experiments, we simulate a multi-
agent community and allow the agents to use a combination of ABN, evasion and
re-planning techniques to overcome conflicts that arise within the community.
Analysing the observed results, we show that, in our domain, ABN presents an effective means of resolving conflicts when the resources are constrained. However,
we also show it is a more costly and less effective means, compared to evasion
and re-planning methods, when resources are more abundant.

Keywords: Argumentation-based Negotiation, Conflict Resolution.

1 Introduction

Conflicts are inevitable in multi-agent systems in which autonomous entities pursue
their own goals (whether they do so in a self-interested or in a collaborative manner) [1].
They cover physical conflicts arising due to resource limitations (e.g., multiple agents
attempting to use a non-shareable resource at the same time) and knowledge conflicts
resulting due to discrepancies in viewpoints or opinions (e.g., a contradiction between
agents' beliefs about a particular proposition) [1, 2, 3]. In either case, however, they
present hurdles for the agents to overcome if they are to achieve their goals and actions
in a coordinated manner. Against this background, *Argumentation-Based Negotiation*
(ABN) is advocated as a promising means of interaction that can allow the agents to
resolve these conflicts [4]. In its simplest form, ABN allows agents to exchange proposals
that are accompanied by meta-information, which provides support and justification for
the proposals. It also allows the exchange of explicit arguments, such as critics, appeals
and other forms of persuasive locutions, to influence and persuade the opponent to accept
the proposals and come to a mutual agreement [4, 5, 6].

I. Rahwan et al. (Eds.): ArgMAS 2004, LNAI 3366, pp. 234–250, 2005.

Although ABN can be effective at resolving conflicts, there are a number of overheads associated with its use. It takes time to persuade and convince an opponent to change its stance and yield to a less favourable agreement. It takes computational effort for both parties of the conflict to carry out the reasoning required to generate and select a set of convincing arguments, and to evaluate the incoming arguments and reason whether to accept or reject them. However, not all conflicts need to be resolved. Thus, for example, when faced with a conflict, an agent could find an alternative means to work around the situation; thereby *evading the conflict* rather than attempting to resolve it. By way of an example, consider the case where an agent (A) requires the service of another (B) which is also demanded by a third agent (C). Now if B is unwilling to provide its service, instead of attempting to persuade it to change its conflicting stance, A could simply attempt to find another more willing partner (D) who has a similar capability. The result would still be A overcoming the conflict situation, but not through argumentation. In addition to either evading the conflict or arguing and resolving it, an agent could also attempt to *re-plan and alter the means* by which it intends to achieve the objective so that the conflict situation is removed (e.g., A could delay its task until B becomes available).

Given the overheads of argumentation, and the alternative methods available for overcoming conflicts (evade and re-plan), we believe it is important for agents to be able to weigh up the relative advantages and disadvantages of arguing, before attempting to resolve conflicts through argumentation. This is the main long-term motivation of our research. Specifically, we aim to empirically evaluate the effectiveness and efficiency of argumentation as a conflict resolution mechanism with respect to these other non-arguing alternatives available to the agents. To date, this issue has largely been overlooked in existing literature. Current ABN assumes that the agent has already made the decision to argue (typically without any consideration) and the focus is on the internal mechanisms of argumentation (i.e., how agents can generate, select and evaluate arguments). Our work presents an initial step in this direction.

Against this background, this work advances the state of the art in the following ways. *First*, our main contribution is to evaluate the relative effectiveness and efficiency of using simple forms of ABN, as opposed to evasion and re-planning, to overcome conflicts in a multi-agent system. Specifically, we consider an ABN system in which agents exchange meta-information, alongside their decisions, either to explain the internal constraints that prompt them to make their decisions, or to suggest alternative solutions that satisfy their internal constraints (e.g., I reject this proposal, since I am fully committed at this time or I reject this proposal for the suggested time, but for this price I am willing to perform this service at the following alternative times).[1] Through an empirical evaluation, in an idealised task allocation scenario, we show that such ABN does indeed present a better means of conflict resolution than evasion when the resources are constrained. However, we also demonstrate the diminishing impact (both in effectiveness and in efficiency) of the ABN method as the resource levels increase within the community.

---

[1] Clearly, this is toward the simpler end of the possibilities in argumentation. However, our purpose here is not to exhaustively cover all forms of argumentation. Rather we seek to evaluate the trade-offs involved in engaging in argumentation and concentrating on the simpler models provides an initial point of departure.

Second, we demonstrate the superior performance of hybrid strategies (i.e., those that use both ABN and evasion in a combined manner) as opposed to pure strategies that always attempt to use either one or another in conflict resolution. *Third*, to empirically illustrate our concepts, we present a simple, but well-defined multi-agent context, where conflicts occur naturally through interaction of agents with different motivations. Even though, our experimental context embodies a series of simplifying assumptions made for implementation purposes (detailed in Section 3.1), we demonstrate its versatility by replicating both Kraus et al.'s [5] and Jung et al.'s [7] main experimental observations.

The remainder of the paper is structured as follows. Section 2 discusses the related work and establishes our contribution within the current literature. Section 3 details our argumentation context, the conflicts arising within it and presents the different methods and strategies used by the agents to resolve these conflicts. Subsequently, Section 4 details the experimental setting, presents our results and an analysis of the key observations. Section 5 concludes, and details our future directions.

2   Related Work

Argumentation-based negotiation is fast emerging as an important means of interaction for agents within multi-agent communities [4]. To date, most of the work in this area has focused on the internal mechanisms of argumentation; that is how arguments are generated [6, 8, 9], selected [5, 10, 11] and evaluated [12, 13], and how the process of argumentation can resolve conflicts and achieve agreements [7, 14]. However, no real attention is given to the overall impact of the decision made by the agents to resolve their conflicts by arguing. Rather, it is simply assumed that the agent has already made that decision and the focus is on how the agent can use arguments to resolve the conflict. Thus, unanswered questions remain such as when to use argumentation?, under what conditions does it yield better results than non-arguing strategies?, and what are its implications for the performance of the multi-agent community?

In tackling this problem we draw inspiration from a number of previous efforts in the ABN literature. Specifically, Jung, Tambe and Kulkarni's empirical work [7] acted as an important impetus for our effort. Their work attempts to evaluate the overall impact of using meta-information within a negotiation process to resolve conflicts. To do so, this work models a set of collaborative agents attempting to solve a distributed constraint satisfaction problem (DCSP) [15] and it maps the DCSP into an argumentation context. More specifically, the conflicts are mapped as external constraints affecting the local variables in the DCSP, the pure negotiation process involves the exchange of values for these internal variables, and the meta-information (argument) exchange is mapped as the propagation of internal constraints. Motivated by the desire to resolve the DCSP, the agents can either interact to resolve these conflicts via pure negotiation (without arguments) or ABN. However, the main motivations of our work are quite different from theirs. In particular, their work assumes that all conflicts need to be resolved, and thus they compare ABN to negotiation without argumentation in order to assess the impact of meta-information exchange on the conflict resolution effort. In contrast, we do not believe that all conflicts need to be resolved because they can sometimes be avoided through evasion or re-planning. Therefore, our motivation is to evaluate the importance of ABN as a conflict resolution mechanism as opposed to using other non-arguing means to overcome conflicts.

Kraus, Sycara and Evenchik [5], to a limited extent, consider whether argumentation should be used when faced with a conflict situation. They use a fixed heuristic to enable the agent to decide when to argue and when to stop the argument and re-plan. In their experiments, two self-interested agents are assigned a particular task, which neither has the capability to achieve alone. Thus, the agents must cooperate to achieve the task. The mechanism of achieving cooperation is by using negotiation and persuasion dialogues. According to their heuristic, the agent will *always* first try to argue and reason with the other party and try to achieve an agreement. However, if the agent is unsuccessful in achieving an agreement in a given fixed time schedule, it will stop the argument. In the next time slot it will re-plan, generate a new set of goals and intentions, and will start the process all over again. However, this heuristic is rather rigid and is but one possibility. Moreover, it was tested in a two-agent context where the only option available to an agent was to make the other agent agree (otherwise, it could not complete its task). Generally speaking, when there are only two agents, the alternative options available for the arguer are limited. Thus, the *always argue* approach becomes more viable. Avoiding conflicts is not a possibility, because the agent that wants to achieve the task has to somehow convince the only other agent within the system to provide its services. However, its usage in a multi-agent context, where there are many other potential alternative agents that might be willing to cooperate, is questionable.

3 The Argumentation Context

To evaluate the overall performance of argumentation as a means of conflict resolution, we require a computational context in which a number of agents interact and conflicts arise as a natural consequence of these interactions. To this end, Section 3.1 presents an overall description of the experimental setting, clearly specifying the task environment, which presents the agents with the motivation to interact. Subsequently, Section 3.2 explains how these interactions give rise to conflicts and then proceeds to explain the three different methods the agents can use to overcome them; namely *argue*, *evade* and *re-plan*. Finally, Section 3.3 details the strategies that agents use to combine these three methods for conflict resolution.

3.1 The Scenario

The scenario simulates a collection of self-interested agents, each with a specific capability and a specific task to achieve. Each task requires a particular series of actions to be achieved in a predefined order, and each action requires a specific capability. However, none of the agents possess the capability to achieve all their actions, thus they need to negotiate for the services of one another. When an agent manages to attain all the capabilities required to execute its actions in the predefined order, the task is completed. Upon completion of the task, the agent receives a specific reward. It is this reward that motivates the self-interested agents to complete their tasks, which, in turn, results in agents interacting within the system.

Table 1. A Sample Problem: Presents a three agent society, each having their own capability and their assigned task schedule

Time Slot	**A** (α) £6,000	**B** (β) £4,000	**C** (γ) £10,000
TS0	α	β	β
TS1	β	α	β
TS2	γ	α	α
TS3	α	β	γ

In more detail, Table 1 depicts a sample scenario of a multi-agent community with three such agents; namely A, B and C. Agent A has the capability to perform the action α, while B and C are capable of performing β and γ respectively. Each task is presented as a series of actions. For example, agent A's task involves four actions, which requires capabilities α, β, γ and α respectively. The notion of time is an important parameter in the scenario. Not only must agents achieve their actions in the specified order, but also they need to achieve them in the specified time. Any delays on this time will incur a penalty charge (this penalty calculation is discussed later). All agents operate to a unified clock and an atomic unit of time is termed a time slot. For example, A's task spans four time slots TS0 to TS3. Thus, for A to attain the complete £6,000 reward, it will have to find capable agents to perform α, β, γ and α at TS0, TS1, TS2 and TS3.

How the agents interact to find their task partners is a central issue in this work. In the simplest case, when an agent needs to find a certain capability to achieve some action for a specific time slot, it will first look to see if it possesses the necessary capability to perform the action on its own. If it does so, it assigns that action to itself. However, if it does not possess the required capability, it must attempt to convince another agent to sell its services for that specific time slot.[2] In the above example, agent A does not have the required capability to perform the action at TS1 (since it does not possess capability β). Therefore, it will attempt to convince another agent B (who has capability β) to sell its services for the time slot TS1.

If an agent does not manage to convince any of its known acquaintances to sell it their service, it has to *delay* that action. Delaying means, it will not accomplish any action within that time slot. Since the agents need to achieve their actions in the strictly prescribed sequence, adding these delays naturally lengthens the time required to accomplish the task.[3] As mentioned above, any task completed after the initially assigned time incurs a *penalty*, which, in turn, reduces the task's reward available for the agent upon completion. The amount of penalty is a fixed value per extended time slot and is proportional to the task's initial reward. However, if the agent loses all its initial reward as penalty charges, any further delays will not incur any additional charge. This is an

---

[2] It is worth noting that in certain situations, even though the agent does possess the capability to accomplish its own action, it may find it more rewarding to find another to perform it. This may occur, if the agent has already agreed to sell its services to another, and it is more rewarding for it to maintain this agreement than to pay another agent to perform its action.

[3] Here a delay slot is inserted in place of *TS1*, and the action β at *TS1* will be scheduled at *TS2*. This process would result in the shift of all subsequent actions by one time slot.

implementation choice made to prevent agents incurring greater penalty charges than their initial allocated reward:

$$\text{Penalty} = \begin{cases} \frac{R_{init}}{T_{init} \times d_{\max}} & \text{if } T_{init} < T_{ext} < (T_{init} \times d_{\max}), \\ 0 & \text{if } (T_{ext} \leq T_{init}) \vee (T_{ext} \geq (T_{init} \times d_{\max})) \end{cases} \qquad (1)$$

where:

- T_{ext} is the extended task duration taken to achieve the task,
- T_{init} is the initial allocated task duration,
- R_{init} is the assigned task reward, and
- $d_{\max}$ is the maximum delay factor, which is a constant for all agents in our case.[4]

If a certain agent (in the above example B) agrees to provide its services to a specific agent (A) for a particular time slot (TS1), B will not be able to agree to provide any other action for TS1, unless it cancels its current agreement with A. For example, if C requests B to perform its action, which requires capability β (refer to Table 1) at TS1, it cannot do so unless it reneges on its current contract with A. Our framework allows agents to *renege upon their agreements* if they perceive a more profitable opportunity.[5] This ability to renege current agreements is important because it promotes opportunities for the agents that seek services later in the scheduling process to achieve agreements if they are willing to pay sufficiently high premiums for these services.

In this scenario, the main objective of the agents is to maximise their individual earnings. There are two methods of doing so. First, they can complete their assigned tasks. Once an agent completes its task, it will receive the allocated reward (less the penalty charges due to delays). This we term the agent's *task earnings* (TE). Second, they can sell their services to other agents (which we term the agent's *service earnings* (SE)). Both components contribute toward the overall *individual earnings* (IE) of the agent.

$$\text{TE} = R_{init} - \sum(\text{Penalty}) - \sum(\text{External Service Payment}) \qquad (2)$$

$$\text{SE} = \sum(\text{External Service Earning}) \qquad (3)$$

$$\text{IE} = \text{TE} + \text{SE}. \qquad (4)$$

Given an overall description of the scenario, we, however, make a number of simplifying assumptions. First, we assume that each agent within the system has complete and accurate knowledge of its own task (i.e., its reward, the actions required, and the sequence in which they need to occur to achieve the task). Thus, during the interaction, the service providers would not be able to give any new information about the task that

---

[4] For example, an agent with a task worth £10,000 spanning 50 time slots, and an $d_{\max}$ set to 4, will incur a penalty of £50 (i.e. $\frac{£10000}{(50 \times 4)}$) per each additional time slot taken to complete the task. If the agent takes more than 200 (i.e. 50×4) slots its reward would be zero, and, thereafter, it will not incur penalties.

[5] At this time, the agents do not incur an extra charge for reneging upon their agreements. As explained in Section 5, we aim to investigate these effects in our future experiments.

the buyer would not already know, or be able to convince the buyers on anything contrary about their task specification. For example, the sellers won't be able to suggest that the actual task is worth less than its initial estimate or be able to recommend different sequences of actions (other than the one specified) to achieve the same task. Second, we assume that the agents are truthful when they communicate information to others, and do not attempt to deceive them into making incorrect decisions. Third, we assume the interactions consist of single encounters, thus, issues such as trust and reputation do not have a material effect within the context.

Even though, all the above are real issues present in multi-agent environments, our motivation for excluding them from the initial experiments is to attain simplicity within the argumentation context. Our desire is to design a context that is simple, yet expressive enough to simulate conflicts and methods of overcoming them (i.e., argue, evade and re-plan as explained in Section 3.2), but not to simulate the most sophisticated simulations of these behaviours. Additionally, excluding these parameters limits the variability present in the system. This allows us to predict more accurate hypotheses about the system, gain a better understanding of the dynamics of the multi-agent interaction, and explain the reasons for the observations with more ease. Given the broad overview of the multi-agent scenario and the assumptions made, we now proceed to explain how interaction within the context leads to conflicts and the three distinct methods used to overcome them.

3.2   Conflicts and Methods of Resolution

The self-interested motivations of our agents give rise to conflicts within the system. Thus, when agents attempt to acquire the services of another, they are motivated to pay the lowest amount they possibly can for that service. This is because the lower an agent's external service payments are, the higher its own TE will be (formula 2). However, on the other hand, when agents sell their services, they are motivated to attain the highest payment they possibly can to maximise their SE (formula 3). Thus, whenever an agent attempts to convince another to provide its services, it naturally gives rise to conflicts of interests between buyer and seller agents within the system.

The dynamics of interaction become more complicated due to the presence of penalty charges and the ability of agents to renege on their present agreements. Since agents are motivated to maximise their TE, they want to avoid penalties (formula 2). However, if a buyer is only willing to offer a very low reward for the service, it is more likely to be rejected, and, in turn, stands a higher chance of incurring a penalty. This motivates the agent to make high rewarding proposals. Secondly, because sellers can renege on their present agreements if they receive more rewarding proposals, agreements made at low values are more likely to be revoked than higher rewarding ones. This may also motivate buyers to make higher rewarding offers to ensure their agreements are more secure. Together these opposing motivations dynamically generate conflicts within the system[6] providing a good context to test the performance of our various methods for overcoming conflicts.

---

[6] Here we consider only one form of conflict; namely conflicts resulting from discrepancies of interests. Conflicts of knowledge due to discrepancies of viewpoints or opinions are not considered in this work.

Following presents the three distinct methods we use to overcome these conflicts:

1. *Argue*: **Use ABN to resolve conflicts**

   When an agent requires a capability from an acquaintance, it generates a *proposal* and forwards it to an agent who has that capability. Once received, the agent evaluates the proposal and decides whether to accept or reject it. The agent will then, communicate its decision, either as an *acceptance* or as a *rejection*, to the original agent. If it decides to accept, the interaction ends in an agreement. However, if the decision is to reject, the onus is transferred back to the original buyer agent to generate and forward an alternative proposal. To help this interaction process, the seller agent, will accompany its rejection with two additional forms of meta-information (arguments) that it will convey back to the original buyer agent:

   - *Reasons for refusal:* This details the reason that prompted the refusal. In our system, seller agents reject due to two types of reasons. First, the agent may be fully committed to a prior arrangement in the requested time slot, so it returns an argument indicating that the reason for failure is unavailability (rather than the offer price being too low). Second, the offer value may not be sufficiently valuable to the agent, in which case it will return an argument accompanied with its rejection indicating the minimal threshold that must be exceeded before the proposal will be considered. The return of such arguments should assist the buyer in its attempt to choose the next proposal to forward. For example, if the reason is unavailability, the buyer would not make an increased value proposal since doing so would be futile. On the other hand, if the threshold is returned as reason for refusal, the buyer can use this to gauge whether to make another proposal to that agent and if it does then value that should be used in such circumstances. These form of arguments are analogues to the types of meta-information exchanged in Jung et al. [7].

   - *Alternative suggestions:* If the seller is willing to work for the suggested value of the offer, but not in the proposed time slot, it will send a number of its neighbouring time slots as alternative suggestions. This meta-information helps the buyer agent in finding agents for those future time slots. For example, assume that in the attempt to find a partner for TS1, agent B indicates to A that it is willing to work for TS2 as an alternative. If agent A requires the same capability for the same price (the price offered when it got the alternative) in TS2, before requesting other random agents, A will first ask B who has already expressed its willingness. Thus, alternatives provide agents with information about their partners' schedules, which they will, in turn, use to selectively choose the order (instead of strictly adhering to a random one) in which they request their partners.

   If any such proposal results in an agreement the argue method is said to have succeeded in its objective. However, if all possible proposals fail to make an agreement the argue process ends in failure.

2. *Evade*: **Find an alternative method to achieve the same plan**

   Unlike the previous method, here the agent does not attempt to use ABN to resolve its conflicts. The agent will only make a single proposal. This is to establish the willingness of the potential partner. If that offer is rejected the agent will not attempt to convince the non-willing partner, but will move on to the next known acquaintance, which has the required capability. However, in this scenario the buyer chooses to offer the maximum price it can in its single proposal. The rationale for this choice is to maximise the chances of success of its single proposal, thus this represents the maximally effective evade strategy. Since the sellers are always motivated to accept higher offers (formula 3), making the highest offer possible maximises the chances of success in its single proposal. If the seller refuses this proposal the evade method fails. On the other hand, if it accepts, then evade method succeeds.

3. *Re-plan*: **Change the original plan**
   When a conflict arises at a particular time slot, the buyer agent simply places a delay slot in its schedule and tries to arrange for the desired capability to be scheduled to the next time slot. This delays the whole sequence of remaining activities, thus, will extend the task's overall duration by one time slot. While the argue and evade methods remain the main methods in our strategies, re-plan represents the fall back option (refer to Section 3.3). Thus, re-planning through delays (since theoretically an agent can delay forever) will always ensure success in overcoming any specific conflict. However, delays may cause subsequent conflict situations to arise and will render the task less rewarding via penalties.

3.3   Conflict Resolution Strategies

In this section, we presents six different strategies for conflict resolution which differ in terms of the way they order the argue, evade and re-plan methods. These strategies are defined to give a range of different behaviours in resolving conflicts in a multi-agent context. However, they are neither meant to be the most optimal, nor an exhaustive list. Rather their designed purpose is to allow us to perform a comparative analysis of the relative performance of arguing versus evasion in conflict resolution.

- *Evade_1:* Randomly select one agent. *Evade* with that agent. If fail, re-plan.
- *Argue_1:* Randomly select one agent. *Argue* with that agent. If fail, re-plan.
- *Always_Evade:* Randomly select one agent at a time and *evade*. Continue *evade* till either an agent agrees or the last agent is reached. If fail with last agent, re-plan.
- *Evade_Finally_Argue:* Similar to *Always_Evade*, thus, continue to *evade* till penultimate agent. However, with the *last* agent *argue*. If fail with the last agent, re-plan.
- *Argue_First_then_Evade:* Similar to *Always_Evade*, but *argue* with the *first* agent. If fail with this agent continue *evade* till either an agent agrees or last agent is reached. If fail with last agent, re-plan.
- *Always_Argue:* Similar to *Always_Evade*, but in *all* encounters *argue* till either an agent agrees or the last agent is reached. If fail with last agent, re-plan.

From the above, *Evade_1* and *Argue_1* only allow the agents to interact with a single partner. Strategies *Always_Evade* and *Always_Argue* allow agents to interact with all potential partners (one at a time). However, they only allow the agents a single method to resolve conflicts (either evade or argue), thus are termed pure strategies. In contrast, *Evade_Finally_Argue* and *Argue_First_then_Evade* are hybrid strategies that selectively use argumentation with evasion; the former gives priority to evasion, while the later gives priority to argumentation. Having introduced our argumentation context, we now turn to our empirical evaluation.

4   Experimental Evaluation

The aim of these experiments is to evaluate the overall effectiveness and efficiency of using a simple ABN, as opposed to evasion and/or re-planning, to overcome conflicts in our chosen scenario. In particular, we simulate a multi-agent context (as per Section 3.1) and endow the agents with different resolution strategies (as per Section 3.3). The observed overall performance of the society is measured and used to carry out a comparative analysis between these strategies.

4.1   Experimental Setting

The experiments are set within a society of 75 agents, each having one out of three capabilities (α, β or γ). These capabilities are equally distributed within the society with 25 agents per capability. All agents are assigned a single task spanning 50 time slots. Each time slot contains a single action that requires a single capability. These actions are randomly distributed within a task. The initial rewards for the tasks are set according to a normal distribution with a mean £10,000 and a standard deviation of £2,500. The d_{max} parameter (formula 1) for the penalty charge is set to 4 (based on initial experiments).

In each experiment, the society differs in terms of its resource settings (RS). In the maximum resource setting (RS_{25}), each agent knows about all the other agents, hence it has maximum access to the resources within the system. On the other hand, in the most constrained setting (RS_1), each agent is only aware of the existence of a single (randomly selected) agent per capability. In between we define a series of 12 intermediate settings, where each agent is aware of the existence of 2, 4, ..., 24 (referred to as RS_2, RS_4 etc.) other agents per capability. Thus, for example, at RS_4, each agent is aware of the existence of 4 other agents with capability α, 4 with β and 4 with γ. We use the following metrics to evaluate the overall performance of the different strategies [7, 10]:

- **Effectiveness of the Strategy**
  We use the *total accumulated penalty* incurred by all agents within the society as a measure of effectiveness. If this value is low, the strategy has been effective in handling the conflicts that have arisen.

- **Efficiency of the Strategy**
  This reflects the computational cost of interaction incurred by the society, while using a particular strategy to resolve conflicts. As interaction takes longer, more resources are consumed by the agents. On the other hand, these longer interactions also increase the number of messages. Thus, the *total number of messages* provides us a good method to measure computational resources used by the agents during interaction. This covers the messages used to overcome conflicts and reach agreements (including reasons and alternatives exchanged as meta-information), and the messages associated with reneging from agreements. In this context, a strategy that

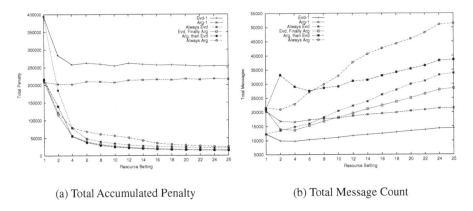

(a) Total Accumulated Penalty   (b) Total Message Count

Fig. 1. Variation of Total Penalty and Total Messages with different resource settings

involves fewer messages is said to have performed more efficiently than one that uses a higher number.

4.2   Results and Observations

Given these experimental settings, we can now turn to the actual results. Here all reported results are averaged over 50 simulation runs to diminish the impact of random noise, and all observations emphasised are statistically significant at the 99% confidence level.

Observation 1: *In highly resource constrained settings, argumentation significantly enhances the overall effectiveness of the society.*

In Figure 1(a), we observe that at highly resource constrained levels (i.e., RS_1 and RS_2), the strategies that use argumentation to resolve conflicts (namely *Argue_1*, *Evade_Finally_Argue*, *Argue_First_then_Evade* and *Always_Argue*) incur a significantly lower penalty charge than those that merely evade (i.e., *Evade_1* and *Always_Evade*). The impact is most apparent in RS_1, where the resources are most constrained. The difference is approximately of a magnitude of 1.84 (i.e., *Evade_1* and *Always_Evade* have an average penalty of £394,250, whereas *Argue_1*, *Evade_Finally_Argue*, *Argue_First_-then_Evade* and *Always_Argue* have an average of £213,487). Although slightly reduced, this effect is also observable in RS_2 approximately a magnitude of 1.41 between *Evade_1* and *Argue_1*, and 1.47 between *Always_Evade* and *Evade_Finally_Argue*, *Argue_First_then_Evade* and *Always_Argue*. In such scarce resource settings, the number of alternative solutions available to the agent to overcome conflicts is highly constrained. Due to the absence of such alternatives, the evasion techniques (*Evade_1* and *Always_Evade*), tend to fail more as they evade conflicts in search of the non-existent alternatives and thereby incur higher penalties. On the other hand, strategies that attempt to resolve the conflicts through ABN tend to form more agreements and, thus, incur fewer penalty charges.

Further support for this observation can be drawn by comparing the behaviour of strategies *Evade_1* and *Argue_1* over all resource settings. Both of these strategies attempt to overcome conflicts by interacting with a single randomly chosen partner. Although from the outset this does not appear to be a very prudent strategy (constraining oneself to a single partner when there are more potential partners available) these agents were specifically designed to experiment with the relative impact of using argumentation in resource-constrained settings. To this end, Figure 1(a) shows how *Argue_1* continuously incurs low penalties than *Evade_1*. Since these strategies constrain the agents to interact with just a single partner, irrespective of how much resources are available to them, the agents still operate in limited resource settings. Thus, the alternatives available to them are limited. These observations further justify our conclusion that using ABN to resolve conflicts tends to be a more effective method than evasion in resource-constrained settings. This finding is also consistent with the experimental results observed by Kraus et al. [5], where they presented the benefits of the *Always_Argue* strategy in a two agent setting.

Observation 2: *As resource levels increase, both the argue and evade methods become more effective, but the relative difference between them decreases.*

Figure 1(a) also shows that the penalty charges for the strategies *Always_Evade*, *Evade_Finally_Argue*, *Argue_First_then_Evade* and *Always_Argue* reduce as resource levels increase. This effect is seen more clearly in Figure 2(a), which presents a magnified view of the penalty variation for these four strategies. The primary reason for these reductions is the increase in resource level. Thus, as resources increase, so does the potential to find an alternative agreeable partner. Thus, a higher number of conflicts can be overcome, which, in turn, reduces the delay. The net result being a reduction in penalty charges for all strategies.

Arguably, a more interesting observation is the differences in the rate of penalty reduction for the strategies that use argumentation and the ones that use evasion. Specifically, the penalty charge of *Always_Evade* decreases more rapidly than *Always_Argue*. Figure 2(a) shows *Always_Evade* surpassing *Always_Argue* between RS_4 and RS_6 and thereafter maintaining its performance. The reason for this difference is as follows. As the potential alternatives increase within the society, the need to convince a non-willing partner decreases. Arguing strategies, which attempt to convince their non-willing partners before attempting to search for these alternatives, do not use these options to the same degree as evasion strategies do, which explains the observable differences in the rate reduction between *Always_Evade* and *Always_Argue*. Furthermore, Figure 1(b) shows evasion strategies using a lower number of messages than arguing ones. This is because unlike evasion strategies, arguing strategies in their attempt to convince non-willing partners tend to use more messages in their interaction. Thus, even when both arguing and evasion strategies are equally effective, evasion strategies tend to be more efficient. This observation allows us to conclude that as resources become more abundant, evasion increasingly becomes the more preferable option.

Observation 3: *Using argumentation indiscriminately has an negative impact on the systems' overall effectiveness.*

Figure 2(a) also allows us to compare the performance of strategy *Always_Argue* versus *Evade_Finally_Argue* and *Argue_First_then_Evade*. Unlike the selective argumentation used by *Evade_Finally_Argue* and *Argue_First_then_Evade*, *Always_Argue* indis-

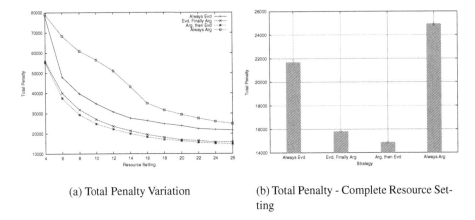

(a) Total Penalty Variation   (b) Total Penalty - Complete Resource Setting

Fig. 2. Magnified Penalty Variations for the high resource settings

Table 2. Summarised Penalty Charges and the Message Counts for the complete resource setting

Strategy	Total Messages		Total Penalty ($£$)	
	Mean	Std Div	Mean	Std Div
Evade_1	14397.7	142.95	254634.0	9113.30
Argue_1	21473.4	274.07	216523.0	7913.68
Always Evade	33836.8	1347.78	21688.5	1452.01
Evade, finally Argue	28500.3	361.04	15800.8	439.64
First Argue, then Evade	38607.7	578.20	14873.9	445.52
Always Argue	51425.3	1188.25	24918.7	866.41

criminately argues in all interactions. However, in both Figures 2(a) and 2(b) it can be seen that *Always_Argue* incurs a higher penalty value than those strategies that selectively argue.

To help us analyse the reasons for this effect, Figure 3 presents the number of conflicts for all six strategies in RS_{25}. These conflicts are divided into two sections; namely, the primary conflicts that arise when the agents first attempt to find partners and the secondary conflicts that arise due to agents reneging upon their agreements. It can be observed that the strategies *Always_Evade*, *Evade_Finally_Argue*, *Argue_First_then_Evade* and *Always_Argue* incur approximately the same number of primary conflicts. However, the strategies *Evade_Finally_Argue* and *Argue_First_then_Evade*, which give priority to the argue method, incur a significantly higher number of secondary conflicts. The reason being when agents argue to form agreements, they manage to convince the sellers to make lower price agreements. However, another arguing agent can potentially come forward and, using ABN, negotiate a higher valued contract, which breaks the previous agreement. On the other hand, when agents evade, as they tend to offer the maximum possible reward, they formulate agreements that are difficult to break.

Given the reasons for the discrepancy in the number of conflicts, we proceed to explain the negative impact of indiscriminate argumentation. The differences in the

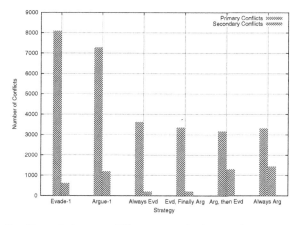

Fig. 3. Conflict variation over different strategies in complete resource setting

number of conflicts allow us to explain the difference between *Evade_Finally_Argue* and *Always_Argue*. Specifically, Figure 3 shows a lower number of conflicts arise within the society when using *Evade_Finally_Argue*, which, in turn, results in a lower number of delays (i.e., on average 521 delays were caused by 3545 conflicts with *Evade_Finally-_Argue*, as opposed to 720 delays caused due to 4731 conflicts with *Always_Argue*). Even though *Argue_First_then_Evade* caused only a small number of conflicts fewer than *Always_Argue* (4442 conflicts as opposed to 4731), most of them got resolved (only 508 (11.5%) delays occurred with *Argue_First_then_Evade* as compared to 720 (15.2%) delays with *Always_Argue*). This leads us to conclude that the ABN in combination with evasion is a more effective strategy than indiscriminate argumentation.

Observation 4: *Using argumentation as the last resort tends to produce a higher overall performance.*

Figures 2(a) and 2(b) show a small difference in penalty between strategies *Evade-_Finally_Argue* and *Argue_First_then_Evade* (£15,800.8 as opposed to £14,873.9 as per Table 2). However, Figure 1(b) shows the difference between the number of messages used to achieve this outcome as significantly higher between *Evade_Finally_Argue* and *Argue_First_then_Evade* (i.e., the difference is of a magnitude of 1.35 times; 28,500.3 message units for *Evade_Finally_Argue* versus 38,607.7 for *Argue_First_then_Evade*). The reason for this large difference is that when the agents use *Argue_First_then_Evade*, they always argue with the first agent. In some instances, this argumentation may not yield any agreement. However, since it has already argued with that agent, its message count has already increased. On the other hand, when using *Evade_Finally_Argue*, the agent will attempt to argue only if it gets to the very last encounter. Thus, in many cases, it resolves the conflict before it gets to the last agent. Another observation worth noting is the differences in the number of messages used by *Always_Evade* and *Evade_Finally_Argue*. The former uses more messages than the latter (Table 2 shows that *Always_Evade* use an average 33,836.8 messages, as opposed to *Evade_Finally-_Argue* which uses only 28,500.3). Therefore, this shows that selective argumentation not only improves the effectiveness, but also efficiency of the system. Thus, when both efficiency and effec-

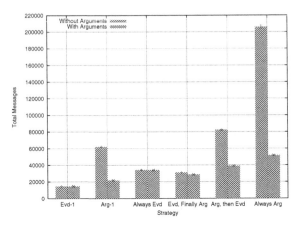

Fig. 4. Total Messages - Complete Resource Setting: both with and without Meta-Information

tiveness are taken together we can conclude that evading first and arguing as the last resort tends to be the most preferable option among these strategies.

Observation 5: *Exchange of meta-information, such as reasons and alternatives, allow agents to resolve their conflicts more efficiently than using a simple negotiation approach without such an exchange.*

Finally, we observe the impact of exchanging meta-information within the negotiation process. To this end, Figure 4 presents the total number of messages used by the society in the complete resource setting (RS_{25}), both when negotiation involves the exchange of meta-information and when it does not. When negotiating without exchanging meta-information, the seller agents do not incorporate reasons and alternatives when they respond to proposals, whereas when they do incorporate them, they argue in the way we have described throughout this paper (refer to Section 3.2). In Figure 4, it is clearly observable that incorporating meta-information into the interaction process allows the agents to reduce the number of messages used to resolve their conflicts. This is most apparent in the *Argue-1* and *Always_Argue* strategies, which predominantly use the argue method to resolve conflicts. The improvement is also present to a lesser degree in *Argue_First_then_Evade*, which gives priority to argue, but only marginally present in *Evade_Finally_Argue* strategy that argues only in the last encounter. The reason for this reduction is due to buyer agents using the additional information provided by the sellers in their proposal selection and partner selection techniques. Specifically, as explained in Section 3.2, when agents receive reasons, either as an *unavailable* message or as *recommended prices*, they, in turn, use this information to decide on their next proposal. On the other hand, alternative suggested by the sellers are used to select the order of contacting potential partners in future interactions. Both of these uses help to reduce the number of unnecessary proposals exchanged within the society so they increase the efficiency of the argue method. This finding is consistent with the experimental results observed by Jung et al. [7], which presents the positive contribution of incorporating meta-information on the negotiation effort. The ability to consistently replicate their observations within our domain, adds further support to our formulated argumentation context.

5   Conclusions and Future Work

ABN has been proposed as a promising means for agents to resolve conflicts in multi-agent systems. However, in many cases, not all conflicts need to be resolved; some can be overcome through evasion or re-planning. In such a context, it is important for the agents to identify the specific situations where arguing is beneficial and those in which it is not. To this end, this paper presented a preliminary empirical evaluation and assessed the efficiency and effectiveness of argumentation as a conflict resolution mechanism with respect to evasion in our particular domain.

Our results can be summarised as three main points. *First*, the relative variation of effectiveness of the methods is very much related to the resources available in the system. The chosen ABN presents a far more effective method of conflict resolution than evasion when the resources are more constrained. However, this effect tends to diminish as resources become more abundant. Furthermore, it is shown that attempting to always argue in high resource settings yields an inferior outcome (both in terms of efficiency and effectiveness) than always using evasion. *Second*, we show that selective use of argumentation is a far more effective and efficient strategy than indiscriminate argumentation. *Finally*, we show the strategy of evading first and arguing as the last resort tends to yield the most favourable overall performance among these strategies. However, this final point needs further investigation to see whether this is an artefact of our domain or is something that is more generally true. Obviously all these results are couched in the context of our particular domain and further investigation is needed to see whether they generalise.

In addition to the generalisation aspect, there are a number of different ways in which the experiments themselves can be extended. To date, our agents only use a handful of simple arguments (reasons and alternatives). It would be interesting to observe the overall effect of incorporating more persuasive forms of locutions such as appeals, threats and promises [5]. Second, in our experiments we maintained the level of commitment for all agreements at zero. This allowed agents to renege without suffering a loss. As a next step we plan to implement the concept of charging a decommitment penalty [16] and observe its impact on the performance of the strategies. Third, in the current implementation, the society has no structure and all agents operate within a peer-to-peer environment. In future developments, we plan to incorporate a social structure governed by roles and relationships [17] within agents and observe its impact on the relative effectiveness of the strategies.

Acknowledgements

This research is funded by the EPSRC project Information Exchange (GR/S03706/01). We thank Chris Reed, Tim Norman, Sarvapali Ramchurn and Partha Dutta for their thoughts, contributions and discussions. We specially thank the two anonymous reviewers for their valuable comments and suggestions, and also express our gratitude to AOS Ltd. for their JACK agent framework and support.

References

1. Tessier, C., Chaudron, L., Müller, H.J., eds.: Agents' Conflicts: New Issues. In: Conflicting Agents Conflict Management in Multi-Agent Systems. Kluwer Academic Publishers, Dordrecht, Netherlands (2000) 1–30
2. Castelfranchi, C.: Conflict Ontology. In: Computational Conflicts, Conflict Modeling for Distributed Intelligent Systems. Springer (2000) 21–40
3. Walton, D.N., Krabbe, E.C.: Dialgoues: Types, Goals, and Shifts. In: Commitment in Dialogue: Basic Concepts of Interpersonal Reasoning. State Univ of New York Press, Albany, NY, USA (1995) 65–117
4. Rahwan, I., Ramchurn, S.D., Jennings, N.R., McBurney, P., Parsons, S., Sonenberg, L.: Argumentation-based negotiation. The Knowledge Engineering Review **18** (2004)
5. Kraus, S., Sycara, K., Evenchik, A.: Reaching agreements through argumentation. Artificial Intelligence **104** (1998) 1–69
6. Sycara, K.: Persuasive argumentation in negotiation. Theory and Decision **28** (1990) 203–242
7. Jung, H., Tambe, M., Kulkarni, S.: Argumentation as distributed constraint satisfaction: Applications and results. In: Proceedings of the Fifth International Conference on Autonomous Agents (Agents'01), Montreal, Canada, ACM Press (2001) 324–331
8. Rahwan, I., Sonenberg, L., Dignum, F.: Towards interest-based negotiation. In Rosenschein, J.S., Sandholm, T., Wooldridge, M., Yokoo, M., eds.: Proceedings of the 2nd International Joint Conference on Autonomas Agents and Multi-Agent Systems (AAMAS'03), Melbourne, Australia (2003) 773–780
9. Reed, C., Long, D., Fox, M., Garagnani, M.: Persuasion as a form of inter-agent negotiation. In: Selected Papers of the 2nd Australian Workshop on Distributed Artificial Intelligence (DAI'96), Cairns, Australia, Springer-Verlag (1996) 120–136
10. Ramchurn, S.D., Jennings, N.R., Sierra, C.: Persuasive negotiation for autonomous agents: A rhetorical approach. In: IJCAI Workshop on Computational Models of Natural Argument, Acapulco, Mexico (2003) 9–18
11. Amgoud, L., Maudet, N.: Strategical considerations for argumentative agents (preliminary report). In: Proceedings of the 9th International Workshop on Non-Monotonic Reasoning (NMR'02): Special session on Argument, dialogue, decision, Toulouse, France (2002) 399–407
12. Parsons, S., Sierra, C., Jennings, N.R.: Agents that reason and negotiate by arguing. Journal of Logic and Computation **8** (1998) 261–292
13. Sierra, C., Jennings, N.R., Noriega, P., Parsons, S.: A framework for argumentation-based negotiation. In Singh, M.P., Rao, A., Wooldridge, M.J., eds.: Proceedings of Fourth International Workshop on Agent Theories Architectures and Languages (ATAL'97). Volume 1365 of Lecture Notes in Computer Science., Springer-Verlag (1998) 177–192
14. McBurney, P., van Eijk, R., Parsons, S., Amgoud, L.: A dialogue-game protocol for agent purchase negotiations. Autonomous Agents and Multi-Agent Systems **7** (2003) 235–273
15. Yokoo, M., Hirayama, K.: Distributed constraint satisfaction algorithm for complex local problems. In: Proceedings of the Third International Conference on Multiagent Systems (ICMAS'98), Paris, France (1998) 372–379
16. Sandholm, T.W., Lesser, V.R.: Advantages of a leveled commitment contracting protocol. In: Proceedings of the Thirteenth National Conference on Artificial Intelligence (AAAI'96), Portland, OR, USA (1996) 126–133
17. Panzarasa, P., Jennings, N.R., Norman, T.: Social mental shaping: Modelling the impact of sociality on the mental states of autonomous agents. Computational Intelligence **17** (2001) 738–782

When Is It Okay to Lie? A Simple Model of Contradiction in Agent-Based Dialogues

Elizabeth Sklar[1], Simon Parsons[2], and Mathew Davies[1]

[1] Dept of Computer Science, Columbia University,
1214 Amsterdam Avenue, Mailcode 0401,
New York, NY 10027, USA
{sklar, mdavies}@cs.columbia.edu
[2] Department of Computer and Information Science, Brooklyn College,
City University of New York, 2900 Bedford Avenue, Brooklyn,
New York, NY 11210, USA
parsons@sci.brooklyn.cuny.edu

Abstract. When is it okay to lie? And what constitutes a lie, anyway? This paper examines the notion of lying in agent-based systems, focusing on dialogues and situations where it is acceptable for agents to utter locutions that contradict their beliefs. We examine situations in human and animal behavior where lying — acting or making statements that contradict one's set of beliefs — is considered to be socially acceptable or even necessary for survival.

1 Introduction

When is it okay to lie? And what constitutes a lie, anyway? This paper examines the notion of lying in agent-based systems, focusing on dialogues and situations where it is acceptable for agents to utter locutions that contradict their beliefs. We examine situations in human and animal behavior where lying — acting or making statements that contradict one's set of beliefs — is considered to be socially acceptable or even necessary for survival.

Consider the following examples:

- a teacher presents a contradictory example to her students in order to motivate them to think about and explain the contradiction
- a parent uses "reverse psychology" to convince his child to finish eating her vegetables
- an opossum pretends that it is dead so that a predator will not attack it
- a wife tells a "white lie" in order to hide from her husband her plans for giving him a surprise birthday party
- a buyer in an art auction hides his "private value" so that he can make bids that are lower than he would truthfully be willing to pay
- a chameleon changes its color as a camouflage mechanism

In each of these situations, one actor is lying but with good reason. Webster defines the verb "lie" as follows: "to make an untrue statement with intent to

I. Rahwan et al. (Eds.): ArgMAS 2004, LNAI 3366, pp. 251–261, 2005.

deceive; to create a false or misleading impression" [1]. The level or purpose of the deception is what makes these types of untruths socially acceptable.

We have been examining the use of *dialogues* as interaction mechanisms in agent-based systems. In earlier work of Parsons and colleagues [9, 10], the semantics of the dialogue framework restrict an agent from uttering locutions that contradict its belief set. The reason for this restriction is as follows. Following Singh [11], we wish to provide agents using our dialogue framework with a form of *social semantics* in which other agents can contest any assertion, and refuse to accept it until it has been proven truthful to their satisfaction. The simplest way to achieve this is to restrict agents to only assert things that are, as far as they know, true. In this paper we develop the notion that, as illustrated above, there exist socially acceptable, rational situations in which it may be necessary for agents to contradict their own beliefs in a dialogue. As we shall see, doing this while maintaining the social semantics is considerably trickier than when agents have to tell the truth.

We begin by reviewing previous work on dialogues, highlighting terminology and describing the theoretical framework in which we are working. Next, we present a structure for expanding this dialogue framework in order to be able to model contradiction. Then we outline some examples of how we might apply this contradictory behavior to two of the domains we are actively modelling: classroom management in an education setting and negotiation in a car market.

2   Background

A *dialogue game* is structured in terms of *moves* made by two players. An influential model devised by Walton and Krabbe [15] defines six basic types of argumentation that can be combined to create complex dialogues:

- *Information-Seeking Dialogues* — where one participant seeks the answer to some question(s) from another participant, who is believed by the first to know the answer(s);
- *Inquiry Dialogues* — where the participants collaborate to answer some question or questions whose answers are not known to any participant;
- *Persuasion Dialogues* — where one party seeks to persuade another party to adopt a belief or point-of-view he or she does not currently hold;
- *Negotiation Dialogues* — where the participants bargain over the division of some scarce resource in a way acceptable to all, with each individual party aiming to maximize his or her share;
- *Deliberation Dialogues* — where participants collaborate to decide what course of action to take in some situation. Participants share a responsibility to decide the course of action, and either share a common set of intentions or a willingness to discuss rationally whether they have shared intentions;
- *Eristic Dialogues* — where participants quarrel verbally as a substitute for physical fighting, with each aiming to win the exchange.

Walton and Krabbe do not claim that these are the only possible kinds of dialogue, and indeed others have introduced additional types. Girle [4] discusses a *command dialogue* in which one agent tells another what to do. McBurney [5] presents *chance discovery dialogue* where two agents arrive at an idea that neither one had prior to the exchange; instead, the idea arises from or is realized by the agents' discussion. Gabbay and Woods [3] have analysed *non-cooperation* dialogues in which the participants, who may be hostile to one another, do not share the goal of necessarily completing the dialogue. Sklar and Parsons [13] have described *education dialogues* where two types of agents, tutor and learner, interact with the goal of the learner to acquire knowledge about a particular subject and the goal of the tutor to acquire "meta-knowledge" about what the learner knows.

Within these types of dialogues, in particular *information seeking, inquiry* and *negotiation,* Parsons and colleagues have defined six locutions [9, 10, 13]:

- *assert*(p) — This locution is used in any dialogue where the agent making the assertion has knowledge of the proposal p from its belief set and wants the other agent to accept it.
- *accept*(p) — This locution is uttered in response to an assertion and indicates that the agent making proposition p is deciding to agree with the assertion.
- *question*(p) — An agent that does not know whether p is true or not uses *question* to request this information from another agent.
- *challenge*(p) — This is when an agent is unsure of proposition p and so questions the agent who uttered it; it is a way of forcing the utterer to reveal their arguments in support of the proposition. An agent has to respond to this by stating its reasons for having asserted p.
- *quiz*(p) — This type of locution belongs to the class of *education dialogues*; a tutor asks a question (p) of the learner, but the tutor already knows the answer to the question and is interested in determining whether or not the learner knows the answer.
- *answer*(p) — This locution also belongs to *education dialogues* and is used by a learner in response to a quiz.

Associated with each of these locutions is a set of rules or *axiomatic semantics* [14] which describe the pre-conditions under which an agent may utter a locution and the post-conditions or changes in the agent's belief state that occur as a result of the utterance.

We follow the notational conventions developed previously (see [10] or [8]) and highlight the elements pertinent to the work discussed herein:

- Σ_i represents the *knowledge base*, or beliefs, of each agent i. If the dialogue takes place between two agents M (me) and U (you), then their corresponding knowledge bases are referred to as Σ_M and Σ_U, respectively. This term loosely refers to all the beliefs of an agent.
- An argument (S, p) is a pair, where p is a conclusive proposition and S is its support. p is a logical consequence of S, and S is a minimal subset of Σ_i from which it can be inferred.
- $\mathcal{A}(\Sigma)$ is the set of all arguments that can be made from Σ.

Table 1. Axiomatic semantics for *assert*, uttered by M as the ith locution of a dialogue

---

assert

LOCUTION:

- $M \rightarrow U : assert(p)$

PRE-CONDITIONS:

1. $(S, p) \in \underline{S}(\Sigma_M \cup CS_U)$

POST-CONDITIONS:

1. $CS_{M,i} = CS_{M,i-1} \cup \{p\}$ (update)
2. $CS_{U,i} = CS_{U,i-1}$ (no change)

- $\underline{S}(\Sigma)$ is the set of all *acceptable* arguments in Σ — that is, arguments that an agent has no reason to doubt (i.e., there are either no arguments that *undercut* them, or all the arguments that undercut them are themselves undercut).
- We can partition an agent's belief set Σ by identifying relevant portions of it. The agent's *commitment store* (CS) refers to statements that have been made in the dialogue and which the agents are prepared to defend. We think of Σ as the agent's private knowledge base — all of the agent's beliefs — whereas CS is the agent's public knowledge base — all the beliefs that the agent has discussed in public (i.e., with other agents), and hence are known to the other agents.

[10] shows how these simple elements can be used to construct information-seeking, inquiry, and persuasion dialogues.

Table 1 shows the axiomatic semantics associated with the locution **assert**. In order for agent M to be able to assert a proposal, p, agent M has to either:

1. have direct knowledge about that assertion in its set of beliefs;
2. contain an argument that will support the assertion in its set of beliefs; or
3. contain an argument that will support the assertion either in its set of beliefs or in the set of utterances made by the other agent(s) involved in the dialogue.

We summarize these three conditions as

$$(S, p) \in \underline{S}(\Sigma_M \cup CS_U)$$

meaning that M can assert a proposition if there is an argument to support it in its belief set or in the commitment store of agent U, the other agent engaged in the dialogue.

There is an additional precondition, which refines the three conditions given above, and is not stated in Tab 1 since it varies depending on the agent's *attitude*

[10]. The idea of attitude captures the fact that different agents may be more or less strict about the things it asserts. In particular in [10], an agent may adopt one of three *assertion* attitudes. If agent M is engaged in a dialogue with agent U, then:

- if M is *confident*, then it can assert any proposition p for which $(S, p) \in \mathcal{A}(\Sigma_M, CS_U)$
- if M is *careful*, then it can assert any proposition p for which there is an argument (S, p) and no stronger argument $(S, \neg p)$ exists in $\mathcal{A}(\Sigma_M, CS_U)$
- if M is *thoughtful*, then it can assert any proposition p for which there is an *acceptable* argument $(S, p) \in \mathcal{A}(\Sigma_M, CS_U)$

These constraints were designed under the assumption that uttering a false proposal, or at least one that cannot be backed up in some way — is considered to be socially unacceptable and ruled out by the social semantics. However, as indicated by the examples in the opening paragraphs of this paper, there are nontrivial circumstances in which an agent may need to utter locutions which contradict its beliefs. How, then, can we allow our agents to lie when they need to, without sacrificing the social semantics? The next section explains how this may be done.

3   Contradiction in Dialogues

While the dialogue game can serve as the mechanism for a wide variety of interactions among agents, the axiomatic semantics of **assert** within a dialogue do not permit an agent M to make an assertion that contradicts its own beliefs, which we define as a *lie*, or a false proposal. To assert a truth p, an agent M must have an *acceptable* argument for (S, p). Given the semantics of argumentation, as described in [10] for example, this implies two things[1]. The first is that M has no argument $(S', \neg p)$ that is as strong as the argument for p. The second is that there is no $r \in S$ such that M believes $\neg r$ more strongly than r.

More formally, we mean that an assertion q ($\neg p$ above) is a *direct lie* if M knows of a stronger argument supporting $\neg q$ (p) in $\underline{S}(\Sigma_M \cup CS_U)$. A direct lie, then, is the assertion of a fact that is believed to be false. This is a violation of the first condition on assertion. We can also distinguish an *indirect lie*, where M asserts some q for which it has an argument (S'', q) even though there is some $r \in S''$ which M believes less strongly than $\neg r$. M is therefore asserting something that it does not believe to be supported by what it believes to be true. This is a violation of the second condition of assertion. (A particular assertion can be both a direct and an indirect lie, as when $\neg q \in \Sigma_M$ but M asserts q anyway.) For the remainder of this paper we will only consider direct lies, but a

---

[1] The precise formal distinction is a little more subtle than this, but without introducing the dialogue system in its full detail — which we do not have room to do here — we have to skate over this subtlety. Suffice it to say that it makes no difference to the validity of the argument we are making here.

similar analysis can be carried out for indirect lies (which will require a direct lie if the indirect lie is challenged).

So then, how can M assert a direct lie q, since by definition the agent can find no argument in Σ_M or CS_U supporting q that wins out over the counterargument? Our solution to this problem is to construct a set of false beliefs, which we call J, that an agent can use as the logical basis for *justification* of q, when $\neg q$ is supported by Σ_M and/or CS_U. Using the same conventions for notation, we define J_M informally as the set of all beliefs t_i, such that M asserts q where:

- $(S', \neg q) \in \underline{S}(\Sigma_M \cup CS_U)$, and
- $(S'', q) \in \underline{S}(\Sigma_M \cup CS_U \cup (\bigcup_i \{t_i\}))$.

In other words J_M is exactly that set of propositions necessary to justify the lies that M has told. Note that this includes the case in which some $t_i = q$, that is M doesn't try to construct a reason why q is the case, but just claims it is true — a barefaced lie. The agent M does not *believe* the proposals in J_M, but in effect holds them for use in passing off the lie, as if they were genuine beliefs in Σ_M.

This, then, provides a way of maintaining the social semantics. If and when another agent questions the lie, M can respond with the argument that draws on J_M. This is not guaranteed to be convincing. Depending on how obvious the falsehoods are, the other agent may be able to spot them easily. However, if M chooses its justifications well, then it may be able to remain undetected. This is, of course, exactly the way that lying works in human society. A lie remains undetected so long as the party that is being lied to has no way to uncover the falsehood on which the lie is based.

Allowing contradiction thus requires a modification of the original semantics of **assert** given in Tab 1. In order for an agent M to utter q as a lie, two pre-conditions must hold:

- support for an acceptable argument for q exists in its justification set J, taken together with the set of utterances made by the other agent(s) involved in the dialogue (i.e., $(S, q) \in \underline{S}(\Sigma_M \cup CS_U \cup J_M)$, and
- support for an acceptable argument for $\neg q$ exists either in its set of beliefs or in the set of utterances made by the other agent(s) involved in the dialogue (i.e., $(S, \neg q) \in \underline{S}(\Sigma_M \cup CS_U)$).

The first condition states that q can be asserted as a contradiction, and the second condition states that q cannot be asserted as a truth. Taken together, these conditions imply that $(S, q) \notin \underline{S}(\Sigma_M \cup CS_U)$; in other words, the existence of J as a non-empty set is instrumental to the assertion of q.

Now that we have defined a way of justifying a lie within our dialogue framework, we need a way of being able to express that lie. We note that we cannot simply create a new locution **lie(p)** because, by definition of our dialogue framework, the type of locution being uttered is actually *included in the utterance*. So for an agent to say **lie(p)**, it would be revealing the fact that it is lying.

In order to get around this, we introduce the notion of a *contradictory* attitude in which the pre-conditions of an assertion are modified in order to allow

Table 2. Axiomatic semantics for *assert*, contradictory, uttered by M as the ith locution of a dialogue

---

contradictory **assert**

LOCUTION:

- $M \rightarrow U : assert(p)$

PRE-CONDITIONS:

1. $(S, \neg p) \in \underline{S}(\Sigma_M \cup CS_U)$ AND
   $(S, p) \in \underline{S}(\Sigma_M \cup CS_U \cup J_M)$

POST-CONDITIONS:

1. $CS_{M,i} = CS_{M,i-1} \cup p$ (update)
2. $CS_{U,i} = CS_{U,i-1}$ (no change)

---

an agent to utter a proposition that opposes its belief set. A contradictory attitude may also be, at the same time, confident, careful, or thoughtful, as defined earlier (but considering the set of possible arguments whose support includes J.) The full axiomatic semantics of contradictory assertion are contained in Tab 2. Again the additional "attitude" condition applies.

4   Carrying Off a Lie

To knowingly assert even a single falsehood may entail some difficulty for an agent, at least if the agent intends that the lie remain undiscovered. First, if the lie is challenged, the agent may have to assert other contradictions (possibly members of J), which may in turn require commitment to even more false assertions, resulting in a potential cascade of false commitments — with no guarantee that the original lie q will even be accepted. Second, even if the lie is accepted, with or without challenge, it may turn out to contradict other (possibly true) proposals the agent may wish to assert in the future. Third, agent M may wish to maintain consistency with regard to lies uttered in dialogues with particular agents, but may not want to carry the lies into dialogues with *all* agents. In any of these cases, uttering lies is problematic, because each lie potentially impacts the present and future consistency of the agent's commitment store.

As a method for addressing these issues, we put forth the notion that each lie, q, has a lifetime. Figuratively speaking, the lie is born when it is first uttered; and the lie dies when the agent who uttered the lie retracts it. We can think of this as adding and subtracting elements from J. When all lies have been retracted, J is the empty set. As soon as an agent utters a single lie, it is inserted into J.

Further, we introduce the notion of "personalized" Js, whereby agent M maintains a separate set $J_{M,j}$ which contains all the lies that M told to agent j

(that have not been retracted). $J_{M,j}$ could be thought of as a partition of J_M. There could be multiple partitions within J_M. For example, suppose that M engages in separate dialogues with agents U, V and W. We will assume here that each dialogue is private, i.e., V and W do not "hear" what is said between M and U, and so forth. In talking to U, any true statement p that is uttered by M is just part of Σ_M or CS_U; just as in talking to V, any true statement r that is uttered by M is part of Σ_M or CS_V. But if M tells a lie, q, in a dialogue with U, and then tells another lie, s, in a dialogue with V, it is important that M not assume knowledge of s when talking to U nor of r when talking to V. The crucial aspect is that M remember which lies it told to which agents; so in our example, $q \in J_{M,U}$ and $s \in J_{M,V}$, and $q \notin J_{M,V}$ and $s \notin J_{M,U}$. It is also possible that M *wants* to maintain a lie amongst all agents it interacts with, in which case that lie would be a member of each $J_{M,*}$. This latter case would circumvent the problem that M has told q to U and $\neg q$ to V, but because U and V are in contact, these two agents discover the contradiction.

5   Why Lie?

We have not yet addressed the most important question concerning contradictory dialogues: why do agents lie? As described in the foregoing analysis, the task of agent M who has asserted proposal p (that it believes to be true) is to find an acceptable argument $(S, p) \in \underline{S}(\Sigma_M \cup CS_U)$. The complexity of this task is several steps above the complexity of checking the consistency of p in $\Sigma_M \cup CS_U$ in the hierarchy of computational complexity [10]. It is evident, then, that the task of constructing a set J of justifications to support the lie q is not any more difficult, generally speaking, than finding an acceptable argument for some p that is not a lie.

Suppose agent M is engaged in a dialogue with a particular goal in mind. With experience, M will be able to judge the relative merits and difficulties entailed in employing truthful assertions in arguing towards the goal, as compared to employing contradictory ones. Let p and q be contradictory and non-contradictory proposals, respectively, each of which, if uttered, could move M closer to its goal. Since M can at best only estimate the difficulty of justifying either proposal, inventing an acceptable argument for the lie q may indeed be considerably easier than finding an acceptable argument for p, at least in the short term. As previous discussion suggests, the goal may ultimately be defeated if q results in an unforeseen inconsistency that contradicts some other necessary proposal, as discussed above, or if q is exposed as a lie.

In natural environments, agents may lie or deceive one another without regard to complexity. However, the goal behind such contradictory behavior need not be socially unacceptable, as indicated in the opening of the paper. For instance, a teacher may assert a contradiction in an education dialogue with students (a form of dialogue we have begun formalizing in [13]), either playing the devil's advocate or to present a counter-example or to provoke the students to challenge the teacher and in so doing explore a set of arguments around some topic.

As another example, both humans and animals are known to exhibit feigned behaviors (such as aggression or flight) both in play, and when learning the purpose and meaning of such behaviors through imitation. [2] has suggested that artificial agents may only develop intelligence recognizable to people through human-like social conditioning, which may require assertions of contradiction either in dialogue or in behavior. Such contradictions may be not just socially condoned, but actually constitute a part of the social and economic fabric of a society. In the next section, we explore several well-known examples of contradictory locution and behavior in human and animal societies that help illuminate the role and necessity of contradiction in complex societies.

6   Application Domains

Two application areas in which we are actively working show more concretely why we believe that it is important to be able to lie. The first is drawn from our work on simulating aspects of the education system [12], while the second comes from an ecommerce application.

6.1   SimEd

The SimEd project is constructing models of a number of aspects of the educational system in the US [12]. One of these describes interactions at the classroom level — we are building models that simulate the effects on learning outcomes of different teaching strategies. As a result we are interested in student-teacher dialogues, and recently proposed a formal model of such dialogues [13] which focuses on kinds of dialogue that are common in the classroom but which have not been studied formally before now. (These dialogues do not yet include contradiction.)

Now, while teachers usually tell the truth to their students, there are occasions upon which lying may be an appropriate action. For example, one way to encourage a child to think through a problem is to present them with a problem and a false solution, and, when they object to the solution, asking them to justify their reaction. The reason for doing this, of course, is to get the student to explain the route to obtaining the correct answer.

Such an interaction is precisely what our framework is capable of providing. The teacher **assert**s the wrong answer, the student then **assert**s the contrary, the teacher **challenge**s the student's assertion, and the student has to provide their reasoning. When this is complete there is an explicit ("so what I said to begin with was wrong") or implicit ("yes, you're right") retraction of the initial lie.

6.2   Car Market

Our second example comes from [7]. Consider a dialogue about the purchase of a car between the agent for a buyer and a sales agent. This may involve a combination of a number of the kinds of dialogue identified by Walton and Krabbe [15] (combined, for example, as discussed in [6]).

The dialogue might open with an information seeking dialogue in which the sales agent attempts to find out how much money the buyer is prepared to spend, and what features the buyer is looking for. It might then pass into an inquiry stage, during which the two agents attempt to identify the best car, then a negotiation to settle the price, and this latter may include some persuasion on the part of the sales agent in order to get the buyer to agree.

There are several points here where the buyer might find it advantageous to lie. It might be beneficial for the buyer to misrepresent the price that she is prepared to pay, mentioning a smaller amount than is really the case (to avoid the inflation of prices, for example, and also to rule out any attempt by the sales agent to present unsuitably expensive vehicles). It might also be beneficial to lie about the features sought — covering up a weakness for small red sporty cars for example — if these might be exploited to the agent's disutility, or to be able to pretend that a figure mentioned during the negotiation is so high that negotiations should be broken off then and there (in the hope of gaining a concession).

Again, these forms of lying are exactly those provided for in our model.

7   Summary

This paper has presented a formal model of lying in agent-based systems. Arguing that lying can be a useful, and under certain circumstances, desirable feature of agent-based systems, we have adapted a dialogue framework from our previous work to allow the assertion of untruths. We have presented an axiomatic semantics for the new part of this framework and have discussed some of the consequences of the modification.

Our work on this topic is ongoing, and there are many areas that we need to explore in order to have a comprehensive treatment of lying. What we have provided here is the start of a semantics for lying in the context of argumentation. That formalisation needs to be completed. However, the formal semantics alone is not enough. We also need to develop our understanding of the *pragmatics* of lying as well. When is it acceptable to lie? When is it better (and in what sense) to lie than to tell the truth? If we are going to lie, what basis shall we use for our lies? These and other questions need to be answered. In addition, we are also looking to implement the dialogue framework to allow us to experimentally evaluate the utility of allowing agents to lie.

Acknowledgements. This work was made possible by funding from NSF #REC-02-19347 and NSF #IIS-03-29037. We are grateful to the reviewers for their helpful comments.

References

1. Miriam Webster Online Dictionary. http://www.m-w.com.
2. K. Dautenhahn. Getting to know each other – artificial social intelligence for autonomous robots. *Robotics and Autonomous Systems*, 16:333–356, 1995.

3. D. M. Gabbay and J. Woods. Non-cooperation in dialogue logic. *Synthese*, 127(12):161–186, 2001.
4. R. Girle. Commands in Dialogue Logic. In D. M. Gabbay and H. J. Ohlbach, editors, *Practical Reasoning: Proceedings of the First International Conference on Formal and Applied Practical Reasoning (FAPR 1996), Bonn, Germany*, Lecture Notes in Artificial Intelligence 1085, pages 246–260, Berlin, Germany, 1996. Springer.
5. P. McBurney and S. Parsons. Chance discovery using dialectical argumentation. In *Proceedings of the Workshop on Chance Discovery, Fifteenth Annual Conference of the Japanese Society for Artificial Intelligence*, Matsue, Japan, 2001.
6. P. McBurney and S. Parsons. Games that agents play: A formal framework for dialogues between autonomous agents. *J. Logic, Language, and Information*, 11(3):315–334, 2002.
7. P. McBurney, R. M. van Eijk, S. Parsons, and L. Amgoud. A dialogue-game protocol for agent purchase negotiations. *Journal of Autonomous Agents and Multi-Agent Systems*, 7(3):235–273, 2003.
8. S. Parsons, P. McBurney, and M. Wooldridge. Some preliminray steps towards a meta-theory for formal inter-agent dialogues. In I. Rahwan, editor, *Proceedings of the First International Workshop on Argumentation in Multi-Agent Systems.* (this volume), 2004.
9. S. Parsons, M. Wooldridge, and L. Amgoud. On the outcomes of formal inter-agent dialogues. In *2nd International Conference on Autonomous Agents and Multi-Agent Systems.* ACM Press, 2003.
10. S. Parsons, M. Wooldridge, and L. Amgoud. Properties and complexity of formal inter-agent dialogues. *Journal of Logic and Computation*, 13(3):347–376, 2003.
11. M. P. Singh. Agent communication languages: Rethinking the principles. In *IEEE Computer 31*, pages 40–47, 1998.
12. E. Sklar, M. Davies, and M. Co. SimEd: Simulating Education as a Multi Agent System. In C. Sierra and E. Sonenberg, editors, *Proceedings of the 3rd International Conference on Autonomous Agents and Multi-Agent Systems.* IEEE Press, 2004.
13. E. Sklar and S. Parsons. Towards the application of argumentation-based dialogues for education. In C. Sierra and E. Sonenberg, editors, *Proceedings of the 3rd International Conference on Autonomous Agents and Multi-Agent Systems.* IEEE Press, 2004.
14. R. D. Tennent. *Semantics of Programming Languages.* International Series in Computer Science. Prentice Hall, Hemel Hempstead, UK, 1991.
15. D. N. Walton and E. C. W. Krabbe. *Commitment in Dialogue: Basic Concepts of Interpersonal Reasoning.* State University of New York Press, Albany, NY, USA, 1995.

Author Index

Lecture Notes in Artificial Intelligence (LNAI)